The 83rd Pennsylvania Volunteers in the Civil War

The 83rd Pennsylvania Volunteers in the Civil War

Michael Schellhammer

Foreword by P. J. O'Rourke

McFarland & Company, Inc., Publishers
Jefferson, North Carolina, and London

The present work is a reprint of the illustrated case bound edition of The 83rd Pennsylvania Volunteers in the Civil War, *first published in 2003 by McFarland.*

LIBRARY OF CONGRESS CATALOGUING-IN-PUBLICATION DATA

Schellhammer, Michael.
The 83rd Pennsylvania Volunteers in the Civil War /
Michael Schellhammer ; foreword by P.J. O'Rourke.
       p.   cm.
Includes bibliographical references (p.) and index.

ISBN 978-0-7864-4078-8
softcover : 50# alkaline paper ∞

1. United States. Army. Pennsylvania Infantry Regiment, 83rd (1861–1865)
2. Pennsylvania—History—Civil War, 1861–1865—Regimental histories.
3. United States—History—Civil War, 1861–1865—Regimental histories.   I. Title.
E527.5 83rd .S34   2009   973.7'448—dc21   2002015004

British Library cataloguing data are available

©2003 Michael Schellhammer. All rights reserved

No part of this book may be reproduced or transmitted in any form or by any means, electronic or mechanical, including photocopying or recording, or by any information storage and retrieval system, without permission in writing from the publisher.

Manufactured in the United States of America

Cover illustration: *The Battle of Hanover Court House,* sketched by eyewitness Alfred Waud (Library of Congress)

McFarland & Company, Inc., Publishers
Box 611, Jefferson, North Carolina 28640
www.mcfarlandpub.com

For Lisa and Sean

Acknowledgments

I want to thank my friends and colleagues whose assistance made this book possible. Jenna Stephens was a thorough and persistent research assistant in Erie. Russ Miller gave me valuable advice on the book's basic construction. Jerry English, of the Erie Civil War Round Table, introduced me to the collectors and students of the 83rd and was an insightful sounding board for the length of this project. The late Irwin Rider kindly offered his 83rd memorabilia, artifacts, photos and correspondence to me. The Rider family continues Irwin's tradition of generosity. Don Judson, the great grandson of Amos Judson, graciously provided me with fascinating information on his ancestor. Ronn Palm was a tremendous help with obtaining photos of 83rd soldiers. James Wright provided me with excellent information on Strong Vincent. Howard Maddeus, the renowned expert on Confederate battle flags, helped me track down the Rebel banner that the 83rd captured at Malvern Hill, which is explained in Chapter VI.

I also owe a debt of thanks to the archivists and historians who so kindly cooperated with my queries for information. Most prominently, Annita Andrick of the Erie County Historical Society and Museum, Rose Dekka of the Crawford County Historical Society, the late Ed Morrison of the Ft. LeBoeuf Historical Society, Joanna McDonald of the Pennsylvania Capitol Preservation Committee, Louise Arnold-Friend at the U.S. Army Military History Institute, John Heiser of the Gettysburg National Military Park, James Burgess at the Manassas National Battlefield Park and Donald Pfanz at the Fredericksburg & Spotsylvania National Military Park. Their assistance was invaluable.

Robert E. L. Krick of the Richmond National Battlefield Park deserves special notice and thanks for all the time he devoted to helping me dissect the 83rd's activities during the Peninsula Campaign.

Thanks also go to Jean Rodgers Hall, the Charles Alcorn family, Karen Steinlight, Lee Zuver, and Cynthia Campbell, who donated their family letters. It is an honor to give voice to their ancestors.

Special thanks go to Nancy and Dennis Belmont of Belmont Design, who turned a series of draft maps, drawn by my singularly untalented hands, into the works of cartographic art that grace the following pages. Caroline Bruckner took valuable time away from her legal studies to proofread the manuscript, and she is also the only person who has ever hugged me while discussing the Civil War. For their patience, talent and generosity, Nancy, Dennis and Caroline have my eternal gratitude.

This book would not have been possible without the tutelage and guidance of my good friend and mentor, P. J. O'Rourke.

The most important help I received

came from my lovely wife, Lisa. Lisa is an artist and not naturally inclined to discuss military science or history. For six years she endured countless conversations about the 83rd, occupied herself while I spent hours at the computer or was off researching somewhere, and tromped over miles of battlefields in all types of weather. She encouraged, listened, sympathized and politely prodded, as only a wife can. This is as much her book as it is mine.

Contents

Acknowledgments — vii
Foreword by P. J. O'Rourke — 1
Preface — 3

    I. Here Am I, Let Me Go — 7
   II. It Seemed a Little Like War — 26
  III. Hard Marches to Yorktown — 46
  IV. A Promise of Perfect Success — 62
    V. You Will See Enough of Them Before Night — 80
  VI. Revenge for McLane — 100
 VII. An Unlucky Field — 116
VIII. Armies Broken and Divided — 129
  IX. Mournful Cries in the Stillness of the Night — 137
    X. The Tempest and Whirlwind of Battle — 150
  XI. The Rocky Hill — 167

Epilogue: For None Others Can Know — 187
Notes — 199
Bibliography — 213
Index — 217

Foreword

by P. J. O'Rourke

The voice of the common soldier has been heard, now and then, since Homer reported the bellyaching hoplite Thersites mouthing-off to Agamemnon:

What's wrong, son of Atreus, something you need?
   Your huts are filled with bronze, and with women

But that was a sound bite. We know very little about what common soldiers, through history, thought of their wars. The American Civil War was the first conflict fought by literate armies. The genius of *The 83rd Pennsylvania Volunteers* is that it allows us to listen to the regular people who populate a battlefield and who, until 1861, didn't get to tell their stories unless they said something clever within earshot of a Homer.

Michael Schellhammer researched daily life in the 83rd Pennsylvania down to details the size of the lice that infested it. He pushed through the thicket of red tape surrounding primary sources and made his way across the desert of tedium within. He read all the available letters and diaries, also the Civil War memoirs written in a style that can hardly be read. As a result, when Schellhammer's soldiers speak, they say more than just what they thought they should say, and we hear more than just what we want to hear.

We do not hear a simple "War is hell." What surprises us—after the charnel house of the 20th century—is how few people knew this in 1861. For the soldiers of the 83rd, the Mexican War was something that had taken place far away and while they were boys—the two conditions that make war seem most glorious. The Mexican War had been the Persian Gulf War of its day, plus America got to keep the Kuwait in question. The War of 1812 was as remote in time to Civil War combatants as the Korean War is to today's Special Forces in Afghanistan (without intervening *M*A*S*H** reruns). When the South seceded hardly a living person could remember the countrywide devastation of the Revolution. In fact, until William Tecumseh Sherman said so in 1879, no one had ever flatly stated, "War is hell."

The American Civil War was the beginning of modern, centralized nation states using mass armies in conjunction with the products of industrialization. The story of the 83rd Pennsylvania is the story of men experiencing a great change in the nature of war. Hellish aspects war has always had, but the 83rd volunteers were right on time to see human warfare turn into nothing but hell.

Even to call war hell is to give a too romantic and theatrical name to what the

83rd went through. The first thing gleaned from this book is that war is work. The most harrowing passages of the book are not tales of battle but descriptions of the marches to get there. The 83rd's maiden journey into combat was a rush hour that lasted from 4AM to 4PM. Think 70 pounds of briefcase, a deep mud freeway, and the only SUV is your feet. War is ditch-digging with an enemy howitzer for a backhoe, a job in a garbage dump where the garbage is also trying to bury you, plantation field labor except what gets planted is, too often, your dead body.

Another lesson of this work is to borrow other people's eyes to look at other people's wars. For us, the mission of the Civil War was to eliminate human bondage. For the soldiers of the 83rd, though they opposed slavery, the mission was to preserve political union. Colonel Strong Vincent, the 83rd's commander, put it coldly when he wrote to his wife that the North must make the South believe "that to break this band in twain is monstrous and impossible; that the life of every man, yea, of every weak woman or helpless child in the entire South, is of no value whatever compared with the integrity of the Union." But the men of the 83rd were not moral idiots. The greatest American statesman of the pre-war era, Daniel Webster, had sacrificed his political ambitions, his reputation among his peers, and his abolitionist cause to hold the Union together with the Compromise of 1850. The idea of government of, for, and by the people (if not exactly all the people) was still new to the world and fragile at the dawn of the Civil War. Every global freedom acquired since stems from that idea. We should resist the temptation to travel back in time and lecture the Pennsylvanians.

As significant as what is said in the pages that follow is what goes without saying. We hear very little about fear. Perhaps the best example of the very little comes not from the 83rd but from one of their Confederate opponents at the battle of Gaines's Mill: "It was the worst place I ever saw. We went in but came back out again in a hurry, and didn't keer to go back." What else was there to say about a thing so pervasive? Of the 1,808 men who served in the 83rd over the course of the war, 971 were killed, wounded, or captured and at least 130 died from disease. We hear very little about fear from the 83rd for the same reason that, although every person on earth is at pains not to fall down, we hear very little from them about gravity.

There are other eloquent silences in this book. Narrations of war from the common soldier's point of view are no longer rare. The genre began, perhaps, with Stephen Crane's 1895 Civil War novel, *The Red Badge of Courage*. From World War I on, everyman-at-war has been a staple of literature. But these sensitive, artistic portrayals of war have the disadvantage of being—how else to put it kindly?—sensitive and artistic. Most of us are not so finely attuned to the horrors around us, nor would we wish to be. And the men of the 83rd were insensitive enough to fight until victory in the battle for Little Round Top. They did their duty. As Robert E. Lee said, "You cannot do more." They tell us about the sacrifices that duty entails, but they don't presume to say what, finally, cannot be communicated.

Seth Waid served from the 83rd's mustering through Gettysburg. In the last entry of his war diary he speaks for everyone who has endured terrors with honor: "*I am at home.* Who can describe the deeply interesting emotions of the Soul, as it passes over the road described in the forgoing? I cannot. My pen is too feeble, my lips to dumb for the task, and I leave it to be imagined, aye, to be experienced by those who are of the like Sencibilitys for none others can know."

Preface

At the beginning of the Civil War, over 1,000 farmers, tradesmen and laborers in northwestern Pennsylvania formed a unit of the Union Army that became the 83rd Pennsylvania Infantry Regiment. Their commander, Colonel John McLane, was a middle-aged county sheriff. The second-in-command, Lieutenant-colonel Strong Vincent, was an attorney in his early-twenties.

In their first year of combat from the spring of 1862 to the summer of 1863, over 400 of those soldiers were killed and wounded during seven major battles. Hundreds more were disabled by disease, missing, or captured. In campaigns through Virginia, Maryland and Pennsylvania, they endured conditions too terrible for most modern Americans to comprehend; battle horrors that defy description, choking dust, drenching rains, freezing winters, rotten food, and the violent death of friends. Those that returned home were changed forever.

Many of these soldiers' voices, left behind in letters and diaries, have been silent for over 140 years. I wrote this book so that these ordinary men, who fought so extraordinarily, would be remembered.

Erie, Pennsylvania, where the 83rd was raised, is my hometown. Attention on the Civil War was not evident in the area during my childhood years of the 1960s and '70s, and I grew up totally unaware of my hometown's role in the war. It wasn't until the fall of 1983 that I discovered the regiment's existence, and even that was by accident.

I was a student at Erie's Mercyhurst College and in search of a subject for a locally-oriented thesis, which was the final requirement for a bachelor's degree in history. At the age of twenty-one I was an authority on several local bars but little local history. Wandering through the County Library, I found the regiment's colors, wrapped in plastic and barely recognizable, encased in glass.

The idea that my hometown had contributed such a large contingent of men for the Civil War was fascinating. Research on the regiment occupied the weeks and months of the remaining school year. I learned that the 83rd had a proud battle record, that charismatic leaders like McLane and Vincent had commanded the regiment through some of the most dramatic actions in the war, and that the regiment's soldiers had been as heroic as any I had read about before. By the time I finished the paper in May 1984, I was proud of those men and of my hometown.

I became an Army officer after college, and the Civil War remained a subject of great professional and personal interest. The more I learned about the war, the more I appreciated the significance of the campaigns of 1862 and 1863. During this crucial year, the Union's Army of the Potomac suffered a string of demoralizing defeats in the eastern theater, but eventually turned the Confederacy back at the battle of Gettysburg. The heartiness of the northern troops, men that fought bravely despite their failures, fascinated me.

The experiences of the 83rd and the Army of the Potomac are, of course, intertwined. The hardships suffered by the men of the 83rd are an example of the brutality of the Army of the Potomac's campaigns from the Peninsula to Gettysburg. Over half of all the 83rd's battle-related deaths of the entire war occurred during that one terrible year. Over a third of the regiment's ranks were killed, wounded or captured at the battle of Gaines's Mill in late June 1862. Within a week half of those men still in the ranks were killed or wounded at the battle of Malvern Hill. At the second battle of Bull Run two months later, the regiment lost over 40 percent of its remaining soldiers. The fact that the regiment continued to serve with distinction is a testament to the toughness of the Union soldier. In his book *For Cause and Comrades; Why Men Fought in the Civil War*, historian James McPherson observed, "Studies of modern armies have shown that a unit is wrecked psychologically if it twice suffers casualties equivalent to one-third of its strength." From Gaines's Mill to Bull Run, the 83rd lost well over one-third of its strength three times in as many months. Instead of becoming "wrecked" as many units did, these Pennsylvanians fought on during the time when the Union needed them most. By the time the 83rd moved onto Little Round Top at Gettysburg in the summer of 1863, less than 300 able-bodied soldiers held their line against the Confederates. Had these men been made of weaker material, our history would be different.

Though the 83rd Pennsylvania served so honorably, no history of the unit has appeared since 1865, when Amos Judson, a former captain in the regiment, wrote *A History of the 83rd Regiment Pennsylvania Volunteers*. Though it incorporates official government records and the remembrances of other soldiers, Judson's book is not an objective history. Its nineteenth century style can also be difficult to digest. I felt that a more readable and thorough review of the regiment's most critical years in service was needed to make the story of the 83rd more accessible to modern readers.

The U.S. Government's *Official Records of the War of the Rebellion*, Judson's *History of the 83rd*, and Oliver Norton's *Army Letters, 1861-1865* formed the foundation for this book. The best way to tell this story is to let the troops speak as much as possible. To that end, I also scoured the country for other letters or diaries from 83rd soldiers. Every county that contributed men to the 83rd was queried for sources, as was every county where they fought. My search extended to battlefield archives, national museums, Civil War veterans' newspapers like the *National Tribune*, western Pennsylvania historical journals, histories of units that fought alongside the 83rd, and archives in areas where I knew the regiment's veterans retired, like Neosho, Kansas.

The U.S. Army Military History Institute has large holdings on the regiment. The original muster rolls and records at the National Archives also yielded much information on the unit orders and composition throughout the war. Letters and diaries came from descendants of 83rd soldiers and collectors. Period newspapers, such as the *Erie Weekly Gazette* and the *Crawford Journal* were excellent sources of soldier correspondence and background on northwestern Pennsylvania during the Civil War. I hope that by combining these sources the result is a story that honors the soldiers of northwestern Pennsylvania.

Those interested in reading about the 83rd's final two years in the war should read Judson's *History of the 83rd*. For a glimpse into the views of a Union enlisted soldier, see Norton's *Army Letters*. Norton also published two thorough reviews of the 83rd's activities at Gettysburg in *The Attack and Defense of Little Round Top* and *Strong Vincent and his Brigade at Little Round Top*. *What Death More Glorious, A Biography of General Strong Vincent*, by James H. Nevins and William B. Styple, is the only biography of Vincent, one of the Union's most gifted officers.

MICHAEL SCHELLHAMMER
ARLINGTON, VIRGINIA
FALL 2002

Here Am I, Let Me Go

From the summit of the hill that Gettysburg locals called Little Round Top, you could see the entire battlefield that surrounded the small Pennsylvania town on the afternoon of Thursday, July 2, 1863.

Looking north, a long and low rise known as Cemetery Ridge began in the trees at the base of the hill and ran about a mile and a half to the knoll that was the site of the area's burial grounds, the descriptively named Cemetery Hill. Another half mile beyond Cemetery Hill were the white clapboard houses of Gettysburg. To their right was the wooded Culp's Hill. A mile to the left, or west, the Seminary Ridge, another low rise, ran almost parallel with Cemetery Ridge to a point past Gettysburg. More ridges rolled beyond it farther west. Most of the ground in between the landmarks was a patchwork of farmer's fields. Acres of trees covered parts of the ridges and hilltops, and all of the foliage had the lush greens, browns and tans of rural America in the bloom of summer.

The oval-shaped Little Round Top stood 150 feet over the surrounding countryside at the south end of Cemetery Ridge, with its long sides facing roughly west and east. Its west side had been recently cleared but the eastern half was still covered with tall trees. About one hundred yards to the south, the completely wooded and conical height of Big Round Top rose fifty feet above the smaller hill. Both dominated the area.

For the past month the Confederate Army of Northern Virginia had moved north from its camps in Virginia with the Union Army of the Potomac in pursuit. The Rebels had advanced into Pennsylvania in the last week and had turned to concentrate their scattered formations at Gettysburg. The Federal army, maneuvering between the Confederates and Washington, marched to meet them. On Wednesday, July 1, the lead portions of both armies met northwest of Gettysburg and fought hard all day in a battle with over 15,000 killed and wounded. The Union troops had been pushed back to Cemetery Ridge, leaving the Rebels in possession of the town of Gettysburg and Seminary Ridge. By the morning of July 2, most of the soldiers on both sides were exhausted from marching and fighting. It was a hot day and many of the men rested in their ranks well past the noon hour. An observer on Little Round Top would have seen thousands of soldiers of both armies formed in neat lines, interspersed with groups of black cannon, along the ridges, fields and hills. Except for an occasional cannon shot, there was little indication that the most costly battle in American history was taking place.

At about 3:30 PM, artillery thundered from Seminary Ridge and broke the languid afternoon. Within minutes 20,000 Mississippians, Georgians, and Texans of the Confederate 1st and 3rd Corps emerged from the woods on Seminary Ridge and rushed the Federal line at a point a mile northwest of Little Round Top. Startled but not broken, the Unionists held and rushed reinforcements to the fight. As more troops from both sides joined the melee, the noise of musket volleys rose to a continuous roar. The booms of artillery shook the ground, and the fields around Cemetery Ridge became enveloped in thick gunpowder smoke. Orange explosions of artillery shells burst among the troops and in the air. The Northerners held their lines vigorously as the Rebels pushed them, and the fighting was hand-to-hand in some places. The screams and pleas of men rose above the din.

About a half mile behind the fighting, at the base of Cemetery Ridge, the 1,336 Yankee soldiers that made up the 3rd Brigade, 1st Division, of the 13,000 strong 5th Army Corps waited to be sent into the action. Their commander, Col. Strong Vincent of Erie, Pennsylvania, watched the battle unfold. Next to Vincent was his bugler, Pvt. Oliver Norton. Vincent, Norton, and the four infantry regiments that composed the Brigade—the 16th Michigan, 20th Maine, 44th New York and 83rd Pennsylvania—arrived at Gettysburg early that morning after an all-night march. Although they had shifted position a couple of times that day, the brigade had not been sent into the action. As Vincent waited for orders, the men lounged in their ranks.

The armies of the Civil War were almost completely composed of volunteer soldiers who had left their civilian lives to fight, and many men rose to high rank at early ages. Generals in their thirties or even late twenties were not uncommon, but even among them, Strong Vincent stood out. Educated at Harvard, he was an attorney in Erie when the war began and had risen from a private in the 83rd Pennsylvania to its colonel in little more than a year. Though he was not a professional soldier, Vincent epitomized an officer. He was considered a handsome man, with a determined gaze that was framed by bushy brown sideburns. Brave in battle—he had the habit of carrying his wife's riding crop with him instead of sword—he was also a firm but fair disciplinarian in camp. He was a fine horseman who sat ramrod-straight in the saddle. Though his views on slavery are unknown, Vincent strongly believed in the Federal Union and detested the Confederate cause. With the full respect of his troops, peers and superiors, Vincent was given command of the 3rd Brigade two months before reaching Gettysburg and had handled it admirably on the march into Pennsylvania. He was twenty-six years old.

His bugler, Oliver Norton, was a minister's son from the small farming town of Springfield, Pennsylvania, located west of Erie. Though his formal education had ended when he was sixteen, Norton claimed to be a teacher upon his enlistment as a private in the 83rd Pennsylvania in September 1861. As Vincent epitomized the Federal officer, Norton was the true picture of a Yankee private soldier. He believed strongly in the Union and regarded the Rebels as traitors for their secession. Having seen slaves in Virginia, Norton considered himself an abolitionist against a system he said was one of "cruelty and inhumanity." He had seen action in four campaigns before Gettysburg and had been wounded at the battle of Gaines's Mill in June 1862. Though stalwart under enemy fire, Norton found much fault with the army. He made his own personal comfort his first priority in camp. He had been the Brigade Bugler for nine months, a duty which suited him well since he was relieved from most of the fatigue work common to privates in the infantry regiments. Norton was a prolific writer and keen observer of his surroundings. At twenty-three years old he was two years younger than the average enlisted man. He had a boyish face that probably could not have supported a full beard and a mop of light brown hair. As the colonel's bugler, it was

Norton's job to mark Vincent's position with the 3rd Brigade flag so other officers could locate Vincent on smoky and confusing battlefields. The pennant, a large white triangle bordered by blue with a red Maltese cross in the center, floated from a staff that Norton rested in his stirrup.

The infantrymen of Vincent's Brigade were some of the hardiest veterans of the war. The 16th Michigan, 44th New York and the 83rd Pennsylvania had trained and fought together since the fall of 1861 and the 20th Maine had joined the brigade the previous autumn. Collectively, the regiments had fought at the battles of Yorktown, Hanover Court House, The Seven Days, Second Bull Run, Antietam, Fredericksburg and Chancellorsville. By the time they reached Gettysburg, the men were expert fighters. They were tanned, lean, and wore uniforms tattered from two years of war. As the brigade rested at Gettysburg, the dozing veterans listened to the fighting with practiced ears and lifted their heads as the sounds grew closer and more fierce.

Still on their horses in front of the troops, Vincent and Norton saw a messenger from Gen. Sykes, commander of the 5th Corps, on a galloping horse nearby. Intercepting him, Vincent asked: "Captain, what are your orders?"

The junior officer was visibly agitated and, asking for Vincent's division commander, only replied: "Where is General Barnes?"

Vincent was not put off and demanded: "What are your orders? Give me your orders."

Little Round Top dominated the sky behind Vincent's troops, and indicating the hill, the captain answered, "General Sykes told me to direct General Barnes to send one of his brigades to occupy that rocky hill yonder."

Vincent glanced at the hill for a moment and instantly realized its importance. With its commanding position over the Union line, control of it was a key to victory for either side. Sykes' urgent request for soldiers to hold the hill meant that it was unoccupied and vulnerable to the Rebel attack. Turning back to the courier, Vincent told him: "I will take the responsibility of taking my brigade there." The colonel galloped back to his troops and hastily gave orders for the four regiments to form ranks and to quickly march to the hill. That done, he rode off with Norton to scout out the ground.

The two men were alone on the hill when they arrived. They had only looked at the area for a few moments when a cannon shell whistled in and exploded near them, announcing that they had become the target of Confederate artillery. The 3rd Brigade pennant that Norton carried had attracted fire from Rebel batteries on Seminary Ridge. The colonel barked, "Down with that flag, Norton!" The rebuke was a rare one from the even-tempered Vincent and it may have warranted a curious look from the private for a moment. Two more shells landed in quick succession and threw rocks and dirt over the men and Vincent quickly added, "Damn it, go behind the rocks with it!" Norton trotted his horse back to the crest of the hill where the trees and boulders provided some cover and placed his banner that had attracted the fire against a rock. A moment later Vincent followed and left his own horse there as he went back out in the open to survey the hill.

The west side of Little Round Top, where Vincent looked for the best position to place his brigade, rises steeply from a low-lying boulder field known as the Devil's Den. More granite boulders and rocks are scattered on the open hillside. Sparse grass, weeds and wildflowers are its only vegetation. The opposite, or east, side is completely wooded up to the spine of the oblong hill. A few trails cut up the hill but most of the wooded area is thick enough to make ascent difficult. The slope of Big Round Top meets the south edge of Little Round Top to form a valley between the two hills. The Confederates were fighting their way through the Devil's Den only a few hundred yards away, and the noise from the action filled the air as Vincent analyzed the ground.

The rocks and steep incline perfectly suited defense, but the colonel had no idea how many Rebels his men would have to fight or from which direction they would come. As far as Vincent knew, his soldiers were the only ones coming and there were too few of them to occupy the entire hill. The Confederates were probably moving up behind Big Round Top, and they could emerge from anywhere among the trees at any moment. Vincent had to place his troops exactly where the Rebels would appear, otherwise it would be easy for his advancing enemy move around his line, seize the summit, and control the rise. His brigade would arrive in a few minutes. But so would the Rebels.

As Vincent pondered this problem, Pvt. Norton heard the brigade coming over the spine of the hill from the east. Turning to look, he saw the 44th New York lead the column, followed by the 16th Michigan, the 83rd Pennsylvania and the 20th Maine last. The flag of the Union and distinctive blue regimental colors marked the head of each regiment, but the four units from different states moved as if they were one. The troops picked their way through the trees and rocks at the double-quick step, sweating and breathing heavily from their run. The sounds of rattling equipment and tramping feet mixed with the noise of officers and sergeants hurrying the soldiers along. The Confederate artillery was still firing and shells exploded in the tree tops and on the ground, so the men received alternating showers of leaves, splinters, and rock fragments. The troops stepped quickly under the bursting shells, but did not give the fire much notice. The column jogged over the crest and onto the open west slope.

It was after four in the afternoon and the sun streamed through the trees as the commanders of the four regiments found Col. Vincent and dismounted from their horses to receive their orders. Vincent told them that the brigade would form in a semicircular line near the base of Little Round Top where it could control the valley between the two hills. The 44th New York would take the right of the brigade, the 16th Michigan and 83rd in the center, and the 20th Maine on the far left in a line. Col. James Rice, the commander of the 44th, was not satisfied with the alignment and told Vincent, "In every battle in which we have engaged, the 83rd and the 44th have fought side by side…. I wish it might be so today." Vincent sympathized, "All right. Let the 16th pass you."

The regiments hurried into line as their commander directed, and the New Yorkers took their position in the brigade's center alongside the 83rd. In about five minutes the line had taken shape and the soldiers prepared to face the Confederates.

Commanding the 83rd Pennsylvania that day was a twenty-eight year old captain named Orpheus Woodward, a seasoned veteran who had already been wounded in the Seven Days battles a year earlier. He sent some of his soldiers down the slope to watch for Rebels and had the rest of the men pile stones to make a wall, as the other regiments were doing. With rifled muskets that could only be loaded while standing, the soldiers needed a wall at least a few feet high for protection. There was not enough time to stack the stones high enough to provide real safety, but at that point, any cover was better than none at all.

In the fields west of Devil's Den, Confederates were rushing towards Little Round Top, unseen by Vincent's men from their position near the valley. A battery of Federal artillery set up on the crest of the hill. Rebel positions all over the battlefield were within their range and the gunners began firing at the Confederate formations that headed for the Union line. The muzzle of a Civil War field cannon could only depress a few degrees below the horizontal plane and the slope of Little Round Top was so steep that the gunners could not cover the front of Vincent's line. Though the battery had more effect on the fight in Devil's Den, the sound of the guns were reassuring to the men on Little Round Top. The soldiers piled their rocks, loaded rifles, and made private peace with their maker or themselves, as soldiers often did before a fight.

The men were in the midst of their work when they heard firing and shouting from the direction of Big Round Top. The thick woods hid the source of the commotion at first, but in a few moments they saw the soldiers who had been posted to watch for the enemy come running back to the main line. Just visible through the trees and close behind the running Union soldiers were the tough Texas and Alabama troops of Gen. Hood's division, moving up the slope, picking their way around boulders and trees. Hood's men, like Vincent's, were veterans of the war's bloodiest battles. The Rebel officers and sergeants were hurrying them along, just as the leaders of the 83rd had done a few minutes before. A Federal battery somewhere managed to land a few shells in their formation. Some of the Rebels dropped from the ranks, but the mass kept moving at a steady pace. When they reached the base of the hill, the Confederates screamed the high-pitched wail of the Rebel Yell and charged up the slope with their bayonets fixed.

The Rebels were every bit as determined to take Little Round Top as the 3rd Brigade was to hold it, and they headed straight for the portion of the line held by the 83rd Pennsylvania.

❋ ❋ ❋

The battle of Gettysburg was one of the bloodiest and most decisive of the Civil War, and Union possession of Little Round Top was a key part of the victory. Though other Federal units fought on the hill, much of the credit for holding the height has justly gone to Col. Vincent and his brigade.

By the time the men of the 83rd reached Gettysburg, most of them had endured over a year of the most intense combat that ever occurred in North America. The regiment's first face-to-face confrontation with Confederate infantry had been in May 1862, at Hanover Court House, Virginia, and had ended with an easy victory for the Pennsylvanians. They were confident of continued success and a quick end to the war, but one month later at Gaines's Mill, they fought off Rebel attacks for hours and were eventually outflanked and forced to scatter with heavy casualties. Four days later they helped repulse six Rebel brigades at Malvern Hill, but again lost heavily and retreated from the battlefield along with the rest of the Army of the Potomac. At the Second Battle of Bull Run in August, the 83rd charged uphill against Confederates and was turned back after nearly half of its soldiers were killed, wounded, or captured. The Federal tactics, and the regiment's retreat, were repeated at Fredericksburg in December. Instead of victory, the year 1862 brought the 83rd demoralizing defeats.

Roughly 1,000 men had joined the unit when it was formed in October 1861, and in less than two years 144 of them had been killed and over 250 were wounded, some more than once. Sickness and disease were so prevalent that in August 1862, 495 soldiers—more than half of the men on the regiment's roll books and over twice the number still fit for duty—were in the hospital. Conditions were so severe in the 83rd's first campaign that Pvt. Oliver Norton pleaded with his family not to allow his younger brother to join the army. "It is more than probable that I shall not outlive the war," he wrote his father, "and you will want him left." Forty-eight soldiers deserted over the winter of 1862-63. By the time the regiment moved onto Little Round Top there were fewer than 300 able-bodied soldiers left in the ranks.[1]

After Gettysburg, the 83rd continued to fight in all of the major battles of the eastern theater up to the final campaign at Appomattox. The regiment would have a total of 1,808 members before the end of the war, and 971 of them were killed, wounded, or captured, which gave the men of the 83rd roughly even odds of becoming some type of casualty. Out of that number, 282 soldiers were killed in battle or died directly from their wounds. Of all the Union regiments in all the theaters of war, only the 5th New Hampshire Infantry, with 295 battle deaths, lost more men to the same causes.

Though the men of the 83rd had seen more than half of their comrades killed or carried away sick or wounded, the survivors pulled themselves together after each battle, mourned their lost comrades, and fought with valor. The soldiers who survived to fight on Little Round Top had been lucky, but they were also the toughest of the lot. There were few units in the war, or in any army at that time, that knew more about death and were better at inflicting it, but none of the men who followed Col. Vincent and Capt. Woodward into battle at Gettysburg were professional soldiers.[2]

In 1861, the Regular United States Army consisted of about 16,000 men and officers who were mostly spread out in posts on the frontier or at seacoast forts. Soon after the first shots of the war were fired at Ft. Sumter, Confederate President Jefferson Davis began organizing an army, planned to exceed 100,000 men, to defend Southern territory from the Federal government. Most of the Regular U.S. Army units were recalled to fight the rebellion, but the defeat of an insurrection of the size the Confederacy required a massive expansion.[3]

Since the days of the Revolution, the American ideal of a national army was one that consisted of short-term citizen-soldiers who interrupted their civilian lives to fight wars and then returned to their homes. With this goal in mind, the Military Act of 1792 authorized the President to federalize the volunteer state militias for limited time periods to suppress insurrections. The Government had employed the militia in many of its wars with varying levels of success, and the law provided the best means to quickly raise the number of men needed to meet a national emergency.

President Lincoln recognized the need for a large army to crush the Confederacy. On April 15, 1861, he requested 75,000 militiamen for ninety days of Federal service. States that had recently joined the Confederacy openly rejected the call or ignored it. The North enthusiastically endorsed the proclamation. The War Department apportioned quotas of the total to each state, to be filled by regiments of 780 soldiers divided into ten companies of roughly seventy-five men each.[4]

The Revolution and War of 1812 had ended a full generation before, the Regular Army had borne the brunt of the Mexican War, and so the harsh realities of combat were far removed from the minds of most Americans. With dreams of glory and adventure, thousands of men signed up to do their part in the destruction of the rebellion. Pennsylvania was requested to send 16 regiments of infantry, and as in the rest of the north, men rushed to join their local militia companies. The men from the northwest corner of the state were no exception. They represented an area with a long tradition of conflict and frontier toughness.

Before Europeans settled the lands west of the Allegheny Mountains, the area that became northwestern Pennsylvania was inhabited by several tribes of Native Americans. Senecas and Pymatuming Delawares lived on the western foothills of the mountains. The Eriez (also called the Erie or

Eries) held the glacier-scraped lands that sloped to the shores of the Great Lakes, until they were wiped out by the Senecas. French soldiers and trappers came to the region in the mid-eighteenth century. Great Britain also made claims to the area, and the French built a series of forts from Lake Erie to what would become Pittsburgh to protect their interests from the English. The forts were evacuated during the French and Indian War, rebuilt by the British, and lost again during Pontiac's Rebellion in the years afterward. The British closed the volatile area to white settlers until crown rule ended after the Revolutionary War. When the area was re-opened by the new United States, resistance from the tribes of the Six Nations inhibited settlement until their western allies were defeated at the battle of Fallen Timbers near present day Toledo, Ohio, in 1794. In 1800, the Pennsylvania Legislature divided the huge Allegheny and Lycoming counties into the counties of Erie, Crawford, Warren, Mercer and Venango.[5]

The state designated much of the area as "donation lands" to be given to war veterans in reward for their service in the Revolution, and settlers began coming west with their land grants in the early nineteenth century. Scottish Presbyterians and Irish from eastern Pennsylvania settled Mercer County. Iron ore and coal were discovered and several blast furnaces operated throughout the county. Iron was also discovered in Venango County, east of Mercer, in 1825. There were already twenty smelters operating there in 1859 when Edwin Drake sank a petroleum well in the northwest corner of the county and began the nation's oil boom. Warren County, north of Venango, was home to the first sawmill built on the Allegheny River and was also a major producer of oats, potatoes, wheat, corn, rye, and barley. Crawford County lies west of Warren. French Creek, part of the headwaters of the Allegheny River, flows south through Crawford County and shipping was a major industry, as well as beaver trapping, logging and farming. In addition to the land-grant veterans who settled there, many citizens were German, French, Scots and Irish immigrants. Overall the four counties covered 3,247 square miles and had a combined population of over 129,000 at the beginning of the Civil War. Over 31,000 of that number were men between the ages of fifteen and forty-nine who were eligible for military service.[6]

Erie County lies on Crawford's northern border and extends to the shore of the Great Lake from which it takes its name. To gain access to the lake, Pennsylvania had purchased the area, then known as "the Erie Triangle," in 1792. A peninsula that forms a sheltered bay, located midway between the borders with Ohio and New York, was also a potential harbor for the state's entry into the lucrative lake commerce. The French had built one of their first forts there as did the English after them. The foreign posts were destroyed and abandoned by the end of the Revolutionary War, and after 1794, Indian resistance in the region was quieted. The Erie Township was founded at the base of the peninsula—named "Presqu'ile," or "almost an island," by the French—and within a year the town plan was surveyed and the first settlers arrived.

When Pennsylvania carved up Allegheny County in 1800, the Erie Triangle became the 804-square-mile Erie County. With eighty-one residents, Erie was designated the county seat. It was considered the western frontier by the pioneers of the early nineteenth century, and the area's population increased with America's westward expansion. In 1805 Erie Township had grown enough to be named a borough and by 1830 it was home to over 1,300 citizens. The bay and peninsula (Anglicized as "Presque Isle") proved to be an excellent harbor. As Pennsylvania's only lake port, the shipping business prospered early. The iron milling, fishing and lumber industries also boomed.

Farms flourished throughout the county. A telegraph office opened in 1847. In 1851 Erie had nearly 6,000 residents and was incorporated as a city.

Lake shipping dominated Erie's commerce in the early 1860s. The city also boasted three foundries, two breweries, nine hotels and a collection of service industries that included two photographers. Erie's heart was close to the bay at the foot of State Street, the main thoroughfare. Though most of the city's roads were still dirt or gravel, much of State Street was paved. Shops of all kinds ran along both sides of the street and a spacious park overlooked the bay at its lower end. Gas lighting gave a modern air to the downtown area. Two newspapers, the Republican-leaning *Erie Weekly Gazette* and the more moderate *Erie Observer*, served the area along with several rural and special interest papers. The railroad had opened nine years earlier and passenger and freight traffic to Pittsburgh, Cleveland and Buffalo ran regularly. The train stopped at the villages along its way, but travel to other towns in the county was by foot, horse or a horse-drawn conveyance over dirt or plank roads. Though Erie was barely one generation removed from being a rough frontier town, it was on the verge of nineteenth century industrialization as the Civil War loomed.

With about 9,000 people, Erie was the largest city in northwestern Pennsylvania after Pittsburgh (the next in size was Meadville, Crawford County's seat, which was fifty miles south of Erie and had almost 4,000 citizens). More than half of the city's adult work force was foreign-born. The German immigrants had their own native language newspaper and a primary school, and comprised much of the town's artisans and craftsmen. The Irish often worked as laborers and domestic help. There were a small number of British, Canadian and French immigrants. Also, more than 180 free blacks lived in Erie County and worked as manual laborers. The diverse citizenry supported one parochial and two public schools. Secondary education was available, for private tuition, at the Erie Academy. One Sunday school offered education for African Americans. The population was predominantly Protestant. Only two churches out of its eleven were for the Catholic faith, one built by the Irish and one by the Germans. There was a small Jewish community. Politically, Erie was Republican territory and 70 percent of the electorate voted for Abraham Lincoln in the 1861 election. The city's abolitionists clandestinely operated stations of the Underground Railroad for escaped slaves on their way to Canada.

About 40,000 people lived on farms and in towns that sprouted outside the city limits. The towns of Fairview, Girard, and Springfield were to the west, between Erie and the Ohio border. Moorheadville and the (fittingly-named) borough of North East are northeast of the city along the lake shore, towards New York. Edinboro, Waterford and Ft. LeBoeuf (an old French post named for the cattle, or "beef," that were native to the area in the seventeenth century) are in the southern portion of the county.[7]

The county had maintained companies of militia since 1801 and the tradition for military service was still strong at the beginning of the Civil War. Erie was home to the "Wayne Guards" named for Gen. Anthony Wayne, who had died in the town during his return east after the battle of Fallen Timbers in 1794. The "Perry Artillery Company" honored Commodore Oliver Hazard Perry, who had built part of his fleet at Erie in 1813 and sailed from Presque Isle Bay to defeat the British at the battle of Lake Erie. The "Franklin Pierce Rifle Guards" were named for America's fourteenth president. The village of North East had the "Burgettstown Blues" and in Waterford there were the "Invincibles." Grandiose names were common to American militias, and they reflected the romantic notions that many Americans held about the military and warfare. These organizations and others like them throughout the United States were the target of Lincoln's call for troops in 1861.[8]

On April 18, the *Erie Weekly Gazette* printed the President's proclamation in its entirety, and as the one of the paper's writers opined, the militia companies were expected to answer Lincoln's request. "It is understood that the Wayne Guards will respond to the call for volunteers to defend the Government," he wrote, "Their gallant Captain has held himself in readiness for months to comply with any demand which might be made for his services, and a considerable number of the company now manifest a willingness to accompany him." The unidentified, but apparently well known, "gallant captain" was John W. McLane, and his name appeared on the paper's fourth page as the Sheriff of Erie County, at the bottom of the column that listed public auctions. Three days after he was so identified in the *Gazette*, McLane telegraphed Pennsylvania Governor Andrew Curtain and offered to raise a regiment for the service of the Union.[9]

Born in Wilmington, Delaware, in 1820, John McLane had lived in Erie County since his family had moved to Moorheadville (later Harborcreek), northeast of the city of Erie, in 1829. At twenty-one, he became the manager of Joseph Neely's gristmill in the same town. A year later McLane showed an early martial aptitude and formed a militia company named "The Wayne Grays" in honor of Gen. Anthony Wayne. In 1845, he married Neely's daughter, Jane, and continued managing the grist mill and commanding the Wayne Grays until 1846 when the family moved to Indiana.

War with Mexico was declared that year and McLane raised a company of the 1st Indiana Volunteer Infantry under a Presidential request for militia similar to the one

Colonel John McLane, the first commander of the 83rd Pennsylvania. (Ronn Palm)

that was issued in 1861. Although the regiment joined the Army in Mexico, its service was limited to garrison duty in Matamoras and Monterey. The McLanes returned to Harborcreek, but Jane died of fever in 1854. Two years later John married Rosanna Moorhead. In 1857 he and other county businessmen founded the Farmer's Mutual Fire Insurance Company of Harborcreek. The business prospered and McLane was elected Sheriff of Erie County the next year.

In 1859, tensions between North and South indicated a coming war, and McLane formed "The Wayne Guards" militia company with himself as its captain. A staunch Unionist, he attended Abraham Lincoln's inauguration in March 1861. Two days after the national request for militia, Governor Curtain offered him the politically prestigious post of Pennsylvania's Commissary General. A source reported that he responded, "I am not lame. I am sound and strong. I want active work in the field. Give me that." As a Crawford County newspaper reported, "The captain is a noble man, but we think he would prefer to meet his foe upon the tented field, rather than be shut up dealing out victuals to those who do the fighting." Curtain responded to McLane's request with a colonel's commission and the authorization to raise his infantry regiment.[10]

To help recruit the required soldiers, towns held "war meetings" where civic leaders and militia officers gave patriotic speeches and extolled men to join up. Crawford County held three rallies in one week and soon sent an equal number of companies—the Conneautville Rifles, the Titusville Volunteers, and the Spartansburg Volunteers—to join McLane's regiment. Forty-two men signed on after one meeting in Warren. Seventy students at Allegheny College near Meadville formed a company. The town of Waterford sent its own "Ft. LeBoeuf Volunteers" to join. The *Erie Weekly Gazette* asked readers, "Will you take up arms in your country's defence, [sic] in its present time of imperative need?... We rejoice to witness, here, and elsewhere, striking proofs of a prevailing willingness to stand by the Administration and its patriotic determination to preserve and perpetuate our admirable form of Government." (The news writer noted that he would join "without a moment's hesitation, if our personal health, and consequently our physical strength, warranted.")[11]

Citizens of the county showered their militiamen with patriotic attention. Erie County war meetings voted to raise $7,000 for the regiment's equipment and support for the soldiers' families, and then added $10,000 to the sum a few days later. Farmers from the county donated food. The women of Erie made each man a blue uniform with a yellow flannel shirt. At least two men who called themselves "old soldiers" wrote to the local newspapers with advice for the new troops on what clothes to pack, accessories to carry, and such tips as "Keep your entire person clean; this prevents fevers and bowel complaints in warm climates. Avoid strong coffee and oily meat."[12]

The United States Hotel in Erie housed many of the new soldiers in the first few days of recruitment, but over 1,000 men came to Erie in less than ten days to join the regiment and the hotel was soon overwhelmed. McLane moved the men to a vacant lot at Parade and Sixth Streets and dubbed it "The Wayne Camp Ground." In the tradition of the American militia, McLane held elections for the regiment's senior officers on April 27, where the men unanimously voted him as their colonel, Benjamin Grant as the lieutenant-colonel, and Matthias Schlaudecker as major. Col. McLane telegraphed the governor for permission to swear all the men into service and proceed to action. Limited by the War Department regulations, Curtain authorized him to accept ten companies of eighty men each. Lt. Col. Grant swore the 800 men into their companies the day after the elections, and the rest were sent home.[13]

Col. McLane's Erie Regiment was fully manned, sworn in, and uniformed (but without muskets) and ready to join the war by the end of April. Fairgrounds outside Pittsburgh were named "Camp Wilkins" and designated the point for all regiments raised in western Pennsylvania to report for acceptance into Federal service. In a pouring rain on the first of May, the soldiers left the Wayne Camp Ground and marched to the State Street railroad station to board the train for Pittsburgh. Even in the wet weather their spirits were high, and a crowd that was both tearful and cheering met them at the station to bid farewell. The next evening the regiment arrived at Camp Wilkins.[14]

Though Col. McLane's men were anxious to meet the enemies of the Union, most had little or no military experience and needed much training before they were ready for action. For the first few weeks of May the soldiers' main activity was a twelve-hour-a-day drilling regimen. Late that month a sergeant wrote home that the men were "fast improving in the rudiments of military knowledge. [The regiment] is composed of men who are anxious to learn that they may best know how to fight, and such men learn quickly." Col. McLane was named commander of Camp Wilkins, and one newspaperman reported after a visit there: "If any of the boasting Rebels down South imagine that one of their traitor crew can whip three Northern men, they will experience a terrible disappointment when the Erie boys happen along."[15]

By early June a Union army was forming to counter a secessionist force in western Virginia. Some of McLane's soldiers expected to join the expedition, but they still had not been accepted into Federal service and did not even have weapons. Rumors of action were plentiful, and one report of a Confederate move toward the Pennsylvania-Virginia border generated such a scare that the regiments at Camp Wilkins were quickly issued muskets and prepared to march to the emergency. The orders were rescinded when the report was proven false, and the rifles were packed away, much to the dismay of McLane's men. One soldier wrote home, "It would be the height of folly, you know, to let the Erie Regiment—with not a personal friend of the Governor in it and no funds on hand to buy favors—have a musket to handle before they were needed to stop the balls of the rebellion." Another panic and marching orders came in late June, but were again canceled. McLane's troops moved to a more comfortable camp that month and received their muskets, but the *Weekly Gazette* reported, "The Erie Regiment, located at Camp Wright ... seems doomed to disappointment ... the Regiment is confessedly one of the best in the State, and anxious for active service, but the opportunity is denied it. Consequently both officers and privates are disheartened and depressed."[16]

A frustrated Col. McLane visited the War Department in Washington to ask when his troops would be sworn in to Federal service. By that time the government had realized that the war was likely to last longer than the militia's ninety-day terms of enlistment and called for 42,000 more soldiers to serve for three years. The ninety-day men were not what was needed, and the War Department told McLane that the Government would accept his regiment immediately if the men signed on for three-year terms. McLane returned to the camp and offered the idea to the troops. Many soldiers believed that the war would be over within months and were skeptical of the need for such a long commitment. Pvt. Plympton White said as much in a letter home: "I understand the report has gone to Erie that we have all enlisted for three years' but that is a mistake: for my part I will not enlist for a longer period than three months unless the country needs me, in which case I would enlist for life." Some of McLane's men favored the three-year proposal, but not enough to form a complete regiment. Those that wished to could have stayed on with other units, but that would have excluded McLane and his officers from leading them. With the difficult choice of disbanding or languishing in camp, the men elected to stay together and serve their time as a cohesive unit until ordered to war or home.[17]

By early July, weeks had gone by with no orders. In contrast to their earlier long training days, one soldier of Company B complained, "Our greatest trouble is inactivity and idleness, too much sleep and rest." An officer recorded that their main summer activity was the crafting of jewelry from clamshells found on the banks of the Allegheny River. By mid-July the regiment was still in camp with no prospect of leaving and to make matters worse, they had received no pay. Complaints grew, but Col. McLane took immediate action to head off any un-soldierly conduct. After a grueling, three-hour drill one morning, he formed the regiment in a hollow square and told them to maintain their bearing under the trying times. "I have spent $1,000 and have not received a cent in return," he told them, "but I am determined to do my duty; and if the state of Pennsylvania is too poor to repay me, I will make a free gift of my services to her. And if there is one among you who is not willing to do the same, I will pay him his wages out of my own pocket.... Let us honor ourselves and those we represent at home by behaving like gentlemen and soldiers." McLane followed his speech with three more hours of drill, and one officer later remembered, "The starch had been so completely taken out of the malcontents that not a word of complaint was heard from them afterwards."[18]

Within days of McLane's speech, the men were resigned to the fact that they would not be Federalized. There is no definitive explanation for why the regiment was never called, but it was probably because the government had been overwhelmed by the response of the militias. Unfortunately for the men who had joined, states all through the north, including Pennsylvania, had raised more soldiers than they were prepared to transport or equip. Thousands of volunteers sat as idle as McLane's men. Some units camped near Harrisburg became so discontented that they mutinied. The *Erie Weekly Gazette* reported that Gov. Curtain had originally marked the Erie troops to be the fourteenth of the sixteen required Pennsylvania regiments, but when Washington feared a march by the Rebels that summer, Curtain sent another more available unit to the capital in their place. Curtain expected another requisition for troops and intended to send the Erie men on with the second group, but the expected request was rescinded. After the call for three-year volunteers in mid–July, there was simply no need for McLane's three-month soldiers. The state had no choice but to discharge the men and let them go home. Released from camp, they returned to Erie on July 20. Though they had seen no action, another cheering crowd welcomed the men at the train station. Still proud, the men formed their ranks and marched to Erie's Central Park where the town hosted their returning soldiers to a picnic. After the refreshments, Col. McLane dismissed his soldiers and allowed them to serve the remainder of their enlistment time, which would end on August 1, on furlough.[19]

The day after McLane released his men, events in Virginia offered them a second chance to join the war. Though the men from northwestern Pennsylvania had been rebuffed in their efforts to fight for the Union, thousands of other soldiers succeeded in joining the Federal army, then camped at Washington. With only rudimentary training, 37,000 troops were formed into an army under Brig. Gen. Irvin McDowell. Likewise, the Confederates marshaled an army of 21,000 under Brig. Gen. P.G.T. Beauregard at the Manassas Junction railhead, thirty-five miles west of the capital. At the same time that McLane's Erie Regiment was returning to Erie, McDowell moved his troops out of Washington with the intent of destroying the Rebels at Bull Run Creek. The battle started early on July 21. At first all went well for McDowell, but by the end of the day the Confederates rallied and fought off the attack. Many Washington residents and members of Government had journeyed out to Manassas to watch the battle, and when McDowell's men began retreating, so did the spectators. In the rush to get out of the way of the advancing Rebels, Union soldiers, Congressmen, families, and hangers-on got mixed together in a very confusing fight for possession of the roads back to Washington. Only the fact that the Confederates were too tired and disorganized to manage an organized pursuit saved them from capture. The South clearly claimed victory in the first large battle of the war, and the Rebel army in Virginia became a very real threat for the citizens of Washington.

Though President Lincoln had already intended to raise 500,000 more three-year troops, the defeat at Bull Run proved that the Confederates could fight and that the war would be a long one. The day after the battle, Congress passed the Military Act that officially called for the volunteers that Lincoln sought. Even before leaving Pittsburgh, John McLane had let it be known that he meant to form another unit, and when news of the Military Act reached Erie, he received a second colonel's commission and permission to recruit a new regiment. Within days, newspapers and bulletins appeared all over the five counties of northwestern Pennsylvania. McLane also took advantage of the telegraph as a means to rapidly communicate with militia leaders. One message was later printed in a Crawford County newspaper under the header "RECRUITS WANTED! U.S. VOLUNTEERS!!" It was a typical announcement:

Erie, July 29, 1861, Capt. Shaw, Meadeville:
I have orders from the War Department for a Regiment. Fill up your Company.
Col. John W. McLane."[20]

The new Military Act called for regiments of 1,048 officers and men. Organized according to Federal Regulations, the regiment was led by the Field Staff, which consisted of 1 colonel, 1 major, 1 quartermaster (first lieutenant), 1 surgeon, 1 sergeant major, 1 commissary sergeant, 1 hospital steward, 2 principal musicians, 1 chaplain, a band with 24 musicians, 1 lieutenant colonel, 1 adjutant (first lieutenant), 1 quartermaster sergeant, and 1 assistant surgeon.

The fighting strength of the regiment was found in ten infantry companies of about 100 men each, lettered "A" through "K" (traditionally there was no "J" company, because of the similarity to the letter "I" when written in longhand). Each company had 1 captain, 1 second lieutenant, 4 sergeants, 2 musicians, 64 to 82 privates, 1 first lieutenant, 1 first sergeant, 8 corporals, and 1 wagoner.[21]

Though there was much support for the war in the northwestern counties, McLane would find the recruitment of over 1,000 men more difficult than he had in April. By late July, the U.S. Regulars and the Navy were also looking for volunteers in Erie, and some men had gone to join other units in neighboring Ohio or New York. The boredom of life at Camp Wright had also no doubt soured many militiamen to the experience of full-time service, and in the face of such competition, even a man of McLane's reputation would have trouble rapidly raising so many men. There are no records of exactly how the colonel recruited the second regiment, but if McLane followed the standard method, he would have relied on the northwestern Pennsylvania county leadership to help him bring the men in. Just as Gov. Curtain had promised him a colonel's commission, McLane would have offered a captain's position to any man who could bring a fully formed company to the regiment. The captain-designees, in turn, garnered assistance with recruiting their units by offering lieutenant's commissions to other men with education, reputation, or any form of influence who convinced others to join. Through this system, the natural leaders, well-connected, or educated men gained positions as the regimental leadership, and the citizenry signed on as private soldiers to follow them. Once the requisite number had joined, the entire company would move to the regiment's designated muster-site in Erie and report for service.[22]

It is unknown what happened to the Capt. Shaw that McLane directed to recruit troops in Meadville, but another Crawford County Company named the "Finney Guards" (named for a Pennsylvania senator) under Capt. DeWitt McCoy was the first filled and left for Erie on August 3.

Companies from Waterford, Titusville, Conneauteville, Edinbroro and Erie gathered in the next few weeks. About 300 men from the three-months regiment returned. When Forest County's "Tionesta Rangers" mustered, a delegation of ladies bestowed them with a handmade flag and made patriotic speeches about how well the soldiers would perform against the Rebels. The company left for Erie as bands played and a crowd cheered. In two days they covered the sixty-two miles to Erie by foot, flatboat and train, and joined the regiment on September 6. One member later wrote that the young men of Tionesta exuded a spirit that said, "Here am I, let me go."[23]

The companies arrived under the command of the captains that had recruited them and as required by Army regulation, any vacancies in their leadership were soon filled by a soldiers' vote. McLane had received his colonel's commission directly from the governor, and the positions of lieutenant-colonel and major were to be elected by the junior officers. Though more extensive elections were not required, McLane allowed the enlisted men to vote for the senior officers in order to validate the soldiers' trust in their leadership. His confidence in the men was confirmed when he secured the commander's position and Strong Vincent, former adjutant of the Three Months' regiment, was elected to major. The position of lieutenant-colonel was left vacant for the expected appointment of Capt. Fleming, a Regular Army officer.[24]

The company officers represented the many levels of Pennsylvania social strata. Capt. David S. Knox, who led Company G, was a merchant in Tionesta. His 1st Lieutenant, George Stowe, was a laborer and the company's 2nd Lieutenant, Daniel Clark, was a clerk. Thomas Austin, Captain of Waterford's Company K, operated a watch and jewelry store in Erie. Lt. David P. Jones of Company A and Daniel Sager of Company G were farmers. Capt. Hugh Campbell was also a farmer before raising Company E, but he had been born in Scotland, emigrated to America at the age of twenty, and still spoke with a soft Scottish burr. In the same company was Amos Judson, who had graduated from Yale with honors. Though he was a member of the Pennsylvania Bar, Judson was the editor of the *Waterford Enquirer* when he joined the regiment. Before that he had spent five years in the Southern states as a teacher and published a book of poetry called *The Wanderer*. A well-known citizen of Waterford and an outspoken critic of slavery, it took Judson only four days to raise Company E and accept a commission as its first lieutenant. Plympton White, who had earlier stated that he would "enlist for life" if the country needed him, was also studying law in Erie and signed on as Company D's 1st Lieutenant. Capt. Orpheus Woodward was a schoolmaster in Edinboro. The commander of Company I, Hiram Brown, operated Brown's Hotel in Erie (at the north corner of State Street and the Public Square). Brown had grown up in Erie but had also lived in Chicago and California. Details of his activities in California are sketchy but one biographer referred to him as an "adventurer." Brown's 2nd Lieutenant, John Clark, was a shop clerk. Strong Vincent, the regiment's new Major, was an attorney in Erie when he enlisted, and he had been a man of distinction for many years.[25]

Vincent was born in Waterford in 1837 to Bethuel Boyd Vincent and the former Sarah Strong. Both parents came from proud, prosperous families. His father's line had been in America since 1687, and the Strongs had been one of the first families of the Massachusetts Bay Colony. Like their ancestors, the Vincents were well established when Strong was born. His grandfather, John Vincent, was a judge and also made a substantial fortune in Erie and Waterford mercantile and freight businesses.

Bethuel Boyd Vincent raised his sons under strict Christian morality and ethics. Strong's younger brother Boyd remembered their regimen: "Bible-reading, family prayer, study of Sunday-school lessons, strict Sunday observance, carefully regulated amusements.... Each boy had to take his share, too, of the daily 'chores' about the house, caring for the horses and cows, building fires, carrying coal and ashes and blacking all the shoes every Saturday night. 'No lazy boys about me. Don't stand back and wait for the other fellow. Jump in and put your own hand to it': these were constant injunctions. [Our father] was nearly six feet tall and weighed 225 pounds; when he said 'Come' we came, and when he said 'Go' we went."

Strong entered the Erie Academy, the city's private secondary school, after the family moved into the city of Erie in 1843. He continued until age fourteen, when the curriculum bored him and he saw no reason to continue school. Strong's father allowed him to leave the Academy only if he went to work in the family foundry, Vincent, Himrod & Co, to which Strong agreed. He was soon known for his remarkable physical strength and considered to be a bright boy around the ironworks. After six months in the foundries he was transferred to the counting-room, where Strong oversaw the company's books and then advanced to manage much of the labor.

Strong Vincent as a first lieutenant in 1861. (Ronn Palm)

In 1854, Strong was seventeen and he left Erie to attend the Scientific School at Trinity College. In his second year there he began calling upon Miss Elizabeth Carter, a teacher at a nearby women's school. A fellow student later recorded that at some point of the courtship a guard or watchman uttered a caustic remark on Miss Carter's reputation, and Vincent reportedly pummeled the man into unconsciousness. The incident may have prompted his early release from Trinity in 1857.

Whatever the circumstances, Vincent moved on to Harvard University the same year. His grades were average, but Vincent was well known. "Harvard Memorial Biographies" describes him as "a man of mark in his Class and in the College. There was not a student, from Senior to Sophomore, who did not on first meeting him seek to learn who he was. Physically he seemed fully developed. Of rather above medium height, he had a well-formed and powerful frame, and his face was remarkably striking and

Amos Judson, first lieutenant of Company E.

handsome. He looked many years older than he really was, and in every respect his mind corresponded to his body. One would have said, on hearing him converse, that he was twenty-five years old." Though outwardly impressive, Vincent led his class in absences from prayers and was also admonished for "smoking in the yard." He graduated with a law degree in the class of 1859, fifty-first out of ninety-two students.

After his return to Erie, Strong joined the law practice of William S. Lane, one of the county's leading attorneys. He followed politics, and supported Abraham Lincoln's candidacy in 1860. A year later he passed the Bar and became Lane's partner. When John McLane announced his recruitment for the three-months regiment, Vincent enlisted as a private. He was selected to be Company A's 2nd Lt., and then the Regimental Adjutant, one of the colonel's key assistants.

Before McLane's regiment left for Pittsburgh, Strong telegraphed Elizabeth Carter and asked her to marry him before his departure for the war. Elizabeth accepted the proposal, and they married in Jersey City, New Jersey, on April 25, 1861. Vincent rejoined the regiment in Pittsburgh, and Elizabeth took residence in a hotel near the soldiers' camp.

Just as he was a notable personality at Harvard, Vincent appeared to be the darling of Erie. Soon after his wedding, the *Weekly Gazette* reported: "Our young friend having previously enlisted, is now 'off to the wars' as Adjutant of the Regiment from this District. We trust he may safely return to his fair bride after fulfilling the demands of his country upon his services, and thereafter enjoy long continued and uninterrupted domestic felicity." When recruitment for McLane's second regiment began, Vincent's strong belief in the ideals of the Federal Union drove him to sign on again. He would soon write to his wife: "Surely the right will prevail. If I live, we will rejoice over our country's success. If I fall, remember you have given your husband to a sacrifice to the most righteous cause that ever widowed a woman." There were probably few other soldiers in the regiment that so embodied the Yankee ideals of self-reliance, courage, and patriotism more than the twenty-four year old Vincent.[26]

Like the officers, the soldiers were difficult to typify. About half of McLane's enlisted men were farmers when they joined. Over a quarter of them were some type of craftsman or tradesman such as carpenters, masons, joiners, bricklayers or painters. Oliver Norton, Vincent's color bearer on Little Round Top, was one of the sixteen school teachers who signed on. A large percentage of soldiers listed their occupations simply as "laborer." In this respect they matched the occupational demographics of all Pennsylvania volunteers, of which over nine-tenths were farmers, mechanics or laborers.[27]

There were exceptions to this norm. In Edinboro's Company D, three quarters of the men were laborers and only six were farmers. Company B, from Meadville, had a high percentage of lumbermen and sawyers in their ranks. Though Erie was the center for lake shipping, Company B also had the regiment's highest number of sailors and boatmen on the rolls, probably men who worked the barges on French Creek.

Some soldiers' occupations defied categorization with their comrades. Joseph Scholl and Bryon Smith were both physicians and joined companies as private soldiers, although with their education they probably could have obtained officer's commissions in other units. Company H had one soldier who was a druggist; Company E had a post office clerk. Americans of 1861 were not as accustomed to filling out forms and answering personal inquiries as citizens of the twentieth century are, and the question of "occupation" probably puzzled some of the men. Three members of Erie's Company I listed their occupations as "soldier," possibly because they were unemployed at the time of enlistment, misunderstood the intent of the question, or because they entertained thoughts of making the Army their permanent vocations. The entries were not prophetic. One of them, Belgian immigrant Francis Deschrya, was discharged for a disability six months later. A second, Charles Lewis, would later desert the army while he was a hospital patient. Only one of the three, Abner Edison, would serve through the war. Other men mocked the rigidity of the military with jokes about their occupations. Ezekial Chambers, who stood 5'4" tall, flamboyantly claimed "horse jockey!" as his livelihood. The records of Company K show "Deserter" as the occupation of Pvt. Samuel Calvin and "Pie Eater" was listed as the trade of nineteen year old Allen Johnston. Calvin lived up to his description when he deserted on September 13, six days after his enlistment. It is not known whether Pvt. Johnston particularly enjoyed baked goods, but "Pie Eater" was slang for someone who avoided work, and it is easy to imagine that an angry company commander or clerk made entries like these as fitting records of the service of unimpressive soldiers.[28]

The General Orders accompanying the Military Act required recruits to be "able-bodied men, between the ages of eighteen and forty-five." Minors could join with the written consent of their parents or guardians. James Miller, age sixteen, and fifteen year old Frank Vader both joined Company I and were the unit's youngest soldiers. Stephen Robinson and John Wells both listed themselves as eighteen at enlistment, but were discharged when they were discovered to be underage. On the other end of the spectrum, there were nineteen men over the age of forty who joined that summer. Though over the regulatory age, seven recruits were over fifty. Some of them were discharged soon after they were examined

Pvt. Oliver Norton in his militia uniform, before joining the 83rd.

by the regimental surgeon and found not to be "able-bodied." The regiment's oldest serving soldier was fifty-three year old Pvt. William Robinson of Company C; a stout, 5'6" sailor from Erie who stayed with the unit until doctors discharged him, probably because of illness, in 1863.[29]

Like the enlisted soldiers, the General Orders required officers to be men between the ages of eighteen and forty-five and have "physical strength and vigor." Excluding Col. McLane, who was forty-one years old, and Surgeon William Faulkner who was forty-two, the company officers' average age was twenty-nine. Maj. Strong Vincent was twenty-four, Lt. Joel Smith of Company F was forty-one, illustrating that age did not necessarily equate to rank.[30]

With the companies raised from the same localities, the men were closely related. Three brothers of the Van Giesen family—Thomas, Charles, and John—joined Company G on the same day, as did the Wittich boys—William and Frederick, in Company I. Most of the soldiers probably lived and worked near the towns of their birth, but seventy of them were immigrants and most likely not yet citizens of the United States. Germany and Prussia were the most common countries of origin. Erie's Company A, with sixteen Irishmen, had the highest concentration of immigrant soldiers. There were also men from England, Scotland, Wales, and France throughout the regiment. Many soldiers of all nationalities could not name their birthplaces. One man in Company H listed his home simply as "Europe" and Pvt. William Schlachback of McKean claimed to have been "born at sea."[31]

Although they had no uniforms or muskets, the men established "Camp McLane" on the Buffalo Road about two miles east of Erie and set up regular guards, work details, and training while the ranks continued to fill. By September 8 all ten companies had reported to Erie and were sworn into state service. This time the Government, embarrassed by the loss at Bull Run and panicked by the threat of a Rebel march on Washington, called for the new three-year units to be sent as fast as they were raised. The same day the last of McLane's companies mustered in, a Regular Army officer swore them all into the service of the United States.[32]

One diligent recorder of the regiment's activity was Pvt. Seth Waid of Company F. A farmer from Randolph Township, about seven miles east of Meadville in Crawford County, he was married for less than a year to the former Elethear Cutler when he volunteered for the service of the Union. Elether's brother, Charles Cutler, was in the same company and Waid's own sibling Chauncy was in another Pennsylvania regiment. At twenty-six, Seth was older than most of his comrades. He was a devoted Free Methodist, and rather than carouse with the other troops he spent much time reflecting on his family or how the fortunes of war might treat him. Waid started a diary the day he left home, and in it he recorded that on September 14, Col. McLane called the soldiers out to the parade ground to make an announcement. Waid recalled, "We could see by the movement that there was something unusual on foot ... we faced to the center and the colonel addressed us—Saying that he had received orders from the War department to march his regiment directly to the seat of war [northern Virginia], and he read the dispatches to us giving the orders for us to pack our things immediately and be ready to start tomorrow night.... The news was received by the men with the wildest enthusiasm and three rousing cheers were sent up for the war, and hundreds of hats were thrown into the air in token of the spirits with which the news were received then the companies were marched off the Parade ground and dismissed and most of the men were busy with pen and ink writing to Friends at home. I wrote to Thear [his wife] and the rest of our folks and mailed it."[33]

Three days later, Col. McLane marched his soldiers to the train station again to start their journey to join the army at Washington. As the *Weekly Gazette* reported, "Of course a vast crowd collected for the occasion, embracing fathers, mothers, wives, sisters and people generally from Erie and adjoining counties. The scene was a deeply impressive one, and good many tears were shed and many heart-felt good wishes exchanged." At 3:00 p.m., the train left Erie and headed east for New York, the first leg of a winding route to "the seat of war."[34]

Another correspondent, Daniel Foote, was one of the new privates in Company K. The son of a farmer from Wattsburg in Erie County, he had attended the Waterford Academy until the age of nineteen and afterward taught a few sessions there. He had turned twenty on August 24, less than a week after his enlistment. Foote was friends with Julia Hill, the daughter of a minister

Daniel Foote, in a post-war photo. (U.S. Army Military History Institute)

in the town of North East, and he began correspondence with her when he joined the regiment. Heading for New York, the train carrying the regiment passed through North East and Foote wrote to Julia, "I looked hard to see you or some of your folks but could not. From the birds eye view I got I should think that you lived in a pretty little village." Just before leaving, Seth Waid also wrote: "It is natural that my thoughts should wander back to that home where I have spent the sweetest time of my life and I would breath [sic] an humble prayer that I may be spared to return to that home when peace shall again be restored to my beloved parents in their declining years and to once more clasp the form of my loving wife in my arms."[35]

As soldiers had done since armies had existed, many of Col. John McLane's men felt the same way as they watched their homes disappear in the distance.

II

IT SEEMED A LITTLE LIKE WAR

Though Col. McLane's soldiers in September 1861 were full of confidence and enthusiasm, that was not the case with the citizens and troops in the nation's capital.

The Union army of Gen. Irvin McDowell had retreated to Washington after the debacle at Bull Run. Many of the hastily raised militia regiments were shattered in battle and some units had completely melted away. Few of the units in McDowell's army were positioned for an adequate defense of the capital, and no effective command system was in place to direct those that were. Many officers had lost control of their units and thousands of demoralized men camped all over the city. However, unlike their Yankee counterparts, Gen. Beauregard's Confederates were flush with victory and had pushed their outposts to the hills of northern Virginia within sight of the capitol building itself. Though the Rebels were too weak to advance any farther, the residents of Washington assumed a Confederate move on the city was imminent. With the broken Federal army as their only defense, prospects for holding off Beauregard's troops looked slim.

To defend the capital and eventually defeat the rebellion, the Union needed an army that was fully trained and ready to fight a long war. To build it, President Lincoln appointed Major-General George B. McClellan as its new commander and relegated Gen. McDowell to a lesser post. McClellan arrived in Washington on July 26, 1861, and took charge of an army that he said was "a mere collection of regiments cowering on the banks of the Potomac."[1]

George McClellan had graduated second in his class at West Point in 1846 and served as an engineer officer during the Mexican War. After the war, he held posts in the cavalry, as an instructor at West Point, and as an observer in Russia during the Crimean War until he resigned in 1855. McClellan then applied his engineering skills for the Illinois Central Railroad and by 1861 had risen to be the company vice-president and chief of its Ohio & Mississippi Division.

When the war began McClellan immediately volunteered his services to the governor of Ohio and was commissioned as a major-general in the state volunteers. As a trained engineer, Regular Army officer and railroad executive, George McClellan knew how to organize. His skill at marshaling Ohio's raw troops came to the attention of the War Department and in May, Congress transferred him to the Regular Army. The campaign to clear western Virginia (the one that McLane's men had hoped to join when they were camped outside Pittsburgh) had been his first assignment, and his success there in June and July 1861 caught the attention of the press. A handsome man of thirty-two, McClellan looked like a model soldier, and he spoke to the hearts of his

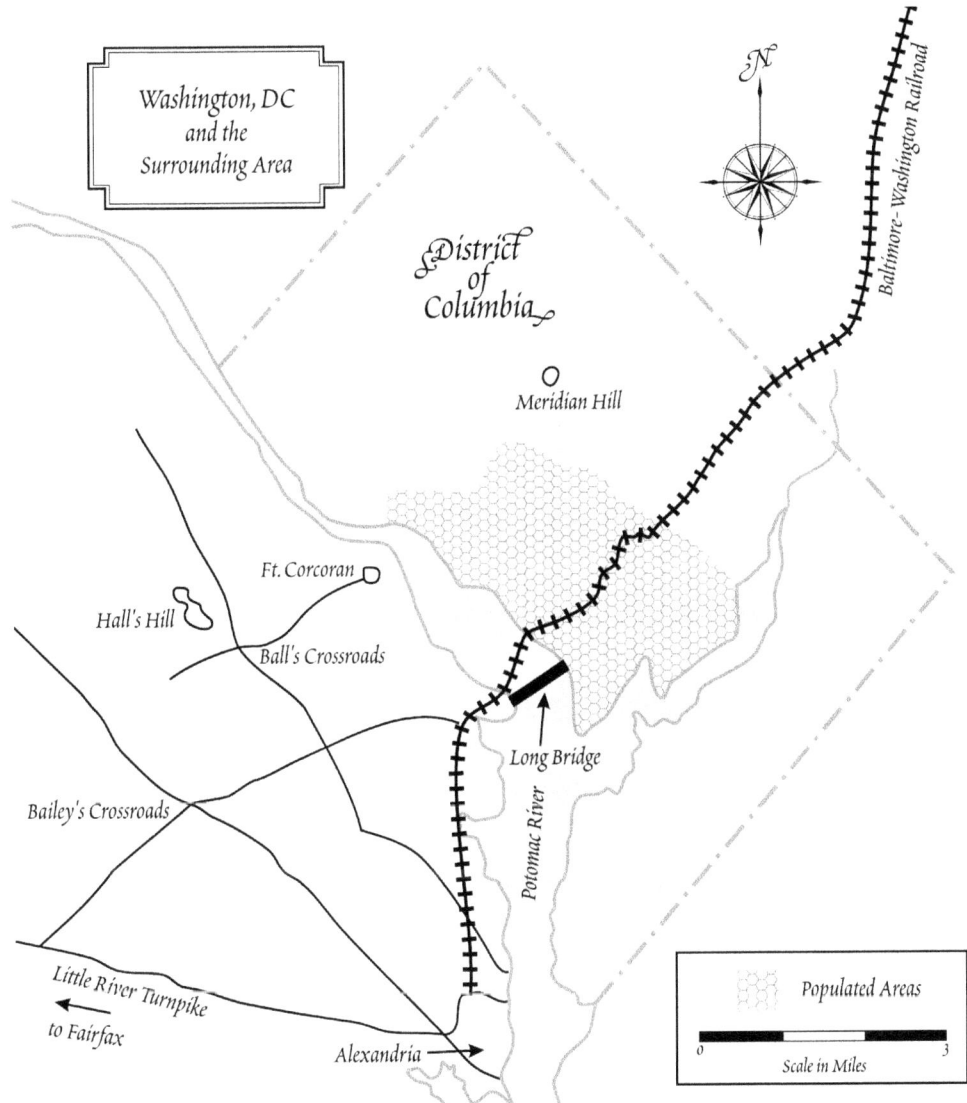

Washington, D.C., and northern Virginia in 1861. Here the 83rd spent its first winter of the war.

men with stirring speeches. One of his addresses that summer went: "Soldiers! I have heard that there was danger here and have come to share it with you. I fear now but one thing—that you will not find foemen worthy of your steel." The troops loved McClellan, and before the campaign was over the newspapers had started calling him "The Young Napoleon" or "Little Mac." Lincoln summoned him by telegram the morning after the defeat at Bull Run, and McClellan set about turning his demoralized soldiers back into a fighting force.

At Little Mac's order, engineers established a system of forts to guard Washington. A Provost Marshal Corps rounded up the soldiers roving around the city and returned them to their regiments. Inept leaders were replaced with Volunteer or Regular officers who had proven their mettle. The supply system was improved so quartermasters could replace lost equipment and issue new uniforms. Above all, McClellan ensured that unit commanders instilled discipline and kept their men on the training field. Every unit was required to drill for at least eight hours daily in camps that were set up according to standards in Army Regulations.

In response to the government's call for troops, new volunteer regiments began arriving in Washington in the late summer and the army grew by the thousands every week. On August 20, Congress organized the units around Washington into "The Army of the Potomac" under McClellan's command. To streamline control, Little Mac divided his new army into four divisions, each composed of three infantry brigades and a cavalry brigade. Brigades were made up of three to five regiments.[2]

The Army was in the midst of this reorganization when McLane's Regiment, as it was still known, arrived in the capital. From Erie, their train had wound its way through New York State to Elmira, south to Harrisburg and Baltimore, and then to Washington with no more than a few hours' stop at any station. Three days after it left Erie, the regiment reached its final destination at the Washington train depot on the evening of Thursday, September 19.

Maj. Vincent had arrived in the capital days ahead of the soldiers in order to arrange their reception, and he met them at the station with wagons full of tentage and other supplies—their first military equipment. Supper was also waiting for the men at the "Soldier's Rest," a reception hall behind the station that was reported to have a capacity of two thousand men. After dinner, Vincent formed the regiment and marched them about three miles northeast through darkened streets to Meridian Hill, on the outskirts of the capital's developed area.[3]

It was the first time that most of Erie's soldiers had seen Washington, and the sight of the capital left lasting impressions. Daniel Foote wrote that the city was "small by the size of Baltimore but is well laid out and the Capital [sic] is as nice a building as I ever saw. The great dome on the top is splendid." As for the condition of Washington, Foote called it "more like a great brick yard than anything else." A bright moon shone as the men moved toward their campground, and Lt. Amos Judson recalled with drama: "Here, beneath the great dome of the Capital [sic] looming up grandly in the distance, we spread our tents upon the ground and made our first bivouac upon the soil of Maryland."* Written after the war, his remembrance may have been romanticized by the passage of time. Another of the regiment's correspondents, writing within days of the event, wrote that the men were so tired that they threw down their blankets and fell asleep without pitching the tents that Maj. Vincent had just delivered.[4]

The next day, Pvt. Seth Waid recorded that the issue of the supplies that Vincent had ordered continued, with privates receiving "One flannel shirt, one white blanket with a blue stripe, one pair of shoes, one knapsack, a haverssack, one canteen apeace…." Old smoothbore muskets, blue "kepi" caps, cartridge boxes, belts, bayonets, and regulation waist-length shell jackets called "roundabouts" of blue serge were issued about a week later. Though they still wore their civilian trousers, the men at least began to look like soldiers.[5]

Capt. Fleming, whom Col. McLane expected to become the regiment's lieutenant-colonel, had never joined the unit and McLane held another round of elections for the staff positions. But in this vote Maj. Vincent was promoted to lieutenant-colonel and Dr. Louis Nahgel, a personal friend of McLane's who had lived in Erie and later

---

*Judson was mistaken about their location. Meridian Hill was on the outskirts of Washington's developed area in 1861 but within the District of Columbia. Part of the army's camping area is now Washington's Meridian Hill Park.

operated a medical practice in Indiana, was selected as the regiment's major.⁶

At the end of September McLane received orders for his troops to join the Army of the Potomac, which was camped throughout Washington and on the hills overlooking the Potomac River in Virginia. On the frosty evening of October 1, the men broke camp and marched across the river on Washington's Long Bridge to Arlington Heights, Virginia. Israel Thickstun, a twenty-three year old 2nd Lieutenant in Company H, wrote his mother his impression of seeing secessionist territory: "For the first time, it seemed a little like war."⁷

Col. McLane had requested assignment to a division of Pennsylvania regiments under Maj. Gen. George W. McCall but after a two-day stay at Fort Corcoran, on the west bank of the Potomac, the regiment was ordered to join Brig. Gen. Fitz-John Porter's Division, camped four miles west at Hall's Hill.⁸

Like McClellan, Porter was a veteran Regular Army Officer. The product of a family which had already produced two famous early nineteenth century naval heroes, Captain John Porter and Commodore David Porter, Fitz-John had graduated from West Point in 1845, eighth in a class of 123. Within a year, Porter was in action in the Mexican War where he was wounded and later promoted to major for distinguished service. Following the war he served in the Indian campaigns and was highly regarded throughout the small pre-

Lt. David Rodgers with Julia Porter. (Jean Rodgers Hall)

war Army. When the Civil War began, the thirty-nine year old Porter succeeded in winning a series of promotions that resulted in his command of the 15th U.S. Infantry Regiment. When McClellan came to the army in July, he immediately commissioned Porter a brigadier-general of volunteers and gave him command of a brigade composed of the 12th and 17th New York regiments and the 16th Michigan (known as "The Michigan Independents") at Hall's Hill. By the time McLane's Pennsylvanians arrived, Porter's Brigade had expanded into a division.⁹

Porter's protégé was Brig. Gen. Daniel

Butterfield, commander of the brigade that McLane's regiment joined. Unlike McClellan and Porter, Butterfield had been a founding member of the American Express Company whose only military experience was as the commander of the 12th Regiment of New York Militia. Though an amateur, Butterfield's leadership talents attracted the favorable attention of his superiors and Porter had personally requested him as a brigade commander in his division.[10]

Butterfield's Brigade set up camp at Hall's Hill, an oblong, 400-foot height north of the city of Alexandria and about three miles west of the Potomac. The hill was actually part of a 327-acre farm owned by Bazil Hall, a prosperous Unionist who had suffered at the hands of local Secessionists. Federals and Confederates had recently skirmished over the area and both sides had damaged the Hall mansion. Despite Hall's Union sympathies, McClellan ordered the hill occupied in September. It was one of the most advanced and important Federal outposts in the area and was still contested. Oliver Norton wrote home after their arrival, "As far as I can see in every direction, the white tents of our enemy dot every hilltop. The rebel camps are within two miles of us, their pickets and ours shooting at each other every night." The proximity of the enemy made the soldiers chafe for action, but McLane's regiment required thorough training before it saw combat.[11]

The Union and Confederate armies fought with tactics that had been adopted in the 1830s from the French, then considered by many American officers to be premier among the world's militaries. Unlike modern soldiers, who move independently and use natural concealment, Civil War infantrymen fought in the open in formations designed to mass their fire. With a few exceptions, regiments moved and fought as single entities under the direction of their colonel. To march from place to place, reg-

Top: Brig. Gen. Daniel Butterfield, commander of the 3rd Brigade. (LOC)
Bottom: Maj. Gen. Fitz-John Porter. (LOC)

iments used a column formation, which looked like this:

To generate effective fire on an enemy, regiments deployed on a broad front, called a "line of battle," where the soldiers would fire their muskets at the same time in volleys that sent masses of bullets at the opposing line. Designed in an age of inaccurate smoothbore muskets, the tactic was designed to ensure as many hits as possible on the enemy.* A line of battle looked like this:[12]

The regimental line of battle was usually composed of 8 to 9 companies formed in two ranks, the second rank 13 inches behind the first. Two companies, usually "A" and "B" went forward and stretched themselves out as a "skirmish line." Company comman-

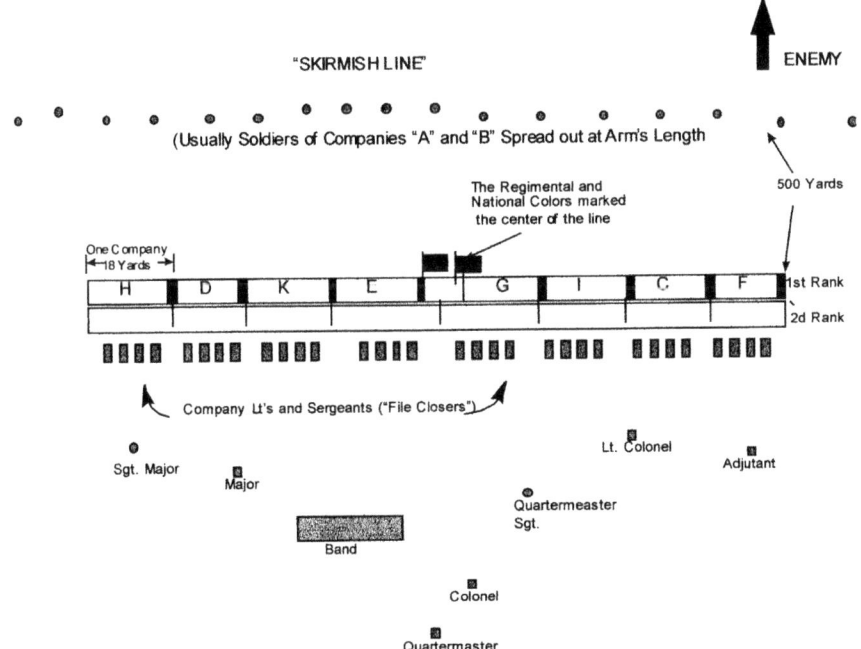

Top: A regiment in column of companies. *Bottom:* The regiment in line of battle (adapted from a chart by Lynn Myers, *The Civil War Infantryman*, Gregory A. Coco, 1996).

Rifled muskets and the Minié bullet came into use just before the Civil War and greatly increased the accuracy and range of the infantry musket. Their use would render these tactics exceptionally deadly and cause huge casualties during the war, a fact the men of the 83rd would learn in their first campaign.

ders stood in the front rank on the right side of their companies. Company positions on the line were based on the dates of their captains' commissions, the most senior always at the right and then staggered according to rules laid out in Army tactics manuals. According to the records of commissions of the captains present in the fall of 1861, the preceding diagram is a likely depiction of the 83rd's line. Company E held the place of honor in the center of the line as "the color company"—the keepers of the regimental flag.

The ability to march and fight in formation required hundreds of hours of continuous practice. Such drilling forced the men to learn to execute maneuvers instantly, without thought or hesitation. Men moved, faced a certain direction, fired or retreated only when ordered. To be able to do so was literally a matter of life or death, since maneuverable units on a battlefield would be able to make a line of battle and fire before less-drilled enemies were ready. Drilling to master the movements was a soldier's most important task. Use of the manual "Infantry Tactics," written by Brig. Gen. Silas Casey, ensured uniform training. Casey's text gave complete instructions for drilling soldiers, companies, regiments, brigades and divisions. It set the rigorous training standards that McLane's men would have to meet.[13]

For example, there were nine separate sub-movements just to load and prepare muskets for firing. They included placing the musket on the ground, removing a cartridge from a box carried on the hip, tearing open the cartridge, pouring the powder and dropping the bullet down the barrel, drawing the rammer, ramming the cartridge down the barrel, returning the rammer, priming the rifle, and returning the weapon to the carrying position. Only at the command "Ready" did the soldier raise the musket to chest height. At the command "Aim" he shouldered the weapon and sighted along the barrel. On the order of "Fire" the troops discharged the weapon and repeated the process on command. Once all nine movements were mastered, troops learned to condense them with the command, "Load in Four Times" or "Load at Will," and with this method a good man could fire about three rounds each minute.

The soldier also needed to learn how to move as a member of the unit. That included four different bodily facings; four movements; and thirteen different ways to march with a squad. Casey's manual even taught the men the proper form for leg and foot movement when marching:

> At the first command, the recruit will throw the weight of the body on the right leg, without bending the left knee. At the third command, he will smartly, but without a jerk, carry straight forward the left foot twenty-eight inches from the right, the sole near the ground, the ham extended, the toe a little depressed, and also the knee, slightly turned out. He will, at the same time, throw the weight of the body forward, and plant flat the left foot, without shock, precisely at the distance where it finds itself from the right when the weight of the body is brought forward, the whole of which will now rest on the advanced foot.

The manual also explained that when executing a long jog at "double quick time" that the men should "breathe as much as possible through the nose, keeping the mouth closed. Experience has proved that, by conforming to this principle, a man can pass over a much longer distance, and with less fatigue."[14]

Although a few of the regiment's officers had been in the militia and would have been somewhat familiar with the tactics and training standards, most of the leaders lacked true military experience. Exceptions were Col. McLane, who was known as "an excellent drill master" and Lt. Chauncey P. Rogers of Company D who campaigned against the Sioux as an engineer. Training in Erie, Seth Waid had noticed "Our officers do not know any more about drill than some of the privates." He wrote of another occasion: "We have just been out on drill under Lieutenant [Thomas] Stebbins and did not learn anything for the most of us know as much as he does." As Waid observed, the 83rd's officers were inexpert at the art of war.[15]

The officers' training regimen was even more difficult than that of the soldiers. Company commanders had to master guiding their men through at least thirty combinations of marching, changing direction and formation, forming lines of battle, and different firing sequences. In addition to the drill, officers were required to learn Army Regulations, management of company equipment and supplies, and the use of forms for every activity. Lieutenants were the commander's assistants and had to learn the workings of the companies as well as their captains. During drill, the lieutenants marched behind the ranks as "file closers" and ensured the lines kept proper alignment. They also had to learn all maneuvers in order to take charge if their commander was out of action. Like the soldiers, company captains and lieutenants also had to learn how to think and direct their units through all conditions, especially under fire. Officers on the Regimental Staff learned how to plan routes of march, provision the regiment and account for personnel. As called for in Casey's manual, Col. McLane personally trained all the officers. McLane and Butterfield were known to frequently quiz leaders on their skills, and many officers continued their studies at night to avoid being caught unprepared for their questions.[16]

All the individual and company movements came together to maneuver as a regiment, where Col. McLane had a choice of over one hundred methods to move the unit though any combination of circumstances. There were also six methods for the regiment to fire in volleys, which was possibly the most important of all tasks.[17]

To master all these requirements, the soldiers drilled in squads and companies every day in the early morning, followed by regimental practice. Brigade maneuvers occurred three times a week in the afternoons. Soldiers also held regular target practice and the best shots received public acknowledgment. In mock or "sham battles" the soldiers maneuvered, fired blank cartridges at each other, and charged and yelled with great enthusiasm. Pvt. Alexander May of Company K happily wrote of them, "It was active business but just suits me ... it makes a devil of a noise."[18]

The soldiers drilled every day except Sunday, and apart from the mock battles, training was hard work for the farmers-turned-soldiers. Seth Waid recorded soon after reaching Washington: "I think that anyone that will find fault with his fair at home had ought to try Soldiering for a while, and if that don't cure him I don't know what will...." Pvt. Oliver Norton wrote home: "My soldiering now is not play, it is work." In mid–October Norton summed up their routine: "The first thing in the morning is drill, then drill, then drill again. Then drill, a little more drill. Then drill, and lastly, drill. Between drills, we drill, and sometimes stop to eat a little and have a roll call."[19]

Uniformity and adherence to regulations became the watchwords of the soldiers' existence. Bugle calls told the troops when to wake, work and rest. The men woke to the sounds of "reveille" at six-thirty and went to sleep when the bugler blew the "extinguish lights" call at nine-thirty at night. Sergeants regularly inspected the troops' arms and equipment to ensure that they were kept in working order. Though they did not have to learn maneuvers, the regimental staff learned to perform their duties to the same exacting standards as the company officers. Unit supply and personnel records were maintained in precise detail which Gen. Butterfield's Brigade staff checked for accuracy. The Quartermaster, Lt. James Saeger, and the Commissary Sergeant, John C. Rockwell, learned to supply the soldiers with precise amounts of food, clothing, medical stores and ammunition. The Adjutant, Lt. John Clark, kept track of the 1,000 soldiers with a bewildering amount of forms, all of which had to be filled out precisely as called for in regulations. In addition to supplying martial music, the regimental musicians, led by the French-born, twenty-six year old professional musician Michael Mehl, learned to play the standard bugle and drum calls that corresponded to the marching commands and other common events of the day. There were fifteen commands on the drum, twenty-six on the bugle, and another forty-three for skirmishers. Everyone from the colonel down to lowest private had to memorize them all.[20]

Besides maneuvering, the constant training was designed to force the new soldiers, who still retained some level of individual independence, to move as one unit without thought. The idea of the regiment as a single entity was figuratively "drilled" into the minds of the men by constant repetition of the same tasks alongside the same men. By doing so, the soldiers learned to rely on each other and work together in a way few civilians did. Once the men put their trust in one another they would be a true unit and be ready to face the Confederates. They would need such close relationships to survive the hardships of war.

What men did not learn about each other during training, they found out in their close living conditions. The soldiers' quarters were the canvas "wedge" tents that were standard issue to the Army of the Potomac. Named from their shape, the tents were six feet square and designed to accommodate four soldiers. As many as five men slept in them at Camp Leslie,* rolling out their blankets at night on the ground and using knapsacks for pillows. In an example of the ingenuity of the American soldier, troops fashioned wooden ration boxes and ammunition cases into shelves, chairs, and other furniture. Over-filled, the tents were cramped with the soldiers' clothing, equipment and personal living items. In warm weather the men threw back the tent flaps and spent their few off-duty hours lounging on their rough furniture.

No maps of Camp Leslie exist, but Porter likely ordered the regiments to use layouts dictated in military manuals. A company's wedge tents were erected in two rows, with two paces between each tent. A twenty-foot wide aisle or "street" ran between the rows. A kitchen for each company was placed at the end of the street with sergeant's tents beyond that. Captains occupied ten-foot square "wall tents" (named from their short walls on the long sides) placed at the head of their companies. The two lieutenants in each company shared a wall tent next to their captains. The colonel, field officers, and the surgeon were allowed the luxury of two wall tents, although their quarters doubled as work areas, which ran in a line next to the company officers. About a hundred yards to the rear of the soldiers' tents were dug the latrines or "sinks" as they were called. Officers' sinks were placed at the opposite side of the camp. All together a regulation regimental camp consisted of about 250 tents and had the shape of a large rectangle. With this arrangement, any soldier could find his way around in the dark or any visitor could quickly locate those in authority. Beyond its military utility, uniformity gave the regimental camp the feeling of a small town. At night, while the officers sat around their own tents or studied their manuals, the en-

---

The camp at Hall's Hill was often referred to as Camp Leslie, Camp Porter, and Camp Butterfield.

listed men gathered in the company streets. As they did on porches or village stores at home, the troops read their mail or newspapers, complained about the day's training, smoked their pipes, engaged in horseplay and swapped stories. The bonds of camaraderie that were made from sweat on the drill field were cemented in friendship in the company street.[21]

To control entry and exit of the camp and to protect against thievery, desertion, or surprise, companies manned guard posts around Hall's Hill on a rotational basis. As with the drill, the guard mission was performed to exact standards, and Lt. Amos Judson recalled, "Guard mounting was conducted with a precision and conformity to army regulations which we had never before known." Each soldier was required to memorize the daily password and orders for his post, and to be caught sleeping on duty was a court-martial offense. To ensure that the work was taken seriously, Gen. Butterfield ordered that every guard shift be read 27 paragraphs of the Army Regulations (five typed pages in a modern edition) before they assumed their posts. Orders like that probably prompted Pvt. Alexander May in Company K to observe: "Our regiment does not perform here like they did at Camp McLane. A fellow is in danger of his life if he does not toe up. They are mighty strict on the guard."[22]

The soldiers usually stood their posts at key points around the camp in shifts of two hours at a time, and had to stand and stay alert no matter what the conditions or how tired they might have been. Oliver Norton wrote: "It is tiresome work. No sleep nights." Seth Waid used his tour as roving guard as a chance to observe the camp activities: "My duty gives me a good opportunity to get acquainted with the whole camp as I have to walk all about it. While going the round last night I noticed what the men were at and was struck with the number that were engaged in writing to their friends. Some were lying quietly in their tents and some were playing ... and I saw one man that was rolling and tumbling in pain with the cramp."[23]

All the regiments as Hall's Hill also periodically posted soldiers on a "picket" line, four or five miles from the camp to scout Rebel activity and guard against surprise attacks. Often within sight of enemy outposts, the expeditions were exciting but difficult. Occasional mishaps punctuated guard and picket duty and at least three men mishandled their muskets and shot themselves. When one soldier accidentally shot his own finger, Pvt. Daniel Foote wrote of the unfortunate man, "He made a terrible fuss.... I do not know exactly what he will do when he gets his head shot [off]." Some sentries fired at sounds in the night or moving shadows. Norton recalled that a pig wandered through the lines one night and a nervous sentry mistook it for an intruder and shot it in the nose. He also recorded the following exchange, which Norton claimed occurred when an Irishman in the regiment challenged an approaching group:

"Halt! Who goes there?"
"The Grand Rounds" [an officer's inspection].
"Och, to the divil wid yez grand rounds; I thought it was the relafe guard."

As at Camp Wright in Pittsburgh, rumors of Rebel activity circulated almost as soon as the regiment arrived at Hall's Hill. The proximity of actual Confederates gave the reports credibility. Within their first week in Virginia, Norton had written home: "Regiments are moving every night, and though we are ignorant of what is to be done, the universal impression is that a great battle in on the tapis." An anonymous soldier wrote to the *Erie Weekly Gazette* of how the regiment mustered in reaction to an alarm in early October: "Never shall I forget the enthusiasm manifested by our Regiment at the prospect of having a 'set to.'

The sick as well as others turned out...." In his diary, Seth Waid recorded his more private impression of the same event: "We were ordered soon after dinner to pack up and be ready to march immediately and all was wild excitement for a while and soon we were all ready. With knapsacks stuffed full, haversack, canteen, cartridges, caps, guns, & c. Some expecting to go into battle in less than an hour, some looking as badly frightened as if the enemy were really is in sight.—but after all [was] said and done we did not go 60 rods from camp, just out on inspection where we drilled nearly all the afternoon under all that load. For my part, I felt ready to go into battle."[25]

One of the most prevailing discomforts was army food. By regulation, each soldier was authorized a daily ration of twelve ounces of pork or bacon or one pound of beef; one pound six ounces of soft bread or flour, one pound of hard bread or one pound four ounces of cornmeal. Every company was to receive one peck of beans or peas, ten pounds of rice or hominy, ten pounds of green coffee, eight pounds roasted and ground coffee or tea, fifteen pounds sugar, two quarts of salt, four quarts of vinegar, four ounces of pepper, one-half bushel of potatoes, and one quart of molasses. Dried vegetables, fruits, pickles, or cabbage were also authorized. Officers received an allowance of $36 per month to supply their own rations plus an allotment for hiring one servant each.[26]

The Quartermaster drew the rations for the regiment and distributed them to Company 1st Sergeants in uncooked, bulk form. Official cooks were not part of the regimental structure, and it was the responsibility of each company to prepare its own food with whatever resources it could muster. Commanders usually selected some soldier who showed an aptitude for cooking (or unfortunately, one who merely had no aptitude for soldiering) to perform the cook's duties. Companies also issued the food straight to the men as a day's subsistence and the soldiers sometimes pooled rations with friends to form a small dining group known as a "mess" and cooked it themselves. The men of Company G hired a black servant, possibly an escaped slave, to cook for them.

The food was of many styles and quality, regardless of what the regulations called for or how it was cooked and distributed. Seth Waid's record of the following meals served at Hall's Hill indicates the variety of the soldier's diet:[27]

Oct 3: Dinner of bread, beef, beans, vinegar soup
Oct 13: Breakfast of crackers and coffee
Oct 22: Dinner of liver and salt-bread
Oct 27: Breakfast of potatoes, bread, beef, tea, pickled tongue
Nov 16: Breakfast of cabbage and bread; dinner of potatoes and milk
Nov 28: Thanksgiving Day: an oyster supper

Waid did not find many faults with army food, but other soldiers were not as tolerant. Oliver Norton wrote his friends: "You need not envy us much for our vegetables. They seem to be a failure. Our cooks don't know how to cook them and no one likes them." Norton later derided the staple army-issue cracker, known as "hardtack" or "pilot bread": "Some of this was good, but the greater part very poor, moldy, wormy, and made of poor flour, etc. Several barrels had crackers stamped 'T. Weld & Co., Boston, 1810', Company 'I' say they had a barrel marked 'B.C. 97' I don't know whether the crackers or the barrel was made before Christ, but I think it must have been the barrel." (Although the rations did not impress Norton, he apparently ate enough of it. By mid–December he wrote that his weight had increased to 135 pounds.) In Company G, Pvt. Thomas Van Giesen, one of the three brothers from Tionesta, echoed Norton's opinion of hardtack in mid–October: "We have plenty to eat ... but some of the time we have crackers that is hard enough to kill brush, but I can stand it if I git plenty of them."

To supplement the rations, every regiment was authorized one licensed peddler known as a "sutler" that sold, usually at high prices, pies, cakes, vegetables, fruit and other goods. Foraging parties were authorized to purchase food from local farmers, although they also often forced the civilians to sell their wares. Some expeditions outright stole food even though official orders forbade the practice. Daniel Foote's description of one foraging trip shows how callous the soldiers could be towards the Virginians: "We succeeded in finding 13 loads of hay about two miles over our lines. The [owner] came out as we were taking his last stack and said 'Boys leave me one stack', but our officer said 'Pitch it on, boys' and on it went. It is a hard thing but they are finding war is war."[29]

Other soldiers scavenged from Rebel homes in the area when on picket or scouting duty. Oliver Norton, who detested the Confederates and considered them traitors, wrote of one expedition in October: "We are in Secessia and the meanest part of it, too, and anything the boys can forage they consider theirs. A field of potatoes, five acres, was emptied of its contents in short order. H. [Norton's friend, Pvt. Henry Bushnell] and I got enough for a mess, and some parsnips. You ought to see us clean out the fences. The rails answer first-rate to boil our rations, and they have to do it."[30]

The regiment's lack of complete uniforms was another irritant. Officers purchased their own custom-made outfits but after a month in Federal service the enlisted men had not received their entire issue. When Gen. McClellan and Gen. Porter visited the camp in early October, Norton heard Little Mac say, "There, those boys haven't got their pants yet. That's a shame." Another soldier wrote home: "It was heart rending to see so many of our brave fellows try and hide their shame with the old rags they had on....." Gen. Butterfield demanded clothing from the Army Quartermaster, and on October 11 the same soldier recorded: "To-day (Friday,) lo! and behold! Our Regiment received their pants, or rather part of them, say about 90 pairs per company...." That issue brought the soldier's total kit to, as he explained: "1 Blue flannel Blouse Jacket; 1 cloth Cap—blue; 1 Haversack; 1 Water Bottle; 2 Shirts; 1 Blanket; 2 Pairs Drawers; 1 Pair Shoes; 2 pair Socks; 1 Knapsack; 1 Old flint musket; 40 rounds Ammunition."[31]

The uniforms were exceptionally uncomfortable by today's standards. The wool coats and trousers fit loosely, but were exceedingly hot in the summer. Also of wool, their forage caps kept body heat from escaping through the head, and the leather bill was too short to keep rain or sun out of the soldier's eyes. If wet, the entire suit was scratchy and dried out slowly. Ankle-high boots known as "brogans" were comfortable enough for most conditions, but the smooth leather soles were slippery on ice or wet stones. Over time many soldiers found ways to improve the utility and comfort of their uniforms, such as sewing linen liners or small pockets inside their coats, but regardless of their discomfort, the men were proud to be fully outfitted at last.

In late October the 44th New York Regiment arrived at Hall's Hill and became the fourth unit in Butterfield's Brigade. Known as "The Ellsworth Avengers," the 44th was named in honor of Col. Elmer Ellsworth, the late commander of the 1st New York Infantry and one of the North's first heroes of the war. In a tribute to deceased Ellsworth, New York State formed regiments that were composed of members that were specially selected for their worthiness as soldiers. The regiment reached Camp Leslie the evening of October 28 cold, exhausted from their trip south, and lost in the darkness. They had no welcome arranged and their immediate concern was to eat and bed down for the night. An officer of the 44th, Lt. Eugene Nash, later recorded, "To provide supper and sleeping accommodations for ten hundred men was not a small undertaking. A good Samaritan, numerous, generous, and hospitable, embodied in the 83rd Pa. Regiment, encamped near the spot where we halted, came to our relief."[32]

The Pennsylvanians helped the New Yorkers pitch their tents and later, Col. McLane's field officers and companies hosted their counterparts to dinner. Daniel Foote told Julia Hill of the new regiment, "They are made up of a man from each town in the state of New York and a noble set of men they are. They have come into our brigade now and the night they arrived we treated them to hot coffee and they fairly raised the dead with their cheers for old Penn. and her boys." From that time the regiments had a special fondness for each other. They also developed a friendly rivalry, as Alexander May wrote, "A New York Regt came in since [the last letter] and we had to try them and we beat them. They are picked men and better looking than we are but we are better drilled." Soon the two units would become so close that they earned the nickname "Butterfield's Twins."[33]

By November there were over 11,000 soldiers in Porter's Division and Camp Leslie was the largest in the Washington vicinity. McLane's regiment was officially designated the 83rd Regiment of Pennsylvania Volunteers,* and as May's comment indicates, they had become a well-trained unit. Gen. Butterfield officially commended the regiment for their "spirit of attention to duty" and called them "a worthy example to the rest of the brigade." After one parade, Gen. McClellan himself rode up to McLane and told him, "Colonel, I congratulate you on having one of the very best regiments of the army!" McClellan had also called the 44th "the best drilled regiment in the army" on another occasion, and it was the kind of comment that he made to units to build up their confidence. Regardless of the general's sincerity, he did not compliment soldiers that were not deserving.[34]

By November the entire army was better organized, led, equipped and trained than they had been before the Battle of Bull Run. Morale and confidence were high. Gen. McClellan frequently held reviews to demonstrate the prowess of his new troops, and in mid-November, one of McLane's soldiers wrote:

> It rained during the entire review, yet we went through it all as soldiers only know how to do and came to our quarters at night covered with mud and feeling somewhat damp. The news which was received the next evening, however, abundantly paid us for all we had gone through the day before. A full French Zouave uniform was to be given to the best drilled regiment in the division. But little did we think that the 83rd Pa. regiment was to be the happy recipients of so great an honor. After dress parade Col. McLane announced to the regiment that we had won the prize. The news was received with much surprise and three cheers were given for Gen. Porter and three for Col. McLane.

The Zouave uniform, worn by France's Algerian troops, was characterized by colorful, Arab-style trousers, short jackets and gaudy accouterments. Ridiculous to the modern eye, it was considered particularly attractive by soldiers of the 1860s. The army admired the French uniforms as it did their tactics and in August 1861 the Quartermaster

---

*It is a mystery exactly when the regiment was designated the 83rd. Nelson's History of Erie County states that the regiment was officially designated the "83rd" on December 21, but Pvts. Foote, Norton, May, Van Giesen and others began using "83rd Regiment" as their return address on letters as early as mid-November. On the assumption that the soldiers are the best sources for when they received their numerical designation, we can assume that the regiment was known as "McLane's" until late October or early November.

Top Left: Pvt. Samuel Islett of the 83rd in his *Chasseur de Vincennes* uniform. Islett wears the complete outfit with wide trousers, short jacket, shoulder epaulets and feather-adorned shako. (USAMHI, Randall C. Smythe Collection)

Top Right: Maj. Gen. George McClellan. (LOC)

Bottom Right: An unidentified private in the 83rd poses in his *Chasseur* uniform (USAMHI, Gill Barnett Collection)

Top: A sketch of Union soldiers stealing fence rails, by *Harper's Weekly* artist Alfred Waud. (LOC)
Bottom: Thanksgiving in a Union camp near Washington. The soldiers of the 83rd enjoyed a similar scene in 1861. (LOC)

Union soldiers crowd a sutler's wagon. The sutler sold food and other items at high prices, but without them the Union troops were consigned to eating military rations. (LOC)

General ordered 10,000 "chasseur a pied" (light infantry) style suits along with associated equipment as models for Federal uniforms. They were to be issued to the ten best drilled regiments in the Army, and Gen. Porter gave them to the winners of drill competitions held in each brigade of his division.[36]

Many units had styled themselves "Zouave" when they formed, as some Erie militia companies and the 44th New York had, but to be awarded the distinction by the government was a special honor. After winning the uniforms, Daniel Foote boasted in a letter to Julia Hill: "I presume that you have noticed in the papers that our reg't won the prize a week ago yesterday by doing the best marching, maneuvering and firing of any reg't in Porter's division. The prize consists in a zouave suit for the reg't costing $40. per suit." Oliver Norton beamed, "It is no small thing for a new regiment to beat a number of regiments that have been in the field all summer, and the far-famed 'Ellsworth Avengers,' but we have done it. We have earned a good reputation and we mean to keep it."[37]

The "chasseur a pied" uniform had a tight-fitting blue jacket with nine brass buttons, yellow or orange trim, and green epaulets with yellow crescents. It also had baggy blue trousers, leather gaiters to fit over the boots and lower leg, a cape, a tall plumed shako hat for dress parades and a soft, tasseled folding cap for regular wear. The accompanying equipment included hair-tanned leather knapsacks, cartridge boxes and belts, a variety of tents, picks, hatchets, shovels, nightcaps, neckties, handkerchiefs, white cotton gloves, blankets, haversacks, canteens, camp stools, medical kits, gun cleaning equipment, and pack equipment for mules, as well as small "needle books" with sewing tools and "sacs le petite"—small bags for carrying personal items. Alexander May observed that the outfits contained "all the camp equipment and all that a soldier needs from a kettle to a camp tent." Norton may not have been exaggerating when he wrote that the regiment was to have "the most complete outfit ever seen in this country."[38]

An agent of the French government fitted each man for his uniform, and the officers had special tailored suits ordered from France. The new tents were immediately available and issued while the men waited for the uniforms. With enough room for ten men (the standard American version held five) and interior fittings such as hanging shelves, portable tables and stoves, the tents made winter camp life more comfortable and delighted the soldiers as much as the uniforms. The complete outfits finally arrived in early December. Alexander May wrote to his cousin that the uniforms looked "grand" but qualified his fondness for them by observing that "the pants looks as much like ladies bloomers as anything else." Oliver Norton was steadfast in his view that the uniforms made the soldiers look wonderful, and most men shared his opinion.[39]

Although the men were immensely proud, Col. McLane soon wrote to General Butterfield, "The Frenchmen set to fit them report, after a thorough trial, that one third of the whole are too small a size." McLane had to write to Gen. Porter to exchange the small jackets for the correct sizes, but even when properly fitted, they were impractical for field use. The tight jackets restricted the soldier's movement and would be exceedingly hot in Virginia; the baggy trousers would catch brush in wooded country and the uniform's colorful trim and extras would have little use on a campaign. Perhaps in realization of their faults, McLane restricted his men from wearing any part of the Zouave suits without his authorization. The men would have to be content with the standard, government issue blue uniforms.[40]

The men of the 83rd had always had high spirits, but as winter began at Hall's Hill they showed the confidence that comes from hard training and the true unity of an elite regiment. They had left Erie as a group of raw militiamen, farmers and tradesmen, but they entered winter as a unit of solid soldiers. The drill that had led so many to complain in the autumn became a source of pride. Pvt. James Masiker of Company F wrote home: "The boys seem in good cheer and feel well, I am harty as ever, tough saucy and ruged." Arthur Cleeland, a 17 year old private in Company F, wrote to his sister: "I am getting so used to drilling that when we get a hollow day it seems like the sabbath day." Having drilled hard and been recognized as one of the army's elite regiments, McLane's men were anxious for a chance at the Rebels. Thomas Van Giesen told his siblings in one letter: "I think we can lick them if they let us try it."[41]

They had reason to be proud and look forward to action, but snow came in late November and the Virginia roads turned to mud. McClellan's army stayed in its camps at Washington for the winter. If the soldiers were disheartened by their lack of action, few wrote home about it. Snows caused frequent drill cancellations and the men probably enjoyed their respite. Some of the soldiers started a debating society. Lt. Amos Judson recalled that the men stayed near their fires, "smoking their pipes, and playing at their favorite games of euchre, cribbage, and old sledge." Oliver Norton wrote to his friends at home, "In the daytime we sit round the tents, reading, telling stories, grumbling about the rations, discussing the prospects of marching, cursing the English about the Mason and Slidell affair, expressing a willingness to devote our lives to humbling that proud nation,* and talking of this, that, and the other. Those whose tastes incline them that way are playing with the 'spotted papers,' but you will be glad to know that not one game of cards has been played in our tent since I lived in it, or in the old one either, and more than that, I have not played a game since I've been in

---

*The "Mason and Slidell affair" that Norton refers to occurred in December 1861, when a U.S. Navy ship seized two representatives of the Confederacy from a British vessel in international waters. Great Britain threatened war with the United States until President Lincoln released the prisoners and negotiated a diplomatic response.

the U.S. service. I don't know that as I am principled against it so much, but don't know how to play and don't care to learn. I spend much time writing."[42]

The Union and Confederate armies were the most literate that had ever taken the field up to that time and letter-writing played a larger part in the Civil War soldier's life than the men of any previous wars. Through the mail, the troops received pledges that they were loved, missed, and fought for a righteous cause. In return, families heard tales of military events that were exciting to civilians and more importantly, received reassurance that their men in the field were safe. The mail was vital to maintaining the morale of the soldiers. Anxious to tell their loved ones about army life and the sights of "secessionist" Virginia, the men wrote as often as their duties allowed. It took about a week for letters to travel between Hall's Hill and northwestern Pennsylvania and the men were surprisingly able to keep up with events at home. Norton maintained a weekly correspondence with his family. Daniel Foote traded letters with his relations and Julia Hill several times a month. A German speaker, Foote also helped soldiers from the Deutsche principalities draft their letters.

Pens, pencils, stationery (often adorned with McClellan's image or patriotic slogans) and postage stamps were available from the sutler and were precious items. Night at Camp Leslie usually was the time when troops would sit on their blankets and write home by the light of a candle. Men in tents with handmade furniture sometimes had the luxury of stable writing surfaces, but knapsacks and ration boxes were the soldiers' most common desks. The men thrived on any scrap of news from home and "mail call" was a highlight of every day. A note that described the most mundane events from the hearth filled a man's head with images of loved ones and the comfortable life he hoped to return to. Hometown newspapers were read, re-read, and then shared until they were in tatters. Some families sent packages of food or winter clothing (wool socks and mittens were coveted items) and many soldiers sent portions of their pay home. Letters were among a man's most cherished possessions, and the troops always yearned for more. Pvt. James Masiker told his friend Eliza in one late November note, "I want you to answer this as soon as you get it and let me know how you and the rest of the family is." Arthur Cleeland also implored his sister that month, "Tell Lewis and Phebe to write often and Eliza and Morrison to write often and you just write often and if you all write often it will do first rate." After his signature he added, "write soon soon very soon."[43]

Sicknesses were a frequent topic in soldiers' letters home. Disease had been a persistent problem since the regiment's formation and had caused its first death, Pvt. John Kerr, in late October. The regiment had been inoculated against smallpox in November, but the number of sick rose steadily as the winter wore on. The cold weather caused the men to gather less in the company streets and confined them to their tents. Ample fresh water was available from a stream at the foot of Hall's Hill, but complete bathing was infrequent among Civil War soldiers. The effects of bacteria were unknown to medical science of the time, but doctors recognized a relationship between poor hygiene, crowded camps and disease. "Mephitic effluvia" was believed to accumulate above garbage heaps or latrines and extended life in close quarters could lead to "crowd poisoning." Acting against these perceived maladies, military surgeons urged the soldiers to use the regimental sinks and to get as much fresh air as possible. Despite the warnings, the men often used the camp sinks only when it was convenient to do so and sanitary conditions deteriorated. Diseases passed easily in the poorly ventilated quarters and preyed on soldiers exhausted by tough training. Alexander May had written home that fall, "I have not seen a sick hour since we came to Washington but it is not so with every one. There is a great many sick just now. Our Capt. [James Austin] and orderly sergeant is very sick. They think that neither one of them [are] yet able to take their place again. The colonel drills us to hard for the weakest of them to stand it. Its not hard on me though."[44]

No mere cold would excuse soldiers from duty. At "Sick Call" held every morning after reveille, the regimental surgeon examined each man who claimed illness. Some troops frequently claimed infirmity to escape a day of drill, but McLane's physician, Dr. William Faulkner, had practiced medicine in Erie for at least ten years and was probably a good judge of legitimate maladies. Malingerers or those with minor complaints were sent back to the ranks. Soldiers with sicknesses short of disease were confined to their quarters and treated by the unit medical staff until recovery. Men were not sent to the hospital until they could be either positively diagnosed with a disease or they lost consciousness. It was not unusual for men to spend days in their tents with serious ailments. Seth Waid had been sick with dysentery for four days at their Erie campground, and after Thanksgiving he entered the hospital with an illness he only described as a "cough." He was discharged the day after Christmas and resumed normal duties with his company. Oliver Norton's friend Henry Bushnell was also in the hospital with the measles. By the end of November ninety-four men, nearly a full company's worth, were on the sick list.[45]

Though whiskey was sometimes given to the troops as reward for excelling at drill, recreational alcohol was only available outside of the camp. Like many soldiers away from home for the first time, some used it to excess. In November Lt. Col. Vincent had ordered the regimental sutler closed after five in the afternoon, probably to prevent the late-night sale of liquor, but soldiers still found their libations in the local taverns or other sutlers. Daniel Foote wrote later that month: "Many a boy has gone on a pass who will return tonight reeling and swearing while many another will throw away his money for that which will do him no good." One day in early December, Lt. John Wilson of Company H, serving as the Regimental Provost Guard, reported he observed "a soldier of the 83d Regiment assisted into camp by two of his comrades, he being intoxicated." Lt. Wilson's inquiries into the matter disclosed that another regiment's sutler was illegally selling liquor near Camp Leslie. Wilson sent one of his sergeants to buy a bottle to secure evidence, and when the sale was complete the guard force went to arrest the peddler. Lt. Wilson reported, "I again returned to the sutler and enquired his name, he answered 'If you want my name you can go to my Colonel.' By this time a large crowd of intoxicated soldiers had congregated about the Guard undoubtedly for the purpose of assaulting them and followed us several hundred yards shouting, yelling and brandishing clubs in a threatening manner." Wilson withdrew, but in response to this incident, Gen. Porter ordered the illegal sutler closed and alcohol sales prohibited completely.[46]

Although the drills were canceled during the worst weather, other duties such as guard, picket, and forage detail continued. The soldiers also initiated a camp-beautification project, as Oliver Norton wrote home: "Many of the tents have arches and bowers of evergreens before the doors. At the head of each street a grand arch is made with the letter of the company or some other device suspended, all made of the evergreen trees and branches." Former newspaper editor Amos Judson thought that the camp "brought to mind some of those enchanting scenes of which we read in Spencer's Faerie Queen." On December 21,

Pennsylvania Senator Edward Cowan arrived at Hall's Hill and presented the 83rd its first set of State Colors: a brilliant, six-foot square United States flag with the seal of the Commonwealth of Pennsylvania in its blue field. Lt. Israel Thickstun recorded that the regiment celebrated what he called a "sort-o-merry Christmas," with, "all kinds of amusement—such as fantastic parades, drinking 'medicine,' playing football, fighting (the result of drinking the 'medicine') in which eyes were blacked, heads cut open, etc." Marksmanship training continued and new Springfield rifled muskets were issued to replace the old smoothbore muskets. One of the finest weapons of its time, trained soldiers could hit targets at ranges greater than 400 yards with a Springfield. Arthur Cleeland told his parents that they could shoot 500 yards with theirs, "and from that to a half a mile [or] so I think we can shoot the Rebels."[47]

Late December brought a spell of warm weather but the roads were still too muddy to support a campaign, and the 83rd finished the year 1861 in their camp of French tents and pine bough decorations. McLane's troops were fully uniformed, equipped, and trained, but would have to wait until spring for their chance face the Confederates. As Arthur Cleeland wrote to his mother at the end of December, "There has been some talk of this regiment a going down further south, but we are fixed for winter very comfortable." He signed his letter, "Your Son. A soldier."[48]

III

HARD MARCHES TO YORKTOWN

Instead of combat against the Confederates, the soldiers of the 83rd met the year 1862 fighting the unpredictable Virginia weather. The men were used to the harsh winters of northwestern Pennsylvania, and were frequently exasperated by the varying temperatures and precipitation of the South. In January, Daniel Foote called the season "the meanest weather you can imagine. The snow will fall one day so as to be two or three inches deep then it will begin to grow warm and in two or three days rain and the mud will be about four inches deep." The grass of Camp Leslie probably had been pounded into non-existence by marching feet during the previous fall, and as Foote had described, the melting ice, snow and rains combined into mud that reached impressive proportions. Oliver Norton, now the Regimental Bugler, recorded in February, "Byron's bittersweet and most sarcastic strains were, I believe, written in just such weather," he wrote. "It snowed last night and rains this morning and now two or three inches of slush cover unfathomable mud." In another February letter, he said, "Mud is triumphant and all business except guard and picket duty is suspended, unless I should mention a little target practice." By the end of the month, Norton listed his return address on his letters as "Camp of the Penn. Mudturtles."[1]

Restricted by the weather, the soldiers became frustrated with the lack of action. Alexander May wrote his parents, "One reason I did not write sooner was because there was nothing to write about. Everything has been dull...." Another soldier complained to his friends in Crawford County, "You can see by the heading of this letter that we are still in the same old camp. We have been here so long that it seems like home...." Idleness often causes lapses in discipline, and Gen. Butterfield notified his officers, "Constant attention to duty, careful drill and discipline is absolutely necessary that we maintain our reputation and be ready for any emergency." Tempers flared despite Butterfield's warning. Some men turned to fighting. Pvt. G.A. Goodell described a brawl in February where one soldier was stabbed and another was put under arrest. Alcohol use likely rose. Pvt. John Rice, a twenty-five year old in Company E, wrote home in mid–January about a soldier who slipped out of camp, "got tite," and was put under arrest after officers discovered him and others absent. Lt. Pierce Hanrahan of Company A was also dismissed in January after he was found in Washington, drunk, by the Provost Guard.[2]

Confinement continued to contribute to sickness. In February, the Army of the Potomac's Medical Director, Dr. Charles Tripler, reported that out of 161,524 soldiers on the roll books, 18,177 of them were on the sick list. Typhoid fever, measles and venereal disease were the most common illnesses. The records do not indicate how many of the 83rd's soldiers were afflicted with the diseases Tripler described, but they show that the regiment had 76 men sick as of the end of February, or roughly 7 percent of its total strength. There were many other regiments in the army that had a higher number—some had well over 200 sick—but the 83rd had the highest average for Butterfield's Brigade. Of the fourteen other units in Porter's Division, only one other, the 2nd Maine Infantry, had more. After he recovered from his "cough" in November, Seth Waid returned to the sick list in February with the "fever," which was his only description of the ailment, and had to be carried to the camp hospital. He would later record in his diary that he lapsed into and out of consciousness for weeks. Waid was sent to an Army hospital in Georgetown for further care, and would not return to the 83rd for a year.[3]

By February, eight soldiers of the regiment had been discharged because of disease and four others had died. In addition to those losses fourteen men had been detached, or "detailed" in military parlance, to support the brigade as clerks, hospital nurses, butchers, commissary assistants, cooks and other required positions. Two soldiers had been transferred to other organizations. Now with only 997 men on the rolls, Col. McLane sent recruiting details back to Pennsylvania to fill the ranks. That month Capt. McCoy led one drive in Crawford County and offered a bounty of $100 for new men. Lt. Yale of Company C also drummed up men in Erie. By the end of the month Yale had ten men ready to join the 83rd, two of them minors that struggled with getting the necessary parental permission to sign on.[4]

That month Alexander May wrote his parents, "It is time we was doing something here." Despite the sickness, boredom, mud and weather, McLane's soldiers were still eager to face the Confederates, much like the rest of the army. In February Gen. McClellan reported to the War Department that his troops were fully trained and capable of taking the offensive. But though his regiments were ready, the general had done nothing to remove the Confederates under Gen. Joe Johnston who were still entrenched twenty miles away near Manassas and Centreville.

That fact that the army had not moved against Johnston was not unnoticed in the Government. The previous November, President Lincoln had enough confidence in McClellan to appoint him the Commander of all the Union Armies, and through the winter Lincoln tried, without success, to get his new Commanding General to develop some plan for defeating the Confederacy. By January Lincoln was losing his patience, and the next month he ordered McClellan to move out of the training camps and eliminate Johnston's army. In response, McClellan ordered one attempt to clear a small enemy force on the upper Potomac. Poor planning by the army staff caused the expedition to prematurely halt and the regiments returned to their camps.

The state of affairs looked even worse when the Union began making great gains in other theaters of the war. In mid–February, a little-known Brig. Gen. Ulysses S. Grant captured 14,000 Confederates and opened up the Cumberland River by seizing Forts Henry and Donelson in western Tennessee. He went on to occupy Nashville, making it the first Confederate state capital to fall to the Union. In North Carolina, Brig. Gen. Ambrose Burnside occupied Roanoke Island, captured 2,500 men and was positioned to seize the port of Norfolk. In light of the other Union successes, McClellan appeared to be dragging his feet, and his popularity began to wane.[5]

The soldiers continued to bristle at their inactivity as the weather warmed. In early March, Oliver Norton wrote home, "We are still here on Hall's Hill with no prospect that I can see of leaving very soon. To be sure we have marching orders occasionally, were under orders last week. They kept us two or three days with everything in readiness to leave at a moment's notice and turned us out into ranks several times, but the whole thing flashed in the pan, as it always does." Daniel Foote also wondered when their chance for combat would come: "It seems hard to lay here so long and do nothing, only play soldier when our enemies lay in force only twenty miles from us. I suppose that it is all for the best if I can not see it so." David Rodgers, a twenty-three year old sergeant in Company A, was so dismayed by the rain and lack of action that he wrote, "I think when we leave we will go on *water*."[6]

Many of McLane's men probably still believed that they would have an easy victory over the Rebels once they met them. Even those who held few illusions about war felt that combat would be the test of all their endless training, drilling, guard duty and mock battles. The soldiers that had been part of the Three-Months regiment in April 1861 had already been turned away by the government once and returned home dejected. Since returning to the ranks they had trained hard and been recognized as one of the finest units in the Army. McClellan himself had said it! All they needed to complete their journey was to meet the Rebels face to face, and after that they would have done their part to defeat the rebellion. Later generations would call first combat "baptism by fire" but in Civil War slang, to hear bullets fly was to "See the Elephant," and that was what soldiers yearned to do. As Norton wrote to his cousin in February, "A man is not a hero until he is shot at and missed."[7]

As the soldiers' frustrations mounted in March, Gen. McClellan was finally developing his plan for a spring offensive to take Richmond and end the Confederacy. Amateur strategists suggested the Federals march south from Washington straight to Richmond, but Johnston's army, which McClellan estimated at 150,000, was firmly entrenched at Centreville blocking the most direct route. A Confederate force that large could inflict heavy casualties if attacked in their trenches. If the "Young Napoleon" was to defeat them and seize Richmond, he would have to find another way to do it besides a direct assault.

Instead, McClellan planned to move the bulk of the army by ship to the town of Urbanna on the Rappahannock River, one hundred miles to the south and behind Johnston. A token force would man the Washington defenses to guard against a counterstrike. From Urbanna, the army would have to advance only fifty miles to Richmond. This would cut off the force at Centreville from the rear. Once isolated, Johnston would be forced to abandon his trench line to re-open the communications and supply with Richmond. When the Confederates were out of their defenses the Union could maneuver against them in open country and fight on advantageous ground. As McClellan himself summarized it, he would "leave the enemy where he was, and fight him where he was not."[8]

The plan was strategically sound, but in the government's eyes, it would leave Washington vulnerable while the army slipped one hundred miles away to campaign in Virginia. President Lincoln was skeptical and only approved the plan after a council of the army's senior generals also voted their support on March 7, 1862. Even then, Lincoln qualified his approval by requiring McClellan to ensure Washington remained completely defended, and that the operation had to begin by March 18. The President also directed that the Army would be formed into four corps, each composed of two or three of the existing divisions and commanded by a veteran general from the Regular Army. Porter's Division became the 1st Division of the 3rd Corps under Brig. Gen. Samuel P. Heintzelman.

III. Hard Marches to Yorktown

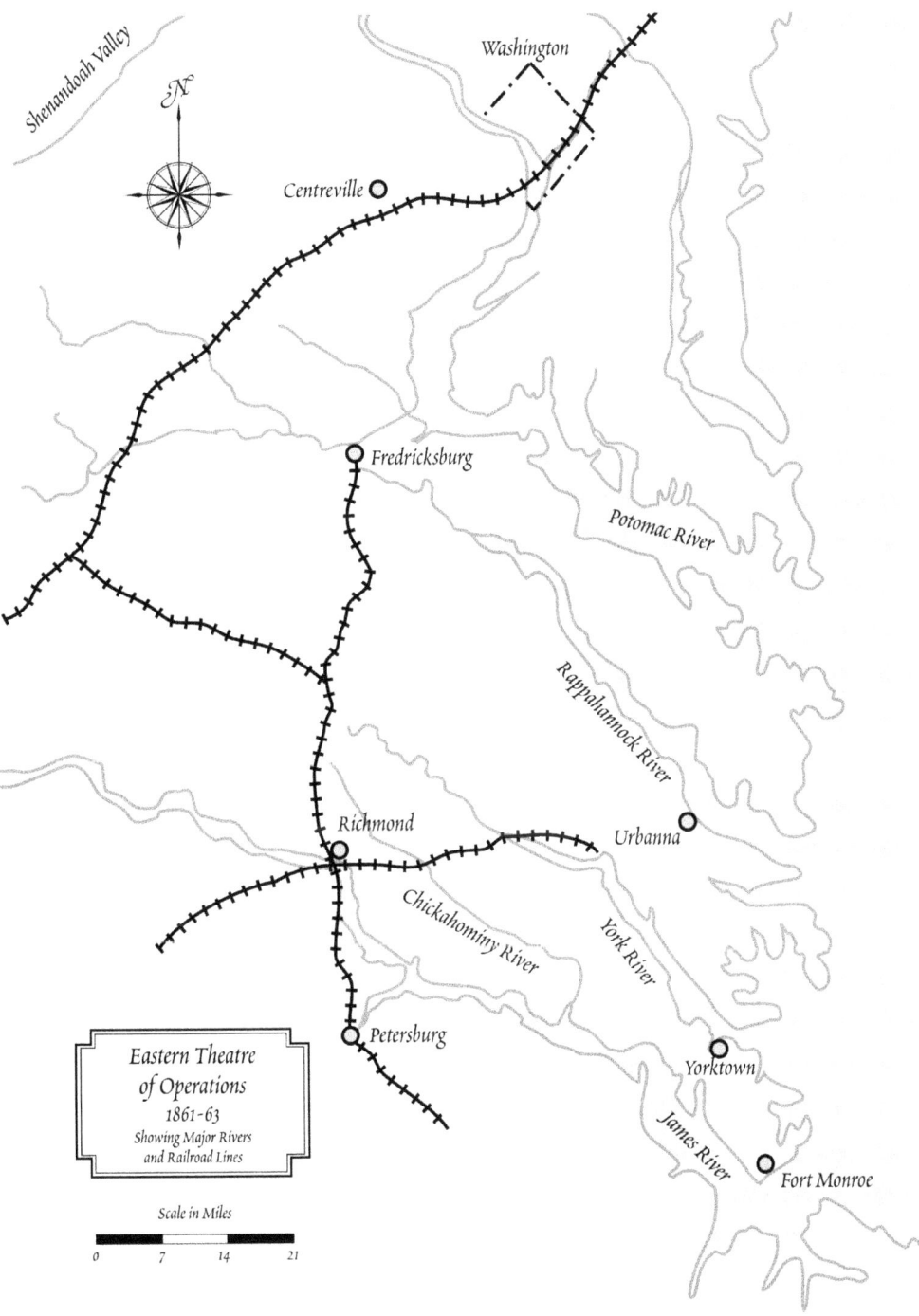

The Eastern Theater of operations. This was the world of the 83rd from 1861 to 1865.

Brig. Gen. Samuel P. Heintzelman, commander of the 3rd Army Corps. (LOC)

The organization of Gen. Porter's Division was also formalized, and as the campaign began, it consisted of three infantry brigades, four artillery batteries, a sharpshooter company and a cavalry regiment. Butterfield's Brigade, enumerated as the 3rd Brigade of the 1st Division, consisted of the 12th New York Infantry, known as the "Onadaga Regiment" under Col. H.A. Weeks, the 16th Michigan ("Michigan Independents") led by Col. T. W. B. Stockton, the 17th New York ("Westchester Chasseurs") under Col. Hugh Lansing, the 44th New York, commanded by S. W. Stryker, and the 83rd Pennsylvania.[9]

The army began preparations for the campaign immediately, and on March 9 the 83rd received instructions to prepare for movement against the enemy. The effect of finally receiving real marching orders was electric. Company E's Lt. Amos Judson later wrote, "The long-expected and long-talked about movement of the Army of the Potomac was about to commence.... All was bustle and preparation in camp." The men packed away all excess clothing and equipment (including the Zouave uniforms) for storage in government warehouses in Georgetown. Three days' rations were issued and cooked. Judson went on, "There was but little repose during the remainder of that night."[10]

Unknown to McClellan and the men of the 83rd, the Confederates were also preparing to move.

The Federal intelligence service had greatly overestimated the size of the enemy at Centreville. Gen. Johnston had only 43,000 men at his disposal, and there was no way they could hold against the 160,000 soldiers in Army of the Potomac. To save his army, Johnston planned to establish a new line below the Rappahannock River, forty miles to the south and closer to Richmond. The Rebels began the withdrawal on March 8, the same day Lincoln approved McClellan's plan for outflanking the phantom force that existed only in the Young Napoleon's mind.

Union scouts had been watching the enemy lines, and when they reported that the Rebels were evacuating Centreville on March 9, McClellan seized the opportunity to begin his campaign with a victory. He announced that the army would immediately advance to Centreville "to push the retreat of the rebels as far as possible." The next day the Federals marched out of Washington, and Oliver Norton recorded the relief that many of the men must have felt: "The 'grand army' has at last moved."[11]

Butterfield's Brigade left Camp Leslie at dawn in a pouring rain. Though the army's divisions took different routes to avoid overcrowding the narrow country lanes, the roads were jammed with troops. Pvt. John F. Rice of Company G wrote, "We left camp in good spirits and the band played Yankee Dudel. Before we got 9 miles from camp we came in contact with so many other Brigades that we were obliged to wate for some time before we could get along. The sean was realy more than I can describe."[12]

Centreville was nearly twenty miles away and the soldiers carried loads of muskets, cartridges, and packs that Daniel Foote estimated to be about seventy pounds each. The conditions combined for a difficult trip, as Oliver Norton wrote home afterward, "We had a hard march. After we had gone some three or four miles the men began to throw off blankets, coats, and knapsacks, and towards night the road was strewn with them. I saw men fall down who could not rise without help. The rain soaked everything woolen full of water and made our loads almost mule loads." The men had learned that campaigning was not as easy it seemed and they were off to an unimpressive start.[13]

Near sundown the regiment reached the town of Fairfax, six miles from Centreville, and word arrived that the Rebels had slipped away. In fact, they had been gone for over twenty-four hours, and so was McClellan's chance to "push the retreat as far as possible." Not knowing that Johnston had ordered the retreat days ago, the soldiers concluded that the threat of the Federal advance had forced the Rebels out of their lines and they considered this their first victory. Amos Judson wrote that when "Little Mac" rode past their ranks, "loud and repeated cheers burst forth from the Union hosts, indicating their joy as this their first triumph as well as their confidence in the strategy of their young commander." With the bands playing and colors flying, the regiment entered camp at Fairfax and waited for their next order. Regimental Bugler Norton recalled that by the time they halted that night, he was "too tired to blow a note" and John Rice called the regiment "the tiredest set of boys you ever saw."[14]

Two days after they began their withdrawal, the Confederates were safely in their new line behind the Rappahannock and only thirty miles from Urbanna, which put McClellan's original plan out of the question. The escape of the Rebel army was a tremendous embarrassment for the Union Government, and Lincoln concluded that McClellan was overtaxed as General-in-Chief of all Union armies and relieved him of all but command of the Army of the Potomac. The crestfallen general's plan to move the army by water to outflank the Confederates was still sound, but the Army of the Potomac needed a base safer than Urbanna from which to assault Richmond.

The answer was Fortress Monroe, a bastion at the tip of the peninsula formed by the York and James Rivers that had remained in Federal hands when Virginia seceded from the Union. From there, the army would have a seventy-five mile march to Richmond, but Union gunboats could patrol the James and the York to protect the army's flanks from attack as it moved up the long narrow peninsula. As McClellan reasoned, the march to Richmond would be longer, but safer with this new route.

On March 12 McClellan offered the plan to the corps commanders for their consideration, and they unanimously agreed to adopt the Ft. Monroe strategy with the provision that 25,000 men should remain to defend Washington. Anxious for action, President Lincoln wired his approval the next day. Gen. McClellan was confident of victory, and issued another stirring speech to the army, "The moment for action has arrived, and I know that I can trust you to save our country.... I will bring you now to face the rebels ... where I know you wish to be,—on the decisive battlefield."[15]

On Saturday morning, March 15, Gen. Porter's Division marched to Alexandria where it was to meet its transports for the trip to Ft. Monroe. As when they had left Hall's Hill, a drenching rain fell. It was eighteen wet, difficult miles to Alexandria. Years later, Lt. Judson remembered the march as "a severe one." Two days after the movement Oliver Norton observed, "We marched eighteen miles, every step in the rain, but we had a good road and the men stood it much better than they did the other march."[16]

Once in Alexandria, the 83rd occupied a former camp of the 69th New York Infantry at the base of Shuter's Hill.* Mud, brush and "refuse" had been washed into tents by the recent rains and the tired men found little comfort. Daniel Foote wrote about how some members of Company K made the conditions worse: "Part of our company were quartered in a Roman Catholic Chapel tent from which they carried off the images. It would [have] pleased you to see how mad the Irish were Sunday." The next day the men pitched their own tents higher on the hill.[17]

Fielding 120,000 men, the Army of the Potomac was nearly three times as large as any previous American army. The movement to Ft. Monroe was an operation of unprecedented size and complexity. To ship the army to central Virginia, the War Department had hired hundreds of schooners, charter boats, side-wheelers, barges and canal boats, and they were all gathering at the Alexandria wharves. From their vantage point on Shuter's Hill, Foote wrote that the men "had a fine view of the Potomac ... the river is full of boats and the troops are embarking as fast as possible. There is about 200,000 men going on the expedition and if the rebels will show grit enough to give us battle it will be fun indeed."[18]

Even with the Government's massive contracting effort, it took days to gather the ships necessary and the army embarked at the rate of one division per day. On the morning of March 22 the 83rd boarded the steamer *Sea Shore* and along with about thirty other transports, headed down the Chesapeake Bay. Though Erie prided itself as a lake port, the sea was a new sight to many of the Pennsylvania men as was rough water. David Rodgers wrote home, "Some of the boys got a little sea sick when they got on the salt water in the bay but I think it done them no harm. It took some of the bile off their stomachs." Arthur Cleeland happily wrote his parents of how he had seen what must have been a dolphin, though he described it as "a sea hog."[19]

They arrived off Ft. Monroe on the afternoon of the next day, and on March 24 the ships took Porter's Division one mile further up an inlet to Hampton, Virginia, where the troops landed and bivouacked for the first time on real enemy territory. Confederate soldiers had burned Hampton the previous fall, and not much was left of the historic town as the 83rd moved through it, as Norton's letter home described: "I saw the walls of the old stone church in which [George] Washington used to worship. It was burned with the town by [the Rebel commander, Maj. Gen. John] Magruder. Hampton was a beautiful old town built almost wholly of brick and stone, but it looks now like pictures of ancient ruins." Daniel Foote said that the town "must have been a beautiful village but now nothing but bare brick walls with streets running in between."[20]

By late March enough troops had landed at Ft. Monroe for the Federals to prepare for their advance up the peninsula. With Johnston's army still on the Rappahannock, Confederate resistance was not expected to be significant. Union intelligence indicated that Maj. Gen. John B. Magruder had 15,000 Confederate soldiers near Yorktown on the north side of the peninsula, but the Army of the Potomac outnumbered them by a ratio of 6 to 1, and Magruder's force presented no great obstacle to the march toward Richmond. Rebel strong points also existed at several places between Yorktown and Ft. Monroe, and the

---

The present day site of the George Washington Masonic Temple in Alexandria.

Union troops landing at Hampton at the beginning of the Peninsula Campaign. (LOC)

army would need to ascertain their correct strengths before moving forward. Reports that 2,000 enemy soldiers held the church crossroads called Big Bethel, six miles from the camp at Hampton, prompted the 3rd Corps commander, Brig. Gen. Samuel P. Heintzelman, to send Porter's Division to reconnoiter the site in late March.[21]

Porter's Division left for Big Bethel on Thursday, March 27, a "bright and beautiful" morning according to Amos Judson, in contrast to the weather during their previous movements. Either by intention to maintain secrecy, or because of inexperience, the officers of the 83rd failed to inform the soldiers of the division's mission. Rumors passed through the ranks that they were marching to meet a force of 2,000 enemy. Judson remembered, "It was not known exactly for what purpose we were going, but as fighting is the business of a soldier's life, it was supposed that fighting was the object." Confused or not, the regiment left their camp at about 8:00 AM, with their colors flying.

The troops moved northwest out of Hampton on the main road toward Big Bethel. It was humid and unseasonably hot, and the men sweated and slipped on the soft, sandy road through the morning. At about noon, the tired column sighted the Rebel works. Oliver Norton described the soldiers' view of their steaming field of action, "There is a line of earthworks in the edge of a pine woods. In front of these is a large level field of two or three hundred acres, and in front of the field an extensive swamp full of wet holes, thickets, briars and vines. The road leads through this swamp to the field." For a few moments, adrenaline surged and the soldiers forgot their aching feet and soggy uniforms as Gen. Butterfield began maneuvering for action.

Butterfield formed the Brigade in a line of battle with the 16th Michigan and 17th New York to the right of the road, the 83rd to its left, and the 44th New York on the far left flank. The division artillery battery unlimbered and set up on the road in the middle of the brigade. Although they still had not seen any enemy soldiers, Judson remembered: "Expectations of a sharp fight and hopes of a brilliant victory ran high...." Col. McLane walked along the line of battle and told the men to stay aligned on their colors, as they had learned to do at Hall's

Hill. Norton remembered that the colonel told them, "Great Bethel would be ours before night."

Butterfield ordered the Brigade forward toward the enemy works. The men pushed through a thicket and heard the crack of rifles ahead. Judson recalled, "All was now bustle and excitement in the 83rd. The field officers of the regiment hurried to and fro, with revolvers in their hands, hurrying forward both officers and men." The excitement level rose, and Norton wrote, "I thought the ball had opened at last." Moving through the thick brush caused the soldiers to lose their shoulder-to-shoulder alignment, and they straightened their lines as they emerged on the far side of the brush. At the same time, the firing ahead ceased as suddenly as it had began. The men could now clearly see the earthworks in front of them and expected to receive fire, but none came. Either by McLane's order or as a spontaneous release of tension, the ranks charged with a yell. When they reached the works, Color-Sergeant McKinley triumphantly planted the 83rd's flag on the post's earthen walls, but there were no enemy soldiers to be seen. The Rebels had abandoned the position, and by the time Butterfield's Brigade arrived the only enemy at Big Bethel was a small Confederate cavalry detachment and some pickets who fired a few shots and then fled. Not a man had been hurt in the regiment's first advance on the enemy, except those that Judson wryly noted afterwards "were badly scratched among the briers while forming for the charge."

Porter's Division continued its reconnaissance for a few miles around Big Bethel, but found no other Confederates. Having accomplished their mission of probing the enemy, they returned to Hampton the next day.[22]

By early April three corps of Union infantry were on the peninsula. Gen. McClellan arrived at Ft. Monroe on April 1, and three days later the army began moving toward Richmond. As far as McClellan knew, Gen. Magruder's position at Yorktown was the only obstacle to his advance. To outflank and eliminate the outpost, Brig. Gen. Keyes' 2nd Corps was to bypass Yorktown to the south and take position on its western side. Heintzelman's 3rd Corps was to take the road directly to Yorktown and advance on Magruder's troops from the east, pinning them down while the 2nd Corps cut them off.

On the first day, the Rebels presented no serious resistance and by dusk both corps were halfway to Yorktown. The next morning heavy rains drenched the area and the soil turned into sand and clay marshes that mired the army. Army engineers had previously reported that the roads were firm enough to support the movement of thousands of troops, cannon, wagons, and draft animals. But within hours of the rain the roads turned to ankle-deep, and then knee-deep, mud. Men, guns and all the army's traffic became hopelessly stuck. Lt. Judson recalled how the men of the 83rd endured another hard, wet march: "Though we only had six miles to go, it proved to be one of the most difficult marches we ever made. A few hours of rain had completely soaked the low, swampy soil of the Peninsula, and the artillery wagons had worked it into a perfect mire." The army also had little information on all the roads that led to Yorktown, and the 3rd Corps spent much of the day as lost as it was stuck.[23]

By the afternoon of April 5 the 3rd Corps had slogged through the roads, overcome their poor maps and were within two miles of Yorktown. Confederate batteries east of the town began firing at the lead troops, and the tired, mud-spattered and foot-sore men of the 83rd could hear cannonading as they reached the scene.

Although the 3rd Corps found the enemy positions exactly where it expected them, the 2nd Corps encountered stiff re-

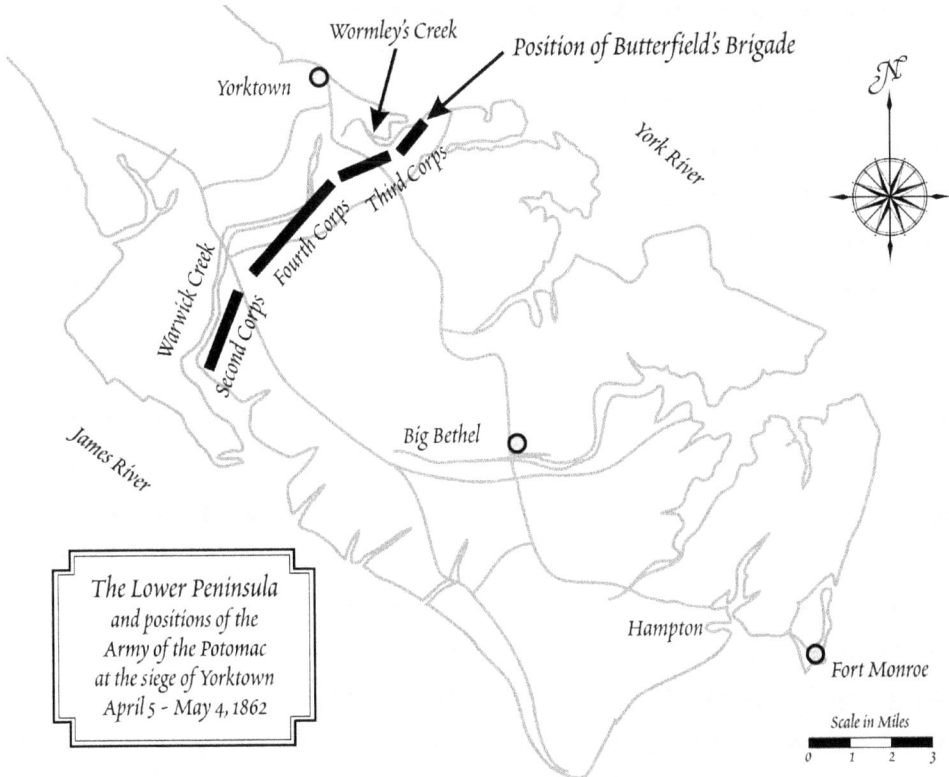

The area between Hampton and Yorktown, where the 83rd began the Peninsula campaign and suffered their first hostile fire.

sistance that thwarted any flanking movement. Their advance, which was supposed to seal the town off from any reinforcements, ground to a halt. While the infantry advance stalled, other events worked against Little Mac's plan for a rapid advance to Richmond.

The advance up the peninsula depended on the ability of the Navy to control the James and York Rivers and guard the army's flanks. Just before the campaign began, the Confederate ironclad warship *Merrimac* began operating in the Hampton Roads area, and the Federal Navy was severely distracted by the fear of it destroying their ships. Assisting the army's move up the peninsula became the Navy's second priority after destruction of the ironclad. Almost all of the ships needed to bombard the fortifications at Yorktown were withheld, and the army would have to use its own heavy artillery to do the job.

The Confederates had also begun to react to the Federal Army's advance. As soon as the Union began moving up the peninsula, President Davis' chief of staff, Maj. Gen. Robert E. Lee, ordered Gen. Johnston to reinforce Yorktown as fast as possible. The Rebel brigades were moving toward Yorktown by rail from the west as McClellan's troops approached on foot from the south and east. To further frustrate the Army of the Potomac, Maj. Gen. Thomas J. "Stonewall" Jackson threatened Washington from the Shenandoah Valley. President Lincoln had already detached one of Little Mac's divisions to counter Jackson, but the threat brought the attention of the War Department to the fact that McClellan had left an inadequate force, many of them untrained recruits, to guard the capital. Not at all satisfied that Washington was properly protected, Lincoln ordered McDowell's 1st Corps, the one that had not yet been transported to Ft. Monroe, to remain behind.

The move outraged McClellan. The loss of McDowell's Corps cut his forces by a third (which left about 67,000 troops on the peninsula) and stymied his plan for the reduction of Yorktown. The 2nd Corps was unable to turn the Confederate defenses and surround the town, nor could the Navy operate on the York or James Rivers. Although his forces still greatly outnumbered Magruder's, in the General's mind there was no other alternative but to eliminate Yorktown by a direct frontal assault. A siege.[24]

In the nineteenth century, the siege was a systematic method of combat. The process called for Union field artillery to pin the Rebel soldiers down with a steady bombardment, while the infantry dug a series of trenches (called "parallels" because they usually mirrored the track of the enemy fortifications) near the opposing lines. When the parallels were within close artillery range, heavy siege cannon would be brought forward to blast the enemy positions. Once the Confederate artillery was silenced, the Union infantry would storm the works and move into Yorktown. Having witnessed sieges during his observer service in the Crimean War, McClellan understood the process very well. He appointed Gen. Porter as the director of the assault, and the army began the slow approach toward Yorktown.[25]

Porter's Division occupied an area that would become known as "Camp Winfield Scott" on the far right of the 3rd Corps' line on an inlet to the York called Wormley's Creek. Across the creek to the west was a large stand of trees that shielded the division from direct view of the enemy. Past the trees, a plain level field extended to the low, brown earthworks of the Rebel lines about a two thousand yards distant. The York River was only a few hundred yards to the right and the rest of the peninsula rolled off to the left. Porter selected Lt. Col. Vincent as an aide, and though he had never seen a siege before, the young Erie lawyer took charge of much of the division's work details that began to dig their way toward the enemy lines.[26]

To conceal the activity as much as possible, the soldiers began the work on the trenches under cover of darkness. 1st, to prevent surprise, a picket line went out beyond the woods to within a few hundred yards of the Rebels. Then, armed with only shovels and picks, work parties of soldiers moved into the field and dug "rifle pits" three feet deep and three feet wide.* Each night, the soldiers returned to widen and extend the holes until they connected to form trenches. When those were deep enough to protect the men, work continued during the day. Then the trenches themselves were improved with log and earthen roofs. When the trenches were complete, the engineers supervised the building of embrasures and emplacements for heavy artillery.

As the regimental bugler, Oliver Norton was normally excused from fatigue details like trench-digging, but with the Rebels within hearing distance of the bugles, the regiments sent orders only by drummers so as not to broadcast their activities. Norton volunteered to take his turn on picket duty and in the work parties, and he described, "Six of our companies including Company K went out at daylight yesterday and worked all day in the rain. It was a very disagreeable day and we came back at night soaked through, cold, and hungry, but as merry a lot of fellows as you ever saw." It was backbreaking work, and despite Norton's description of the men as

---

*The rifle pit would later become familiar to later generations of American soldiers as the "foxhole."

III. Hard Marches to Yorktown

A party of Union soldiers leaves Camp Winfield Scott to work on the trenches at Yorktown. A sketch by Alfred Waud. (LOC)

a "merry lot," the siege must have seemed more like a labor camp than a war.[27]

Danger was added to drudgery when Rebel artillery fired on the work details, and Col. McLane wisely kept sentries above the trenches to watch for the flash of the enemy guns and to warn the men to take cover. Soldiers on the picket line were prime targets for Rebel sharpshooters. Pvt. Jacob Snyder of Company K wrote to his family of their turns as pickets, "We dare not move much er if perceived by the enemy we would have the bullets whistle past us or over us...." Daniel Foote also noted that to rise out of the prone position brought immediate shots from the enemy, and that soldiers "generally try the experiment but once." The 83rd's pickets used the woods or rifle pits for concealment and protection and remained on duty for twelve hours at a time (to relieve them more often would reveal their positions). With nine men on duty, they took turns on guard or resting. If any Rebel soldier showed himself, they were to "blaze away at him" as Norton put it, although there is no record of McLane's soldiers actually killing any enemy soldiers in this manner at Yorktown.[28]

Though the 83rd lost no soldiers to enemy marksmen or cannon, there were plenty of close calls. Norton wrote, "I have seen some fellows who had narrow escapes. One had his knapsack shot off his back by a solid shot and was not hurt. One had a ball go through a cup that he was about to drink from. One had a Minie ball pass through fifteen thickness of cloth (a knot on his cape) and lodge against a rib. Another had the tassel shot off his cap."[29]*

Gen. McClellan had ordered over one hundred pieces of heavy artillery brought up to bombard the Confederate lines, and in addition to the trenches, McLane's men had other projects to support the movement of the guns. Under the direction of the army's engineers, roads and bridges were built by laying hundreds of logs along dirt tracks in a manner known as "corduroy."

---

*The fact that soldiers had capes and caps with tassels indicates that some of them were still wearing parts of the Zouave uniform that had been ordered packed away. It is possible that some of them were so proud of their uniforms that they disregarded orders and kept portions, or that Col. McLane allowed some pieces to be brought on the campaign.

A heavy siege mortar in its position near Yorktown. This is battery No. 4 on Wormley's Creek, where Butterfield's Brigade worked. (LOC)

To lay corduroy, teams of soldiers chopped down trees and trimmed the branches with axes. Then they placed logs lengthwise down the sides of a prepared trail like a railway. The last step was to lay the trimmed logs closely against each other, across the track, perpendicular to direction of travel. This manner resulted in a road that was exceptionally rough for wagons to travel on, but kept vehicles and cannon from becoming mired. Good corduroy had a layer of earth spread over it to soften the ride. Though exceptionally rugged, the soldiers took pride in this work as well. In mid–April Norton wrote home: "Our regiment and the Avengers [44th New York] have made nearly six miles of corduroy road beside doing picket duty every four days, reconnoitering, etc. I assure you the work is being pushed forward with all the speed possible."[30]

Despite the drama of the shelling and sharpshooting, there was not an overwhelming threat of death. Their remembrances show the awe with which they watched their first battle. Even after the war, when he had seen sights that would disillusion the heartiest men, Amos Judson recalled:

When our two hundred pounders opened the earth shook as if in the convulsions of an earthquake for a mile around, and their ponderous projectiles could be heard screaming through the air for several minutes until they plunged with a terrible explosion into the enemy's works.... In the midst of the darkness and stillness of the night, the effect was what might have been called sublime. At first a flash like that of vapor lightning, suddenly illuminating the skies, would be seen; then, as you stood eagerly listening to catch the report, counting one, two, three, five-ten-fifteen-twenty, and even thirty—the deep, heavy roar broke upon your ears, echoing and re-echoing for miles up and down the vast forests of the Peninsula; and then came rushing along the tremendous projectile, with a whizzing sound resembling that of a meteor; and bursting in mid air, the fragments would fly off in every direction, whirling and convolving with a sound conforming to their size—some like the distant buzz of a threshing machine, and some not unlike the shrill of a steam engine. Other times the shells would fail to burst, and we could hear their

III. Hard Marches to Yorktown

heavy "thug" into the fort, although a mile distant, that reminded one of something like the concussion of two planets coming together.

Daniel Foote's description of the experience of shelling was less eloquent than Judson's, but probably very honest: "It is a grand and beautiful sight to see a shell start from the gun and watch it till it bursts. Still when it looks as though it was coming directly at you it creates no very pleasant feeling." John Rice wrote during the midst of one cannon duel: "Just whilst I was writing that last line [of this letter] thare was a large shell came singing down half a mile this side of the works and exploded. They fairly make our ears ring. Thare goes another. Whis. Whis. Goes the peaces.... The gun boats throw one into the fort of the rebels once in a while just for to bother them."[31]

Oliver Norton's description, written in mid—April, summed up the conditions in which the men existed: "They have kept up this cannonading ever since we came here on the 5th," he wrote home, "and there is scarcely ten minutes in the day when we do not hear the report of cannon. We are getting used to it so we pay no more attention than to the birds singing, unless the firing is unusually sharp." Norton may have been boasting a little, but another of Daniel Foote's observations lends some credence to how lackadaisical the men had become. "Even while I write I hear the bombing of cannon and whistling of the shells as they pass to our right," he wrote. "Still the boys lay around unconcerned as though they were at home." Easing their way into combat, the men had an innocence and comfort with their situation that they would not experience again.[32]*

The weather and the swamps around Yorktown probably constituted more of a danger to the soldiers than the enemy did. Tidewater Virginia saw 18 days of rain that April with temperatures from the 40s to low 80s, but work continued in all conditions, as Lt. Judson recalled: "On several occasions we descended into the trenches, the rain pouring down and the night so pitchy dark that we could not distinguish each other at the distance of two feet apart." Jacob Snyder also wrote, "It rained like the old nick while we were placed in that swamp. There is where we picked up all our fevers and Rheumatics and by the many storms that we had and were digging trenches, building bridges, and standing sentinels...." By the end of April the 83rd had 99 men on the regiment's sick list, 69 of those were in the hospital, and there were only 921 soldiers present for duty.[33]

In addition to problems caused by weather and enemy activity, the army was working its way through massive logistical problems. Army regulations stipulated that on an active campaign a soldier's daily issue consisted of hard bread, salt pork or fresh meat, plus sugar, coffee and salt for a total of about three pounds per man. To keep the 83rd supplied, the Quartermaster, Lt. Daniel Clark, had to send the regiment's two wagons on daily trips to the nearest Federal depot at Cheesman's Creek, three miles to the rear. In good conditions each wagon could carry 4,500 pounds of provisions, but the sand-based roads easily mired any type of vehicle and many carried half their prescribed loads to avoid becoming stuck. Wagons rarely moved faster than a walk, and with traffic jams, halts on the road and loading time at the depot, a single

---

*In truth, the danger from the shelling and firing may not have been that high. The only officially recorded injury to any member of the 83rd during this time was to Lt. Israel Thickstun, who had been detached from the regiment as an acting Signal Officer for Army Headquarters. According to the report of the Army's Chief Signal Officer, Thickstun was manning a signal post near the York River on April 7 and came under fire from the Confederate batteries. Fragments from an exploding shell struck Thickstun in the head and knocked him unconscious. Although he was on detached service from the 83rd, Thickstun had porbably susbtained the first combat injury in his regiment.

round-trip to Cheesman's Creek could take an entire day. The 921 soldiers of the 83rd required over 2,700 pounds of food every day—or one wagon dedicated to nothing but rations. Lt. Clark, who had been a shop clerk before the war, also had to bring up ammunition, medicines, camp equipment, shovels, axes, nails, horseshoes, forage for draught animals and hundreds of other items. Most of the Union units digging around Yorktown suffered under the same conditions and despite their quartermaster's best efforts, the circumstances of wartime supply worked against them and rations were constantly short.[34]

As they had done at Hall's Hill, soldiers turned to unauthorized foraging to supplement their rations, in violation of a warning from Gen. Butterfield that pillaging would be "punished with extreme penalty enjoined by the Articles of War." On one evening, Norton and some other soldiers of Company K raided a local farm and tried to return to camp with a very live and noisy pig. Col. McLane spotted the soldiers and asked a soldier named Bowen, who was carrying the pig, how they acquired the squealing animal. Bowen stammered, and as Norton described, answered the Colonel: "Well c-c-confound it Colonel, I c-c-confiscated him." The Colonel asked: "Haven't you heard orders about that?" To which the Private answered: "Well, Colonel, I haven't had a mouthful to eat except five crackers since yesterday, and I can't build corduroy on that." Norton said that McLane forgave them for stealing the pig, and that the next day it was "pretty well disposed of."

Though it was strictly against orders, stealing posed no ethical dilemma for Norton, as he wrote to his cousin, "You may call it stealing to go prowling round nights snatching poultry and pigs, but my conscience is seared. I don't feel the least compunction. I am well satisfied that a man who has a farm and stock here while the rebels have had undisputed possession for months, is nothing else but *secesh*, and when Uncle Sam can't furnish food, I see nothing wrong in acquiring it of our enemies. That is the general sentiment of the soldiers, and if you think it is wrong you need not feel any delicacy in telling me so." There is no record of how many soldiers took part in the practice but if Norton's statement is taken at face value, stealing must have been a common event.[35]

By the end of April the army had been working on their trenches for over three weeks and John Rice observed, "The rodes have bin thronged all day with teams halling Mortars and shells.... I think you may look for the ball to open inside of the next 8 days." Gen. U.S. Grant had stopped the advance of Albert Sidney Johnston's Confederate army at the battle of Shiloh on the Mississippi-Tennessee border earlier in the month, and news of the victory spurred the troops at Yorktown into a spirit of competition with the western armies. Spirits were high as the work on the trenches continued, but the men grew restless for the end of the siege. Arthur Cleeland said to his father, "We will soon be ready to take York Town and then I think that the secech will be prety near run out.... there is some talk that after the fight at yorktown if we are successful in whipping them that all the Pennsylvania volunteers will be sent home but not discharged. I hope it is so." Daniel Foote wrote, "We have them surrounded so that they have nothing to do but surrender when whipped! I hope this will be the closing scene of this war as it was of the old Revolutionary war of 1776." Both Norton and Cleeland looked forward to their reception from the girls of Pennsylvania, although Norton feared, "When we get home and the girls see what rough, sunburned and disgusting fellows we are—I'm afraid soldiers will be at a discount."[36]

Ever since leaving Alexandria, Gen. McClellan had promised the men that he would destroy the Rebel Army in a great battle, a "Waterloo" for the Confederacy. By the end of April, Porter's parallels were only 1,400 yards from the enemy trenches, well within artillery range, and the heavy guns were moving into place. McClellan had also received some intelligence reports that the Rebels were going to abandon their defenses and fall back to Richmond. Not believing that Johnston could accomplish such a move with any speed, McClellan took time to make final preparations for the grand assault. He scheduled the final attack to open at dawn on May 5.[37]

The Confederates in Yorktown were not sitting still and waiting for the Union soldiers' predictions to come true. Gen. Johnston had arrived with his reinforcements in mid–April, and though he had 56,000 soldiers in defenses that spanned the peninsula, the general knew his forces could not hold against a concentrated Federal siege. As the month closed, the Confederates prepared to evacuate their defenses, fall back to Richmond, and deny McClellan the "Waterloo" he expected. Johnston planned to prevent the Federals from observing his move by keeping their heads down with an artillery bombardment. He set the date of the withdrawal for May 3.

The final move of the siege went to the Confederates. On May 1 the enemy cannon fire "became quite brisk," as Gen. Porter reported, and it increased over the next two days. Daniel Foote described the intensity of the bombardment in a letter he wrote during the cannonade: "I presume that during the [last day] there was from three to five hundred shot and shell sent at us some of them striking the outsides of the earthwork and embedding themselves in the fresh dirt would burst and send the dirt in all directions. One or two shells burst directly over the men's heads but only two were hurt and they were hurt by being back in the woods when a shell came crashing through and broke off a pine tree half way up which fell upon them. It is thought they will both recover." In the midst of the shelling, Foote was more confident than ever and wrote: "Gen. McClellan *will take* Yorktown and I hope Jeff Davis." Amos Judson also recalled: "As we lay in our tents their shells came whistling and bursting over and scattering their fragments around us. One fragment passed through the tent of a drummer in the 83rd, and smashed through his drum, which stood between him and his sleeping comrade."[38]

The increased firing had raised Gen. Porter's suspicions that the Rebels were covering a retreat, and in the early morning of May 4 he prepared his troops in the trenches to advance and seize the enemy works in an attempt to prevent the enemy's escape. As the soldiers readied themselves, Porter received word that recently captured Rebel deserters reported the town was evacuated. Perhaps hoping to bag some before they slipped away, he pushed his men forward through the abandoned lines and on into Yorktown, but the Confederates were already gone. When the 83rd entered the town that morning, Alexander May remembered the Confederates had "left amunition and camp kettles and almost everything." Another chance for the regiment to meet their enemies face to face was gone, and John Rice probably summed up the soldiers' feelings; "I was very much disappointed when the rebels left for I would like to have seen our everlasting works open on them. I tell you it would have bin the biggest thing since the war began, but the rebels have run...."[39]

Though the Confederates had retreated, they had not "run" as Rice thought. The Rebels had saved their army, and the test of McLane's men was to come on another field.

IV

A Promise of Perfect Success

Gen. McClellan was surprised by the Confederate withdrawal from Yorktown, but telegraphed Washington that the army had had a "brilliant" success and in statements similar to those he had sent before Centreville a month earlier, promised to "push the enemy to the wall." To capitalize on the retreat, the Union would have to quickly follow on the heels of the Rebels and destroy them as they pulled away. Unfortunately, McClellan had focused solely on the siege and though his divisions were prepared for a frontal assault on Yorktown, none were immediately available to get on the roads and chase Johnston's rear guard. The general organized a pursuit force of cavalry, artillery and one division from each corps, but the last of the Rebels had been gone from Yorktown for twelve hours—a substantial head start—before any Federal soldier chased after them.

Half of McClellan's army pursued Johnston overland. With the Confederate batteries at Yorktown empty, the York River was open to the Navy and McClellan sent the other half of the army twenty-four miles up the York to where it met the Pamunkey River at West Point to cut the enemy off. Both forces would then unite and march west all the way to Richmond.

Even with the Confederates retreating, McClellan moved methodically. The Confederate rear-guard resisted and slowed the land pursuit at Williamsburg on May 5. Then it took two days for the flotilla of steamers to assemble for the movement up the York. It was not until May 7 that Brig. Gen. Franklin's Division moved up the river to Eltham's Landing, near West Point, with orders to cut off Johnston's main force. Brig. Gen. John B. Hood's Brigade of Texas troops was waiting for the Federals, and their delaying action kept Franklin from trapping the Southerners. By May 8, the Confederate army had escaped from the lower peninsula without serious loss, and Gen. Johnston put his troops in full retreat towards Richmond.[1]

Porter's Division was in the second wave of the waterborne-pursuit force. With the delays with the assembly of the transports, the 83rd rested in Yorktown through May 7, boarded the steamers the next day and landed at West Point on the morning of May 9. Dead from Gen. Franklin's skirmish the previous day still lay where they fell, and the Pennsylvania men had their first close look at the human cost of combat. Though the Confederates lost a total of forty-eight men, Company A's Sgt. David Rodgers heard rumors that there were 160 Rebel dead in the area. He wrote Julia Porter of how they were buried in mass graves: "They put from 15 to 20 in one hole, as close [to] each other as they can lay them, then cover them up without anything more than the clothes they were killed in. It looks hard, but it is the best that can be done and

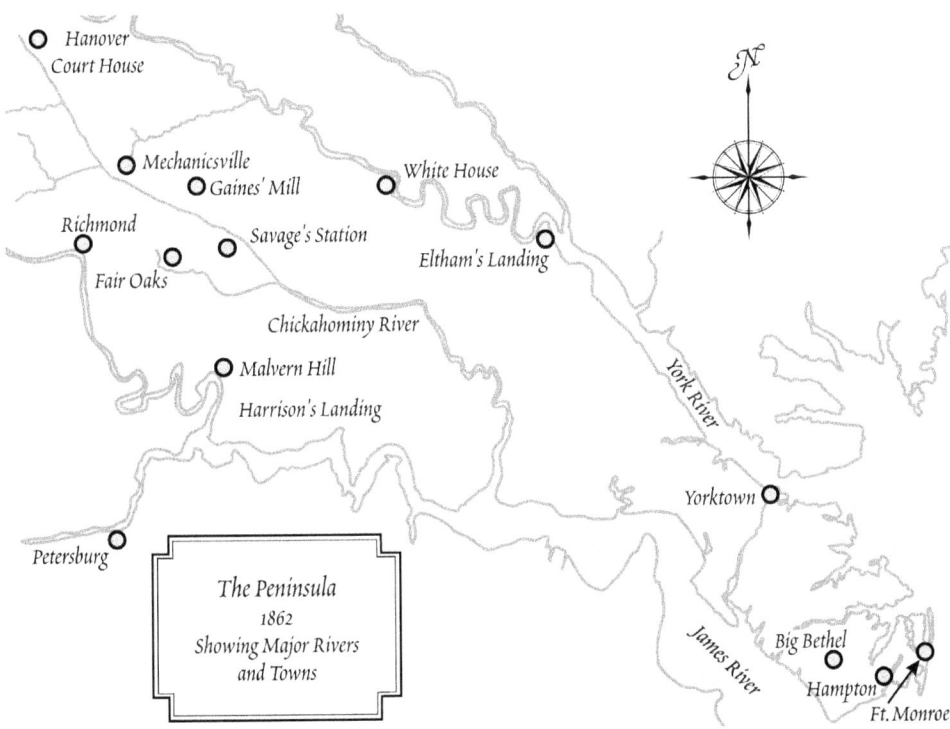

The peninsula formed by the York and James rivers. The 83rd's proving ground in the summer of 1862.

I presume they are just as well off as though they were buried different." Oliver Norton in Company K described: "In Captain Woodward's street considerable blood was still seen on the ground and the boys gathered around it with a curious interest and expressed all sorts of feelings at the novel sight." Pvt. Daniel Foote's first impression of the event was less cavalier: "They were burying the dead the day we landed," he wrote to Julia Hill, "so we had plenty of chance to see dead men if we never have a chance to die ourselves."[2]

Two days later Lt. Col. Vincent led five companies up the Pamunkey on a reconnaissance that met no enemy, but they did encounter some escaped slaves and found significant amounts of forage. Full of confidence, Chaplain Josiah Flower predicted that he would soon preach to them in a Richmond church. David Rodgers mused, "I hope he may, but I don't think he will preach there quite so soon. Although we expect every day to start for Richmond.... I have no doubt but they will be foolish enough to halt us before we get quite in the city." The Army of the Potomac followed the Confederates up the peninsula, and on May 13 the 83rd broke camp again and headed west towards Richmond.[3]

That night they reached Cumberland, eight miles distant, where they had to take time out for a review by Secretary of War William Seward. The regiment was on the march again on May 15, but rains bogged the roads and the men covered only two miles after a full day of marching. The next day they barely made five miles to White House, where they halted for three days. On May 20 the regiment was only three miles closer to Richmond at Turnstall's Station, which led Daniel Foote to tell Julia, "We moved very slow and I cannot see why." It was probably a thought on the minds of many soldiers.[4]

With little terrain favorable to defense on the lower peninsula, Gen. Johnston made no effort to slow McClellan's advance and had rushed his units back to Richmond, where the arrival of the army was particularly disheartening to the Confederacy. Although Yorktown had been evacuated without major losses, there was no disguising the fact that the army had withdrawn before the Federals and was now pushed back to their own capital. The retreat had been long and wearying. Dirty, tired, dispirited Confederate troops streamed into the city and slept wherever they could. As McClellan had done in Washington, Johnston resorted to sending his Provost Guard through Richmond to round up the soldiers and return them to their units. Once the army was back together Johnston formed them in a crescent-shaped defensive line facing west, the closest of the troops only three miles from the city.

Though the Confederate army appeared outwardly ragged, the retreat from Yorktown was no rout and there had been method to their withdrawal. Their defense near Richmond gave them the advantage of a short supply line that would help the shattered units to reconstitute quickly. Its distance from the York and James rivers put Johnston's army out of range of the guns of the Federal navy, and the smaller rivers that ran northwest to southeast outside the city formed substantial barriers against attack. This position also gave them the advantage known as "interior lines," which meant that Johnston could easily shift forces within the defenses to meet any threat from the Union. Johnston's army was in a fine defensive position.[5]

McClellan's army continued up the peninsula in pursuit of the Confederates, buoyed by their victory at Yorktown and other Union triumphs elsewhere in the war. The reversal of the Rebels' advance into Tennessee at the battle of Shiloh (which had so motivated the men in the Yorktown trenches) was the bloodiest battle the war had yet produced and one of the South's most damaging defeats. By mid–May, it looked to McClellan's troops as though the North was winning the war.

With 102,000 men at his disposal, McClellan's army outnumbered Johnston's 75,000 at a ratio of 3:2. A concerted Union push would probably have broken the Confederates but the Federal intelligence service had again greatly overestimated their enemy's strength to be 150,000, a force McClellan deemed too large to attack frontally. On May 15 he attempted to turn Johnston's southern flank with a naval flotilla on the James River, but the expedition ended in failure. Unable to turn Johnston out of his defenses, McClellan decided to take Richmond by the method he knew best, another siege.

In preparation, the general asked Washington to send reinforcements (in particular McDowell's 1st Corps, which had been held back in March and remained near Fredericksburg) at once. McClellan had also been dissatisfied with how his three corps had operated in the early stages of the campaign. To elevate Porter and Brig. Gen. William Franklin, two of his most trusted officers, McClellan decided to split up the nine divisions in the existing corps and reorganize them. The 2nd, 3rd and 4th Corps retained two of their previous three divisions. Porter took command of the new 5th Corps, which consisted of his old division, now led by Brig, Gen. George W. Morell, and a division of mostly Regular regiments under Brig. Gen. George Sykes. The two remaining divisions became the 6th Corps under Gen. Franklin.[6]

On May 20 advanced troops of the 4th Corps reached the Chickahominy River, twelve miles from Richmond. The rest of the army closed on the north bank of the river over the next few days, and Gen. Porter's corps took position as the army's right flank near the town of Mechanicsville.

Organization of the Fifth Army Corps

Morell's Division went into camp near the village of Cold Harbor, and three days after Daniel Foote had fumed at the slow speed of the march, Oliver Norton proudly wrote home, "We are now within ten miles of the rebel capital." McClellan's men had reached the stepping-off point for the final attack into Richmond, the objective of the entire campaign. They were so close that soldiers could hear the city's church bells ring.[7]

The forty-seven mile trip from Yorktown to the Chickahominy had been unopposed, but a long march in the Civil War was still a physically demanding event.

Unless on detached service, regiments usually moved as part of their corps in columns four men abreast. To ease congestion on the roads, corps often took separate, but roughly parallel, routes. Despite splitting the units up, mass movements occupied miles of road. For example, with about 800 soldiers on the march to the Chickahominy River, the 83rd's formation would have consisted of 200 ranks of four men each. Each rank occupied about one yard of lateral space, so the column would have been around 200 yards long. Col. McLane, Lt. Col. Vincent and a few key staff officers were mounted and rode at the front of the regiment or alongside. With four regiments, a brigade formation was over 1,000 yards long. The brigade supply wagons could consist of over 150 vehicles trailing behind the ranks. After the division artillery and baggage transports were added, an entire corps extended over six miles from head to tail.

Marches began in a pleasant enough manner. The regimental band usually supplied some spiriting music to keep the step and the men chatted among themselves. Keeping time was difficult over dirt or sand roads and after a while the band would stop and the men were allowed to walk without keeping in step. The soldiers talked less as they tired, and after the first few miles the only sounds from the column were the shuffling of feet, the creak of leather equipment, and the rattling of tin cups and canteens.

Staff officers, engineers or locals familiar with the roads acted as guides for the corps, but even with experts at the front there were inevitable delays. The column naturally slowed when it forded a stream, crossed a narrow bridge, or, as the men had learned on the way to Yorktown, every time a draught animal, wagon or cannon became mired in mud. The entire body of a six-mile column did not instantaneously halt when a delay was encountered, and the ranks were constantly slowing their pace, stopping and then hurrying to move forward again as obstacles were cleared. The formation became like an accordion, stretching and contracting as it snaked along its path. "Close the gap, men, close the gap," was a never-ending refrain of mounted officers or sergeants that tramped along in the column. Two and a half miles per hour, with periodic rest-halts, was considered a fair march rate.[8]

The week that it took the 83rd to march from the Pamunkey River to the Chickahominy saw alternating days of rain and humid heat. On wet days McLane's men slogged through mud similar to what they had encountered going to Yorktown. When the sun dried the roads, the thousands of tramping feet of the 5th Corps raised clouds of choking grime. Of one day in the middle of the advance, Pvt. John Rice wrote, "The day was very warm and the rodes very dusty and such a looking set of fellows we ware before night you never saw. Our clothes and eyes and whiskers and eye brows ware white with dust and our faces were ringed, streaked and speckled whare the swet had corsed its way down the thick layers of dust."[9]

The soldiers carried what Army regulations termed "light marching order;" rifles, half-shelter tents, blankets, rain ponchos, ammunition, rations, and extra clothing and accouterments in leather knapsacks. Pvt. Daniel Foote estimated their loads to be seventy pounds per man, and there were probably few troops who considered their marching order "light" at all. Temperatures ranged in the 60s on rainy days but reached the mid-80s by the end of the march. Even with a pace of one mile an hour, a full day's hike in the dust was an exhausting event. On improved roads, soldiers were expected to cover fifteen to thirty miles a day, but most of the time units traveled on dirt tracks and an average Civil War march was between eight and thirteen miles. Moving up the peninsula, Pvt. Alexander May wrote to his father, "we dont go over 9 miles in one day for it is so warm that we cant stand it."[10]

Though they were used to hard marches by this time, many soldiers could not "stand it," as May mentioned. Within hours of every journey, troops began dropping out of the formation with foot trouble, dehydration or heat stroke. Soldiers who were legitimately unable to continue were given slips, carried by company commanders, that stated, "The bearer has my permission to fall out of the ranks, being unable to proceed with the regiment." Men with such papers received medical attention or caught up when they were able. Malingerers who skulked away for unauthorized breaks were rounded up by Provost Guards and faced military justice. Commanders were often judged by the number of stragglers from their units, and it was the job of sergeants and junior officers to continually prod the men along in an effort to complete the movement with as many men as possible. Short respites, such as to answer nature's call, were allowed. In those instances, a man handed his rifle and equipment to his comrades, hurried into the bush for his business, and ran back to his place in line. Soldiers who left their friends carrying the extra equipment for long periods of time faced the ire of their tent mates, which was possibly a worse fate than official punishment.[11]

By the time the 83rd reached the Chickahominy River they had the look and attitude of seasoned soldiers. The weak and lazy men would have become known during the campaign and probably detailed to less strenuous duties. The troops were lean and tanned; their uniforms faded and worn. As evidenced by some of the incidents at Yorktown, when soldiers had bullets go through their capes and hat tassels, it appears that some of the men brought parts of their Zouave outfits with them. The coveted suits did not survive the Virginia summer, and Oliver Norton wrote them off with two curt sentences: "We have lately got a set of government uniforms. The Zouave sets are all played out." When they entered their camp at Cold Harbor, there may not have been much difference between the men of the 83rd and their exhausted Confederate counterparts.[12]

McClellan's siege plan called for the steady advance of his infantry corps and heavy artillery, but the Chickahominy River, which ran across the Federal line of advance, would make that difficult. The Chickahominy was a sluggish stream that began about ten miles northwest of Richmond, passed within three miles of the city at one point, and then flowed southeast for thirty-six miles until it emptied into the James. It had low, marshy banks that overflowed and spread into the lowlands during rains and made bridging difficult. The 4th Corps' position at Bottom's Bridge was the army's only foothold over the Chickahominy, and the siege's first objective would be to bridge the river at several locations to enable full movement of the Union forces. Then the bulk of the army would shift across the river, advance to within close artillery range, and storm the Confederate defenses.[13]

Col. McLane's soldiers provided a few work details for this operation but not to the same extent they had at Yorktown. Their camp at Cold Harbor was located about three miles north of the Chickahominy, well out of the swamps, and Lt. Amos Judson in Company E recalled that they undertook "the usual routine of camp duties" there. Pvt. Oliver Norton had time to tell his sister that the area was "as beautiful a section as I ever saw. Lovely scenery, glorious landscapes, everything is beautiful.... Great clover fields in full bloom spreading over gentle swells of ground and broad fields of wheat all headed out abound." It was one of the few times that Norton had anything favorable to say about the Southern states. Still, a few days' inactivity put Norton to restlessness. On May 26 he wrote his friends: "Half a day's march now without special delay would bring us to Richmond. And yet we've seen no rebels except prisoners and deserters, and they are but very poorly calculated to inspire a high opinion of their associates in arms."[12]

In Richmond, Generals Johnston and Lee watched the Union preparations with great concern. Their outnumbered soldiers would have a hard time holding off the Yankee attack, and there was still the possibility that McDowell's 40,000 soldiers at Fredericksburg could move south to reinforce McClellan's army. To guard against the Yankee reinforcements, Johnston ordered a small division commanded by Brig. Gen. Joseph Anderson and a brigade of about 4,000 North Carolina troops led by Brig. Gen. Lawrence Branch to the village of Hanover Court House, north of Richmond, in late May.[15]

Gen. McClellan received reports that the Confederates were advancing near Hanover Court House on May 26, and he immediately perceived the Rebels as a threat to the army's supply line, which ran back to White House on the Pamunkey River. McClellan quickly ordered Gen. Fitz-John Porter to eliminate the menacing Confederates. On May 26, Porter ordered Morell's Division and a squadron of cavalry to mount a raiding force to Hanover Court House the next day. That night, the 83rd's Lt. Amos Judson remembered, "Col. McLane called the commandants of companies together and informed them that an important movement was on foot, and ordered them to have their companies in readiness to march at daylight the next morning."[16]

It was pouring rain when at about 3:30 AM on Tuesday, May 27, sergeants and officers called the men of the 83rd out of their sleep. Each man packed a shelter-half, three day's rations and sixty rounds of ammunition. Cooking fires were impossible in the rain—breakfast consisted of hardtack and water. Although the soldiers were doubtless confused about their early-morning wake up, their preparations soon indicated that the day's activity would not be another routine patrol or continuation of the march. As one member of the brigade recalled: "The order had a telling look. Sixty rounds of ammunition meant something."[17]

Morell's Division began moving at around 4:00 AM. The 1st Regiment of U.S. Sharpshooters led the column, followed in order by the 1st, 3rd and 2nd Brigades. A battery of the division artillery accompanied each unit. The rain continued and soon the road to Hanover was a muddy mess crowded with troops. Norton wrote that the 83rd "traveled as fast as men could travel" but as the men had found out earlier in the campaign, the artillery was constantly getting stuck in the mud and causing delays. The march continued at a slow pace, filled with stops and starts in the knee-deep mud. The downpour stopped in mid-morning, but the heat and humidity were almost as uncomfortable as the rain. Streams crossed the road along the way but the bridges had all been burned, so if the men dried out at all they immediately were wet again each time they waded across. The road itself was just hilly enough to make wet, tired men even more worn out as they slipped in the mud with their smooth-bottomed shoes. Norton later wrote home, "Officers could not stand it any better than the men, for we had not very heavy loads, and the officers and men gave out and lay by the roadside together, utterly unable to go any farther without rest. Captain Austin, Captain Carpenter, Captain Stowe, and Captain Graham all gave out, and half the lieutenants in the regiment with scores of the men fell out and lay down to rest." Even Gen. Butterfield, who was on horseback, called the movement "the most severe I have ever experienced."[18]

At a road junction four miles southeast of Hanover Court House were the Confederate soldiers of Branch's Brigade. Their orders were to guard a section of the Virginia Central Railroad, a key supply line to Richmond, against "small parties" of Federal soldiers. With five North Carolina infantry regiments, two from Georgia, an artillery battery and a detachment of cavalry, Branch's command amounted to about 4,000 soldiers—one-third of the force Porter was bringing to fight them. That morning, Branch had received reports of a Federal advance up the road toward his position and sent the 28th North Carolina Regiment and a section of artillery to watch for the approach of the Union soldiers at the junction of the Ashland and Hanover Roads, which put them directly across Porter's path. For some reason the soldiers had no tents and had been forced to endure the previous night's downpour with little shelter. Like the Yankees marching to meet them, the Rebel troops were wet, tired and miserable.[19]

It was about noon when Porter's vanguard, the 25th New York, arrived at the road junction and encountered the outposts of the 28th North Carolina. A bitter fight between the two units began. Coming up behind the New Yorkers on the road were the soaked, mud-splashed and tired soldiers of the 83rd, who lifted their heads at the sound of the skirmish. Company K's Capt. Henry Austin recalled: "The rapid firing soon told that somebody must get hurt, and that soon."[20]

For over an hour the battle between the 28th North Carolina and the 25th New York see-sawed over the crossroads and lulled when the New Yorkers gave ground. The Tar Heel commander, Col. James Lane, took the opportunity to regroup his unit near the residence of Dr. Thomas H. Kinney, the sole structure in the middle of a wheat field north of the intersection. As the rest of the Yankees closed on the scene, Capt. Henry Benson unlimbered his battery of four three-inch rifled guns and opened fire on Lane's line. Gen. Porter met Butterfield as the 3rd Brigade came up the road and ordered them after the North Carolina troops in the field. As the 1st Brigade swung off the road to the left, Butterfield's troops filed off the track and into the fields to the right.[21]

The Hanover Road curved away to the north, but a stand of woods hid the Rebels from view and Butterfield climbed a tree to pinpoint the Confederate line. Seeing them north and a little east of his brigade's position, he formed the units in a line of battle with the 83rd on the left front and the 17th New York on their right. The 16th Michigan, behind the 83rd, and the 12th New York made up the second line. The tension as the men stepped off the road, dropped their knapsacks, and formed a line of battle would have been electric. Benson's battery boomed from less a quarter-mile away, close enough for the men to feel the concussion of the guns and see the shells exploding on the Rebel position near Dr. Kinney's. Col. McLane sent Companies A and B out to the front as skirmishers under the command of Lt. Col. Vincent. As the excited and nervous Pennsylvanians dressed their lines in final preparation for the attack, Butterfield ordered them forward.[22]

The soldiers stepped off in the manner they had practiced hundreds of times at Hall's Hill. They crossed the dirt road, into the woods and pushed on out to the other side where their first battlefield finally came into view. A rail fence bordered the north edge of the woods directly in front of them. Beyond that, a wheat field with recently harvested shocks rose in a steady slope and crested about two miles in the distance. More woods bordered the field on the left and smaller clumps of trees spotted the low slope where it drifted off to the right along with the Hanover Road. Small ravines and thickets crossed the field. Dr. Kinney's house and the 28th North Carolina, along with two artillery pieces, was in the right-center of the clearing amid the haystacks. After a brief halt at the edge of the woods, the brigade pushed forward through the fence and into the field.

Having been ordered to guard against "small parties" of Federals, the Confederates had not expected to face a force as large as Morell's Division. Col. Lane, the commander of the 890-man 28th North Carolina, was probably shocked to see an entire Yankee brigade emerge from the trees and head toward his line. This was the North Carolinians' first battle, and it would have been prudent for the Tar Heels to withdraw at that point. Shells from Benson's battery were already exploding around the Rebel position, and retrograde movements under fire were difficult to perform even for veterans. By the time he assessed the situation it was probably too late for Lane to retreat his inexperienced troops without Butterfield's line rushing forward and catching them in mid-flight. With no other recourse but to make a fight of it, Lane ordered his artillery to open fire on the Unionists as they moved out of the trees.[23]

The Confederate shells landed near the 3rd Brigade ranks as they moved forward, but as Norton noted: "They shelled us as well as they could, but only one man was hurt." The experience of seeing the Rebel line and the cannon firing directly at them made the difference between a parade field and a battlefield alarmingly evident to the soldiers, but they kept moving. Gen. Morell was watching the attack, and he later wrote that the brigade was in "admirable order" as it moved toward the enemy.[24]

At last, the 83rd had arrived at the field of combat they had anticipated for nine months. Success was not guaranteed—many other regiments had equal training and shrank in the face of battle. The soldiers did not record their exact feelings as they moved closer to the enemy, but their reactions would have been the same of infantrymen of any time. Every man would have feverishly tried to remember the lessons of the training camp; their brains would have

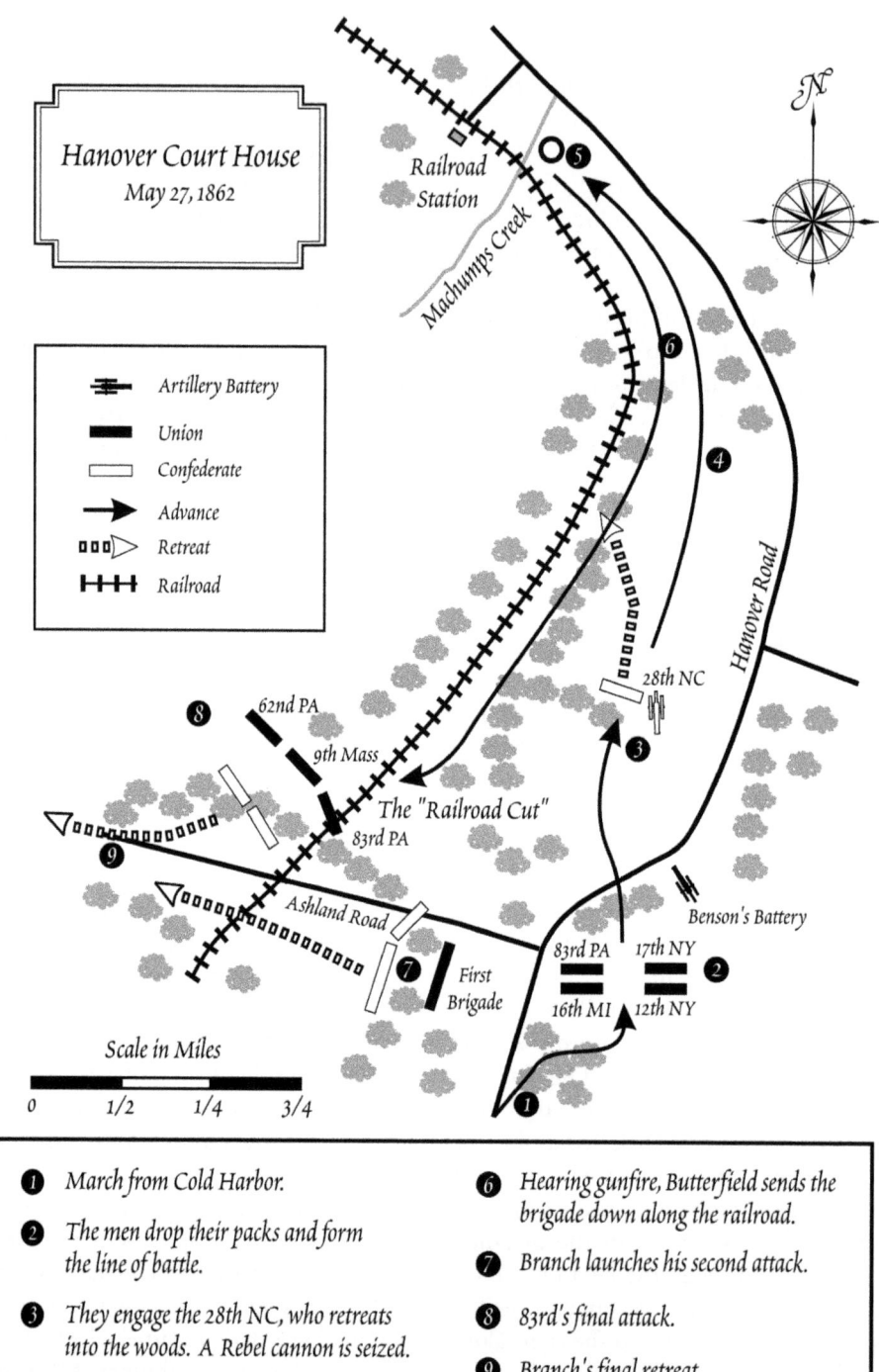

The battle of Hanover Court House, Virginia, where the 83rd saw their first close combat.

IV. A Promise of Perfect Success   71

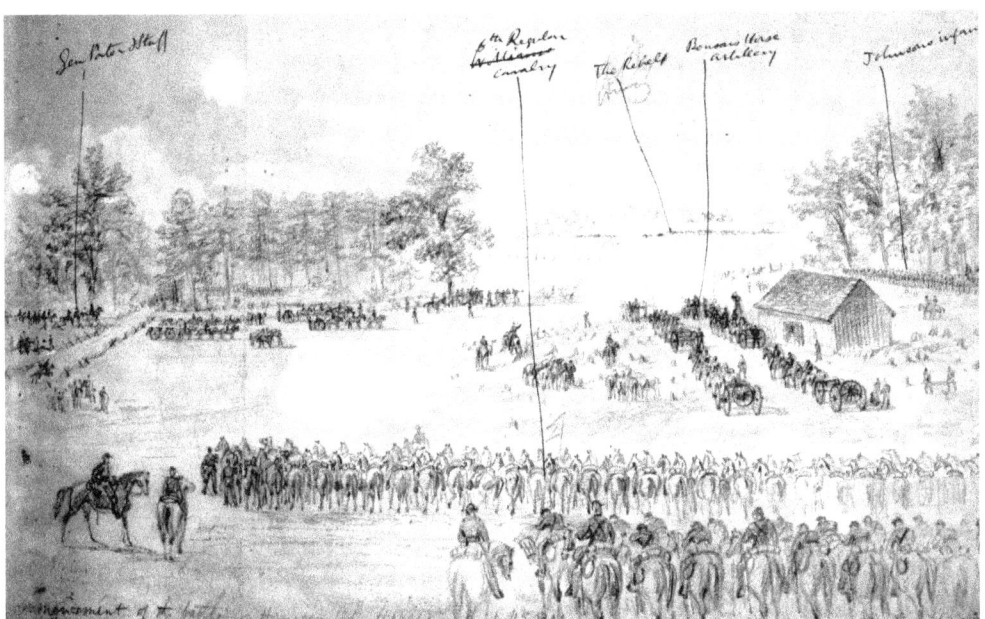

Top: The battle of Hanover Court House, sketched by eyewitness Alfred Waud. This view looks north across the battlefield. Capt. Benson's battery, next to the house in the right center, shells Col. Lane's 28th North Carolina, in the distance marked by Waud's notation, "The Rebels." In the trees at left, Federal infantry, probably Butterfield's Brigade, forms for the attack. The station where Butterfield halted his brigade is in the distance at right. (LOC)
Bottom: The Rebel 12-pounder cannon that the 83rd captured at Hanover Court House, displayed here at the headquarters of the 17th New York. Though the 83rd captured the piece first, the 17th claimed the gun and received the official credit over Col. McLane's protest. (LOC)

Left: Lt. David P. Jones of the 83rd's Company A. (Irwin Rider)
Right: Maj. Gen. George Morell, commander of the 1st Division, 5th Corps. (LOC)

worked to recall the exact sequence of the firing, as their ears would have strained with a new intensity to hear orders on the drum or bugle. As the adrenaline pumped into their veins, the men would have forgotten the fatigue of the hard march and their limbs would move almost automatically. As a second nature, each man would march with his squad, shoulder to shoulder with the same men on the left and right, as they had for hundreds of hours on the drill field. Some men were doubtless very aware of their own mortality, but they could take strength from seeing that the other men kept moving, and that they surely didn't feel the same pangs of fear. Although many of the soldiers had the same feelings, they kept marching just the same.

Moving across the broken ground, the 17th New York slowed as it negotiated a gully and was forced to the right and behind the 83rd. McLane's men took the lead by ten or twenty yards. The 83rd's skirmishers fired at their opposites in the North Carolina line as they advanced. As Butterfield's troops neared the Rebels' right flank, Col. Lane "refused" his line (bent the formation at a right angle) to meet the threat. The Union troops were closing on them when the outnumbered Confederates suddenly abandoned their position and ran for the woods. The Rebels retreated so quickly that they left their dead, wounded, knapsacks, an ambulance, a wagon, and a 12-pounder brass howitzer behind. The 83rd's right flank passed the piece as they continued the advance, but had no time to stop and seize it. The Pennsylvanians could not help but capture a few Confederates who had lagged behind as the Tar Heels withdrew. Norton jumped over a fence and stumbled upon two that he and his comrades quickly disarmed. As the Yankee line continued forward, the separated 17th New York came up behind the 83rd and claimed the abandoned cannon for their own trophy with a triumphant yell.[25]

Overwhelmed, Col. Lane had "deemed it advisable to retire" (as he reported later) and moved his regiment back into the woods north of the wheat field and out of sight of the 83rd. His summary of the situation was, "Exposed all the previous night to a drenching rain, without tents, deprived of food, having marched over a horribly muddy road with unusually heavy knapsacks, and having fought bravely and willingly for three hours in anticipation of being reinforced, we were not in a condition to retreat. Many of my brave men fell from exhaustion on the road-side ... many of them are still missing...." The 83rd's skirmish line, under Lt. Col. Vincent's command, followed the Rebels into the woods, and David Rodgers in Company A wrote home, "We had an interesting time ... the skirmishers was close after them. We took squads of prisoners...." But the Tar Heels disappeared from the field and most of Col. McLane's men never engaged their first foes. Lt. Amos Judson recalled: "It seemed that our brigade was destined to chase something, but we could not see what it was, and have never yet ascertained."[26]

In pursuit of the Confederates, Gen. Butterfield continued the advance to the train depot near Hanover Court House, which the men could see on the top of the rise about a mile ahead. Still in their line of battle, the brigade changed direction slightly to the left and moved on between two belts of woods toward the railroad tracks. Col. McLane sent Maj. Nahgel with Company G to search the woods for the enemy, but the only Rebels in sight were a few scattered horsemen who quickly rode off. When they reached the station, Butterfield assumed he had pushed back the bulk of the Confederates and achieved his day's objective. He halted the brigade and two regiments even stacked their weapons while they rested.[27]

The 28th North Carolina was not the main enemy force, as the Federal officers had assumed. While Butterfield's Brigade had been pursuing the Tar Heels in the wheat field, Branch had pushed two other regiments (the 18th and 37th North Carolina) through the woods from the west to counterattack the Union troops at the intersection of the Hanover and Ashcake Roads. The commander of the 1st Brigade, Brig. Gen. James Martindale, reported the situation to Porter, but the Confederates pressed their attack.[28]

The fight at the crossroads was over a mile away from Butterfield's position at the railroad station. Though the woods around Dr. Kinney's farm blocked the battle from their view, the rattle of fire was clear enough to the men in the ranks, as Amos Judson recalled: "We had not been [there] five minutes when we heard sharp and rapid musketry from the very spot where the engagement had commenced." At about the same time, orders from Porter arrived to move immediately to the support of the 1st Brigade. Judging from the sounds of the battle only, Butterfield determined that the tracks of the Virginia Central Railroad were the most direct route to take his troops into a position on Martindale's flank, and ordered the 83rd and the 16th Michigan to get up and follow the tracks back to the action.[29]

The regiments moved quickly and the 83rd outpaced the 16th. By that time in the late afternoon the men had been marching for about twelve hours and the strain of the day was taking effect, as Pvt. Daniel Foote wrote: "We had come then over 30 miles and in our co. there was nearly 20 men who had tired out and fell in the rear, and the rest of us began to feel very tired...." Oliver Norton also reported his own exhaustion: "I fell out to get some water and bathe my head," he said. "My tongue was so swollen with the heat and thirst, and I so faint I could hardly stand. I followed on, however the regiment was some distance ahead. I came up to Denny and Henry. Henry could not walk but a little way without stopping...." It is likely that many men fell out as the 83rd rushed toward the action.[30]

The regiments had moved south along the tracks for about a mile when they neared the wooded area that the noise indicated to be the scene of the fighting. Gen. Butterfield reported hearing "unceasing volleys of musketry" and cheering that he believed came from the Rebels. It sounded as if the enemy was gaining the upper hand in their attack. With chests heaving from their run and sweat streaming down their faces, the 83rd swung off the railroad track and formed a line of battle. Butterfield was with them as they neared the end of the woods and he urged the men to charge forward with a cheer. Daniel Foote wrote, "The Gen. came along and lifting his fist shouted 'Forward 83rd forward, Double Quick,' We took a dead run...."[31]

Army tactics manuals dictated that the colonel was to stay behind the ranks and direct their movements, but American soldiers have always responded to leadership by example. In practice, it was more common for a colonel to go forward of the ranks and inspire the troops to follow him into the battle. In the Civil War, spontaneous cheers often followed such a gesture from their commander from the men and the line would surge forward in an adrenaline rush. McLane had a strong bond with his troops, and as the 83rd turned off the railroad track and formed its line, he stepped out ahead of them, turned and faced the ranks, and shouted, "Now is the time to prove yourselves soldiers!" The regiment charged through the woods with the yell Butterfield had called for.[32]

The woods were several dozen yards wide, and Amos Judson remembered the anticipation the men felt as they moved toward their second action of the day, "The roar of the artillery becoming nearer, clearer, deadlier ... we could hear [other Union troops] pouring whole broadsides at once into the ranks of the enemy, till finally the fire slackened; and, at the very moment we debouched from the woods, it entirely ceased." As the 83rd had sped down the railroad, Gen. Porter had launched the 9th Massachusetts and 62nd Pennsylvania from the 2nd Brigade against the attacking Confederates, and the two units had beaten Butterfield's troops to the scene and pushed back the Rebels as McLane's men came up. Col. McLane reported that the firing ahead of the regiment was "sharp and constant" and he sent Capt. Hiram Brown's Company I and Company H under Lt. John Wilson out in front as skirmishers. Both companies traded shots with the retreating soldiers and grabbed up more prisoners, which were probably stragglers of the 37th North Carolina that had been pushed out by the 2nd Brigade counterattack. McLane could not spare many soldiers to guard the captured men, so a single sentry from the 83rd sometimes disarmed squads of Confederates and escorted them to the rear.[33]

Some of the prisoners had stated that there were still two Rebel regiments in woods off to the 83rd's right, and at about the same time, Capt. Brown's and Lt. Wilson's skirmishers there came under fire. McLane passed the information to Butterfield but still pressed his regiment forward. Along with the 2nd Brigade soldiers, the Pennsylvanians came through the trees and saw the Rebel troops withdrawing west through an open field towards the Ashland Road. Two sections of Capt. Charles Griffin's artillery battery set up at the edge of the woods and shelled the Confederates as they pulled away.[34]

Overwhelmed, Gen. Branch ordered his regiments to break off the battle and retreat west along the Ashland Road. According to McLane, Butterfield recognized the Rebel retreat to be "the decisive moment of the day" and the general sent the 83rd to attack the withdrawing enemy in the fields. McLane again took the lead, and moved the regiment past Griffin's artillery toward the Ashland Road.[35]

A ten-foot deep cut of the Virginia

Central Railroad cut diagonally across the 83rd's path. Rushing to catch their retreating enemy, the soldiers skidded down the bank and climbed up the other side. Crossing the cut ruined the alignment of the line of battle and some soldiers reached the top as others were still clambering through it. The 83rd was in this disorganized formation when they were surprised to see a Rebel regiment in front of them about three hundred yards away. Daniel Foote coolly recalled, "The Col. shouted 'they are coming boys' ... and I watched them until I saw them halt and bring their guns to a level...." The Confederates, possibly the 7th North Carolina, fired what McLane called "a terrible volley" into their ranks. Instead of following the standard tactic of the day and keeping his men in ranks while bullets flew at them, McLane instantly ordered them to lay down, as Alexander May wrote: "We seen the flash of the guns and we all fell to the ground and there bullets done us no harm."[36]

Companies H and I were walking ahead of the regiment as skirmishers and it is not known why they did not discover the Confederates before Col. McLane did. It is possible that the two companies had moved so far ahead of the regiment that the enemy troops had slipped in between the skirmish line and the 83rd's line of battle. McLane had been surprised but through his quick thinking had avoided the first volley. In the mock battles at Hall's Hill, the 83rd had maneuvered against formations that were several hundred yards distant and clearly visible in open fields and the circumstances at the railroad cut were some that the Pennsylvanians had not trained for. Previously unseen and prepared to fight, the Tar Heels had the advantage over the 83rd. Some commanders would have been unnerved, but as soon as the enemy bullets flew overhead, McLane ordered "Up!" and sent his regiment's first full volley of the war against the Confederates.

Rebel bullets flew back at the 83rd in return. With three companies detached as skirmishers there were around six hundred men on McLane's line. The Pennsylvanians reloaded and shot as fast as they could, sending about 1,800 shots toward the Confederates every minute. The noise was deafening, drowning out orders and even drum calls. The guns gave off billows of smoke so thick that the men fired blindly after the first volley. Foote recalled: "We rose and fired and I loaded and fired again but did not get any aim." Though they could not see the Rebel soldiers, orange muzzle flashes from the enemy guns were clear through the smoke. Minié bullets from the Tar Heels' muskets passed the Yankees with a "hiss" or "whisp" sound. The Confederates also fired blindly but eight of McLane's men fell wounded.

The Minié bullets fired by both armies traveled at relatively low velocities, but were made of soft lead that flattened upon impact. The projectiles, oddly shaped as they entered the body, tore away large chunks of flesh and carried particles of clothing, dirt and gunpowder into the wound. Getting hit was like having a red-hot wire running through the body with a jarring thud if the bullet struck bone, which usually splintered. Shock caused initial numbness, followed by intense pain. Instead of a hiss, the big, .58 caliber bullets made a sickening "whack" when they struck bodies. Standing shoulder to shoulder, soldiers could hear the sound clearly over the din. Blood and bits of flesh spattered on soldiers near those who were hit.[37]

The melee between the opposing lines continued for about ten or fifteen minutes, and then the 83rd advanced, the men firing as they went. With the 9th Massachusetts on the right, the two regiments moved forward for about 200 yards, and as the smoke cleared the soldiers saw the Rebels in full retreat through the woods. A section of 10-pounder Parrot guns commanded by Lt.

Charles Hazlett wheeled into position and shelled the Confederates as they moved away to the west along the Ashland road, but Gen. Butterfield did not intend to let the enemy escape so easily. "Everything was going on handsomely in front," he wrote. "My only desire now was to push forward troops enough to utterly rout the enemy and capture all the prisoners possible." The 83rd followed the Rebels for a few hundred yards in an attempt to fulfill Butterfield's order, but it was now near dark, and Branch's regiments quickly moved out of range. As Alexander May told his parents, "We advanced after them as quick as possibel and they retreated in to the woods so fast and us so tired that we could not catch them...." Still lagging behind the regiment, the fighting had spurred Oliver Norton and his friends to catch up: "Soon we heard the sharp rattle of musketry ahead and the third fight had commenced," he wrote. "We tried to get Henry along, but finally left him and he came on slowly while Denny and I pushed on as fast as we could, but the firing was done when we caught up."[38]

The Confederates' quick retreat had ended the battle. Col. McLane marched his men back to the crossroads where they had earlier dropped their packs and set up a camp for the night. The companies detailed as skirmishers returned with 118 prisoners. The men were no doubt excited at their victory, but exhaustion soon took hold over elation. They had been marching and fighting since before dawn, and most fell quickly to sleep without any bivouac, as Norton described: "Night closed in and we went back to our blankets and, wrapping up, lay down between the rows of corn to sleep. Generals and privates alike spent the night on the ground."[39]

The 83rd's medical staff did not sleep with the rest of the regiment. Porter's force had suffered 285 men killed and wounded, and many of the Confederates' 400 battle casualties had fallen into Union hands.

Most of the injured were collected in the late afternoon, and work for the surgeons began when the infantrymen finished.[40]

As a battle unfolded, it was the job of the regimental surgeon and his team of two assistants and one steward to identify a sheltered area for use as their unit's field hospital. Houses usually served this purpose but any structure or even shade trees were acceptable. The surgeons of brigades or divisions often shared the same facilities. Whatever the hospital was, the assistants fashioned operating tables out of any flat surfaces on hand such as dinner tables, planks on sawhorses or unhinged doors. Stewards arranged the medical supplies and anesthetics such as opiates and whiskey. If time allowed, the company cooks boiled water, soaked sponges and prepared coffee, tea or soup. Straw was strewn about for the comfort of those who would be waiting for treatment. Half of the regimental band was usually assigned to help at the hospital while the other half accompanied the line companies as stretcher bearers. While the surgeon stayed at the field hospital, the assistant surgeon and an orderly carried a small amount of medical supplies behind the regiment as it advanced and set up a "primary station" a few hundred yards behind the line of battle. The division's ambulances, carts specially designed to carry stretchers, also marshaled there.

Those stretcher bearers who actually followed the regiment carried incapacitated men to the primary station. An injured man who could walk was usually ordered to go directly to the station on his own but in practice, even they were often helped off by their tent mates. In this manner, one wounded man sometimes caused as many as three or more to leave the line of battle.

At the primary station, the assistant surgeon administered first aid and often gave the wounded men whiskey as a painkiller. Those with slight wounds sometimes received no further care. Seriously injured soldiers were loaded into ambulances and taken to the field hospital. There, the most severely wounded went to the operating table while the less critical cases were laid out in the straw to await their turn. Though anesthetics were available, the surgeons often probed wounds while the men were fully conscious. The discomfort of those waiting grew as shock wore off, and the shrieks and groans of those waiting or being examined carried far around the hospitals. Before cutting, the surgeon gave the patient an opium pill or from an eighth to a quarter gram of morphine.

Then the surgeon, usually with his sleeves rolled up, smeared with blood, and his instruments sometimes held between his teeth, went to work. The doctor wiped the excess blood from his instruments on his apron and made his cuts and sutures. Limbs with shattered bones were almost always amputated. Arms and legs were unceremoniously piled outside the medical tents. As soon as the procedure was finished the doctor cried, "Next!" and another soldier was delivered to his table.[41]

At Hanover Court House, the medical staffs of Morell's Division turned Dr. Kinney's house, the sheds, slave cabins and barns into field hospitals. A war correspondent at the battle reported, "The floors were littered with cornshucks and fodder, and the maimed, gashed, and dying lay confusedly together ... these poor fellows were frightfully convulsed, breaking into shrieks and shouts, some of them iterated a single word, as 'Doctor!' or 'Help!' or 'Oh!' Commencing with a loud spasmodic cry, and continuing the same word till it died away in sighs." Capt. Henry Austin of the 83rd's K Company visited the hospital and wrote, "I have seen many hard sights within the last 24 hours, but to see the horrors of war you must see a battlefield. The Hospital is a dreadful sight. The one we are using is stained with blood; through every room a sickening contrast to the splendid furniture....* Out on the piazza in front the surgeons are very busy at work taking off limbs of our poor fellows."[42]

One of the "poor fellows" was Company K's 2nd Sergeant, Egbert Hurlbert, who had been shot in the ankle and had his leg amputated below the knee. Daniel Foote told his parents that his tent mate Frank McBride had also been hit in the foot, but noted that "it is a slight wound that is not dangerous." Pvt. Jacob Shriver of Company G would die within two weeks and become the regiment's first battle death. The next day Capt. Austin wrote that "The rebels are poorly armed, but they fight well...." and the myth that Confederate soldiers were an armed rabble with few martial skills was probably ended for the men of the 83rd.[43]

In addition to the wounded, the Federals had taken another 730 Rebels, though the Confederate commander, Gen. Lawrence Branch reported, "The enemy may have captured stragglers enough to offset the prisoners we took from them in the open field, but they took no body of my troops." Butterfield's Brigade alone took 225 prisoners, and the 83rd accounted for over half of that total. Porter passed the news of the victory to Army headquarters, and ever eager for victories, Gen. McClellan telegraphed Washington: "Have this moment heard from F. J. Porter, with his division. He has taken Hanover Court House.... Rebels, 13,000 in number, commanded by General Branch. The expedition promises perfect success in all its objects...." Porter also reported defeating a command of "8,000" enemy, and commended his troops: "I take great pleasure in bearing testimony to the admirable manner in which the command has acquitted itself. The behavior of the officers and men showed the benefit of the good training at Hall's Hill

---

Austin's comment may indicate that he was in Dr. Kinney's House.

and elsewhere, given last winter by their brigade and regimental commanders." Butterfield was also pleased: "The splendid bearing, under their baptismal of fire, of the 83rd Pennsylvania and the 17th New York was worthy of the highest praise. The 83rd was in both fights, and behaved like veterans in the last as in the first." Butterfield would also praise McLane and Vincent in private letters to their wives, saying that the two officers "should never think of being anything else but soldiers."[44]

Although Gen. Martindale's 1st Brigade had borne the brunt of the fighting, McLane's soldiers had entered the battle after a fatiguing march and proved their mettle in every opportunity. After brushing away Lane's 28th North Carolina in Dr. Kinney's field, their drive along the railroad made them the only of Butterfield's regiments to reach the second part of the battle in time. They had been surprised at the railroad cut, but had kept cool enough to return fire and inflicted such damage a prisoner later told McLane that only two men out of one Rebel company were left standing after the fight. The prisoner's claim may have been flattery designed for favorable treatment from his captors, but overall, the 83rd had passed its first combat test with high marks.[45]

Porter's troops stayed on the battlefield, and the next day the men awoke "stiff and sore" as Norton recalled. Their first task was to bury the enemy dead. Although they had glimpsed dead Rebels before at Eltham's Landing, the men seemed to have a particular fascination with these bodies, the results of their own fire. Norton recalled: "The woods were full of dead rebels who lay, as they fell, in all shapes. They were carried out and laid in a ghastly row on the grass. One fine looking man was shot through the heart as he was loading his gun. His hands had not changed their position, one extended above his head drawing his rammer and the other grasping his gun by his side. His eyes were open and the expression of countenance as calm as though he was sleeping, but the fearful wound in his breast told that he would never wake on earth again. We buried over one hundred of them."[46]

Porter's troops continued their mission of burning railroad bridges and tearing up track for the next two days. Amos Judson recalled that the soldiers' rations had "given out" (although they had packed enough for three days), and the men were allowed to forage. It was rich country, previously untouched by the war, and there was plenty of livestock. Many soldiers considered the Rebel property free for the taking. Daniel Foote's statement that "Our neighbors gardens, poultry yards, cellars and pantries as well as the flocks and herds grazing on the hillsides were at our disposal...." hints at the attitude some of the men had for the citizens of Hanover County. Lt. Judson recalled that the troops returned with pigs, turkeys, fowl, and "several demijohns of good liquor captured from the cellars of fleeing inhabitants." At one point some soldiers captured several train cars filled with coveted tobacco, sugar and salt. None of the items the soldiers collected survive, but Norton also described how the men took whatever they could find: "Secesh knapsacks were scattered everywhere, and our boys, if they could have carried away the things, would have got a good many comforts, but we could not. We got a good many love letters, etc., bowie knives, and pistols, and I got a great bowie but I threw it away, I couldn't carry it. I send you a letter that I got in a knapsack, and a secesh stamp. The letter is an excellent specimen of secesh literature and love." Alexander May also found amusement from the litter of the dead: "I wish you could of read some of the letters that was taken from the rebs out to Hanover that their sweethearts have written them," he wrote home, "such loving talk you never heard or read of." Capt. Henry Austin sent home what he called "curiosities" from North Carolina knapsacks, and wrote a letter on what he carefully noted was "secesh paper."[47]

Escaped slaves, an unexpected human dividend, poured into the camp. At that stage of the war, slaves were considered legitimate civilian property, and there were orders against the practice of providing them refuge. Despite the rules, the soldiers let the escaped slaves into the camp and put them to work as paid servants or laborers. Daniel Foote described one incident: "There was a great number of slaves left the plantations and came into camp of both sexes wishing to go as waiters. Among others a colored man of middle age making complaint that his master had flogged him severely of late. Soon his master came after him. In order to claim protection [the slave owner] had taken the oath of allegiance and the negro showed [us] his back. It was awful, one raw mess. The boys began to shout for a rope and the Major on Butterfield's staff [possibly Maj. Von Vegesack, who would give great help to the 83rd in the next battle] ordered him back to his home. He called for his slave. The major drew a revolver and told him to leave and he went that time and the negro goes as a waiter for the Major."[48]

Porter's raiding activities were complete on May 29, and at about 3:00 PM the troops left Hanover for their camp on the Chickahominy. With the roads still muddy from the rains, the march home was a mirror of the first. Again, the artillery and wagons stuck frequently and caused delays that sometimes lasted hours. Without the anticipation of combat and the adrenaline to keep them moving, many of the soldiers simply sat down to rest on the side of the road and fell asleep. The men finally arrived back at Cold Harbor nearly twelve hours after their start. Some of the stragglers did not catch up for another day.[49]

In general, McLane's soldiers must have been elated with their battle at Hanover Court House and morale was probably the highest it had been since their departure from Erie. Three days after the battle, young Arthur Cleeland told his parents, "I never felt better in my life than I did while we was in the fight." Knowing that the army was preparing for its assault into Richmond, they looked forward to what they thought would be the final battle of the war. Alexander May's opinion was that, "After everything is ready the rebel army must give way before our brave boys. We have every reason to expect a desperate resistance on their part and hard fighting on our own before the stars and stripes will float in triumph over the Confederate capital." Daniel Foote closed one early June letter to Julia Hill expectantly with: "I hope to receive an answer while in Richmond." Oliver Norton was one of those who believed that the long-anticipated battle would begin soon, and told his sister, "[McClellan] wants to end the war here and he has not got everything ready yet." Bugler Norton finished his letter of June 10 with the prediction, "There is a good time coming yet, boys."[50]

V

YOU WILL SEE ENOUGH OF THEM BEFORE NIGHT

If Gen. McClellan shared the optimism that the men of the 83rd felt after Hanover Court House, he gave little evidence of it. The battle had been the first major clash of the armies near Richmond and McClellan called it "a glorious victory," but in reality the action had distracted the general from securing more crossings over the Chickahominy for almost a full week, and that gave Gen. Johnston more time to organize the Confederate defenses. Weeks passed, but by mid–June the Army of the Potomac was still on the Chickahominy with the 2nd, 5th, and 6th Corps on the north side of the river, the 3rd and 4th Corps south of it, and none of them substantially closer to Richmond than they had been at the end of May. Army engineers had built pontoon bridges over the river but crossing large numbers of troops and artillery was still difficult. Although McClellan had enough men to brush through the Confederates in their defenses, he remained determined to continue with his methodical siege.

In contrast, Gen. Johnston planned to attack the Union line as soon as an opportunity presented itself. The heavy rains in late May that had annoyed the men of the 83rd also had caused the Chickahominy to overflow and sweep away most of McClellan's new bridges. The Union 3rd and 4th Corps were cut off from the troops north of the river, and Johnston quickly concentrated his power to destroy the isolated corps in detail before the rest of the Federal Army could cross to assist them. On May 31 Johnston attacked at a crossroads six miles east of Richmond known as Seven Pines. Surprised, the Union troops lost ground until reinforcements arrived and bolstered the line.[1]

At their camp four miles north of Seven Pines, the men of the 83rd heard the battle develop and were ordered into the fight along with the rest of Morell's Division. At about 11:00 PM that night the regiment packed up and moved south, where engineers attempted to bridge what Amos Judson called the "black Stygian waves" of the overflowing Chickahominy. All night the men waited for the engineers' success, but swampy banks and swift, rising water defeated their efforts and the regiment remained on the north side of the river. The contest continued the next day. The fighting was intense but troops of the 2nd Corps eventually reached the field and the Union held their positions. The closest that the 83rd came to the action was as spectators on the north bank of the river, as Judson remembered: "We heard every shot and every volley that was fired, every yell of our men as they charged the enemy, and the cheers that followed; and had our corps been thrown across, it is possible that the enemy might have been pursued to the walls of Richmond."[2]

Neither side gained or lost much ground at Seven Pines, and although the opposing formations had been roughly equal, McClellan believed that his troops had repelled a force much larger than its actual size. After the battle the General's intelligence service still estimated the Confederate army to have over 180,000 soldiers (almost twice their actual strength) and the Young Napoleon was convinced of the need to move more carefully than ever. "I have to be very cautious now," he wrote to President Lincoln in early June, "you can see that the Army of the Potomac has had serious work & that no child's play is before it." In reality, the Confederates had failed to achieve the decisive victory they had hoped for and lost over 6,000 soldiers in the fight. One of them was Gen. Johnston himself, who was badly wounded while he directed the action from a forward position. With Johnston incapacitated, General Robert E. Lee took command of the Army of Northern Virginia the same day.[3]

Continuing with McClellan's cautious siege plan, Union engineers repaired the bridges over the Chickahominy and built more until there were seven crossing sites. All through June, soldiers laid miles of corduroy road and the four corps located south of the river dug in behind earthwork barricades. More heavy artillery came forward on the new roads and more supplies were stockpiled. McClellan continued to badger Washington for more troops, and in mid-June the War Department added Brig. Gen. George McCall's Division of Pennsylvania Reserves to the Army of the Potomac. Assigned to Gen. Porter's command, McCall's Division made the 5th Corps the largest in the army and brought McClellan's troop strength up to 105,900 soldiers.[4]

Much of the siege work was done by the engineers and the men of the 83rd settled into a lazy routine of drill, picketing along the river, and ordinary camp duties. Daniel Foote described their schedule to his family: "Reveille 4:30 o'clock, drill from 5:30 to 6:30 o'clock. From that time if we stay in camp or near by it is all that is wished of us until 5 o'clock PM when we have another hour drill and there ends the days labor. So you see we are not having it hard at all, in fact I enjoy it. [If] I had plenty of interesting books I should be in paradise almost I think." Foote saved his sole complaint for another letter to Julia Hill: "The worst of it is it troubles us seriously to get water and make coffee in an hour and troubles us a little worse to eat nothing until near 8 o'clock." The soldiers were worn out after two months of hard campaigning and the inactivity was the delight of some of them. Alexander May described the regiment's relaxed, summertime attitude in one of his letters: "We are having [a] splendid time now. Nothing much to do. Our drill is to go to the dam for a bathe, a little picket duty and fatigue which amounts to nothing. Hall's Hill discipline is all done away with, so it makes very pleasant soldiering. No telling how long we will remain inactive." May was confident of victory, and he looked forward to his return to Erie. He asked a friend: "Speak a good word for me to some of the prity girls for I am coming home. The rebs can't get me." Picket duty away from the regiment seemed to be a particular treat, as Foote wrote, "All is quiet along the lines save now and then a little skirmishing between the pickets who are in speaking distance of each other and often when the officers are not in sight they hold conversations with each other and in one or two instances have exchanged some of our daily papers for copies of theirs." John Rice also told his friends, "I was on picket at New bridge 10 days & I tell you I had a musical time of it. I never enjoyed myself better."[5]

Visitors from Washington flocked to

the peninsula during this lull in the fighting, among them were military observers from European powers. Officers of professional foreign armies were very interested in what soldiers the American citizens made, and often visited the new volunteer regiments. The 83rd had their chance to impress one of them on June 19 when General Prim y Prats of the Spanish Army came to their camp. Norton observed that Prim was "quite a contrast to the plain dress of 'our George' [McClellan], as he rode by in his gold lace and trimmings."[6]

Some of the new machines of war were also in operation nearby, to the amusement of the soldiers. The men had watched Professor Thaddeus Lowe's hot-air balloon ascend to report on enemy movements during the battle of Seven Pines, as Alexander May wrote: "Our baloons is their worst enemy. We wach their movements to much ... there is where we have the advantage of them. They havent the inginuity about them to get up one." Lowe's balloon continued to ascend near their camp throughout June and the Confederates eventually launched their own, disproving May's prediction.* Later in the month Norton was fortunate to be able to see a forerunner of the machine gun called a "coffee grinder" which he described as "a cannon drawn by one horse that one man can fire two hundred times a minute by merely turning a crank," and as "a curious Yankee contrivance ... it makes a noise like the dogs of war let loose."†

The soldiers enjoyed their easy and interesting environment. Few probably recognized that the time for advancing on Richmond was slipping away. Norton's mid–June observation was: "This is great country for rain. It rains for two days and the next day it rains, and then we have some rain and wet weather," which meant that that the weather was keeping the Chickahominy high and the ground soft, and complicating the progress of the siege.

In addition to the strategic disadvantage for the Union, the rain made the hot Virginia summer even more humid and contributed to the breeding of disease-carrying insects along the river. A debilitating ailment the men called the "Chickahominy Fever," which may have been typhoid or typhus, became common. The soldier's constant diet of salt pork, salt beef, and hardtack also produced outbreaks of scurvy. Dysentery and chronic diarrhea were also frequent maladies (with the humor typical of a veteran soldier, Lt. Israel Thickstun would joke a year later, "A signal officer dreamed he had the diarrhia and on waking found it to be a 'dirreality'"). By the end of June, the Army of the Potomac had 11,000 men unfit for duty due to disease.[9]

Camped a mile north of the river on the farm of Dr. William Gaines, the 83rd began the month of June with 130 soldiers in the hospital and another 35 sick but still present for duty. Even Col. McLane had been ill with "intermittent fever" in May but had remained with regiment. By the end of the month the regiment reported 180 men in the hospital and 131 soldiers sick and in the ranks. One of those in the hospital was Lt. Col. Vincent, who had contracted Chickahominy Fever. Twenty-six of the Pennsylvanians had died of disease since leaving Hall's Hill. Thirteen men had been detailed to work outside the regiment as staff clerks, butchers or ambulance drivers. Three soldiers, most likely Lake Erie sailors, had been transferred to serve on gunboats in the western theater. All ten companies were

---

*Though an innovative use of technology, balloon observation was not as useful to the military as it was expected to be and neither side used it much after the Peninsula campaign.
†Pennsylvania Governor Andrew Curtain supplied a number of the coffee-grinder guns to some of his infantry regiments in the 6th Corps. The guns apparently did not work as well as predicted, because they saw limited field use. The Confederates later captured most of them, and there is no record of their use on their side.

The Army Engineers' bridge over the Chickahominy on the Mechanicsville Road. The low and marshy banks are typical of the conditions that the 83rd found all along the river. (LOC)

significantly reduced in strength, as Daniel Foote wrote about Company K, "We muster about 60 men rank and file now in our Co. and all tough, rugged men. All the weakly ones have died, been discharged and [are] in the hospital. Most of the men are tanned up very black but it makes them look well." The state of the men and the regiment typified the Union units that had crossed the peninsula.[10]

The Confederates suffered the same proportions of sickness that Federal troops did, and Gen. Lee knew that there was little chance that his outnumbered and weakening army would be able to defend against the expected Union assault. With no room to retreat, Lee decided to mass the Confederate forces in the east to counter the Union advantage in numbers. First, he directed Stonewall Jackson to eliminate the Federal forces from the Shenandoah Valley and then to move south to join the Army of Northern Virginia. Jackson's four divisions and

reinforcements from southern Virginia would give Lee 92,400 men. With that number he could afford to maintain the defenses of Richmond with a skeletal force and strike McClellan at a weak point with the rest of the army.

To identify the Union positions and find their weaknesses, Lee dispatched his cavalry brigade under Brig. Gen. J.E.B. Stuart. From June 12 to June 15, Stuart's troopers rode all the way around the Army of the Potomac with little opposition. In addition to being a flamboyant snub at the Yankees, Stuart's ride revealed that Porter's 5th Corps was alone on the north side of the Chickahominy. With no natural or man-made obstacle to anchor it, the northern end of the Federal line was open to attack. Behind the 5th Corps, the Union supply line ran fifteen miles to White House on the Pamunkey River. It was the vulnerability that the Lee looked for.

Lee immediately sent word for Jackson's troops to join the main army as soon as possible. When they arrived, he planned to hold the Richmond defenses with three divisions while three others, commanded by Major-Generals Longstreet, A. P. Hill and D. H. Hill, moved north of the Chickahominy and joined with Jackson's force. Once concentrated, the northern wing of the army would attack Porter's exposed corps on its front, flank, and rear. When the Union flank was crushed and its supply line to White House was threatened, Lee reasoned, McClellan would have to pull the other corps out of their fortifications and fall back. The attack was set to begin at 3:00 AM, on June 26.

Outside Richmond, Gen. McClellan was finally satisfied with the lengthy siege preparations and prepared to begin the assault on the city's defenses. The General planned for the 2nd and 3rd Corps to slowly advance and seize key ground south of the Chickahominy on June 25, while the 5th Corps held the northern flank. In a rare instance of effectiveness, the Union intelligence service learned of Jackson's movement to join Lee's army and the 5th Corps prepared to meet the expected Rebel troops. McCall's Pennsylvania Reserves division dug in near Mechanicsville behind Beaver Dam Creek. Sykes' and Morrel's divisions remained near the Chickahominy, positioned and ready to counter any Confederate attack. Preparing for action on June 25, the men of the 83rd packed their excess baggage and sent it across the Chickahominy with the regimental wagons so it would not encumber them in the coming battle. Little information of their role in the coming fight reached the men. Amos Judson remembered that, as they sent away their equipment, "the air became filled with rumors."[11]

As scheduled, the 3rd Corps attacked the Confederates at Oak Grove (near the Seven Pines battlefield) on June 25. The troops advanced cautiously but steadily pushed the Rebels back, and Gen. McClellan was satisfied with their progress. As the general watched the action, he received more reports that thousands of Confederate troops were massing to attack the Union lines north of the Chickahominy and that Jackson's command was moving towards the army's rear. Always willing to believe the exaggerated estimates of enemy strength, the latest reports confirmed to McClellan that his army was outnumbered. As the 3rd Corps' advance met stiff resistance and ground to a halt, he decided that it was impossible to continue against what he called "overwhelming numbers" and expected an attack by "200,000" enemy. That night McClellan alerted the corps commanders to prepare to receive the Confederate assault all along the line the next day.

Though distracted by the Federal attack at Oak Grove, Gen. Lee continued with his offensive. The attack on the 5th Corps began in the early afternoon on June 26. Brig. Gen. McCall's division of Pennsylvania Reserves was waiting and held firmly from behind their prepared defenses, but by late afternoon Porter ordered up reinforcements from the two reserve divisions near the Chickahominy.[12]

The troops of Brig. Gen. George Morell's Division began June 26 with rumors of nearby enemy activity and spent a tense morning waiting for orders or the sounds of gunfire. Brig. Gen. Martindale's 1st Brigade was posted to reinforce the Mechanicsville line early that morning, and when the attack developed further in the afternoon, Morell dispatched Brig. Gen. Griffin's 2nd brigade into action as well. Lt. Israel Thickstun was visiting his friends in the 83rd that afternoon. He wrote that he had "been there but a few minutes when an order came to prepare to march immediately. In fifteen minutes the brigade was on the move...." Butterfield's 3rd Brigade advanced to the town of Cold Harbor with orders to "take a strong position and hold the enemy in check...." Soon after their arrival, a cavalry regiment rode in and excitedly told them that rebel cavalry was on the loose all around. Gen. Butterfield ordered the regiments to scout the area. The 83rd detached Companies G and B to look for them, but they found none of the enemy that had caused the alarm, if there ever were any. Action seemed imminent but elusive, and Amos Judson recalled, "Various were the conjectures as to our destination, for at that time the plans of the enemy, though perhaps known to the Commanding General, were not known to the rank and file." The soldiers noticed that they were frequently entering action with little or no information on the overall situation. Though their confusion was a trait common to soldiers of any age, it was a frustrating way to begin a battle.[13]

Though they outnumbered the 5th Corps, the Confederates failed to break Porter's line at Mechanicsville and the day ended with the two lines firing away at each other in the gathering darkness. The 3rd Brigade's support at Mechanicsville was no longer needed, and Butterfield marched his troops back to Dr. Gaines's farm.[14]

Watching the Confederate formations withdraw in the twilight, Gen. McClellan proclaimed the battle of Mechanicsville a victory. The general stayed at the 5th Corps headquarters and discussed the situation with Porter, and there the Young Napoleon's optimism waned. Porter believed that with reinforcements, the 5th Corps could hold off Confederate attacks the next day while McClellan stormed Richmond with the rest of the army. Though his forces were well positioned to execute Porter's recommendation, McClellan was concerned by the Rebel threat to the supply line to White House, and he also considered withdrawing his army south to a new base on the James River while the 5th Corps held the Confederates north of the Chickahominy. In preparation for the latter alternative, McClellan dispatched his chief engineer officer, Brig. Gen. Barnard, to select a defensive position for the 5th Corps to block the Chickahominy crossing points. Promising Porter he would consider both plans, he told him, "Now Fitz, you understand my views and the absolute necessity of holding the ground, until arrangements over the river can be completed. Whichever of the two positions you take, *hold* it." Porter replied: "Give yourself no uneasiness. I shall hold it to the last extremity."

But Gen. McClellan was most uneasy. Unnerved by the threat of a Confederate flank attack, he decided to pull the army back to the James River where there would be support from the Union Navy. He would term the operation a "change of base," but in reality the Army of the Potomac was retreating from an enemy that it greatly outnumbered. By attacking at Mechanicsville and convincing McClellan that his army was on the verge of destruction, Gen. Lee had won the battle of wills and seized the initiative for the campaign. About two hours after he left Porter's headquarters, McClellan ordered the 5th Corps to pull back and set up a new defense on the Chickahominy near the cluster of buildings known as Gaines's Mill. The army would begin the thirteen-mile move south to the James the next day, June 27.[15]

The ground Barnard selected as the 5th Corps' new destination was a plateau of wheat fields about two miles wide and one mile from the river. A sluggish stream called Boatswain's Creek came up from the ground on the northeast corner of the fields, flowed west to form its northern edge, and then turned south to empty into the Chickahominy. The 83rd's Capt. Hugh Campbell fairly described the stream as "an intricate, gorged rivulet, thickly overgrown with brier and brushwood," and much of the stream was also known as Boatswain's Swamp. Infantrymen would have to work their way through the swamp, underbrush, and up the wooded banks to attack the 5th Corps, which made the southern side easily defensible. The Adams, Watt and McGehee families owned most of the land, but locals knew the general area for the gristmill located a mile to the north, the property of the area's largest landowner, Dr. William Gaines. Federal troops, the 83rd among them, had been camped on the Gaines plantation for over a month and some units had buried their soldiers that had died of disease on his land. As a devoted Confederate, Gaines had threatened to feed the bodies to his hogs when the Yankees were gone. Unfortunately for him and the other proprietors, their land sat directly astride the roads that led to four bridges over the Chickahominy which Porter would have to hold to keep Lee's army north of the river.[16]

Brig. Gen. Sykes' Division had been camped at Gaines's Mill all day on June 26, and the 83rd arrived there from Cold Harbor that night. The soldiers were worn out from their day of marching and countermarching, and few, if any, appreciated the area's fine defensive qualities. More concerned with sleeping than anything else, the men set up a bivouac but they were still within earshot of the fighting at Mechanicsville. As Amos Judson recalled, the battle was a constant distraction: "We lay down for rest, but not for sleep," he wrote, "for all the indications were that tomorrow's dawn would usher in the most terrible struggle that we had yet seen, and the roar of artillery in our front, lighting up the firmament with its succession of vivid flashes, even until after the hour of nine, gave token of the awful storm that was approaching." The fighting was much more intense that anything the regiment had seen at Yorktown or Hanover Court House, and the soldiers may have begun thinking that their experience in combat was not as complete as they had previously thought.[17]

The battle at Mechanicsville subsided that night, and Porter began ordering the units there to withdraw in the early morning hours. By daylight the blue columns were streaming into Gaines's Mill and moved into a semi-circular defensive line on the south side of Boatswain's Swamp, facing north. Sykes's Division of Regulars took the right half of the line where the swamp began, Morell's Division held the left, and McCall's Division formed in the rear as a reserve. As the sun rose Porter personally posted Butterfield's Brigade on the far left flank of the line in the wooded ravine of the swamp about 400 yards west of the Watt farmhouse. The troops had been roused out of their sleep before daylight to guard the approaches to Gaines's Mill as the other troops took position, and Amos Judson recalled with some bitterness that the regiment was moved around that morning "without having time to take even a hasty breakfast."[18]

The 3rd Brigade was fortunate to have a position where Boatswain's Creek turned south to flow into the Chickahominy, where the banks of the swamp were steeper and higher than anywhere else along the stream. Butterfield put his four regiments in two lines of battle. The front rank, with the 44th on the left and the 83rd to their right, was at the base of the bank and nearly in the swamp. The 16th Michigan made the left half of the second rank, some 25 feet behind the first line and an equal distance higher up the slope, and the 12th New York formed to the rear of the 83rd.* The banks were not as steep to the 83rd's right, where Gen. Morell placed the 1st and 2nd brigades, joining with Sykes' Division. Morell's artillery set up on the top of the plateau behind each brigade, positioned to fire through gaps in the woods. In addition to the 1st Division guns, the 6th Corps sited heavy artillery across the Chickahominy

---

Though part of Butterfield's Brigade, the 17th New York was guarding White House Landing during this action.

which could cover the ground directly in front of Butterfield's line.[19]

Porter ordered the building of barricades of trees and brush in front of the infantry as rough breastworks. As soon as they assumed their line of battle, the men of the 83rd and 44th dropped their knapsacks, stacked their rifles, and went to work. Axes had been requested but never arrived. The artillery batteries lent their tools to the infantrymen, but McLane's men mostly dragged fallen trees, branches, and what Capt. Campbell called "rubbish" into their breastwork. Amos Judson later recalled: "In less than half an hour we had such a line of works erected as not only would save the lives of our men, but enable them to repulse any number that might come against us." Elsewhere along the line, quartermasters evacuated excess stores across the river but many of the mule teams and wagons required for the task were miles away at the White House depot, and some of the supplies had to be destroyed. Lacking his transportation, a sutler in Sykes' Division had to burn much of his wares and some soldiers confiscated his stock of cigars rather than see them wasted. Amazingly, mail was delivered that morning, and the newspaper dealers also came to the defensive line. As the morning wore on, the field of Gaines's Mill became a bustling scene of men building the barricades, sutlers burning supplies, and news boys selling their papers, all with the smell of tobacco drifting from the Regulars as they coolly smoked their cigars.[20]

The tangled bottomland of Boatswain's Swamp extended about 300 feet in front on the 83rd's position at the base of the bank and offered a clear field of fire for McLane's troops. Beyond that, the far bank of the stream and a low hill blocked observation across Dr. Gaines's fields where the Confederates would most likely attack. To compensate for the lack of visibility, Gen. Butterfield sent a skirmish line composed 83rd's A Company, more from the 44th, and sharpshooters from the 16th Michigan to the opposite bank.

By mid-morning the brigade's preparations were complete and there was nothing else to do but wait for the Confederates. Butterfield sent an aide to the 83rd to emphasize the need for the regiment to hold the position if attacked. McLane answered: "Tell General Butterfield he needn't have sent any such orders. I intend to hold it." Morning passed into noon. The day was clear and the sun beat down on the men as they sat behind the barricade and passed the time. Some of them groused about waiting for an enemy that it seemed would never arrive. "Boys," Col. McLane advised them, "you will see enough of them before night."[21]

Confederate troops were at that time moving toward Gaines's Mill, and McLane's statement to his troops was more correct than he could have known. That morning, Gen. Lee was determined to renew the attack of the previous day and turn the Federal flank at Mechanicsville, but when his troops moved forward they found that the 5th Corps had slipped away. Pressing his divisions south, Lee planned to hit the Federals in a repeat of the previous day's attack at Mechanicsville, and Jackson's command was to move around the Yankee position to the north to outflank them while Gen. A.P. Hill's and D.H. Hill's Divisions pinned the Union down in front. A.P. Hill's Division took the lead in the new advance, closely followed by Gen. James Longstreet's Division.[22]

Using the smoke plumes of the burning 5th Corps stores as guides, Longstreet's and Hill's troops headed southeast along the Chickahominy after the Federals. Mystified about the position of the Yankees, both divisions pushed on and Longstreet ordered the three brigades commanded by Brig. Generals Roger Pryor, Cadmus Wilcox, and Winfield Featherston into line of battle to probe for the Union troops as they went forward. At around noon, Pryor's lead

Top: Boatswain's Swamp, looking north from the 83rd's position. (Photograph by author)
Bottom: The position of Butterfield's Brigade at Gaines's Mill, looking northeast. The path in this photo runs near where the 83rd formed their barricade and line of battle. The 12th New York was behind them further up the slope (to the right in this photograph). Boatswain's Swamp is to the left, out of this shot. (Photograph by author)

troops came within sight of Butterfield's skirmish line and within range of the 6th Corps' cannon across the river. The Union guns opened what Pryor called "a galling fire" on the Rebels as they pressed forward. Pryor's reports that the Union was strongly positioned behind Boatswain's Creek spurred Longstreet to push his three lead brigades forward to ascertain as much information as possible. Lt. Col. Ruehle of the 16th Michigan reported that at about that time, "the firing of the skirmishers in front grew louder and nearer...." The 83rd's Company B under Capt. John F. Morris relieved Company A, and within minutes Morris was brought back wounded as the skirmishing grew more intense. Though the main Confederate line had not yet reached the 5th Corps, the battle had begun for Butterfield's Brigade.

As Longstreet's and Butterfield's skirmishers dueled, Gen. A. P. Hill deployed the six brigades of his division and sent them forward against Porter's line at about 2:30

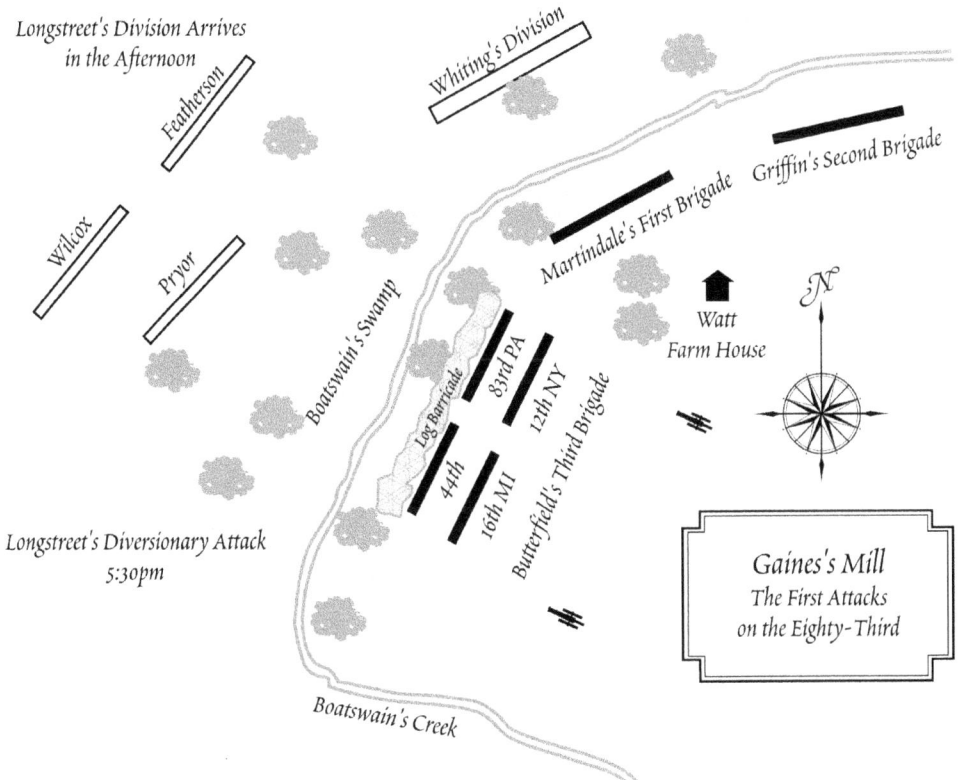

Butterfield's Brigade at the beginning of the battle at Gaines's Mill

PM. The firing increased in front of the 83rd as the Confederates pressed their attack, and the regiment's skirmishers were finally driven back. Judson later remembered that "showers of bursting shells" crashed into the woods around them and announced the proximity of the enemy. Col. McLane increased the regiment's forward protection by sending two men from each company across the stream as sharpshooters, and the rest of the men quit lounging and assumed their positions behind the barricade.[24]

The Rebel brigades advanced steadily towards the Union line, hidden from the sight of the 83rd by the brow of the far bank of Boatswain's Stream. The men stood nervously behind the barricade and watched the top of the hill for enemy. There was little wind that day and the trees barely moved overhead. The foliage made Boatswain's Swamp a shady place, but the high afternoon sun broke through the leaves and speckled the tangled roots with a patchwork of light. Col. McLane stood beneath a beech tree at the center of the regiment and told the men to wait until the enemy came in full sight, and then to fire a volley from the entire line at once. The soldiers strained to see through the sun's glare or the sweat that dripped into their eyes, as the officers stood along the ranks and encouraged the men. Amos Judson perceived that there was "an ominous silence" as they waited that he attributed to "such occasions, when life and death, victory or defeat, are poised in the balance of fate." It was more likely a lull in the firing, but whatever the reason for the silence, no doubt there were a few anxious minutes as the men waited for the assault.[25]

Suddenly, orders rang in the New York regiments behind the 83rd and a volley crashed from their ranks and over the Pennsylvanians' heads. Pryor's Rebels came over the far side of the swamp, still out of the 83rd's sight but under fire from the New Yorkers. McLane's men waited nervously while bullets flew over their heads, and then saw the Rebels come down into Boatswain's Swamp about two hundred yards away. It was the moment the men had waited for. The right half of the regiment let off the first volley, then was joined by the left half and the Union artillery in what Judson called "a living sheet of fire" that made the Rebel line quiver like "a reed shaken in the wind."

To get close enough to effectively fire into Butterfield's line, Pryor's Alabama, Florida, Louisiana, and Virginia regiments had to go down the embankment of the swamp, struggle through the brush and entanglements, and then try to move up the other side, all under concentrated artillery and rifle fire. The volume of lead from Butterfield's four regiments and the cannon made it almost impossible for the Confederates to make much headway in the marsh. Pryor wrote that his line was "staggered by a terrific volley...." Amos Judson wrote, "Huge gaps were made in their ranks, but like brave men they endeavored to close them up and press forward to the charge. Their color bearer fell at the first volley, but some other daring fellow seized the flag and rearing it triumphantly above the smoke of battle, fell pierced by a score of bullets. Again and again it was caught up and the attempt made to rally their men to the charge until five successive color bearers were shot down beneath it."[27]

Gen. Butterfield rode down along the 83rd's line in the midst of the melee, his hat off and sword in hand. Grabbing the regiment's colors and waving them over his head, he extolled the soldiers: "Boys if they come upon you again, I want you give it to them! You are just the boys that can do it!"* The soldiers answered Butterfield with cheers. The Confederates charged through the swamp again, and George Bedient, an eighteen-year-old private in Company I, remembered: "The rebs treated us to one of their favorite yells. In answer we gave them lead hot from our muskets, and those of them that were able went back even faster than they came down." [28]

McLane's men cheered again as Pryor's troops withdrew, but by then the rest of Longstreet's Division had arrived as well as Maj. Gen. Richard Ewell's Division. None of the preceding Confederate attacks had gained a foothold across Boatswain's Stream, and Lee sent Ewell's Division against the center of the Union line in a second attempt to break through. To prevent Porter from reinforcing against the assault, Lee also ordered Longstreet to make a diversionary attack on the Federal left. Longstreet sent his reserve brigade, commanded by Brig. Gen. George Pickett, to make the feint.[29]

Though the Confederates were following the standard tactics of the day, they were having little success. Confederate formations were being riddled before they could get into effective striking distance of the Union line. The tangled Boatswain's Swamp made it difficult for the Rebels to form their lines and many attacks went forward by companies or squads. Most of Porter's men were also behind barricades which protected them from much of the Confederate fire, and the gaps in the line were well covered by Federal artillery. Lee's men suffered under the realization that

---

The accounts of Butterfield's words to the regiment differ. This version is Amos Judson's recollection. Capt. Hugh Campbell reported that Butterfield said: "Your ammunition is never expended while you have your bayonets, my boys, and use them to the socket." Daniel Foote wrote home that Butterfield told the men, "Never let a man pass that ditch in front of you." No matter what Butterfield actually said, he rode in the middle of the firing with the regimental colors and inspired the men to hold their line.

massed infantry attacks against the front of a prepared enemy were among the most deadly of Civil War maneuvers.

It was after 4:00 PM when Gen. Pickett formed his Virginia regiments in a line of battle in one of Dr. Gaines's fields and sent them toward Butterfield's position at the double-quick. The Rebels advanced quickly to Boatswain's Stream, but when they moved down the bank they met the same concentrated fire from Butterfield's regiments that had stalled Pryor's attack. In the ranks with Company I, Pvt. George Bedient recalled, "Another brigade advanced on the charge from the line of timber on the little hill in the same way as did the first line, and were driven back by our well-directed volley at short range." Gen. Pickett was wounded, and his successor reported, "Here the firing became so fearful that the men threw themselves upon the ground and commenced returning the fire with spirit." The son of farmer Wilmer McGehee, who owned the land where Sykes' Division was posted, was a soldier in Pickett's Brigade. Pvt. McGehee did not record if fighting near his own family's farm had any special effect on him, but he recounted his memory to a journalist after the war of going up against Butterfield's line: "It was the worst place I ever saw," he recalled. "We went in but we came back out again in a hurry, and didn't keer to go back." George Bedient went on to say, "That slope was more thickly covered with Confederate dead and wounded than any field of its size during the war," and some of McLane's soldiers jumped over the barricade and took prisoners of the Rebels who were wounded or too slow to escape with their comrades. With their demonstration stalled, Pickett's Brigade held their position in the swamp.[30]

The fighting lulled as Confederate units re-grouped, and the battlefield became quiet again and began to take on an eerie look. The plateau was blanketed in low-hanging gunpowder smoke so thick that from a distance, only the treetops of Gaines's Mill were visible. On the firing line, the low afternoon sun burned red through the haze, illuminating the figures of Union and Confederate wounded and others that moved about, ghost-like in the smoke, carrying their injured comrades away. Bedient recalled that "except for the cries of the wounded on the slope it was so very quiet we thought the rebs had retreated."

Gen. Porter had watched the battle from his headquarters at the Watt farmhouse and also reported that there were "a few hours of ominous silence ... indicating that the [Confederate] troops were being massed for an overwhelming attack." Although he had been optimistic about the battle earlier that afternoon, he became anxious as the Rebel assaults grew more ferocious. "I am pressed hard, very hard," he telegraphed McClellan, and requested reinforcements. Porter's men were doing a splendid job resisting the assaults from behind their barricades but they would not be able to hold off the entire Confederate force for much longer. By the early evening all six of Lee's divisions had arrived at Gaines's Mill and he and Longstreet had concluded that the only way to dislodge the 5th Corps was to overwhelm it with the entire army. Lee deployed his troops along the length of the Yankee line and gave orders for the final assault with his entire force.[31]

At about 7:00 PM, the stillness of Gaines's Mill was shattered as the Confederate artillery opened fire and Rebel brigades began crossing Boatswain's Stream. The right of the Union line was hit first, followed by the center, and then Longstreet's soldiers went forward with a yell that one of the Southerners remembered "sounded like forty thousand wildcats."[32]

The previous attacks against Butterfield's Brigade had been made with determination, but neither was really intended to break through. The final attack, which was meant to drive the Union from the field, was something different. Longstreet's line of five brigades extended beyond both of Butterfield's flanks and they came forward with a fury. The 83rd blasted away at the Rebels as they scrambled through the swamp, but the Confederates of Maj. Gen. W. H. C. Whiting's Division also struck Martindale's 1st Brigade. McLane's soldiers were soon caught in fire that came from their front and right flank. Capt. Campbell wrote: "The battle at this juncture raged furiously. The fire was tremendous. The trees were lopped and branches and leaves fell as thick as snowflakes, whilst the balls flew like a hail-storm, the solid shot, grape, canister, and shrapnel unintermittingly scattering destruction in all directions...."[33]

Off on the 83rd's right, the 1st Brigade became caught in artillery crossfire that Gen. Martindale remembered as "one continuous roar." A brigade of Texas, Georgia and South Carolina troops under Brig. Gen. John B. Hood charged the line and Martindale's overwhelmed soldiers began falling back. Butterfield attempted to stem the Rebel advance by facing the 12th New York to the right, but the 1st Brigade troops "gave way and retired in disorder," according to their commander's official report. Confederates poured through the gap and towards the 83rd's exposed right flank.[34]

Although the position of Gen. Martindale's 1st Brigade was just a few dozen yards from McLane's, a belt of woods between them hid the events from view and it took a few minutes for the Pennsylvanians to see that their line was in jeopardy. Amos Judson remembered, "The first notice served upon us was the enfilading fire from the enemy's artillery, which began to pour on us from the direction of our own troops. One shot came hissing and whirling into our midst, killing one man and severely wounding another." George Bedient noticed the change in troop dispositions: "The 12th New York were no longer on the little hill in our rear," he recalled, "Suddenly a man who had been to fill canteens at a favorite little spring came running towards Col. McLane and yelled: 'The rebs are in our rear—a whole army!" It took a few more moments for McLane to grasp the situation. Even when the Adjutant, Lt. Plympton White, informed him that the enemy had broken through, the colonel doubted that the other brigades of Morell's Division would allow such a thing to happen. As they spoke, fire poured into the right of the regiment from the exposed flank and McLane realized the new threat.[35]

If the 83rd remained in its current position the Rebels would continue raking them with fire and eventually cut them off from the Chickahominy. To remain stationary would be suicidal, so McLane reformed his companies to face north on a line perpendicular to their barricade. George Bedient remembered: "Colonel McLane gave the command: 'On right into line—double quick—march!' which was executed with all the precision of a dress parade." This faced the line of battle directly at the Rebels, but by then Hood's troops had surged across the stream and advanced toward the 83rd, firing as they went and taking shelter behind trees and fences on the north side of the Watt Farm.[36]

Fortunately for the Pennsylvanians, the Rebel advance had become disorganized and a quick volley from the 83rd checked their progress. Some had come within thirty feet of McLane's new line and the fire between both sides was intense. Without the protection of their barricade, the Northerners suffered from the Rebel fire, as Amos Judson recalled, "Now the conflict became almost hand to hand, and the crash of musketry was absolutely appalling.... [Men] began to fall thick and fast all around.... One brave boy of sixteen, who was knocked down with a crushing wound in the head, was seen to grasp his musket and attempt to repeatedly rise, as if determined to fight while the last ebb of life lasted." Daniel

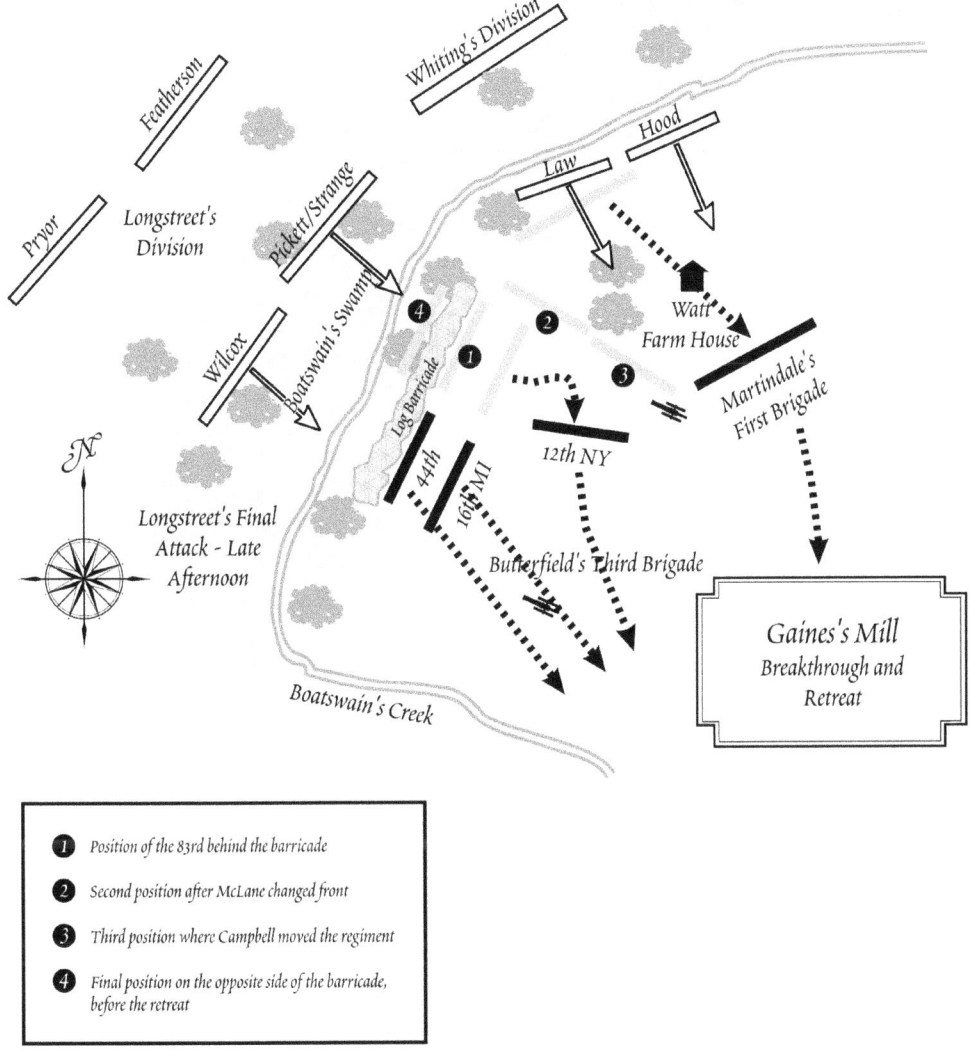

Butterfield's Brigade in the late afternoon at Gaines's Mill.

Foote had nearly been killed earlier in the battle when a Rebel shell fragment ripped through the tin cup he was raising to his lips, and he narrowly missed death again as bullets hit the men around him. He wrote home, "The enemy poured a deadly fire into us.... Two men directly in front of me fell ... my front rank man fell at my feet and I shot at his murderer which put a stop to his shooting whether it killed him or not."[37]

The men may have considered themselves veterans before, but this battle was an alarming education in the reality of close combat. Oliver Norton had taken a place on the line fighting instead of bugling for the colonel, and he came upon his two friends since Hall's Hill, Denny and Henry. Both had been severely wounded and were sitting together, but Norton could offer them no help and left them propped up under a tree. George Bedient also recalled a similar experience: "An old schoolmate of Co. D had just been hit in the thigh by a bullet, and seeing me, appealed to me to help him, as he was bleeding to death. I hastily made a tourniquet using one of his suspenders, which I twisted up with his bayonet, and then cautioned him to keep it tight." With no other chance but to let their friends fend for themselves, Norton and Bedient resumed their places with their companies.[38]

The regiment's officers were prime targets. A bullet slammed into Col. McLane's right chest as a shell fragment hit him over the left eye, killing him instantly.* Almost simultaneously, Maj. Nahgel took a round in his chest. Capts. John Morris, DeWitt McCoy, and Hiram Brown would also fall wounded. Momentarily leaderless, Judson wrote that "no orders could be heard above the rattle of musketry, each man became his own officer and fought on his own score."[39]

With Lt. Col. Vincent still in the hospital, Capt. Hugh Campbell took command as the regiment's senior surviving officer. Now rallied, the regiment fired volleys that forced the Confederates to break off their attack. Campbell took advantage of the respite to move his disorganized companies out of the woods and off to the right to a field that afforded better observation. Completely in the open, the captain formed a new line of battle that faced northeast at the Rebels that had broken through the 5th Corps front. Along with the rest of the regiment's dead and severely wounded, Col. McLane's body remained where he had fallen. Privates Seth Sturtevant and Daniel Hatch of Company K removed the colonel's sword, pistol and shoulder straps and one of his spurs to keep them from becoming some Rebel's war trophies, and in a final token of respect for their commander, they laid out the body as well as they could before moving off.[40]

About half an hour after the Confederate assault began, the Union line was becoming overwhelmed and regiments were falling back all over the field. From their position behind the 83rd, the 12th New York had directed its fire to the brigade's threatened right flank but fleeing Union troops ran through their lines and spread enough confusion to make them also break ranks. The 16th Michigan had stayed in its place until the attack became too fierce to hold off any longer. Their commander, Col. T. B. W. Stockton, prepared to fall back fighting. He later reported, "I had no sooner given the command to march than all started in double-quick, leaving me at once in the rear, and regardless of my commands to halt." Out of the four regiments in Butterfield's Brigade, only the 44th New York had remained in its original position behind the barricade.[41]

Gen. Butterfield could see that his regiments were about to be surrounded and tried to gradually withdraw the brigade under the cover of the artillery to form a new line. He sent a one of his staff officers, a Lt. Fisher, to order the 83rd to pull back, but the lieutenant was killed before he delivered the order and the regiment stayed in place. Parts of the battered 16th Michigan that had not run for the Chickahominy regrouped and formed on the 83rd's right flank. Together, the two regiments prepared to fight on, but more Confederates were coming in through the gap in the lines and moved to cut the 3rd Brigade off from the river.[42]

Campbell was dressing the regiment's

In all probability, McLane died quickly and without a sound. A letter to the Erie Weekly Gazette *dated July 11th, 1862 (signed by "A Subaltern"), quoted McLane as saying, "Boys I can command you no longer!" but that seems too dramatic to be probable. Capt. Campbell did not mention any "last words" in his official report of the battle; neither did Daniel Foote, who wrote home about the fight on July 18. George Bedient wrote that McLane "expired before he hit the ground" (albeit Bedient wrote the account in 1905). Oliver Norton was not with the colonel when he was killed, but as the regimental bugler, Norton was probably around the staff soon after the battle, and heard the first accounts of it before the embellishments began. He wrote on July 7 that McLane "died without a struggle or a word."*

The plateau of Gaines's Mill today, looking southwest from the Watt House. Butterfield's Brigade began the battle in the woods to the right. Capt. Hugh Campbell moved the 83rd out into the area in this photograph after Col. McLane was killed. After being surrounded, Campbell's men retreated to the left to reach the Chickahominy River. (Photograph by author)

line in its new position when another of Butterfield's staff officers, Maj. Vegesack, arrived and took control. Campbell wrote that the major had the 83rd face right, march forward, turn left at an angle and keep marching in a maneuver that kept the front of the regiment toward the Rebels but still allowed the Pennsylvanians to head toward the Chickahominy. Less concerned with the details of the tactics, Daniel Foote recalled that Vegasack simply told them, "See boys, you must fall back."[43]

Pulling the units out was the right thing to do, since the battle was becoming difficult to control. Thick smoke from an afternoon's worth of firing covered the plateau and concealed everything that was more than a few yards away. It was impossible for Butterfield to even see where his four regiments were at that point. Artillery and muskets roared from almost every direction and orders had to be shouted to be heard, if they could be heard at all. But as the men followed Vegesack's directions to retreat, they dimly made out two groups of soldiers about one hundred yards away, one in front of the 83rd and one in front of the 16th. It was impossible to ascertain their identity in the thick smoke, and Vegesack called for an officer to go forward to discover who they were. The 83rd's Lt. White walked toward the unknown men with a handkerchief on the point of his sword as a flag of truce.

Unbeknownst to the Union troops, two of Longstreet's regiments, the 5th South Carolina and the Palmetto Sharpshooters, had penetrated far beyond the main Federal line and were heading toward the Chickahominy when the 83rd's and 16th's column had loomed up out of the smoke and twilight. The commander of the 5th South Carolina, Col. Jackson, and one of his lieutenants went forward and met White halfway between the opposing lines. Jackson demanded the 83rd's surrender, "a proposition," Campbell wrote in his report, "that caused indignant mirth among us." Amos Judson recounted what happened next:

"Who are you?" asked White.

"The Eleventh South Carolina."*

"The 83rd Pennsylvania never surrenders to South Carolinians."

"Then what do you want?"

"I have come to demand that you surrender unconditionally to the forces of the United States."

The historian of the 5th South Carolina wrote that White simply answered that the regiment had no orders to surrender and returned to his lines. What was actually said at the parley will never be known, but if the story occurred the way Judson told it, White deserves praise for demanding surrender when the 83rd was shot-up, outnumbered and in retreat. Either way, the Confederate officers were amazed at White's refusal to give up, and the three officers returned to their respective lines. Before he reached the 83rd, White heard muskets cock behind him. Turning around, he saw the Rebels preparing to deliver a volley.[44]

Capt. Campbell also saw the enemy getting ready to shoot. Maybe remembering Col. McLane's tactic at Hanover Court House, he immediately ordered the men to lie flat as the Carolina troops opened fire. The Confederate volley flew overhead and Campbell's soldiers fired back from the prone or on one knee. Infuriated that the Rebels had violated the flag of truce and shot at White, the 83rd returned the volleys with a vengeance. Judson recalled, "The action now became hot, fierce and determined," and the men yelled angrily: "They have killed White; let's charge! Damn 'em boys, let's charge them!" One of the South Carolina soldiers wrote, "Our boys poured into them at a distance of less than 100 yards a volley which cut them down where they stood by the scores, but they ... promptly gave us back our fire." Maj. Vegesack saw more enemy troops approaching, possibly the Palmetto Sharpshooters, which had also opened fire on the 16th Michigan, and tried to continue the withdrawal to the river, but the men refused to move. Their blood was up, but the regiment was in a precarious position. George Bedient remembered: "This was the time and place that pandemonium with all its fury was let loose on the devoted heads of our regiment. From that day to the close of the war we never met its equal. Our captains were a mark for the best shots of the enemy, and soon many were wounded and others were killed; hundreds of our men were dead or dying, the wounded were everywhere; four lines of battle of the enemy were in plain view across the field we had so thickly strewn their dead; a whole division of rebels were in sight on the left front...."[45]

Norton wrote of the fight: "Our boys were dropping on all sides of me. I was blazing away at the rascals not ten yards off when a ball struck my gun just above the lower band as I was capping it, and cut it in two. The ball flew in pieces and part went to my head to the right and three pieces struck just below my left collar bone. I pulled them out and snatched a gun from Ames in Company H as he fell dead. Before I had fired this at all a ball clipped off a piece of the stock, and an instant after, another struck the seam of my canteen and entered my left groin. I pulled it out, and more maddened than ever, I rushed in again. A few minutes later, another ball took six inches off the muzzle of this gun. I snatched another from a wounded man under a tree, and as I was loading kneeling by the side of the road, a ball cut my rammer in two as I was turning it over my head. Another gun was easier got than a rammer so I threw that one away and picked up a fourth one. Here in the road a buckshot struck me in the left eyebrow, making the third slight scratch I received in the action."[46]

In the midst of their avenging firefight with the Confederates, Lt. White had

---

*Either White or Judson recalled the wrong regimental number.

crawled back to the regiment underneath the barrage, where he appeared, as Judson recalled, "to the surprised vision of the men as one who had just risen from the dead." The Confederate fire began to slacken, but it had taken its toll on the 16th Michigan troops and they began to fall back. What happened to Maj. Vegesack is not known, but Capt. Campbell took command again and moved the 83rd back into the woods near their first position where they would find better cover.[47]

Back on the wooded stream bank, Campbell found Lt. Col. James Rice and the 44th New York still behind their barricade. Campbell asked him: "Do you think we can hold them from behind the defenses?" to which Rice replied, "I think we can." The 83rd moved in beside the 44th on what had formerly been the enemy side of their own breastworks, with the swamp to their backs. This time the barricade offered little safety. Longstreet's troops had penetrated the Federal line at several points and soon the two lone Union regiments were under attack from all sides. The odds caught up with George Bedient. He wrote that he "was struck in the neck with something that seemed to weigh a ton. I was thrown down, and still having my senses I commenced to roll down that little hill away from that line of fire towards what had earlier in the day been our front. I made a survey with my fingers and found a great hole in my neck, into which I ran three of my fingers. The blood was spurting from three to five feet, and the noise made by my breathing could be heard a hundred yards. The bullet had collapsed my windpipe and separated one of the cartilages leaving a whole through which I breathed. There seemed no chance for a tourniquet here and not long to live—perhaps ten minutes. Water I must have, and then make my peace with God. I remember those moments so well in which every mean and bad action came up before me. I kept up that slope, and it seemed there were thousands of dead and wounded, as care was necessary to keep from walking on them. This was the work we had done from 2 until 5 that afternoon and now the work of caring for the wounded was going on, as hundreds of the rebs were assisting their comrades."[48]

Soldiers from five of Longstreet's brigades swarmed around the position. Campbell's men were exhausted and almost out of ammunition. To remain any longer would have ensured their destruction, as Judson later summarized: "It was now no longer a matter of courage or duty to attempt to withstand the numbers that were closing on us. It was downright rashness." Rice told Campbell that it was time to give up the fight and retreat across the Chickahominy. To try to reach the river in formation would have presented too good of a target to the rebel artillery, and the men would have to save themselves the best they could.[49]

For nearly a year, the men of the 83rd had drilled and practiced to become a unit and act as a single entity. Their teamwork had enabled them to survive in this battle as long as they had, but now they could only escape death or capture by acting as individuals again. Although the 44th moved to the Chickahominy in a column, the 83rd's soldiers scattered on Campbell's order and ran for the river in small groups. Judson remembered the shocking scene as the soldiers made their break: "The sun had gone down amid the lurid smoke of battle, and darkness was fast settling upon the field where lay our brave boys stretched in death, or writhing in agony, with mangled limbs and bleeding wounds. Here and there were seen the fugitives running towards the river, but scarcely seeming to know where to find a bridge over which to escape, some wounded in the head, some in the arms, some in the body, and some limping along with ghastly wounds in the legs and still clinging to their muskets."[50]

Some of the men ran west into Boatswain's Swamp. Others like Oliver Norton

Top: The Watt House today. Gen. Porter used this as his headquarters during the battle. Later, doctors used it as a hospital. This is probably where the 83rd's Maj. Nahgel was taken after his wounding and died in the early morning of June 28. (Photograph by author)

Bottom: Confederates sweep the field of Gaines's Mill at dusk in this sketch. The men of the 83rd saw a similar view of their enemy as they made their break for the Chickahominy. (LOC)

went south, straight for the Chickahominy. Having already lost his musket, Norton threw his cartridge box over his shoulder when he reached the river and waded through water up to his armpits to the safety of the other side.[51]

Not all of the men escaped as easily as Norton did. Foote wrote that the soldiers made for the river "but not without great loss for the rebels throwed grape and canister among us thick and fast." A lieutenant of the 44th wrote that one of his regiment's soldiers was helping a wounded 83rd man along, but when the New Yorker told the Pennsylvanian that he was becoming heavy, "The Pa. boy did not answer, and when his companion turned around he found that another bullet had struck him in back of the head, killing him almost instantly." A bullet passed through Amos Judson's left arm as he headed for the Chickahominy. Reaching the water, he straddled a log and paddled across with his good arm. Many men went to cross on the bridge but found the planks torn up, apparently by other retreating troops. Some ran across the sleepers, but the rebel artillery saw them and opened fire. The bodies of those that were hit fell into the river and drifted downstream.[52]

While the rest of the regiment made their escape, George Bedient was still searching for water amid the Rebels down in Boatswain's Swamp. He wrote, "I soon came to the first line of battle which had stacked arms, and a few men were left to guard the line of arms while their comrades were caring for their wounded. When they heard and saw me they took down a stack of guns and I passed through. This was repeated the same way by three lines in the rear. Not a word was addressed to me. They looked sorry, and perhaps thought I was dying. I passed on some distance, and then made a sharp turn towards the Chickahominy where I soon found water in the millrace. Night was now shutting down. I washed my wound and wet a towel, which fortunately was in my haversack, placed it around my neck, sat down against a tree, asked God to be merciful to me, and knew no more." With that, Bedient slipped into unconsciousness.[53]

The 5th Corps had given way under the weight of the final Confederate assault, and there had been other breakthroughs in addition to the one that occurred in Martindale's Brigade. All along the Union line, regiments were gradually retreating toward the river. The Rebels pursued the Union troops as they pulled back, but the Federal artillery posted north of Chickahominy continued firing and forced them to slow. As the men withdrew, two brigades from the 2nd Corps, reinforcements that Porter had requested earlier, finally arrived and formed a line of battle that held the Confederates off about a mile from the river. The Rebel advance ground to a halt and the 5th Corps continued its withdrawal.[54]

It was dark as the men of the 83rd began emerging on the opposite side of the Chickahominy but the flashes of the continued firing of the Federal artillery lit up the sky. The soldiers were exhausted, soaked from swimming the river, most had lost their equipment, and some were probably in shock. Campbell collected his shaken soldiers and the toll of the day's fighting became clear. A full third of the regiment had been killed, wounded, or taken prisoner.* A few of the wounded, like Maj. Nahgel, had been taken to field hospitals, but most were left where they fell. George Bedient and Oliver Norton's friends Denny and Henry were some of the wounded still there. Col. McLane was among the dead, along with Pvt. Alexander May, who had written home after Hanover Court House that he was looking forward to meeting pretty girls back home in Erie.

Soldiers of the 44h New York were also emerging from the river and gathering on the south bank, and the two regiments grouped together. Campbell and Rice decided to take what was left of their units to the 6th Corps lines, the nearest known Federal position, and the battered 83rd fell into formation. The cannon fire eventually died out, and as it had been at other times of the day, the field of Gaines's Mill was silent again. There were only the groans and cries of the wounded, and the sound followed the men as they marched away from the river.[55]

---

*The 83rd went into battle with 554 soldiers and lost 46 killed, 51 wounded, and 99 missing, for a total of 196 casualties or 35 percent of the beginning strength. Fifteen of those wounded would die later.

VI

REVENGE FOR MCLANE

Many of the 83rd's wounded would continue the trials of Gaines's Mill through the night.

Federal surgeons used the Watt, Adams, and Martin farmhouses as field hospitals on the north side of the Chickahominy. At around midnight, an unidentified group of soldiers from the 83rd delivered Maj. Louis Nahgel to one of them, and the surgeon of Martindale's Brigade, Dr. William White, came across the major among the other casualties. White later wrote that he gave Nahgel special attention, "as he was an officer of rank." A bullet pierced the major's right lung and the doctor could offer little help at the crude hospital. "I gave him the only straw bed remaining, drew off his boots, [and] he handed me a watch and pocket book containing four dollars in small notes," wrote White. "For a short time he conversed freely, but he soon became exhausted by hemorrhage.... His only cry was for water.... I procured him cool water and gave it every few minutes with my own hand." Nahgel told Dr. White that Col. McLane was dead, and then died at about 3:00 AM.[1]*

The retreat of the 5th Corps had continued into the early hours of the morning, and as Nahgel passed away in the hospital, the battle slowly died out as well. As the 83rd crossed the river just after darkness, most of Morell's division fell back fighting and retreated over the Chickahominy in the early morning hours. Sykes' Regulars were the last of the troops to withdraw from Gaines's Mill, and the final act of the battle was played near dawn when they crossed the river and burned the engineer's bridges behind them. Porter's Corps had achieved its objective of holding the Confederates north of the Chickahominy, but it had also paid the price of over 6,000 soldiers killed, wounded or captured. Lee's Army had fared worse with over 7,000 casualties. Gaines's Mill is listed as one of the most brutal battles of the war.[2]

At dawn some Federal soldiers were still isolated north of the river. George Bedient was one of them. "A soldier wakes at the break of day," he continued his account of the battle, "so at 4 o'clock I found I still lived, but quite weak from loss of blood." Bedient washed his wound with a towel and crept through the swamp away from the Confederates. He met an unidentified soldier from Company A in similar straits who said that Bedient's company commander, Capt. Hiram Brown, was nearby but mortally wounded. Bedient crawled through the swamp towards the river and found his captain just as the other man described, shot in

---

*Dr. White described the Nahgel episode in a letter to Mr. Isaac Moorehead, printed in the Erie Weekly Gazette. It does not state where his hospital was located, but it is likely that White's hospital was set up at the Watt House, directly behind the 1st Brigade line, and that it operated even after being overrun by the Confederates.

the abdomen. "What he needed most was some of the water from my canteen and a little skill in dressing a wound," said Bedient, whose wound-dressing skills were probably limited to the work he had performed on his own neck the night before. Skillful or not, he tended to Brown's injuries and as he wrote "soon had him on his feet and quite cheerful."

The two continued on towards the Chickahominy together and found a footbridge across Boatswain's Swamp that the regiment had built in May. The bridge crossed the marsh and led to the river, but the men saw that a Rebel artillery battery covered the area from not far away. They had no choice but to try to make it across the bridge in full view of the enemy. Bedient described what happened next: "As soon as they caught sight of us they let off the whole six guns of the battery which were loaded with grape and canister, which cut great limbs off the trees, knocked the footbridge into splinters, making a noise which nearly split our ears. We ... moved very rapidly for wounded men ... I was again praying.... The shrieking of the shot was the most terrifying noise we heard during the four years."

Reaching the river, they found the bridges torn up by the troops that had crossed during the night. Luckily, some men in the 5th Vermont Regiment on the south bank saw them trying to cross. The Vermonters made a float out of bridge parts and swam over with it to ferry the men back. Capt. Brown went back with them first, and then Bedient followed.[3]

After Naghel's death, Dr. White had launched a search for Col. McLane's body. Probably at about the same time George Bedient was trying to cross to the south bank, White had found the body under a tree—presumably where Seth Sturtevant had laid it out—but minus the colonel's coat, vest, and boots. Though he never explained how, the doctor managed to get the body back to the hospital and had it placed in the same grave as Nahgel and another officer, and marked the spot.[4]

George Bedient and Hiram Brown eventually found the 83rd. The previous night, the regiment and the remnants of the 44th had joined the first Union soldiers they came to, Brig. Gen. Smith's Division of the 6th Corps. Smith told Lt. Col. Rice and Capt. Campbell that he was glad to have the two units join his line because he expected an attack in the morning. Campbell's and Rice's soldiers were exhausted and out of ammunition, and the idea of fighting off another attack understandably alarmed both officers. The soldiers that made up the remnants of the two regiments reluctantly assumed a place in the Sixth Corps defenses and Gen. Smith arranged the issue of rations and ammunition. With hopes of receiving different orders, Rice and Campbell went to find Gen. Butterfield.

On foot, they found the last reported location of Gen. McClellan's headquarters at around midnight. Only the telegraph station and a few tents remained. The headquarters was apparently breaking down and moving towards the James, and the exhausted Rice and Campbell decided to wait to see if any senior officers returned. The telegraph operator refused their requests to send messages to their families, citing that the telegraph was for "government purposes only" and the two sat down to write home that they had survived the battle. After a few minutes McClellan entered the tent along with Gen. Butterfield, and the junior officers explained the state of their units and reported McLane's death. Butterfield promised to move the regiments out of the 6th Corps lines and to safety the next day. Later that night, troops of the 6th Corps relieved the 83rd and 44th. Butterfield's Twins moved into a nearby cornfield and fell asleep.

The men awoke after a few hours of uncomfortable sleep and cooked a meager breakfast from whatever rations they had been issued. Many still suffered from the shock of the battle, and Daniel Foote described the regiment as "a grave looking set of men. Many shed tears over the loss of their mates." The scattered elements of Morell's Division assembled that morning and along with the rest of the army, began their withdrawal to the James in the afternoon.[5]

The Federals had broken contact with the Confederates so thoroughly that on the morning of June 28, Lee was left wondering where the Union Army was and which way it was headed. Federal artillery guarded the crossing points on the Chickahominy and prevented his divisions from following, so Lee sent Ewell's Division and Stuart's cavalry to find a way across the river and monitor the Union retreat while the rest of his army recuperated from the previous day's battle. By the late afternoon reports confirmed that the Yankees were moving toward the James, and Lee issued orders for the pursuit to begin the next morning.

The retreat of an entire army in the face of an attacking enemy is a difficult task, and McClellan's situation was far from ideal. The general planned to take his troops to a sand bar on the James called Harrison's Landing, 17 miles to the southeast. Few roads led directly south to the river, so over 99,000 men, hundreds of pieces of field artillery, wagons, ambulances and siege guns had to snake over narrow tracks that wound through forests and swamps to reach their safe haven.[6]

As the 2nd Corps remained at Savage's Station as the army's rear guard, the 5th Corps joined the mass movement south. The artillery, wagons, pack animals, and other encumbrances caused continuous delays, and columns halted in traffic jams that were miles long and lasted for hours. The soldiers marched in hot, humid dust clouds kicked up by thousands of marching feet, and exhausted men fell asleep where they stood. Many soldiers didn't know the army was retreating and some even thought they were moving towards Richmond. The march continued into the night along a road that was thickly wooded on both sides and so dark that some 5th Corps soldiers would later remember the night as "the blind march." Rebels could have been encountered anywhere, so the soldiers moved in enforced silence.

Confusion, exhaustion, darkness, and silence began to take effect. The corps guide, supposedly knowledgeable about the area's roads, lost his way. The column headed toward the enemy lines before another general corrected the error. Rumors of Rebel cavalry operating in the area kept the soldiers tense. At one point, two mules broke loose near the 83rd, made enough noise to sound like the clattering of a dozen horses in the darkness, and the men threw themselves into the woods in an embarrassing panic. At daylight, the troops found that they had marched in a circle of about six miles, and had returned, even more exhausted, to a point not far from their start. The soldiers collapsed on the side of the road but orders soon came to continue the march. By midmorning on June 30 they reached Turkey Run, their intended destination of the previous night, and halted. Now a true veteran, Foote wrote home, "I saw a drowned man [in the stream] but a dead man is no new sight."[7]

The Army of the Potomac had not escaped the Confederate pursuit unharmed. The previous day, only hours after the 5th Corps had left, Lee's lead division struck the Federal 2nd Corps at Savage's Station. The Union troops blunted the attack but continued the withdrawal, and the Rebels seized the hospital at Savage's Station and captured hundreds of wounded Unionists, including Amos Judson. On the morning of June 30 Lee attacked the 2nd, 3rd and 6th Corps at the town of Glendale. Both sides took equal losses and again, the Fed-

The Union hospital at Savage's Station after the battle of Gaines's Mill. The number of soldiers waiting for treatment point to the huge problem of treating so many injured soldiers. Amos Judson was captured at this hospital when advancing Confederates moved through the area on June 29. (LOC)

erals managed to hold the Rebels off and continue their retreat. Though the rearguard actions had been successful, McClellan's strung out columns were in constant danger of being cut up by the pursuing Confederates and the army would have to consolidate at some point if it was to reach Harrison's Landing. The most ideal site for a defense was the low rise on the bank of the James known as Malvern Hill.

Malvern Hill was an oblong plateau about 40 feet higher than the surrounding countryside, a mile and a quarter from north to south and three quarters of a mile wide. Marshy creeks bordered the hill on the east and west, and the south (or bottom edge) was almost a mile north of the James. Farmer's fields descended from the top of the hill in a gradual slope, broken occasionally by dips and gullies, to a tree line over two miles north of the river bank.

Country roads divided the ground roughly in quarters. The most prominent was the Quaker Road, a track which bisected the plateau. Recently harvested wheat shocks dotted the west side of the hill, punctuated only by the single farm house of the Crew family. The eastern half, where the (contrarily named) West family owned the sole dwelling, was also an open field. The small Malvern mansion that gave the area its name stood near the James on the southern edge of the hill. A light breeze blew on the morning of June 30, and it was a comfortable place to the soldiers that had suffered in the swamps of the Chickahominy since May.

Those soldiers that were not too exhausted and had military eyes might have noticed that Malvern Hill was superb defensive terrain. The James blocked attack from the south, the marshes on the right and left protected the army's flanks, and there was enough room on the open fields to establish a strong defensive line facing north—the only direction from which the Rebels could approach. If the Confederates chose to attack, they would have to advance up hill across one-half mile of clear terrain under fire from Union guns. Gen. Porter, left in command of the troops there as Gen. McClellan reconnoitered Harrison's Landing, later called the terrain of Malvern Hill, "the best adapted for a battlefield of any with which we have so far been favored."[8]

Porter knew that the Confederates were not far behind the Union columns, and he immediately began setting up a defensive line as the sweating, tired, dirty soldiers of the five army corps streamed onto the plateau. The 5th Corps arrived first, and Porter put Sykes' Division in place near the center of the hill. Morell's Division came in next from its halt on Turkey Run and set up near the Crew House, facing west. Brig. Gen. Couch's Division of the 4th Corps arrived and formed east of the Quaker road as the right of the Union line, facing north. All the divisions set up their batteries among the lines of infantry, and the Army's artillery chief sited more cannon to the crest of the hill to fire over the heads of the infantrymen. Gen. McClellan returned later in the afternoon and posted the 2nd, 3rd, and 6th Corps on the right flank. With all five corps in position, the Union line curved around Malvern Hill like an upside down "U" with the open end on the banks of the James.[9]

It was late afternoon when the 83rd moved out from their halt at Turkey Run and went into line with Morell's Division near the Crew farmhouse. June 30 was the first time that the Army of the Potomac had occupied the same field, and the open ground of Malvern Hill gave the troops full view of the dozens of brigades and batteries moving into position, as Daniel Foote recalled: "It looked as I imagined large battlefields would when I used to read of them. Each regiment and brigade in mass, it was splendid indeed." Gen. McClellan happened to be inspecting Porter's dispositions as the 83rd took position, and troops all along the line cheered as "Little Mac" came by. Foote continued: "Gen. McClellan rode along the lines and we gave him three hearty cheers as we ever did."[10]

Maj. Gen. Theophilus Holmes's Division had been in the van of Lee's pursuit of the Yankees, and that afternoon his scouts had seen what they thought was an isolated detachment of Federals taking position on Malvern Hill. Holmes moved an artillery battery up to bombard the Northerners and on orders from Lee, attacked with his entire division. Holmes's attack coincidentally began just as McClellan reviewed the line, and as the 83rd's band struck up in honor of the general, a Confederate battery also suddenly opened fire. The shells burst around the Pennsylvanians' line, and the Union men saw the gray-clad troops come out of the trees near Turkey Run and head toward them. Surprised but not unready, the Federal cannon quickly returned the fire and Holmes was alarmed to discover that the few troops he had seen at Malvern were not alone. Union gunboats on the river joined the fight and hurled 100-pound shells from their guns into the Rebel ranks. Clearly outgunned, Holmes's troops moved back out of sight. Foote did not write if McClellan continued his review or not.

It was an insignificant attack, but their presence signaled that the Federal position was now known, and Porter could expect a more deliberate assault at any time. Morell's Division moved from the west end of the line to a station near the center on the Quaker Road. The 83rd went forward as a picket line, and the rest of the troops slept in the ranks with their rifles nearby.[11]

Wednesday, July 1, dawned hot, and the 4th Michigan relieved the 83rd from picket duty. It was the first calm morning the Pennsylvanians had seen in five days. As Capt. Campbell had his soldiers rest and cook breakfast, Confederate troops were moving into position north of the hill. Though some Southern officers thought the Union position was too strong to attack, Lee and Longstreet felt that they had the Yankees nearly beaten and wanted to crush McClellan's army before it slipped away again. Both generals personally scouted the ground, and together they developed a plan for what many of their soldiers hoped would be their last battle with the Army of the Potomac.

The restricting terrain of Malvern Hill would channel their attack straight south up the open slope and into the fields of fire of the massed Union infantry and cannon. To overwhelm the Yankees, Lee decided to mass his own artillery in two "grand batteries," one on the left and another on the right of the assault line, which would bombard the Federals and open the battle. Once the Grand Batteries had destroyed the Union artillery, the infantry would storm the position. Lee issued his orders and the divisions moved into their assault positions.[12]

Confederate skirmishers probed the Union line by mid-morning. On the Federal left, Gen. Morell realized that Brig. Gen. Martindale's and Butterfield's brigades were too far to the rear to provide support to the rest of the line and moved them forward to a depression that led west off the Quaker Road. Seven more batteries set up behind Morell's troops, and Berdan's Brigade of sharpshooters went into the wheat field forward of the division as skirmishers. Morell designated the 3rd Brigade as the division reserve for this battle, ready to back-up Martindale or handle any prisoners taken by troops on the main line. Gen. Butterfield kept his regiments in column formation to enable them to move rapidly, with the 83rd and 44th in front and the 16th Michigan and 12th New York in the rear.[13]

It was about noon when the Grand Batteries opened fire. Butterfield reported that the enemy cannonade converged on his brigade's position. Gen. Martindale, who was just forward of the 83rd, later wrote: "I had encountered artillery before, but now it opened as I had never seen it." Shells exploded all around the 83rd and though Capt. Campbell called the barrage a "terrible cannonading," his men enjoyed the protection of their depression in the ground and most of the shot flew over their heads as they waited for orders.[14]

The act of lying still under concentrated artillery fire was one of the Civil War soldiers' most trying experiences. In a line of battle, the men could take strength from their comrades that stood next to them and physically release some fear through the act of shooting back at the enemy. But there was little comfort from friends while the men lay on the ground, and there was no physical method to relieve the tension. The images of Gaines's Mill were fresh in the soldiers' minds—the smoke, noise, shouted orders, confusion, and friends maimed and killed before their eyes. Many of the 83rd had to fight their instincts that told them to get up and run away. In contrast to their previous battles, there is no record of officers making stirring comments as the regiment hugged the ground, or that any of the men expected an easy victory. The troops simply lay still in their ranks and steeled themselves for the inevitable attack.

The duel between the opposing artillery went on for about three hours. The Federal guns outnumbered Lee's Grand Batteries and fired back with such accuracy that they either destroyed the Rebel cannon or forced them to withdraw. The massive barrage that Lee hoped would soften the Union line never occurred, and by around 3:00 PM, he looked for another method to force the Federals out of their defenses. Skirmishers probed the Union line for a weak spot while the artillery battle continued, and then the Confederate infantry assault lurched into motion.

Brig. Gen. Lewis Armistead's Brigade of Virginia troops was positioned not far from Morell's line on the Union left. The brigade was to lead Lee's attack, but as they waited for the artillery battle to end, Federal sharpshooters opened an accurate fire on Armistead's line. Three Virginia regiments advanced to drive off the marksmen, but ran into concentrated volleys from Gen. Martindale's 1st Brigade and the Union artillery. Armistead's men took cover in a shallow depression near the Crew house, but they could not retreat without running the gauntlet of fire. Unable to go forward or

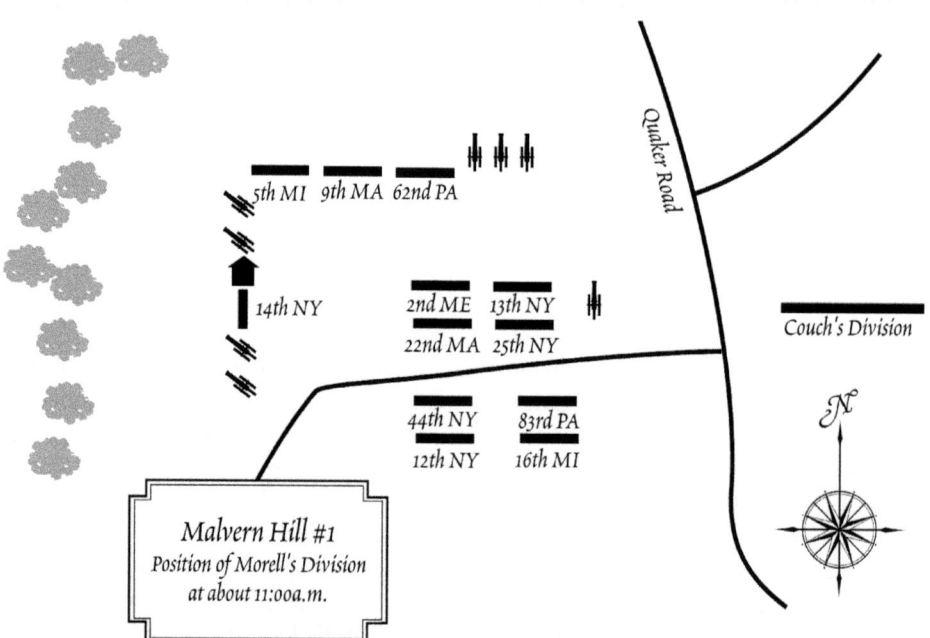

Top: A late nineteenth century view of the Malvern Hill battlefield. This photograph was taken from behind where Butterfield's Brigade formed, looking north. The Crew House is in the left center of the shot. The Confederates emerged from the woods in the distance. (The Gilder Lehrman Collection on deposit at the Pierpont Morgan Library, New York. GLC5111.11.320)
Bottom: The layout of Gen. Morell's Division on the morning of the battle of Malvern Hill.

backward, Armistead's men huddled in the gully and waited for assistance.

Gen. Lee had seen the brigade go forward and mistook it for the beginning of the assault. At about the same time, Union troops on the east side of the hill shifted position, and Gen. W. H. C. Whiting (whose soldiers had broken through Porter's line at Gaines's Mill) mistook their movement as a retreat. In an uncharacteristic misread of his opponent, Lee believed that the Federal army was about to withdraw from Malvern Hill, and he sent word to Gen. Magruder to "press forward, and follow up General Armistead's success." With that order, Magruder sent Brig. Gen. Ambrose Wright's and William Mahone's Brigades to turn the Union left flank while Armistead's troops went for the center. Wright's and Mahone's troops began moving at about 5:00, and Armistead's men rose from the shelter of their gully and charged for Martindale's 1st Brigade. Moving up on their left were the five brigades of Maj. Gen. D. H. Hill's Division, who headed for the center of the Union line at the juncture of Morell's and Couch's troops.[15]

Couch quickly requested reinforcements, and in response Butterfield rode over to the 83rd, where the men were hugging the ground to avoid the artillery, and announced: "83rd, you'll be called on presently. When you advance, let your warcry be, 'Revenge for McLane [!]" With the order to advance, Capt. Campbell ordered his men up, and still in their column formation, they moved out towards Couch's line along with the 16th Michigan. Wounded from the artillery attack were yet being carried away.[16]

In the few minutes it took for the 83rd to form ranks and start moving, the battle took a literal turn. Union sharpshooters spotted the two Rebel brigades moving through the trees towards the Crew House, and the only Union troops in place to oppose them were Griffin's 2nd Brigade and two batteries of artillery. Unless more arrived the Confederates would crush the left of the Federal line. Butterfield immediately recognized that this situation was a greater threat than the enemy infantry attack on the center, and he ordered the 83rd to turn left and back up Griffin's troops. Capt. Campbell reported that the men let out "a wild yell" as they jogged out of their hollow and headed for the impending fight. The

Looking south across the Malvern Hill battlefield in another late nineteenth century photograph. The Crew House, near the position of Butterfield's Brigade, is to the right in this photograph. This view looks toward the position of the Union line, across the open ground where the Confederates advanced. (The Gilder Lehrman Collection on deposit at the Pierpont Morgan Library, New York. GLC 5111.11.319)

view from the ranks was different. Oliver Norton later wrote to his family, "The memory of the scenes of the past few days was fresh in my mind, and as I marched up the hill that concealed us from the enemy, I must admit I felt a reluctance, rather a fear of going in. We were so worn out by the excitement, fatigue, and want of sleep that there was not the spirit in the movement of the men that usually characterized them, but there was the bitter determination to do or die."[17]

Campbell deployed the regiment into a line of battle and reluctantly or not, the men steeled themselves and went forward. The Rebels were coming close to Griffin's line, and one Union battery had already limbered up and had moved to the rear to avoid capture. The 83rd came up out of the depression, moved through the ranks of the 1st Brigade, and came up behind the artillerymen. What they saw was a daunting sight, as Norton continued, "We rushed over the hill on the double quick and there were the rebels. Column behind column was swarming out of the woods and advancing on us." Campbell halted the regiment when they were about 200 yards from the enemy. The soldiers dropped to one knee and fired a volley that slowed the Rebels but did not check their advance. The Confederates came on through what Gen. Wright reported was "a murderous fire of shot, shell, canister, and musketry" until the line finally stalled about 100 yards away from the Federals.[18]

As Gen. Mahone's troops hit the left of Morell's line, the 83rd was caught between their fire and the rifles of Wright's Brigade to the front. With considerable understatement, Capt. Campbell reported that "The battle was now very hot." One enemy bullet splintered the 83rd's flagstaff and killed Corp. Ames, the color bearer. Pvt. Alexander Rogers of Company F picked the flag up and waved it over his head, then went to the front of the regiment and called for the men to follow him and charge the enemy. Another round brought Capt. Campbell to the ground when it hit him in the leg. Norton recalled, "Butterfield and Griffin dashed here and there, cheering on the men—'Go in my gallant 83rd, and give 'em hell,' yelled Butterfield as he dashed along the line, and his inspiring manner cheered the men up." At least one other unit could not stand the intensity of the fight, as Campbell reported, "Another regiment, whose number or name I cannot learn, came to our assistance and formed on our left, and, I regret to say, who, after only receiving a few rounds of the enemy's fire, gave way and fled." The men of the 83rd hooted and catcalled at the unknown unit as it left the scene. As they yelled, the 44th and 12th New York, who Butterfield had also rushed in to hold the line, arrived on their left and went straight into the fight.[19]

The two Confederate brigades continued to try to advance, but the Federal artillery battery that had retreated now returned, set up, and blasted canister and grapeshot at the Southerners. The open wheat field offered little cover for the attackers, and Norton recalled, "As they advanced our artillerists poured in such deadly charges of grape that it was more than any troops could stand.... Each discharge would mow a swath through their lines, from five to eight feet wide. Still they closed up their ranks and came on till they met our fire...."

By the early evening at least six Confederate brigades had attacked an equal number of Union units, which were backed up by several batteries of artillery on a front that was barely 1,000 yards wide. The concentrated fire produced thick clouds of gunpowder smoke that covered the slope and obscured all but the orange flashes of the volleys and cannon, and the men fought savagely and blindly in the growing twilight. Norton wrote, "It was more like the work of fiends than that of human beings. The roar of the artillery, the rattling of musketry

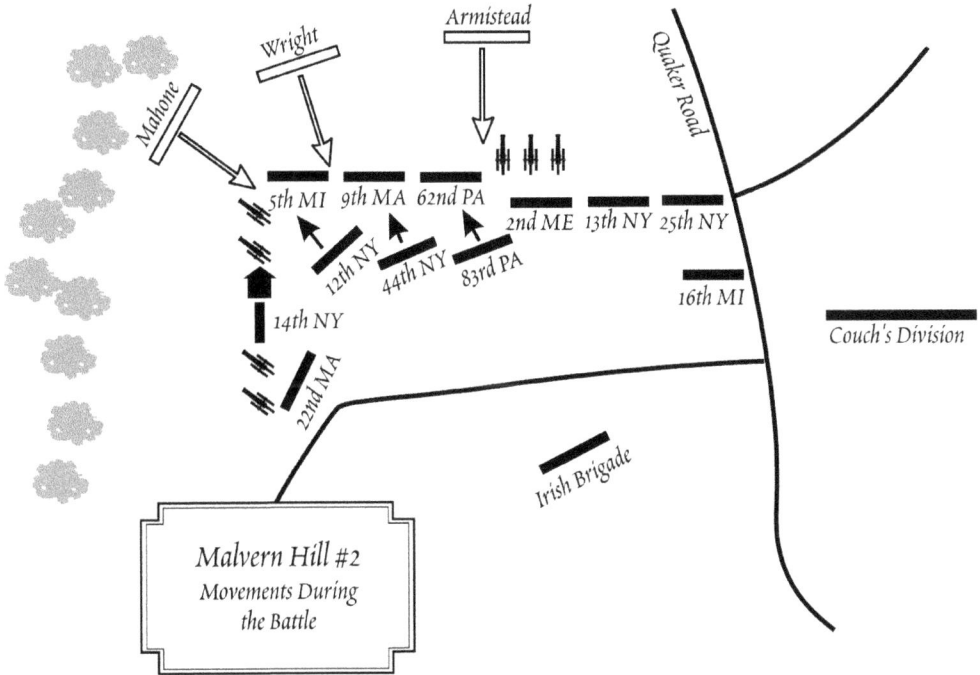

The attacks and counterattacks around Morell's Division in the afternoon at Malvern Hill.

and the unearthly screaming of the great two-foot shells from the gunboats made such music as is only fit for demons, and the appearance of the men was scarcely human. The sweat rolled in streams, for there is nothing like fighting to heat a man's blood, and as the men wiped their faces with powder-grimed or bloody hands, they left the most horrible looking countenances you ever saw." Norton's luck was with him when a bullet hit him but stuck in the folds of a tent he had found that morning and slung over his shoulder: "I picked it out, put it in my pocket, and [continued] firing sixty rounds of my own and a number of a wounded comrade's cartridges," he said. Soldiers usually shot three rounds each minute, but Daniel Foote wrote that they fired so fast there wasn't time to return their ramrods after each shot. Some of the 83rd's guns became so fouled from the powder that the men replaced them with others from fallen comrades and picked up more ammunition in the same way. When the artillery batteries fired their last shells, they cut the traces of their horse teams and shot the chains at the enemy.[20]

Capt. Campbell reported that the effects of the fire was that "the enemy's dead lay in heaps, while he was seen to collect the bodies of his fallen slain and pile them for protection from our fire." The Confederates facing the 83rd attacked with such determination that he added, "We almost felt overpowered—nay, annihilated—from the fury and storm of shot poured into us." Wright's and Mahone's charges broke down, and Brig. Gen. Samuel Garland's Brigade of North Carolina troops joined the Confederate push directly in front of the 83rd. The Yankees kept up their fire, and one of the new attackers, Pvt. E. Franklin Faison of the 20th North Carolina recalled, "As we advanced ... the minie balls from a thousand rifles swept the field and how any of us escaped alive is a mystery."[21]

Butterfield ordered a counterattack as the Rebels staggered under the intense

Union fire. The 12th New York, 44th, and 83rd surged forward for about fifty yards until the Confederates broke and fell back. Company I's Orderly Sergeant, William Wittich, saw the colors of one of the Rebel regiments fall to the ground about a hundred yards from the Union line. A regiment's set of colors were coveted as battle trophies, and Wittich asked his company commander, Lt. John Sell, for permission to seize the flag. With Sell's consent, the sergeant dashed out from the regiment and ran diagonally across the front of the brigade. Another soldier who had seen the flag fall, Pvt. Piepenbrink of the 44th New York, also sprinted for the prize. Though the Rebels had dropped the flag, they had not given up their defense and cannon and musket fire swept the field as both Yankees raced for the colors. Wittich reached the flag first. Taking it by its shattered staff, he held it over his head, walked back to the regiment while bullets hissed by him, and presented the trophy to Gen. Butterfield. Wittich's seizure of the flag made him an instant hero of the 83rd. But the 44th's Lt. J. B. Webber claimed that Pvt. Piepenbrink had reached the colors at the same time and claimed the flag in honor of the for the New Yorker's charge. According to Webber, both soldiers had picked up the flag, and as he wrote, "There they stood and argued for its possession as coolly as if the enemy were not a short distance from them," until an another New York officer stated that the colors fairly belonged to Wittich. In a rare instance of jealously between "Butterfield's Twins," Webber maintained, "Perhaps he was [entitled to it] as an individual, but his regiment certainly was not."[22]*

Mahone's, Wright's and Garland's Brigades were unable to break Morell's line. Near dark, Brig. Gen. G. B. Anderson's North Carolina Brigade came up behind them and charged the Union left. Seeing the new enemy, Butterfield's troops halted their counterattack and fired. Now the men had their blood up, as Norton described: "We poured it into them as fast as we could load and fire, and I tell you my fear was gone then. I felt exultant. We cheered and cheered and shouted our watchword—'Remember McLane'...." Though Norton was exuberant, the 83rd had helped fight off three Confederate brigades in quick succession and their ammunition was almost completely gone. Fortunately, Gen. Porter had sent to the 2nd Corps for reinforcements, and Brig. Gen. Thomas Meagher's tough New York regiments known as the "Irish Brigade" rushed onto the line. The 83rd continued firing with their last rounds of ammunition. Capt. Campbell reported, "With these new troops came new hopes. Energy and devotion now truly showed itself." Oliver Norton was for once was at a loss for words and simply wrote, "God Bless Them!" about the relief. The enemy fell back for the final time, and Butterfield's men continued firing at them until they were out of range.[23]

Though the assaults had waned in front of the 3rd Brigade, the contest came to a climax as darkness set in and the Confederates made a final push in the center of the Union line near the Quaker road. As

---

*After the campaign, the flag was sent to the War Department and labeled "Capture No. 32" with the inscription, "Confederate Battle Flag, captured at Malvern Hill, near James River, Virginia, July 1st 1862 by Butterfield's Brigade, Serg't W.J. Wittich, 83rd Pa. Volunteers; this flag was taken from a South Carolina Regiment who piled up their dead to resist the attack of the Brigade." The regiment that lost the colors was never identified, but based on the inscription, the flag was returned to the state of South Carolina in 1905, when all Confederate trophies held by the Federal government were returned. The Confederate unit that lost the colors remains a mystery. The 2nd, 3rd, 7th and 8th South Carolina regiments of Kershaw's Brigade fought at Malvern Hill, but none reported losing their colors, and none had earned the battle honor of "Seven Pines!" that was sewn on the top of the flag that Wittich captured. A definitive answer remains elusive. Today, the flag is held at the Confederate Relic Room and Museum in Columbia, SC, where it is still known only as "Capture No. 32."

before, the Rebel attack broke down against the strong lines of infantry and artillery, and Lee's troops retreated back to the north from where they started. The opposing artillery batteries continued firing at each other as the infantry lines parted, and soon only the flashes of the cannon in the darkness marked the positions of the two armies.[24]

Relieved by the Irish Brigade, Capt. Campbell took the 83rd back to their first position of the day near the Crew House. The regiment began the day with fewer than 400 soldiers, and battle had cost them nearly half their number. When Gen. Porter saw the regiment forming in the darkness, Campbell told him: "It is all that is left of the 83rd." Porter directed them to a sheltered area to rest, and the last of the cannon firing died off as they went into bivouac. Later, orders came for a detail of two men from each company to help the wounded that were lying all over the battlefield. Daniel Foote was one of them, and he wrote home, "Four of us went back to the battle field and helped off several poor fellows and of all the yelling and groaning I ever heard the rebel wounded made the worst." One of the regiment's dead was Pvt. John Rice, who had written that he had had a "musical time" with the regiment along the Chickahominy in June. Foote may have helped bury him.[25]*

The Federals had repulsed every Confederate attack, and though the battle had been close at times, the Unionists were the clear victors of the field. That night, Porter reported their success to McClellan and requested re-supply to hold the line or to pursue the Rebels next day. But as in the previous battles of the campaign, Gen. Lee eventually won the day. McClellan had abandoned all offensive action and his only objective was to move his army to safe haven at Harrison's Landing. In response to Porter's request to attack, he issued orders to continue the retreat.[26]

Gen. Morell received his instructions to withdraw the 1st Division at about 11:00 PM, and he passed the orders which roused his sleeping soldiers from their well-earned rest. Typical of the inefficiency shown in the retreat from Gaines's Mill, the movement did not begin until around daylight, and heavy rain began soon after the columns began moving. The mud on the road was soon knee-deep, and the inevitable delays followed. Exhausted soldiers fell out all along the way. Though Harrison's Landing was only eight miles from Malvern Hill, it took the 83rd nearly eleven hours to cover the distance and they did not reach their destination until 11:00 the next morning. Some of the soldiers, overcome by the strain, hunger, and shock of the last few days, simply collapsed and fell asleep in the mud when the column finally halted. The next day a few tents were issued and Capt. Campbell had the men set up a rudimentary camp with the what little supplies they had.[27]

The army had been fighting steadily since McClellan opened the attack on Richmond on June 25, and the halt at Harrison's Landing on July 2 was the first chance the officers had to accurately count the casualties. A total of 1,734 men were dead, 8,066 had been wounded, and there were 6,055 missing (out of over 100,000). In the space of one week, McClellan's mighty army had been pushed back from within three miles of the Confederate capital and lost nearly a quarter of its strength. The campaign was soon known on both sides as "The Seven Days."[28]

---

*According to Fox's Regimental Losses in the Civil War, the 83rd began the battle of Gaines's Mill with 554 soldiers and lost 196. Assuming that some of the wounded from the battle stayed in the ranks and that others fell out during the retreat to Malvern Hill, the regiment's strength at Malvern was probably between 300 and 400. The regiment lost 33 men killed at Malvern Hill, 115 wounded (of which 17 would later die) and 18 missing for a total of 166, or roughly 50 percent of the beginning strength.

In the forefront at Mechanicsville, Gaines's Mill, and Malvern Hill, the 5th Corps had borne the brunt of much of the fighting and accounted for almost half of the losses. The 83rd suffered 362 casualties, and only three other regiments in the Army of the Potomac lost more that week.* The 3rd Brigade's losses were the most severe of Morell's entire Division. In his report of the campaign, Gen. Butterfield wrote that "The plains of Hanover, the banks of the Chickahominy, the heights of Malvern are wet with the blood of the gallant dead of this brigade." It was not an exaggeration.[29]

Luckily for the soldiers, the chance of further combat was slim. The Confederates had taken an equally bad beating, and neither army was eager to resume the fighting. McClellan's rapid retreat from Malvern Hill had left Lee once again confused about the location of the Union Army. He knew that McClellan was marching along the river, but didn't know to where and for what purpose. Even with their losses, the Federals still outnumbered the Confederates and were capable of renewing the attack. When Rebel scouts found the Yankees at Harrison's landing on July 4, Lee concluded that the position was too strong to attack. The Confederates left a few cavalry detachments to observe the Yankees and the rest of the Army of Northern Virginia withdrew to Richmond.[30]

With 18 officer casualties, key leadership positions in the 83rd were vacant, and on the evening of July 4 the soldiers continued the regimental tradition of elections to fill the positions. The men chose Strong Vincent as the new colonel (in abstentia since he was still in the hospital), Hugh Campbell as the lieutenant colonel, and Capt. William Lamont was promoted from the adjutant's position to major. Company K promoted their new hero Sgt. Wittich to first lieutenant, and although he was in the hands of the Rebels, Amos Judson was elected captain of Company E.[31]†

Gen. McClellan told the men and the Government that he would continue the campaign, but despite the promise, the army went back to the normal routine of camp duties.[32]

The soldiers needed rest, but Harrison's Landing did not offer the most hospitable environment. Over 90,000 men were crowded onto a sandbar that was four miles wide and one mile deep. One stream ran through the camp. Its banks were low and swampy. Fresh rations were scarce. The poor drainage led to foul water and improper sanitation, and the marshes bred swarms of disease-carrying insects. The men renamed the Chickahominy Fever the James Fever, and by the end of July there were over 42,000 soldiers, nearly half of the army, on the sick list.[33]

The 83rd suffered at Harrison's Landing as much as any unit. The regiment's return for July showed 233 soldiers in the hospital and 163 sick in the ranks. Nine men died of disease that month, another 25 were discharged for disabilities, and 46 died from wounds. At the end of the month, only 301 soldiers were present for duty. Lt. Israel Thickstun was sick with "fevers," in the hospital, and weighed only 125 pounds. He visited the 83rd in late July. He wrote home that Company H consisted of fewer than fifty men, and that only nineteen were fit for duty. Thickstun went on to list thirteen friends who were killed, wounded or captured. Daniel Foote made a similar obser-

---

*The Ninth Massachusetts lost 393 men in the Seven Days, the 4th New Jersey lost 585, the 11th Pennsylvania Reserves 716.

†On July 4 Gen. McClellan held a review of his army where he was scheduled to officially present Sgt. Wittich with the flag he had captured at Malvern Hill. Wittich was sick and came to the parade in an ambulance. The general was called away and could not perform the duty, but the entire 1st Division passed Wittich in review, gave him three cheers and tied the flag to the side of his ambulance.

Sketch by Alfred Waud of A Union burial at Harrison's Landing—a familiar sight to the 83rd. (LOC)

vation of Company K: "Out of fifteen young men from the vicinity of [Wattsburg] five still remain in the co. Four are left at Gaines' Mills, one detached on other duty, one [killed] at Malvern Hill and two wounded and in the hospital, one at home and one died in New York City." The men that were present were not capable of much fighting, as Oliver Norton wrote home on July 9, "Of the small number who remain, not half are strong enough to stand a march of ten miles. A great many are sick, not very sick, but worn out, weak, and unable to endure full duty." Norton himself was down to 117 pounds, but felt fit, and attributed his health to "constant use of woolen drawers and shirts."

The campaign had an effect on minds as well as bodies. Norton had been full of boast earlier in the campaign, but after the Seven Days he wrote to his cousin, "The past ten days seem to me more like some fearful dream than anything else...." and then added in the same letter, "It seems to me almost a miracle that I am yet alive and able to write." Daniel Foote also saw something miraculous in his being alive when he wrote to Julia Hill: "God in his providence spared me and I am very thankful for it."

When Lt. Col. Campbell led a recruiting drive in Erie in late July, Norton feared that his younger brother would join the regiment and wrote to his father, "don't let him...." and continued: "Let him see a ditch half full of dead and wounded men piled on each other; let him see men fall all round him and hear them beg for water; let him see one-quarter of the awful sights of the battlefield, and he would be content to keep away." The men had come a long way from gawking at the sight of blood as they had at Eltham's Landing in May. Arthur Cleeland, who had celebrated his eighteenth birthday in the trenches before Yorktown, wrote to his parents, "I hope that we will never have to go into action again, for we are all satisfied—at least I am." Cleeland died of disease within a month.[35]

Some of the men failed the test of combat. At Hall's Hill, the regiment's chaplain, the Reverend Josiah Flower, had pledged to share the dangers of combat with the soldiers, but the truth was different, as Daniel Foote wrote to Julia, "He deserted us at the battle of Gaines Mills and resigned and went home after the army reached Harrison's Landing and it is my humble opinion that he was not in hearing distance of musketry or artillery...." The *Erie Weekly Gazette* reported that Flower resigned "on account of impaired health," but Norton echoed Foote's story in a letter to his brother and sister, "Our chaplain (Elder Flower) has resigned and gone home, and I don't think the most pious man in the regiment is at all sorry ... when the shells began to fly and the balls to hiss around, he always concluded that fighting was not in his line of business ... if you see or hear him, just ask him how much he saw of it. Ask him where he was at the battle of Malvern Hill." But Norton had not lost his sense of humor. In the same letter, he mentioned a strange bit of news that had reached him from home, "I received a letter from Uncle Newell a few days ago and he said the story was circulated ... that I was to be shot for deserting. What do think of that? Had you heard much about it? I hadn't. I didn't even know that I had been courtmartialed."[36]

Far from facing admonishment by military justice, Norton was called to Gen. Butterfield's tent one July night to fulfill a unique request.

Butterfield had a talent for music. Earlier in the campaign he had developed a special bugle call to be played before all orders, so his soldiers would not confuse the instructions for other brigades with their own. The soldiers had noticed that the beat of the special call matched the rhythm of his name (in a fashion) and they developed their own rhyme to help them remember it. The tune sounded like saying "Dan—Dan—Dan—Butterfield! Butterfield!" When that was played, the men knew the next call they heard would be for their regiment. Norton had not done much bugling in the Seven Days' battles, but he must have earned the general's notice, and Butterfield asked him for help with perfecting a new tune.

The army had a call that could be played on the drum or the bugle to signal "Lights Out in Camp." It had been in use for years, but Butterfield didn't like it. He felt that the song that told soldiers to go to sleep should have a restful, soothing sound, and he worked out a new one in his head. The general hummed a some bars for Norton and had him play them back, made some corrections, and had Norton play again. After a few attempts, Butterfield was satisfied and directed that his new song would be played in the 3rd Brigade to signal "lights out" from then on. The buglers complied, but the soldiers still referred to the new song with title of the old one, which was taken from the sound of the drumsticks beating the drum. "It's lights out soldiers, haven't your heard the Taps?" is how sergeants prodded their men to sleep, and it's how the slow, sad tune that Oliver Norton first played at Harrison's Landing became known as "Taps."[37]

It was appropriate that Butterfield devised a song that became synonymous with sleep and death, because McClellan's grand Peninsula Campaign was dying. President Lincoln was concerned about how the Army of the Potomac had been pushed back onto the James and had visited the camp on July 8. It was then that McClellan announced his intention to renew the Richmond offensive and requested another 100,000 men. The disastrous results of continually reinforcing McClellan over the past three months were fresh in Lincoln's mind, and he was hesitant to commit more troops to a beaten army. The President had recently formed the Army of Virginia under Maj. Gen. John Pope, and he posed the option of withdrawal from the peninsula to cooperate with Pope's force to the five army corps commanders. Three of them voted for staying on the peninsula, two recommended withdrawal, and Lincoln postponed the final decision.

On July 25, McClellan delivered a new plan to attack Richmond, but the War Department deemed it too dangerous to pursue. The general made two more requests to continue the campaign and for more men, but he had lost Lincoln's faith, and the government began seeing Pope's army as their best hope for victory. On July 30, the War Department ordered the Army of the Potomac's sick evacuated to hospitals in northern Virginia, and on August 3, McClellan received instructions to withdraw to Ft. Monroe, where the troops would move by ship to join Pope's army in a new campaign.[38]

The first troops started marching overland to Ft. Monroe in mid-month and the 5th Corps received its orders to move on the afternoon of August 14. Earlier that day, Oliver Norton had written home, "Troops have been going down the river as fast as they could for a week past. Artillery is being loaded up every night, commissary stores are going, and everything looks to me like preparations to abandon the Peninsula."

The corps left Harrison's Landing that night and two days later arrived at their old camp outside Yorktown.[39]

When they had lain siege to Yorktown in the spring, the 83rd consisted of roughly 1,000 healthy, confident, well-equipped and splendidly uniformed soldiers. In August, only about 200 of the same men, in uniforms that were ripped and stained from months of hard campaigning, returned. Most had lost their equipment and many were thin and gaunt from sickness. The next day the regiment continued the march to Hampton, where they were scheduled to meet the steamers that would take them back into northern Virginia. As Norton mused to his father when they left Harrison's Landing, "Thus, I apprehend, ends the campaign on the Peninsula."[40]

VII

AN UNLUCKY FIELD

August's respite from battle gave Gen. McClellan the chance to evacuate his most serious casualties from Harrison's Landing, and when the soldiers of the 83rd left the peninsula that month, many of their sick and wounded comrades had already been taken down the river. By the end of August, the infirm of regiment were scattered among hospitals at Ft. Monroe, Washington, and New York City.[1]

Daniel Foote had fallen ill at Harrison's Landing and was one of those taken to Ft. Monroe. Sick with an ailment that he did not describe in his letters home, Foote was bedridden in a room with two bunks and little else. "The other furniture," he explained to Julia Hill, "consists of two haversacks, two canteens, and two knapsacks and a spittoon, [and] a couple of bottles of medicine." Although his surroundings were doubtless better than the steaming camp at Harrison's Landing, confinement in the hospital was the first event of the campaign that gave him reason to complain, "I am just agoing to tell you what we live on here and make my first complaint against the food." He continued, "For breakfast a slice of bread and a cup of coffee, for dinner a slice of bread, a piece of beef and a cup of soup or a cup of the water the beef is boiled in, for supper a slice of bread and a cup of black tea. I have been here ten days and it has been the same everyday."[2]

Some of the luckier soldiers received furloughs back to Pennsylvania. Company B's commander, Capt. John Morris, was severely wounded at Gaines's Mill and returned to Harmonsburg in Crawford County in late July. When he arrived, a crowd that included the town's fire company greeted him and led him to his house, as the local newspaper reported, "The streets were literally crowded with hundreds of people, all anxious to get a look at the brave soldier who had behaved so nobly on the field and survived wounds which were pronounced mortal by experienced surgeons." Wounded in the leg at Malvern Hill, Lt. Daniel Saeger of the same company had returned to his home in Saegertown that month, where he received a gift of money from the citizens to buy a sword and a sash. When he left to rejoin the regiment in August, his benefactors wished him luck with the confidence that Saeger would "do valiant service against the rebels." Col. Vincent had arrived in Erie in early August after being evacuated from the peninsula and convalescing in New York. One of the Erie newspapers reported that he was "in feeble health," but went on to say that they hoped for a speedy recovery "to the bodily vigor and consequent fitness for the chief command of the gallant boys of the 83rd."[3]

It appears that none of the regiment's wounded went to the military hospital near Philadelphia where Pvt. Seth Waid had worked since May. Waid had been sent to the hospital at Georgetown (with an ailment he only identified as "a lingering fever") back in February, and then was transferred to the hospital near Philadelphia where he recovered. In March, a doctor offered him the position of military nurse. Waid accepted, and from then on he was virtually lost to the regiment.[4]

Waid had fallen into a loophole of the military medical system. Once sent to one of the many hospitals the government had established, soldiers came under the control of the medical authorities that answered only to the Surgeon General of the United States. The Army Medical Department had the power to discharge soldiers, grant furloughs, or detail them to work at the hospital if they showed any particularly useful skills. But hospital patients were completely out of the control of their regiments and could stay away indefinite amounts of time.[5]

Like many other soldiers that were similarly employed, Waid found medical work much more agreeable than soldiering in the field. Although it was not entirely his fault that he had been detailed to the hospital, Waid did not make any extra effort to re-join the 83rd, and he had seen a much easier summer than his comrades on the peninsula. While the regiment fought the Seven Days battles, he had been on leave in Pennsylvania.

Still, hospital service was a necessity, and Waid performed an important duty that he took pride in. His journal entries show him to be a sensitive and caring man, perhaps well suited for the work. As the casualties of the Richmond campaign filled his ward, Waid lamented at their sad state and wrote how they looked "worn out by hardships and toil and privations." He took care to comfort the men (Union and Confederate alike), enjoyed visiting with them, and when one died Waid was deeply moved, as he wrote on August 4; "James Stewart commenced failing verry fast and continued to fail till about ? past 9 in the evening. When he died, his mother, aunt and unkle were with him all day and till he died. It was a very affecting scene to see how much that Mother thot of her Son and how heart broken She was when She knew that he was no more. While we are in the midst of life we are in death." The war took a more personal note for him in July, when he learned that one of his friends from Company F, Pvt. Chauncy Hays, had been wounded in the leg at Malvern Hill. In August his cousin Jairus (serving in the 5th Corps with Gen. McCall's Pennsylvania Reserves) had died from wounds received in the Seven Days. "Oh!" he wrote in his journal, "that this war were ended and all the Rebels hung up by the neck!"[6]

At that time in late August, the 83rd had lost two-thirds of its strength through battle, sickness, and details like Waid's. In addition, a new law that month had eliminated the bands from the regimental organization and the 83rd's had been discharged and shipped home. The regiment critically needed new soldiers, but Army regulations placed the responsibility of recruitment on regimental commanders, which was a difficult task to perform while on active service. The Federal Government had begun imposing conscription on states that failed to meet their volunteer quotas, but Erie County had met their requirements and no draftees came to the 83rd. As men who were forced into service, conscripts were derided by the three-year volunteers. Daniel Foote's brother George was still at home, and earlier that month Daniel had urged his parents, "If George has not enlisted and [been drafted], get a substitute if it costs $50.00 a month. I could see him shot dead by my side or die of fever in a hospital if a volunteer, but he must never come a drafted man." Daniel did not know that George had enlisted in Company K on August 6, and was on his way to the regiment with some other enlistees. Lt. Col. Campbell had also recruited 39 new soldiers while he was home recuperating from his Malvern Hill wound, and when his leave was up in late August he took the men to join the 83rd at as it passed through Hampton. Upon meeting the now-veteran men of the regiment, Pvt. James Harris, one of the new troops, wrote, "The boys as a general thing look rather tough—their features are bronzed by the piercing rays of this hot Southern sun. They have seen hardships enough to harden, and trials enough to sadden the hearts of the bravest." Lt. Col. Campbell apportioned the new soldiers to companies E, H, K, and I and the additions brought the 83rd's strength up to about 225 men present for duty.[7]

On August 20 the 5th Corps boarded steam transports and headed north, and most men probably had no idea that this latest move was the result of months of military and political maneuvering.

The North had mounted a disjointed military effort in the east for most of the preceding year. The Army of the Potomac was the main striking force toward Richmond, but Maj. Gen. Nathaniel Banks' corps also operated in the Shenandoah Valley, Gen. McDowell's 1st Corps stayed near Fredericksburg, and another army under Maj. Gen. John C. Fremont controlled western Virginia. None of the commands really cooperated with one another. The Army's General-in-Chief was supposed to maintain overall control, but the position had been vacant since Lincoln's relief of McClellan from that duty the previous March. The lack of a unified command structure resulted in an uncoordinated war effort, a fact that the President realized by mid-summer and took steps to remedy. Late in June, Lincoln ordered Banks', Fremont's, and McDowell's commands combined into a new field army titled the Army of Virginia, and selected Maj. Gen. John Pope as its commander.

Pope had been in the Regular Army since 1842, had seen extensive service on the frontier, and was a colonel when the war began. He was promoted to command of a brigade, then a division under Grant, and had shown promise in the western campaigns of early 1862. In addition to his good field reputation, he was a personal friend of Lincoln's since before the war and was a loyal member of the President's Republican Party. Like McClellan, Pope also exuded confidence and received the favor of the northern press. He came to Washington on June 22 to an enthusiastic greeting.

Despite the excitement, Pope carried a reputation as an arrogant braggart in the pre-war army, and several senior Union officers, McClellan obviously prominent among them, did not welcome the new general. Animosity between McClellan and Pope rose and the generals began to openly attack each other's competence. Aware of the problems, Lincoln appointed Maj. Gen. Henry Halleck as the Army's General-in-Chief in late July. Halleck also believed in a coordinated offensive against the Confederates; it was he who had ordered the Army of the Potomac off the peninsula to conduct a joint campaign with Pope's forces in northern Virginia.

While Pope's new army gathered near the Rappahannock River in mid–July, Gen. Lee kept his forces near Richmond and waited for the Union to make its next move. The Army of the Potomac remained a threat from the south as long as they were on the peninsula, and Pope's army presented a new danger from the north. With only 60,000 soldiers at his disposal, Lee could not guard against both threats at the same time. In late July he sent the two divisions of the army's Left Wing under Stonewall Jackson to the north to counter Pope while the Right Wing, under Longstreet, protected Richmond from McClellan. As Lee expected, Pope advanced toward Richmond but was repulsed by Jackson at Cedar Mountain on August 9. Three days later, Confederate intelligence confirmed that the Army of the Potomac was leaving the peninsula, and Lee ordered the bulk of his army north to eliminate Pope's force before McClellan's five corps could reinforce it. Jackson's and Pope's formations squared off against each other around the Rappahannock for the last two weeks of August.[8]

While the other armies positioned and skirmished, the Army of the Potomac moved down the peninsula and sailed up the Chesapeake Bay. The troops began landing 35 miles south of Washington on the Potomac River at the wharf at Aquia Creek, but the docks became so overcrowded that 3rd and 6th Corps were forced to land at Alexandria. The 5th Corps had landed at Aquia on August 22, and the same day moved inland to join with Pope's army. The next day they marched eighteen miles to Kelly's Ford on the Rappahannock, and along with Pope's corps, prepared to defend against an expected Confederate thrust across the river.[9]

By the time Porter's divisions moved into place, Gen. Lee could see that the Federals had established a formidable defense on the Rappahannock. To dislodge them, Lee planned to have Longstreet's Wing of five divisions hold a line on the river while Jackson's three-division wing moved ten miles north, around Pope's right flank and into the Union rear. Jackson's presence would sever Pope's supply line and force the Union to retreat out of the Rappahannock defenses into open terrain. Longstreet would join Jackson after the Yankees moved, and from there, Lee would respond to the situation, strike Pope if the opportunity presented itself or even move into Maryland.[10]

Jackson's divisions began their march on August 25. Federal cavalry reported the movement, but instead of realizing his position was being outflanked, Pope believed that the Confederates were retreating. He made no effort to cut Jackson off and the Rebels slipped away unimpeded. Longstreet's divisions followed in their path the next day. On August 26 Jackson's three divisions passed through the Thoroughfare Gap in the Bull Run Mountains, nearly twenty miles behind the Union defenses on the Rappahannock, and captured the Federal supply depot at Manassas Junction. Pope decided to pull out of his defenses, but he also knew that the two wings of Lee's army were vulnerable while they were widely separated. Planning to destroy Jackson's divisions while they were isolated, he ordered all of his corps to converge at Manassas.[11]

On August 28 the 5th Corps broke camp at Kelly's Ford and marched northeast toward Manassas. Since landing at Aquia, the corps had tramped twelve miles south to Falmouth, sixteen miles west to Kelly's Ford, seven miles northwest to Bealeton Station, six miles north to Warrenton Junction and five miles back northeast to Bristoe Station in a track that made a giant "U" across central Virginia. The troops had been following Pope's army for six days and the meandering was beginning to wear on the 83rd. The veterans had experienced plenty of confusion before, but this apparent wandering made even the old soldiers wonder about their elusive destination. Regimental historian Amos Judson recounted that men mused that they were "trying, like Japhet in search of his father, to find somebody; but whether it was Lee, or Jackson, or the holy father (Pope) himself, I am not prepared to say." The 5th Corps had the longest march to Manassas of all the Union units, and much of it was along the Manassas Gap Railroad line. Pvt. James Harris was apparently angered at the concept of having to march along the tracks and wrote, "We took not the *cars,* but the railroad track to Manassas." Some of the old soldiers passed the time by chiding their new recruits about how they would perform in combat.[12]

Following about a day behind Jackson's Corps, Longstreet's formation was moving up from Thoroughfare Gap to join Jackson from the west. It was up to Stonewall's divisions to keep the Union forces fixed until the Confederate wings could unite and bring battle. On the night of August 27 Jackson moved his troops onto Stony Ridge, a low, wooded rise that overlooked intersection of the Warrenton Turnpike and the Groveton-Sudley Road at the six-house village of Groveton. An unfinished railroad bed ran along the ridge just below the crest, and the cuts and fills made a natural entrenchment. From there, Jackson's troops could watch the Warrenton Turnpike and engage Union columns if they tried to move across Bull Run to advantageous defensive positions. On the late afternoon of August 28, the Confederates descended the ridge and engaged Union troops moving east along the pike in the four-hour Battle of Groveton. When Pope received reports of the fight that night, he was convinced that his soldiers had caught Jackson in the midst of a retreat. Once again thinking that he could trap the Confederates, but completely misreading the situation, he ordered a concentration at Groveton the next day. The instructions for gathering the Union army called for the 1st and 5th Corps, halted seven miles south of Groveton at the village of Bristoe, to march northwest to the town of Gainesville. In a spate of confusingly written orders, the general ordered the two corps to move up the Gainesville-Manassas Road to strike what Pope thought was the Confederate flank.[13]

The 5th Corps began moving at around 10:00 AM on August 29, with Gen. Morell's 1st Division in front and Gen. Griffin's 2nd Brigade leading the division. About an hour into the march, Griffin's troops stopped when they were confronted by six regiments of Virginia cavalry that blocked the road at a small bridge on a creek called Dawkins' Branch. The route of the 5th Corps would allow the Unionists to move behind Jackson's Corps, and Confederate Gen. "Jeb" Stuart, who was with the Virginians, knew that if Porter's Corps was allowed to continue on to Gainesville it would block Longstreet's path to unite with Jackson. Though they had surprised the Federals, the cavalrymen would not be able to hold off a concentrated attack for long. Stuart quickly ordered one regiment to drag brush along the road to replicate the dust cloud of a large infantry force coming to their relief.

The woods and hills along Dawkins' Branch made observation difficult and Porter had little idea of the enemy force on the road. Seeing the dust cloud, he halted his column and requested support from the 1st Corps, but Gen. McDowell decided to march his troops off towards Groveton and sent no help. Porter deployed two artillery batteries and Griffin's Brigade to clear away the Rebels but infantry were unable to maneuver in the rugged terrain. McDowell, who was the senior general, further advised Porter to hold his position on the road, and the 5th Corps halted with less than three miles to go to cut off the Southern reinforcements.[14]

The battle of Bull Run was unfolding three miles to northeast. In accordance with Pope's orders, Maj. Gen. Sigel's Corps of the Army of Virginia advanced that morning and found Jackson's men still in place in their railroad cut. They attacked for three hours but retired with heavy losses without dislodging the Confederates. At about noon, Longstreet's Wing began arriving from the west along the Warrenton Turnpike. As they moved into position a brigade of Virginian infantryman backed up the cavalrymen at Dawkins' Branch and the 5th Corps remained stuck on the road.[15]

For some reason Porter, a usually aggressive officer, did not make any concentrated effort to clear the road and block Longstreet before the Rebels assumed their defensive positions. He sent several messages through McDowell to Pope that advised him of the situation, but the failure to attack mystified the soldiers of the 83rd, as Amos Judson later wrote, "While we were diverting ourselves by a desultory artillery fire, the enemy under Longstreet began to pour along, in full view, to the support of Jackson. Our men lay upon their arms all this while ... and wondered why Porter did not attack. Our artillery shelled them as they passed and there the matter ended." In retrospect, Pope's orders for the day did not clearly require Porter to attack at that point. It is also possible that Porter simply judged that his two divisions were too small to take on Longstreet's wing. Regardless of the reasons, his decision to halt his men and not contest the Confederate position would cause much controversy later. Longstreet's men joined the south end of Jackson's position without a serious fight, and by midday the Rebels occupied a doglegged line that extended from Stony Ridge south across the Warrenton Turnpike.[16]

Pope reached the battlefield and took command in the early afternoon. Although the general was still convinced that his forces had caught Jackson while retreating, the Confederates had actually easily repulsed the Federal attacks from their superb defensive position and had moved their entire army onto the field. Despite the failure of the day's earlier assaults, Pope continued to order troops up Stony Ridge in attempts to dislodge Jackson's line. In a turnabout of the battles at Gaines's Mill and Malvern Hill, the Union brigades pushed up the slope of the railroad cut with fixed bayonets and were cut down by massed Rebel rifle and cannon fire within a few yards of their objectives. By the end of August 29 the Union had lost thousands but had gained no ground. Worse, Gen. Pope maintained his belief that the Rebels were badly beaten and would retreat the next day. Porter's and McDowell's corps were near enough to the field to attack, and Pope intended to push forward in the morning to brush aside Longstreet's wing and pursue the "retreating" Rebels. Angry that the 5th Corps had failed to attack, he sent a terse order to Porter to have his troops at the battlefield by daybreak.

The next morning, Saturday, August 30, Pope met with the corps commanders (minus Porter, who was on his way to the battlefield) to discuss the day's attack. Most of the officers were experienced with fighting the Army of Northern Virginia and despite Pope's optimism, they were not at all convinced that the Confederates were retreating. At their urging, Pope altered his plan from a headlong pursuit into a cautious advance by McDowell's, Porter's and Heintzelman's corps. If the Rebels held as the junior commanders expected, the combined assault of the three corps would push them off the ridge. If the Southerners retreated, the Union could easily pursue them as Pope had originally intended. Porter arrived as the meeting closed and argued against any attack until the true strength and location of Longstreet's wing was known. Though Fitz-John Porter probably had more experience with fighting Lee's army than any general present that morning, Pope ignored his advice. He prepared to continue the attack as planned as soon as the Union pickets confirmed that Jackson's troops had not slipped away the previous night.[17]

While the generals argued, the 5th Corps had pulled out of its position on Dawkins' Branch at daybreak, marched north to the Warrenton Turnpike, and at about 9:00 AM had arrived at Dogan's Ridge, the center of the Union line and the staging area for many of the previous day's ill-fated attacks. The five-mile trip from Dawkins' Branch was uneventful except that the 2nd Brigade under Gen. Griffin, along with Gen. Morell, had taken the wrong road and mistakenly marched away towards Centreville. They still hadn't returned by the time the division moved onto Dogan's Ridge, and Gen. Butterfield assumed command of the 1st Division in Morell's absence. Col. Lansing of the 17th New York took charge of the 3rd Brigade. Amos Judson later sarcastically wrote, "This whole affair was in entire keeping with the rest of the splendid management which seemed to bless our arms on that unlucky field."[18]

At about the same time the 5th Corps arrived, Union pickets went warily forward and confirmed that the Rebels had not retreated. The Federal divisions moved into their attack positions. The 5th Corps moved west over Dogan's Ridge and along the turnpike until they were about a mile from the Groveton Woods, where they halted in the open pasture of Dogan's Farm. Col. Lansing kept the 3rd Brigade faced west in column formation with the 17th New York in the lead, "Ellsworth's Avengers" behind them, the 83rd in the middle, and the 12th New York and the "Michigan Independents" in the rear. Lansing was seriously ill (he had arrived at the field in an ambulance) and he asked to be relieved so a more able officer could lead the brigade. Butterfield put Col. Weeks of the 12th New York in charge. Since beginning their march that morning, the brigade had been commanded by Butterfield, Lansing, and now Weeks, its third leader of the day though the battle had not even started.[19]

Col. Weeks had commanded the 12th New York for nearly a year, but he had never led a brigade before and he was one of several officers in the 3rd Brigade that were underqualified for their new leadership positions. Capt. William Huson led Weeks' regiment in his colonel's absence. Maj. William Grower commanded the 17th New York after his commander was detailed to assist Gen. Butterfield, and Capt. Robert Elliot was in charge of the 16th Michigan. Lt. Col. Campbell ably led the 83rd as he had at Malvern Hill, but sixty of the regiment's junior officers, sergeants, and corporals had been killed, wounded, or captured on the peninsula. With so many leaders gone and others stepping into roles for which they probably had little training, the 3rd Brigade and the 83rd were going into the attack severely handicapped.[20]

By mid-morning, Union artillery batteries on Dogan's Ridge began dueling with their opposite numbers on the Confederate line. James Harris wrote, "The boys laid down beside their arms very quietly for awhile as the shot and shell went whistling over our heads," and this battle began in a manner much like their others. There is no doubt that by that point in the war, the men of the 3rd Brigade could be called "veteran," because instead of taking shelter from the cannonade, their thoughts turned to food. The brigade had not been supplied in several days and many of the soldiers began the day's march with empty stomachs. Orders to eat came while they waited in their ranks, but there was little coffee and fewer rations. Accustomed to foraging for their food, the soldiers noticed Farmer Dogan's cornfield nearby and decided to roast the ears as breakfast. They descended on the field with the force that only hungry soldiers can muster, and the men quickly gathered the ears and were having themselves a pleasant picnic until the smoke from their fires attracted the Rebel artillery. With no sympathy for their starved brethren, the Confederates opened fire. Harris described, "Your correspondent had lain humbly down upon the green bosom of his mother earth, a big ear of corn between his masticating organs, something in the style of that peculiar quadruped sometimes called a hog, when bang went a rebel gun, and whiz came a shell down the hill toward our ranks.... It took the shoulder off one of the boys of the 17th, took the leg off one of the 44th, and injured the leg of another, so that it had to be amputated. It lodged in a ditch just before us." The Confederate gunners increased their fire and an officer of the 44th recalled, "The shots and shells of the enemy would go plowing through the air, buzzing, shrieking and bursting, more or less elevated above the ground, and bearing audible evidence of their destructive nature. Then, again, they would strike the ground with great force, diverge from a direct line, continue in a new course until another object was struck when their courses would again change, making their final destination very uncertain and carrying havoc in their irregular trails." The brigade began to take casualties.[21]

About a mile behind the 3rd Brigade, Gen. Pope was at his headquarters and had received more reports that the Confederates were in strong positions and most definitely not retreating. Based mostly on his own observations of the field and stories from captured Rebels, Pope still believed that Lee was about to withdraw. At about 11:30 Pope ordered Porter's Corps to cross the Groveton-Sudley Road with a division of the 3rd Corps and attack what he supposed was the rearguard of Lee's army.[22]

The Groveton Woods was a thick stand of trees that straddled the Groveton-Sudley Road, and the first task for the 5th Corps would be to clear it as the jumping-off point for their attack on Stony Ridge. At about 1:00 PM, the 3rd Brigade moved forward across the cornfield and the 17th New York chased off the few Rebel skirmishers that occupied the woods. The rest of the 3rd Brigade moved into the trees and had their men lay down.[23]

Gen. Butterfield gathered the regimental commanders and gave them their instructions. The 1st Division would lead the attack by crossing the Groveton-Sudley Road and advancing up the slope of Stony Ridge with Weeks' 3rd Brigade on the left and Brig. Gen. Charles Roberts' 1st Brigade to the right. Hatch's Division of the 3rd Corps would attack the Rebel line on the right flank of Butterfield's troops. When they reached the crest of the ridge, Butterfield's brigades were to turn left down the railroad cut to sweep the batteries from the heights while Hatch's troops turned right and cleared out the Rebel infantry. Gen. Porter held Sykes' Division of Regulars in reserve. It probably seemed like a sound plan at the time, but 8,000 soldiers of the 5th Corps were about attack 30,000 experienced, entrenched, and waiting Confederates.[24]

For another hour, the artillery and skirmisher fire steadily increased while the 5th Corps adjusted its lines in the Groveton Woods and waited for the order to attack. The woods were thick and since the men were lying down, they couldn't see much. Tense and anticipating the assault, the men of the 83rd followed the battle by the sounds of the skirmishing, as James Harris remembered: "The infantry firing was now quite brisk; it raged on our right and on our left. A shell from their batteries occasionally came buzzing over and burst away to our left.... Finally the infantry firing began to grow more distant on our left, then it melted slowly away in the center, now it raged with unabated fury on our right; again the rebel lines wavered on our right and it was announced that we had driven them across the field." It was about 2:30 when Porter finally sent Col. Hiram Berdan's 1st U.S. Sharpshooters, the 25th New York, and two companies of the 44th across the Groveton-Sudley Road as his advance skirmish line. A half-hour later the rest of the 5th Corps was ready to follow. Butterfield rode along the lines of the 1st Division in the woods and called for three cheers. The men obliged him, and then stepped out of the woodline and onto the road.[25]

Ahead of them stretched an open meadow almost one mile wide. It dipped slightly for about 50 yards to an intermittent stream called Schoolhouse Branch, then rose sharply for another 200 yards up to the crest of Stony Ridge, about 50 feet higher than the road. The one-room Groveton Schoolhouse stood just across the road off to their right, where Hatch's Division came out of the woods. A few clumps of trees broke the horizon at the top of the ridge, but the slope itself was mostly nothing but wild grasses. The corps' skirmish line had already come under infantry and artillery fire, and though they could not see the hidden Confederates ahead, the Union soldiers must have known that their enemy waited for them as they crossed the road and adjusted their lines in the field.

The Confederates that looked down on Porter's men from the railroad cut belonged to Brig. Gen. W. E. Starke's Division of Jackson's wing, and the sight of the Federal line as it formed for the attack, with each unit in alignment and bayonets gleaming, awed them. Up to this time they had been lounging behind the railroad cut with their weapons stacked (which may explain why they were hidden from the view of Porter's men), but they could see that the attack was heading straight for them and they rushed to grab their muskets and wait for the Yankees.[26]

Forming in the field east of the cut, Col. Weeks put the 17th New York in line of battle, with the 44th, 83rd, 12th New York and 16th Michigan following in column. Weeks gave the order to advance when the brigade was formed. The 17th New York moved quickly to keep pace with Hatch's Division on their right, and pulled ahead of the other regiments. The New Yorkers charged to the railroad cut, but concentrated Confederate rifle and cannon fire staggered the 17th and forced them to take shelter at the base of the hill. Col. Weeks got the rest of the brigade moving, but the tightly packed column formation made an excellent target for the Rebel artillery. Shells ripped through the ranks. The 44th, 12th New York, and 16th Michigan moved up into line as they went forward and the 83rd followed as the brigade reserve. James Harris wrote that Lt. Col. Campbell, "rose, brandished his sword in the air, and with an enthusiasm which sent a fiery thrill of inspiration through the veins of every soldier, gave the command, 'Forward! March!'" The soldiers stepped off into the meadow and toward the ridge.[27]

Advancing over open ground, uphill, against massed artillery and infantry, the men of the 83rd found themselves in the same situation that the Confederates had faced at Gaines's Mill and Malvern Hill. The Yankee troops made easy targets for the Rebel rifles along the crest of Stony Ridge. Confederate cannon sited to the left of Weeks' Brigade fired into the flank of the Union formation. As their enemies had experienced at Malvern, Lt. Col. Campbell's ranks were ripped by the crossfire as they moved forward. Though his men were familiar with the sound of bullets hissing through the air and striking bodies, the Pennsylvanians had never been under concentrated artillery fire before. Canister shot was a metal can filled with half-inch metal balls that came out of cannon like giant shotgun shells. The balls made peculiar "shwoosh" as they went past. If they hit a man, the effects were as deadly as bullets. Cannon balls, known as "solid shot," traveled slow enough to appear as black balls hurtling toward the troops. They dug furrows as they skipped over the ground. Hitting a formation, solid shot cut men in half, cut through entire ranks and continued on until their energy was expended. Exploding rounds blew off limbs or blasted men into bloody fragments. The Confederates threw all of these shells at the Union line as it moved through the field. Through this storm of shot, Lt. Col. Campbell walked his regiment toward Stony Ridge.

The 83rd's closely packed column formation made the regiment too vulnerable to the artillery, and Campbell deployed the 83rd into line of battle and gave the order for the double-quick. With a yell, the regiment rushed for the railroad cut. A musket ball hit Campbell in his leg and brought him to the ground. While he yelled, "Onward, boys!" the regiment passed over him.

VII. An Unlucky Field

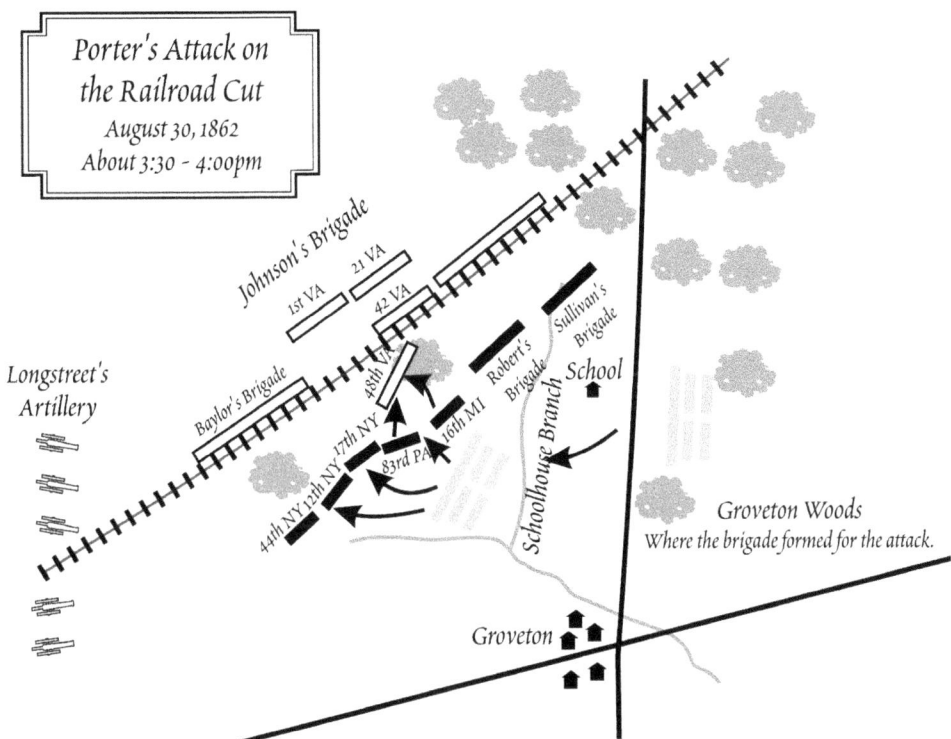

The 5th Corps attack at Bull Run. The men of the 83rd experienced the horror of attacking against firm defenses.

Campbell's Adjutant, Maj. Hugh Lamont, took command.[28]

About 800 Confederates in a brigade of four Virginia regiments commanded by Col. Bradley T. Johnson held the railroad cut directly ahead of the 83rd. Most of the Rebels were well sheltered by the railroad-trench line, but the 48th Virginia occupied a group of trees that extended out from the cut. Bullets from the 48th's volleys showered the flank of the 17th New York, which hugged the base of the ridge as the rest of Weeks' Brigade moved up. Though they were terribly torn by their advance through the Confederate fire, the 83rd and 12th New York surged up the hill with the momentum of the charge behind them. The two regiments angled to the right towards the woods. Col. Johnson later reported, "They stormed my position ... charging on a run...." and the 48th Virginia fell back under the charge. The 83rd and 12th seized the woods.[29]

By that time Johnson's reserves, the 21st Virginia and the 1st Virginia Battalion, had joined the 42nd Virginia on the most dug-out portion of the railroad line called "the Deep Cut." The three regiments shot as fast as they could and Weeks' troops tried to return the fire, but the Confederates had the distinct advantage of being able to re-load in the protection of their cut, as the 83rd's James Harris remembered: "The enemy were secreted behind a little hill a short distance in advance of us. Occasionally they would rise, pour one deadly volley into our ranks and then settle down in their hiding places." Smoke completely blanketed the slope and made the well-protected Rebels exceptionally difficult targets to hit. Capt. DeWitt McCoy of Company F reported that the men were "steadily returning the fire in front, but so far as could be ascertained with but little effect, the enemy being concealed behind some obstacle (I believe the cut of the railroad through the hill)." McCoy's comment shows that the Pennsylvanians had little knowledge of the strength of the position they were attacking.[30]

Though the men of the 83rd could barely see the effects of their fire, the 48th Virginia's retreat left a gap between Johnson's units and Brig. Gen. Alexander Taliaferro's brigade to their right, and the Confederate line was in danger of breaking under the Union attack. The famous Stonewall Brigade under Col. Will Baylor rushed forward to fill the hole, and fire from the Unionists shredded their ranks. Baylor was killed as he urged his men on and the line wavered. The Stonewall Brigade fell back, rallied under their second commander, and plugged the gap in the line.[31]

With Johnson's and Baylor's soldiers shooting down on them from the front and the Rebel artillery still blasting at them from the left, the 83rd was caught in a crossfire of flying bullets and shells. James Harris wrote, "Here the rattle of musketry was almost incessant. Bullets flew thick as hail; shells burst at the root of almost every tree; men were falling like grass before the scythe; some had their faces blown off—some an arm—some a leg—some had great gashes cut in their heads—some received bullets through their hearts, and with one tremendous motion they would fall to the ground, roll up their eyes, give a convulsive twitch, and thus settle down to their last sleep." Maj. Lamont fell with a wound to the left arm, leaving Capt. Graham of Company C in command of the regiment.[32]

The Confederate fire slackened as the troops ran low on ammunition, and Brig. Gen. Charles Field's Brigade of Virginians arrived to bolster the line. Field's four fresh regiments riddled the Federals, who were now becoming exhausted. Pvt. James Harris recalled the confusion in the 83rd, "Batteries to the left were shelling us—everything was confusion. Regiments got mixed up—brigades were intermingled—all was one seething, anxious, excited mess. Men were falling off by scores around us and still we could see no enemy on whom to wreak our vengeance. Some officers were yelling 'Fire!' Others were giving the command to 'Cease, for God's sake! You're shooting our own men!' Those who gave the latter order were grievously disappointed when they looked again and saw the rebel flag flying in front. In the midst of all this confusion there seemed to be no competent head to bring order out of chaos...."[33]

While pandemonium raged all around Pvt. Harris, Gen. Porter watched the assault from Dogan Ridge. The first wave of Hatch's and Butterfield's troops had lost momentum and were pinned down, in some places only a few yards from the railroad cut. Reinforcements could have helped the first wave hold on longer, but at some point Porter realized that another attack would be cut up as badly as the first and he held back his intended sec-

Capt. DeWitt McCoy of Company F. (Irwin Rider)

ond wave. Alone, exhausted, and running out of ammunition, the Union brigades at the railroad cut began to fall back.[34]

When the 83rd's Capt. Graham saw the final group of Rebel reinforcements advance on the regiment's right, he realized that his troops would be outflanked if they stayed where they were. Graham looked to inform the brigade commander, but Col. Weeks had been wounded coming up the ridge. Lacking anyone else, he passed the information to Lt. Col. Rice of the 44th, by then the sole surviving officer of field rank in the brigade. Rice ordered the 44th to fall back, and Graham followed with the 83rd. Although they were still heavily engaged, retreat must have been a difficult step to take for men who had fought so hard for their ground, but as James Harris wrote, "There was no other alternative—there could be no other, when our men were being scattered like chaff before the missiles of an unseen enemy." Still, Graham's order may have been like opening a floodgate for the men who wished only to escape the Rebel crossfire, and Amos Judson's account that "the whole brigade went back, pell mell, together, and without a leader," indicates that the retreat was anything but orderly.[35]*

As the 83rd moved out of their wood lot the other regiments of the 3rd Brigade started down the slope the way they came. The Yankees presented another excellent target when they moved back out into the open meadow, and the Confederate batteries and infantry stepped up their fire. Pvt. Harris recalled, "Bullets pursued us all the faster in our retreat." And Judson wrote, "it is probable that as many men were lost in the retreat as in the advance." Ripped by the fire, the regiments straggled down across the fields and back into the Groveton woods. Some of the Confederates launched a hasty pursuit after the Northerners. Porter had posted a brigade of Regulars from Sykes' Division near the Groveton-Sudley Road in case of a counterattack, and as the Rebels neared the road, the Regulars rose and fired. The blast broke the unorganized pursuers and the Confederates went back up the hill to their own lines.[36]

The withdrawal from the railroad cut was complete by around 3:30. The disorganized soldiers streamed into the trees, and discipline nearly collapsed in the broken regiments that had fallen back from the railroad cut. Officers desperately tried to rally their soldiers and even Porter went up and down the line, yelling, "Form here, men!" As they moved off Dogan's Ridge, Porter had a cavalry detachment set up a picket line to prevent stragglers from sifting to the rear. With all the mixing of units and confusion at a time like that, it was easy for a soldier to slip away to the rear area, and Gen. Butterfield told Capt. Graham to be watchful for stragglers from other regiments and to turn them out of his formation. Graham found a few skulkers hiding in his ranks in an effort to get past the cavalry, but the 83rd kept its own soldiers under control.[37]

The corps rested behind Dogan Ridge into the early evening. Gen. Butterfield returned with Gen. Morell (who had finally found his way back to the battlefield) and they announced that the brigade had been ordered to Centreville, where they would rest, receive rations, and be ready for another battle. The march to Centreville began just after sundown, and Amos Judson

---

*It is unclear who gave the order for the 3rd Brigade to retreat. Judson claims that the brigade was "without a leader" after Weeks' wounding. The Official Report of the 3rd Brigade, written by Col. Lansing, states that Rice took command after Weeks but it does not indicate when that happened. It is entirely possible that Rice was not aware of Weeks' wound and didn't assume command until after the regiments fell back to the Groveton Woods. Rice was severely ill and evacuated right after the battle and filed no report. Only one report from the 3rd Brigade, that of the 12th New York, mentions receiving an order to fall back from Col. Weeks. The others merely use words to the effect that the orders were issued. In all probability, the regiments fell back when they saw all the other units doing the same.

proudly wrote that move was made "in perfect coolness and good order." Pvt. James Harris remembered it as a somber event: "Every tongue was silent—every voice was hushed. We felt that we had been through a terrible ordeal—an unnecessary slaughter—and what was worse, our friends wounded or killed were left on the field to fall into the hands of the enemy."[38]

Out of 224 soldiers of the 83rd that had gone into the battle, 97 had been killed, wounded or captured in about an hour of fighting.* One of the dead was Amos Judson's cousin George. Another was the hero of Malvern Hill, Lt. William Wittich, who had commanded Company I that day. His twin brother serving in the same company, Fredrick, was wounded a few yards from him and taken prisoner. In contrast to the 3rd Brigade's losses, only 120 of Johnson's Virginians had been killed or wounded. Looking at the battlefield afterward, one soldier of the 48th Virginia wrote: "I could walk on bodies for ten steps.... Just think of seeing hundreds of dead and dying men lying on the battlefield. While there are as many wounded ones calling on the name of the Lord, crying for water and dying with thirst."[39]

As the 5th Corps left the battlefield, Jackson's men counterattacked out of their railroad cut. The Federals were slowly overwhelmed and gave ground but a tough Union defense on Henry Hill kept the line from complete collapse, and the Confederate attack died out in the darkness. There was no advantage for the Union to continue holding onto the ground around Bull Run, and Pope was left with no other option but to retreat to the fortified town of Centreville. He issued orders for the army's withdrawal, and by around 11:00 the Union army had retired from the field. Luckily for Pope, Lee's men were too worn out for an organized pursuit.[40]

Far ahead of the rest of the army, the 83rd reached Centreville at about midnight. A light rain pelted the men as they marched into the village, which seemed to fit the general mood of the evening, as James Harris recalled, "It was a dark, cloudy night and the cannon still thundered behind us—streaks of lightning gleamed now and then across the sky.—the outward universe and the inward soul corresponded." Rations of hardtack and coffee were issued, and after a hasty supper the men rolled themselves up in their blankets and went to sleep in the rain.[41]

Gen. Pope's officers met to discuss the situation the next day. Gen. Halleck had recommended that the army stay and defend Centreville, but the senior generals voted to continue the retreat all the way back to the Washington fortifications. The army began their march back to the capital on the evening of September 1, and the 83rd left Centreville at about midnight. James Harris wrote that the men were in their most despondent mood ever: "There had been a cold, drenching rain and the roads were muddy and overflowed at frequent intervals.... We left the strong and boasted fortifications of Centreville in the rear, and were now on the retreat, outnumbered, when our resources were inexhaustible—out generaled, when our generals had been held up to the admiration of the world—retreating from an enemy whom we had not seen, but had *felt*, and bitterly." Now a veteran of hard marches and fierce battle, Harris was qualified to comment.

The next morning the regiment arrived in northern Alexandria County and set up camp. Few of them could have missed the irony in the fact that they had returned to Hall's Hill, and occupied the same regimental streets that they had owned when they had left northern Virginia nearly six months before.[42]

The 83rd suffered 14 killed, 72 wounded, and 11 missing.

Armies Broken and Divided

In September 1862 the 83rd Pennsylvania had been in the service of the Federal government for exactly one year. Within a few months of their departure from Erie, the men had mastered their training and had been recognized as one of the army's elite units. They had experienced the boredom of a soldier's life in a winter camp, followed by the exhilaration of finally marching to meet their enemy. The hard work of digging trenches in the mud and Rebel cannonades had become common to them outside Yorktown. On the advance up the Peninsula, the soldiers learned how exhausting long marches in the Virginia summer could be. They had tasted victory in a deceivingly easy battle at Hanover Court House. In the Seven Days, the men had fought outnumbered and cut-off, but managed to withdraw from the fields of Gaines's Mill and Malvern Hill with honor. A quarter of them had been killed in combat, another quarter had died of disease, and at least fifteen were prisoners of the Confederates. Almost half of the regiment had been wounded at least once, some twice. Less than a quarter of the men that had joined the regiment in Erie still answered the morning roll-call.*

All the hardships and successes aside, the sacrifices of the 83rd, and all the other regiments of the army, had achieved little. The Army of the Potomac had inflicted over 40,000 Confederate casualties, but had returned to the same place it had started out in March and the Rebels were again twenty miles away and in a position to attack Washington.

The main difference between the men who had left Erie in September 1861 and the ones who survived to the same month in 1862 was that the soldiers were no longer naïve enough to believe that the war would be an easy one. If anything, the men that had seen the horrors of the Seven Days and Bull Run were more despondent than they had ever been. Oliver Norton had been a prolific writer of detailed letters to his family all though the Peninsula Campaign, but he only mentioned Bull Run in one letter to his sister, and told her, "We were engaged in the Second Bull Run fight on the same ground as the other, a fight that throws the first one in the shade. If I had the time and felt able, I would like to describe the battle to you and our retreat to Centreville. But I don't know as you would like to hear of such terrible details. Suffice it to say it was another of McDowell's victories—a fearful scene of bloody carnage."† Daniel Foote had been released from the hospital at Ft. Monroe and he made his way back to Alexandria

---

*The Regimental Return filed at the end of August 1862 shows 15 officers and 209 enlisted soldiers present for duty.
†Norton was in error about who commanded the Union forces at Bull Run when he attributed the loss to McDowell. His confusion is typical of the lack of information that most soldiers had about events beyond their own units.

and caught up with the 83rd at Hall's Hill. On September 6, he wrote to Julia Hill, "Our brigade is now cut up badly and we are back where we used to live last winter.... Our whole brigade occupy the [former camps] of the 16th Mich. and our reg't. Out of our squad of 15 that tented together last winter only three familiar faces show themselves. The rest are dead and in the hospital.... Oh! What a dark gloomy picture is this last summer campaign. Thousands of men resting in their long last rest and apparently nothing gained by it."[1]

The other regiments in the 3rd Brigade had suffered equally in the campaigns. The 44th New York had fewer than one hundred soldiers at Hall's Hill and one officer recalled, "Since striking camp on the 10th day of March [1861], had anything been accomplished? If so, what and where?" The 17th New York was down to 87 men, and the 12th New York had 115. Such conditions led Daniel Foote to comment, "This is a dark gloomy time as our nation ever saw since the days of the revolution."[2]

The Army of the Potomac's defeats had generated anger and despair all over the North that September, and internal battles between the army's senior generals made the situation worse. While at Centreville, Gen. Pope began blaming the loss at Bull Run on incompetence and treachery among his subordinates. In his dispatch to Halleck on September 1 he stated, "I think it my duty to call to your attention to the unsoldierly and dangerous conduct of many brigade and some division commanders of the forces sent here from the peninsula.... One commander of a corps, who was ordered to march from Manassas Junction to join me near Groveton, although he was only five miles distant, failed to get up at all, and worse still, fell back to Manassas without a fight, and in plain hearing, at less than three miles distance of a furious battle which raged all day." Pope's letter was a thinly veiled slap at Gen. Porter's halt at Dawkin's Branch on August 30, and if he was to be believed, Porter was guilty of throwing the battle. Rumors that Gen. McClellan had not pushed reinforcements to Bull Run also circulated. Stories of more blunders came out, and the public became equally angry with Pope, Porter, McClellan, McDowell, and other generals whose conduct was subject to question. President Lincoln and the War Department were distraught over the army's losses, and Pope was quickly relieved and sent to Minnesota. Gen. McClellan remained in charge of the Army of the Potomac, and the corps of the defunct Army of Virginia were added to his command.[3]

Much as after the first battle of Bull Run a year before, the soldiers were demoralized, ill-equipped, and tired. Oliver Norton's comments on their campaign summarized the state of the army: "I would not, if I could, tell you how we have suffered on this march," he wrote. "Eating raw beef without salt, and drinking water from mud holes, were done more than once. I have marched forty-six miles on nothing but raw beef and ditch water, and yet I held out to the end. Now I am worn out, and can neither write nor do anything else till I am some rested." As in the previous year, McClellan went to work rebuilding the army.[4]

In contrast to their opponents, Gen. Lee's Army of Northern Virginia had defeated the larger and better equipped Union forces, relieved Richmond, cleared the Shenandoah Valley, and brought the war back to the Federal capital in the space of two months. Success put the Confederacy in a position to take the offensive into Northern territory. In early September Lee pushed his troops across the Potomac into Maryland near the town of Frederick.[5]

Lee had planned that the Army of the Potomac would be unfit for action for at least three weeks, but the Union War Department ordered Gen. McClellan in pursuit of the Confederates within days of their movement. Leaving some troops to guard

Washington, McClellan sent the 1st, 2nd, 6th, 9th, and 12th Corps into Maryland on September 5 and 6, and ordered the 5th Corps to join the columns four days later. Porter's troops broke their camps at 6:00 AM on September 12, passed through Washington, and marched northwest out of the capital along the National Road, paralleling the Potomac River. The soldiers were probably relieved that in this campaign, the 5th Corps was relegated to being the army's reserve.[6]

The same day they left Washington, another division of 6,000 soldiers commanded by Brig. Gen. Andrew A. Humphreys came under the corps and doubled its size. Col. Stockton of the 16th Michigan replaced Gen. Butterfield after the latter was appointed to the 5th Corps staff, and the 20th Maine Volunteer Infantry Regiment under Col. Adelbert Ames and a company of Michigan sharpshooters were also assigned to the 3rd Brigade. Joining the 5th Corps on the march, the new soldiers of the 20th Maine learned that in addition to having a reputation as fighters, the veterans of the 3rd Brigade had earned them the nickname of "Butterfield's Thieves," a testament to their habitual stealing of Rebel property. As the 5th Corps took to the road toward Rockville, Maryland, it was organized like this:[7]

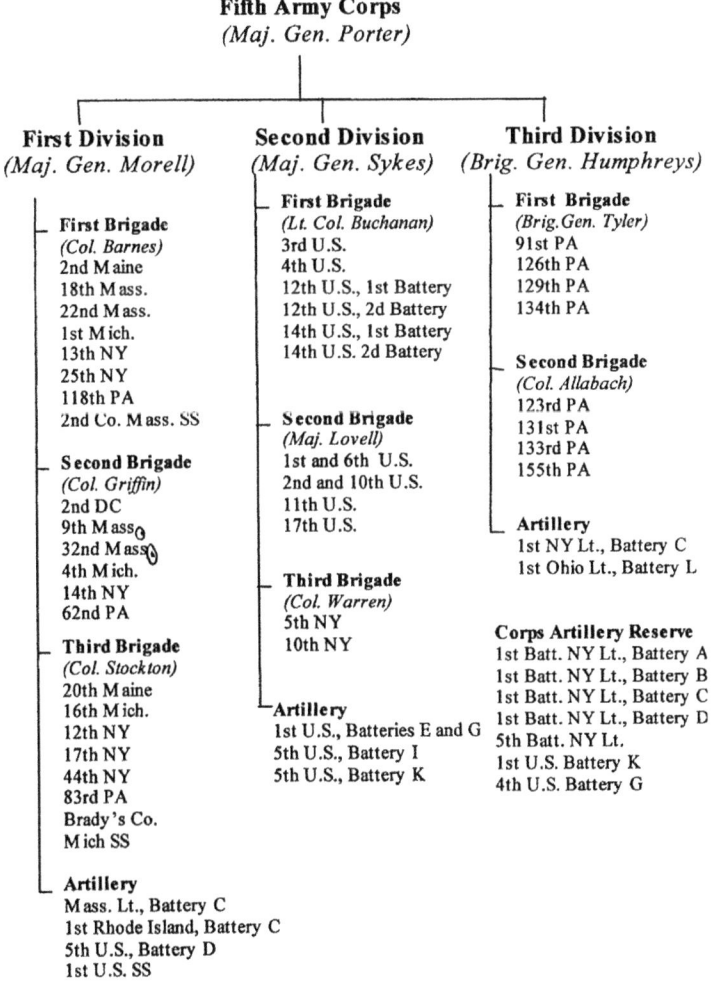

With about 88,000 soldiers, the five corps of the Army of the Potomac moved west towards Frederick on three parallel roads. The soldiers were in high spirits. Although they had felt angry and betrayed in Arlington, it was heartening to be in action again and moving forward in friendly territory to head off the Rebel invasion. After spending a month as a prisoner in Libby Prison in Richmond, Amos Judson was paroled, sent to a hospital in New York, and finally released for active service again after a prisoner exchange. Returning to the regiment, he assumed his post as captain of Company E. Judson remembered that in contrast to the heat, dust, and antagonistic population of Virginia, the weather as they went into Maryland was pleasant, the roads were in good condition, and that smiling citizens greeted the soldiers with Union flags. As an officer of the 44th New York later wrote, "The changed condition was truly exhilarating." Oliver Norton remembered their course in Maryland as "among the most pleasant of my experiences as a soldier. The roads were splendid and the [area] as beautiful a country as I ever saw.... Pretty villages are frequent, and pretty girls more so, and instead of gazing at passing soldiers with scorn and contempt, they are always ready with a pleasant word and a glass of water."[8]

Battlefield intelligence in the Civil War was gained mostly from the cavalry, which, by virtue of its mobility, was capable of the far-ranging scouting necessary to physically observe enemy formations. Since crossing into Maryland, Gen. Lee had shielded his army from observation by Federal horsemen by moving behind the northern tip of the Blue Ridge. McClellan had a fair idea of the general location of Lee's army from the initial reports of the Confederate river crossing, but he would not know their actual position and direction of march until Federal troops pushed through the mountain passes to observe the Rebels. Likewise, Lee's cavalry had not watched their enemy very closely. As his divisions moved deeper into Maryland, Lee was unaware that the Union army had moved from Washington and was advancing from the east.

If Gen. McClellan could have learned the positions of the Confederates, he would have seen that Lee's army was following different routes that scattered them throughout western Maryland and northern Virginia. Lee planned to gather his army at Hagerstown to strike at Harrisburg, Philadelphia, Baltimore, or even Washington, but until they united, the dispersed columns were vulnerable to attack by the more numerous Federals. On September 13, Union troops found a copy of Lee's orders to his division commanders that showed how the Confederates were widely separated and vulnerable. The papers (which would become famous as "Lee's Lost Order") gave McClellan all the information he needed to destroy the Army of Northern Virginia before it could concentrate. That afternoon, he issued orders for his corps to move west to smash Gen. Longstreet's isolated divisions near Hagerstown. The next day, Lee learned that the Yankees had the lost orders and were moving to trap Longstreet. Realizing that his scattered army was in danger, Lee immediately ordered his divisions to concentrate at the town of Sharpsburg, midway between Frederick and Hagerstown on the Potomac.[9]

On September 15, Lee's divisions occupied high ground to the east of Sharpsburg. The same day, Federal troops moved onto the hills over looking the Antietam Creek, one mile further east and within striking distance of the Rebel lines. With characteristic method, McClellan spent all of the next day bringing up the rest of his army and positioning the 1st and 12th Corps north of the town, and the 9th Corps to the south. The 5th Corps came onto the field throughout the day and joined the 2nd Corps as the reserve near the center of the

Union line. Morell's Division arrived at about noon. Except for an artillery duel between the opposing batteries, there was no action on the 16th and most of the troops of both sides spent the day lounging in the sun.[10]

In the early morning on September 17, Gen. McClellan pushed the 1st Corps forward to cut the Rebels off from the Potomac and opened the Battle of Antietam. As the hours went by, three assaults from three Union corps met tenacious Confederate defenses, and the battle raged with a level of intensity that had never been seen on the continent. As the reserve, the 5th Corps made no offensive action, but in the morning Porter moved Morell's Division to help defend the Federal artillery near the Antietam Bridge. The location gave Oliver Norton a vantage point to watch the battle. "I stood on a hill where a battery of twenty-pounders was dealing death to the enemies of our country," he wrote home, "and there, stretched out before me, was a rough, rolling valley sloping away to the Potomac.... Our division was held in reserve near the center of the line, and from where I stood I could trace our lines extending in a semi-circle for several miles. The valley was wrapped in smoke, but the white wreaths curling from the cannon's mouth, the boom of the report and the scream of the shell showed the position of batteries, and the sharp rattle of musketry deepening to a roar told where the most desperate fighting was going on."[11]

The 1st Corps attack in the north ground to a halt a few hours after it began, as did the 12th Corps' assault in the center of the battlefield. Late in the afternoon, Gen. Burnside's 9th Corps succeeded in pushing the Rebels back on the heights over Sharpsburg. Victory was within McClellan's grasp, and Gen. Sykes asked for permission to advance and cut the Confederate line with support from the rest of the 5th Corps. McClellan almost agreed with Sykes, but Porter cautioned against the move. McClellan lost heart for the attack and held Porter's and Sykes' troops in place. Lee's army held their position outside the town, and the two armies disengaged as night fell.[12]

The Army of Northern Virginia had taken over 10,000 casualties and had been pushed to the breaking point. Gen. McClellan, again showing his habit of overestimating the enemy's strength, believed that the Confederates were still capable of offensive action. The general decided to wait all day on September 18 for reinforcements before attacking again, and the lull gave Lee a chance to escape across the Potomac. That afternoon Lee issued orders for the army to retreat into Virginia, and his units pulled out of their positions and crossed back over the river under the cover of darkness. Over 23,000 casualties between both sides made Antietam the single bloodiest day in American history. Except for receiving a few rounds of Confederate artillery, the 83rd had seen no action and had only one man was wounded. When an officer of the regimental staff filled out the Field and Staff Muster Roll (a monthly summary of the regiment's status and activities required by Army Regulations) for September, he sarcastically wrote that the 5th Corps had "vigorously supported" the rest of the army during the battle.[13]

In the early morning of September 19 the Federals discovered that the Confederates had escaped, and the 5th Corps was ordered to move through Sharpsburg in pursuit. When the soldiers arrived on the north bank of the Potomac at Shepardstown Ford, a mile and half southwest of the town, they found that a Confederate rear-guard held the far side. The next morning Gen. Porter set up his artillery along the river and ordered Morell's and Sykes' Divisions to drive the Rebels from their positions. Parts of the 1st and 2nd Brigades of Morell's Division made it across and engaged the Confederates, but through some confusion Sykes' troops never crossed and the 83rd was recalled as they were literally in mid-stream. The Rebels counterattacked the troops on the south side of the river and drove them back to the ford with heavy casualties. Safe on the north bank, the only fire the 83rd received was from a Union battery posted behind them, as Amos Judson recalled: "Our position ... would have been a very desirable one had it not been for the blundering fire of a Dutch [nineteenth century slang for 'German'] battery on the bluff in our rear.... It seemed impossible for them to give the proper length to their fuses or range to their shells, and the consequence was they exploded the half of them the moment they left the cannon's mouth and sent them whiling and leaping into our rear." None of the 83rd was injured from enemy or friendly fire at Shepardstown Ford.[14]

Lee's army retreated into Virginia, but the Union intelligence service estimated it to be twice its actual size, and McClellan decided that it was too strong for his soldiers to immediately pursue. While the Rebels withdrew twenty-eight miles to Winchester, the Union army stayed near Sharpsburg to refit.[15]

The 83rd set up camp a mile south of the town near the mouth of the Antietam Creek. There was no enemy in sight, and a week after the battle, Oliver Norton wrote his family, "All is quiet along the Potomac." Sergeant Thomas Van Giesen, one of the three brothers in Company G, wrote that their schedule included "three hours of drill a day and considerable picketing," but the men still enjoyed their easiest routine in months. Re-equipping the soldiers became the regiment's primary activity. The regimental orderly books are filled with entries such as, "lost knapsack in action, June 27th 1862" or "taken prisoner and lost everything." They made up a testament to the bitter and confusing battles that the soldiers suffered through over the past four months. Many men had gone without equipment since losing it on the Peninsula.[16]

Although the regiment kept an easy pace in pleasant surroundings, there were still 499 soldiers in the hospital, the highest number yet, and replacing losses in personnel was also a major concern. In August the Federal Government had begun imposing conscription on states that failed to meet their volunteer quotas, and in September the 83rd received 67 draftees. Nine former prisoners of the Confederates returned. Col. Vincent also arrived in early October. Incapacitated with the fever which infected his kidneys, bladder, and urinary tract, the colonel had reached Erie in August and was bedridden for the summer. He recuperated under the care of his doctor and wife and left Erie on October 7. "His health was, we are pleased to say, entirely restored," reported the *Weekly Gazette*. Vincent brought twenty-five new enlistees with him. That month the 83rd reported 363 soldiers present for duty, their highest strength since July.[17]

The military atmosphere on the Potomac became more closely related to a rest camp than a campaigning army, and the scene the soldiers faced in the autumn was a striking contrast to their miserable summer in Virginia. Amos Judson later wrote of their stay near Sharpsburg: "Ah, those halcyon days which we passed on the romantic shores of the Potomac! For nearly six weeks did we lie, in perfect repose, in the bosom of that delightful valley ... this proved a season of grateful and beneficial rest. [The regiment] regained their accustomed spirits and strength, received their supplies of clothing and equipment and were again ready for another season of active service." Judson made his comments after the war, but at the time of their encampment in Maryland, the soldiers may not have been as interested in another campaign. Oliver Norton explained to his brother and sister, "I have seen the most of McClellan's, McDowell's, Pope's, Banks' and Sigel's armies, but I would rather see two or three pretty girls and a glee-look this afternoon than the whole of them." Sgt. Thomas Van Giesen wrote his family that month: "[We] are injoying the pleasures of health but while we are spaired many of our comrades have bid fair well to earth & taken there departure for a better land, we hope, & now a stone or some other mark showes the soldier where there comraids is now returning to dust from whence they came." Reflecting on the regiment's dead, Van Giesen also may not have been very enthusiastic about the prospect of facing the Army of Northern Virginia again.[18]

As had happened during the winter at Hall's Hill, inactivity may have also led to boredom and some alcohol excess. Daniel Foote wrote in the end of September, "The inhabitants have been very kind to us in Maryland, often standing for hours when our troops have been passing and given them cool water and they would be much kinder if it were not for many of our own soldiers getting drunk and abusing [them]." In late October two soldiers of Company A, Pvt. Nicholas Akerly and Pvt. George Fales, were charged with being drunk, behaving "in a loud and boisterous manner" and attempting to strike Capt. D. P. Jones. Both soldiers pleaded guilty to the charges and forfeited a month's pay, and Fales received the extra punishment of a public reprimand.[19]*

Though the soldiers enjoyed the inactivity, President Lincoln became frustrated that his troops sat idle while Lee's army regained its strength. On October 7 he ordered McClellan to cross the Potomac and engage the Confederates. The general retorted that his men still needed to refit and were in no condition to take the offensive. Mild temperatures made October perfect campaigning weather, but the season slipped by as the Army of the Potomac lay dormant.[20]

Gen. McClellan's lack of aggressiveness began to bring him public scorn. Oliver Norton's family (apparently questioning the general's suitability for command) asked him his opinion of McClellan's performance on the Peninsula, and he replied, "Those who have seen what he has had to contend with have confidence in him, and although his campaign was a failure, we see that the blame rests not on him, but on those who failed him just on the eve of success.... If I were at home nothing would make me ready to fight sooner than to hear some home guard abuse McClellan." Even after the war, Amos Judson defended McClellan's decision to hold the 5th Corps out of the battle of Antietam: "It would have given the enemy an opportunity to break through, divide the army and capture our trains, besides inflicting upon us a disastrous defeat." It seems that the soldiers of the 83rd stayed loyal to their general.[21]

Under pressure from Lincoln, Gen. McClellan finally sent his army after the Confederates on October 26. The Army of Northern Virginia was still at Winchester, and McClellan planned to move along the eastern slope of the Blue Ridge Mountains and then march south to the town of Warrenton to get between the Lee and Richmond. The 5th Corps crossed the Potomac River on October 30, went through Harper's Ferry, and marched south with the rest of the army during the first week in November. Their route took them through the Loudon Valley in Virginia, an area which had been untouched by the war. Temperatures were mild, there was no contact with the Rebels, and this movement surpassed even the trip through Maryland in September for comfort and encouragement. Amos Judson recalled, "Of all the marches we ever made, none was so pleasant and so romantic as this." Another officer of the 5th Corps recalled that the Union soldiers were in "glo-

---

*Pvt. Akerly deserted from the regiment in June 1863. Fales served out his enlistment without further incident and re-enlisted in February 1864.

rious spirits" as they skirted the Blue Ridge. Daniel Foote, ill with rheumatism and making much of the trip in an ambulance, wrote that the march was "a long 60 miles up Pleasant Valley and a very pleasant valley it is, too." Well-rested and re-equipped, the 83rd was back into fighting trim.[22]

The lead Federal corps began arriving in Warrenton on November 4, but by then, Lee had moved his troops from Winchester to the town of Culpeper, fifteen miles south and in between the Union army and Richmond. It took nine days to move all the corps from Maryland to Warrenton, and now Lee blocked their way to Richmond. McClellan's failure to trap Lee convinced Lincoln that the general had to be replaced, and on November 5, a special messenger from the War Department informed McClellan that he was relieved. As Lincoln instructed, Maj. Gen. Ambrose Burnside of the 9th Corps took command of the Army of the Potomac.[23]

In the same message that fired McClellan, the President also relieved Gen. Porter from the 5th Corps command because of the charges of his misconduct at Bull Run. The men of 83rd learned of the relief of both officers when they reached Warrenton on November 9, and Amos Judson remembered that the news came as "a slight shock ... there was considerable swearing indulged in, and threats of marching on Washington, should but McClellan take the lead."[24]

As Little Mac departed the army's camps on November 11, the officers of the 5th Corps gathered at their headquarters to give him personal farewells. McClellan shook their hands and thanked them for their service, and then boarded a military train to Washington. At the station, the men of the 5th and 2nd Corps waited for him in formation, but broke into cheers when he arrived. They fell silent as McClellan mounted the platform and read a short farewell address that expressed his affection and faith in his soldiers. Some of the men pleaded for the general to disobey the relief order or to lead them on a march on Washington, but McClellan quieted them, boarded his train, and took his leave of the Army of the Potomac. Oliver Norton wrote later, "I think the whole army thinks as much of McClellan to-day as they ever did. We ask no better leader. I believe, too, that the President had as much confidence in his loyalty and ability the day he removed him as he ever had.... Time will show if they were right."[25]

Also ordered to Washington, Fitz-John Porter left the army the next day, and Maj. Gen. "Fighting Joe" Hooker assumed command of the 5th Corps. Two weeks later the War Department convened a court-martial to determine Porter's guilt or innocence of Pope's charges that he had disobeyed orders at Bull Run and negligently sabotaged the battle. In general, Pope accused Porter of disobeying the orders of August 27 and 29 to move the 5th Corps to the attack. Porter was also accused of disobeying the order to march to Manassas on the morning of August 30, and that he had negligently allowed his force to enter the battle undermanned by permitting the 2nd Brigade of Gen. Morell's Division to become lost (there were also sub-specifications for each charge). The military court eventually found Porter guilty of most of the charges and cashiered him from the service in January 1863. The episode was one of the great political dramas of the Civil War, and the men of the 83rd had witnessed the events that caused it while they were halted at Dawkins Branch on August 29, 1862.[26]

The War Department expected one more attempt to destroy Lee's army before the winter turned the Virginia roads into mud, and Gen. Burnside immediately began planning his own campaign. Snow had already fallen. It was the beginning of a cold and bitter winter.

Mournful Cries in the Stillness of the Night

The Confederate invasion of Maryland had failed, as had a similar advance into Kentucky. In the west, the Federal ground and naval forces continued operations on the Mississippi River and threatened to cut the South in two. President Lincoln had issued a preliminary Emancipation Proclamation in the wake of the Union successes, and his armies became the instruments of the policy. The opinions of the Army of the Potomac's soldiers to the Proclamation and their new role varied widely, but Oliver Norton wrote to his sister in early December, "It meets my views exactly. It is broad and deep, but so simple a child can understand it. Nothing [the President] has ever said or done pleased me so much as his reasons for his policy...."[1] In general, the war was turning in favor of the Union in the late fall of 1862, but though the Confederacy had suffered setbacks, the Army of the Potomac caused only one of them. After the disaster on the Peninsula, the retreat from Bull Run, and the loitering after Antietam, the Government and the public were eager for a successful campaign. As the autumn turned to winter, they looked to Maj. Gen. Ambrose E. Burnside to give them a victory.

At thirty-eight, Burnside was a friendly and affable man who people naturally warmed to. Outwardly, he was a burly and imposing six-footer with the distinguishing characteristic of whiskers that ran from ear to ear but left the chin bare that would later become known as "side-burns." Burnside was a man who impressed people, but was known to have bad luck. The son of a South Carolina slave-owner, he graduated from West Point in the midst of the Mexican War in 1847 and saw light service there. Later posted to the southwest, Burnside fought the Apaches and was even wounded, but resigned his army commission in 1853. Three years later he patented a breech-loading rifle and opened a factory for its production. An economic panic in 1857 and the failure to land a government contract for the guns forced the plant into bankruptcy. After that Burnside went to work for his army friend George McClellan at the Illinois Central Railroad. He was later engaged to a Kentucky belle, but was left at the altar. Success finally came in the Rhode Island Militia; Burnside raised the state's 1st Regiment of Volunteers, one of the earliest ninety-day units to reach Washington. Since then he had acquitted himself well at the first battle of Bull Run, led a successful amphibious operation in North Carolina, and had commanded the Ninth Corps at Antietam.[2]

President Lincoln was impressed by the general's strength of character and energy, and he had offered Burnside the command of Army of the Potomac twice before during periods of frustration with McClellan. Frank to a fault, Burnside protested that he was not capable to fill the job and declined, but the President's order in November had left him no choice. After McClellan's departure, the War Department had asked Burnside how he intended to crush Lee, and although reluctant, the general energetically began planning a campaign.

The Army of Northern Virginia was dispersed from the Shenandoah Valley, where Jackson's Corps operated, to Culpeper Court House, where Longstreet's Corps camped.* Stragglers and wounded had returned through the fall, and with new recruits the army began the winter with about 68,000 effective soldiers. The Confederates expected the Union army to strike at them at Culpeper (which is what McClellan intended before he was relieved) but Burnside decided to march his army south to the town of Fredericksburg and cut behind Lee's army for a clear path to Richmond. Successful execution relied on the army's ability to quickly reach Fredericksburg, build pontoon bridges, and cross the Rappahannock before Lee could react. Gen. Halleck viewed the plan with skepticism and deferred final approval to the President. Burnside insisted that it could be successful, and President Lincoln reluctantly approved the plan with a warning to Burnside that he should move quickly or not at all. Halleck promised to order the pontoon bridges to be moved south to Fredericksburg immediately.[3]

Burnside's first concrete step as commander was to restructure the army with three "Grand Divisions," composed of two corps each. The Right Grand Division under

Maj. Gen. Ambrose Burnside. (LOC)

Gen. Sumner consisted of the 2nd and 9th Corps. The Center Grand Division was composed of the 3rd and 5th Corps, and was commanded by Gen. Hooker. The 1st and 6th Corps made up the Left Grand Division under Gen. Franklin. Within the 5th Corps, Gen. Morell had been transferred to command the Union forces on the upper Potomac, and Gen. Griffin succeeded him. Col. T. B. W. Stockton, former commander of the 16th Michigan, took charge of the 3rd Brigade. With Hooker's promotion as the chief of the Center Grand Division, Gen. Butterfield was promoted to command the 5th Corps. The reorganization became effective on November 14, and Burnside put the army in motion towards Fredericksburg the next day.[4]

Situated at the height of navigation on the west bank of the Rappahannock River, Fredericksburg was a picturesque town that had been prosperous since colonial times. George Washington, James Monroe, and John Paul Jones all spent portions of their early lives there. A ridge known as Marye's Heights overlooked the town from the west,

---

*In October, the Confederate Congress authorized the formation of corps in all armies, to be commanded by officers in the grade of Lt. General. In the Army of Northern Virginia, Longstreet and Jackson were subsequently promoted to Lt. General, and the army reorganized to be composed of two corps. The 1st, under Longstreet, had five divisions and the 2nd Corps, commanded by Jackson, had four. Maj. Gen. Stuart commanded the army's cavalry division

as did Stafford Heights on the opposite side of the river. Yankee troops had occupied Fredericksburg from April to September and looted some of the area, but a few strong local commanders stopped the practice and the town escaped significant damage. The Union soldiers withdrew in the Bull Run campaign and burned the bridges over the river behind them. With little strategic importance on its own, Fredericksburg's only military inhabitants in November were a detachment of Confederate scouts.

Gen. Sumner's Right Grand Division led the way out of Warrenton on November 15, and the 5th Corps followed the next day. The lead units reached Fredericksburg two days later, but a hard rain fell and turned the roads into mud. The soldiers slogged through the mire as they had done hundreds of times before and the army had closed on Fredericksburg by November 19. The downpour continued and although the troops were in place, the pontoons that the Union engineers would use to bridge the river were still on the road from Washington. With no way to cross, the soldiers went into camps around Fredericksburg to wait.[5]

The Union corps had moved quickly, but Gen. Lee had suspected Burnside's intent and started sending units to Fredericksburg the same day the Federal march began. The bulk of the Army of Northern Virginia headed for the town when the Union destination was confirmed. Longstreet's Corps began arriving on November 19 and occupied Marye's Heights within days. Jackson's Corps headed toward the town in the next week and deployed on the low ridges south of Fredericksburg. With the surprise gone, the chance of a successful Federal crossing was slipping away.[6]

The Union engineer's pontoons began arriving at Fredericksburg at the same time Lee's units took their positions, but the final pieces were not delivered until the end of November. By that time Burnside knew that the Rebels occupied Marye's Heights, but reasoned that his corps could overpower them if they attacked quickly. President Lincoln again reluctantly authorized the campaign to continue, and Burnside made his final plan for the assault. Gen. Franklin's Grand Division would cross the river south of the city and clear the Rebels from the low ridge. Simultaneously, Gen. Sumner's Grand Division would cross at Fredericksburg, move through the town, and attack up Marye's Heights. Hooker's Grand Division would remain in reserve to back up either assault. River crossings and up-hill attacks were difficult operations, and many of the senior Union generals resisted the plan, but after much debate, most agreed to give it their best effort. The pontoon bridges were to be laid at night on December 10 and the attack was scheduled for the morning of December 11.[7]

While Gen. Sumner's Grand Division waited a mile north of Fredericksburg at the town of Falmouth, Franklin's troops were camped at White Oak Church, four miles to the east. Gen. Hooker's Grand Division was five miles northeast of Fredericksburg along the railroad line that connected the town to Aquia, which was still a Federal landing site. Since November 21, the 5th Corps had been camped at a place called Stoneman's Switch, where the railroad crossed the Potomac Creek. As they were nearly six miles from the scene of action, the soldiers of the 83rd became so detached that Oliver Norton wrote home, "We have been here a couple of weeks now, and things begin to look like winter quarters. The papers still keep up the hue and cry of 'On to Richmond,' but we don't go on to Richmond, and my 'opg.' is that we won't this winter.... My own opinion is (you may have it for what its worth) that we will stay here a month or so until the mud will prevent the rebs from moving north, ... then we will be sent south where winter will not hinder our fighting." Norton had been appointed as one of the brigade buglers in the fall, and his greatest concern in early December appears to have been how to stay warm, as he continued, "I am still established at brigade headquarters and very comfortably fixed, too. I am in a tent with two orderlies. We have built a log house just about seven by nine, five logs high, and covered it with ponchos." The same night Norton wrote those lines, four inches of snow fell and it was so cold that two men of the 20th Maine froze to death in their tents.[8]

The 83rd's detachment from the action ended on December 10 when rumors circulated that the army was ready to move. Reveille came the next morning at 3:00, and as the soldiers packed up their belongings in the cold, the sound of cannon and muskets from Fredericksburg could be clearly heard in the crisp air.[9]

As Burnside had scheduled, the engineers began building the pontoons over the Rappahannock on the night of December 10. The final portions were to be completed at dawn the next day, then Sumner's and Franklin's troops would cross the river and make their assaults. The engineers went to their task before daylight, but a detachment of Mississippi and Florida infantry hidden in Fredericksburg's houses opened fire on them and sent the bridge-builders running for cover. The engineers returned to their task again and again (some Confederates counted nine attempts), but were defenseless against the concealed Rebels and each time retreated to their bank under enemy fire. Gen. Franklin's divisions had crossed the river on their own bridges south of the city without Rebel interference, but by midmorning it was clear that the engineers attempting to cross at Fredericksburg could not complete the task on their own. Burnside ordered a two-hour bombardment that left much of the town rubbled and burning, but even that failed to drive the Rebel infantry away. Eventually, the general sent three regiments of infantry across the river in pontoon boats to clear out the sharpshooters and Gen. Sumner's Grand Division began crossing that afternoon. Four brigades occupied Fredericksburg by the early evening, but by then it was too late to begin the general assault. Burnside ordered the rest of the army to remain on the east bank of the Rappahannock and postponed the attack until the next day.[10]

The 5th Corps had left its camps that morning and the men marched toward the sounds of the battle all day. In the early evening Col. Stockton's Brigade halted near Gen. Burnside's headquarters on Stafford Heights, east of the Rappahannock. Fredericksburg was about a mile east of them across the river, and as an officer of the 44th recalled, "The whole panorama of the battlefields was in full view." In the gray winter twilight, the field was a forbidding site. Most of the residents of Fredericksburg had fled for the Confederate lines and the city was deserted and dark. Beyond the town to the south was a level plain that stretched for three miles to the wooded ridge where Jackson's Corps was preparing to defend. Directly in front of the soldiers to the west another open plain extended from the town and steadily rose to the ridge known as Marye's Heights. An unfinished railway cut and a partially filled millrace slashed through the middle of the slope, and the Telegraph Road ran roughly parallel to the ridgeline of Marye's Heights. To make it level, the road was cut into the ground a few feet and the side towards Fredericksburg had been reinforced with an armpit-high stone wall, which made it a perfect place for a man to fire a musket. Although hidden from the Yankees, Confederate infantry of Longstreet's Corps now filled the road and looked down on the city from behind the stone wall. The Rebels had also dug in over fifty cannon another few hundred feet further up the hill, and sited them to sweep the long, barren slope below. If the Union soldiers were to attack Marye's

Heights, as Burnside planned, they would have to cross half a mile of open ground that was covered by well-protected Confederate infantry and artillery. The significance of the Rebel positions was not unknown—campfires dotted the hillsides. As veterans, the men of the 83rd were well aware that they would be expected to cross a perfect killing ground the next day. Amos Judson later described the field outside Fredericksburg as "the most complete slaughter pen into which a gallant army had ever been led."[11]

The two corps of Gen. Sumner's Grand Division continued crossing the Rappahannock into the city on the morning of December 12, but it took almost the entire day to get all the troops across and for Gen. Franklin's troops to deploy on the plain south of Fredericksburg. By the time the divisions were across it was again too late in the day to begin the assault, and with the knowledge that the Rebels held the hills but his army greatly outnumbered them, Burnside adjusted the plan. The next morning, Franklin's Grand Division would push the Rebels off the low hills south of the city first, and Sumner's Grand Division would follow up their success by advancing to take Marye's Heights. That afternoon, the 5th Corps moved to a position overlooking the pontoon bridges on Stafford Heights, from where they could be ready to join the attack the next day.[12]

The men of the 83rd awoke the morning of Saturday, December 13, with a hard frost on their blankets that Amos Judson recalled was "a quarter of an inch thick." A heavy fog covered the river and low ground, but the sounds of the musketry from Fredericksburg already crackled through the camp. The men ate a quick breakfast of hardtack and coffee, and then fell into ranks to await their orders.[13]

Hours went by while the divisions on the far side of the river got into position to attack. It was not until mid-morning that Col. Vincent's Pennsylvanians heard the booming of cannon that signaled Gen. Franklin's advance on the plains south of Fredericksburg. The fog and dense cannon smoke completely masked Franklin's attack from the view of Union troops waiting on Stafford Heights, but the crash of musketry was clearly audible. For two hours, the men of the 83rd listened with apprehension to the battle. Franklin's troops made some initial progress but stopped when confronted by Jackson's tough defense and well-placed artillery. Burnside could not see the attack either, but by around 10:30 he received sketchy reports that indicated (very incorrectly) that Franklin's attack was succeeding. The reports appear to have convinced Burnside that the time was right to assault Marye's Heights. He ordered Gen. Sumner to advance.[14]

Sumner's brigades were ready to go at about noon. By then the fog burned off and the soldiers emerged from Fredericksburg under a bright sun and formed their lines of battle in the open fields west of the town. The Confederate artillery was waiting for them and opened fire as soon as the soldiers took their first steps up Marye's Heights. Their solid shot mowed down entire squads, taking off limbs and cutting men in half. When the blue line was about halfway to the top, the Rebel infantry of Brig. Gen. Cobb's and Kershaw's Brigades rose from behind the stone wall and fired. Union regiments pressed forward but the Confederate fire was so effective that whole Yankee companies fell at once. Brigade after brigade of Union troops advanced as far as they could in the intense fire and then laid down, each line mixing with one that had preceded it. Lines of infantry that could not breach the wall or retreat through the gauntlet of fire hugged the ground on Marye's Heights, and the slope was carpeted with dead and wounded.[15]

Amos Judson remembered his impressions while the 83rd waited on Stafford Heights: "From early in the morning ... we stood upon the heights and saw the great battle raging below us. The whole of the great amphitheatre, where the two armies, like gladiators, were engaged in a death struggle, was one dense cloud arising from the smoke of battle. After the artillery had ceased nothing was to be heard but the constant rattle and crash of musketry; and there is always something more terrible in the crashing of musketry on the battlefield than in the roar of the heaviest artillery. Occasionally, the firing would die away, for the space of half a minute, not a shot was to be heard. At such moments we would hug the delusive phantom of hope that the carnage was at an end...." In the afternoon the regiment moved down the hill to a position nearer the pontoon bridges. The sounds of the battle did not indicate a Federal success, and the noise grew so brutal that Judson went on to describe it thus: "The demon of war was devouring and crunching the bones of a thousand victims at a time between his iron teeth." Groups of wounded, helped along by those who could not stand the fire, came back across the bridges and gave dire reports of the fight. The prospect of joining the battle did not thrill Vincent's men. Judson continued, "Every soldier in the ranks foresaw that nothing but disaster and defeat was to follow...." An officer of the 44th later wrote that one of his companions stated, "I would consent to give my right arm to be assured that I could escape this day's peril with my life." The noise from the assault was so loud that Lt. Israel Thickstun, still detached to the Signal Corps, heard the cannon booming thirty miles away. Midway into the action, even Gen. Hooker remarked, "There has been enough blood shed to satisfy any reasonable man, and it is time to quit."[16]

Gen. Burnside directed the battle from Stafford Heights but since he could not see the action through the smoke, he judged the events from his subordinate's dispatches. Some reports indicated that one more attack by fresh troops could succeed, and Burnside ordered Hooker to take his Grand Division across the river and storm the stone wall while Franklin made another attempt to break the Confederates south of the city. Hooker protested that his task was impossible, but the commanding general insisted on the advance, and orders for the 5th Corps to join the attack went out at about 3:00 PM.[17]

Col. Stockton's Brigade received their instructions about an hour later and moved across the pontoon bridges. The men of the 20th Maine were going into their first battle, and Lt. Col. Joshua Chamberlain recalled the scene as the 3rd Brigade crossed the Rappahannock: "The air was thick with flying, bursting shells; whooping solid shot swept lengthwise our narrow bridge, fortunately not yet ploughing a furrow through the midst of us, but driving the compressed air so close above our heads that there was an unconquerable instinct to shrink beneath it, although knowing it was then too late. The crowding, swerving column set the pontoons swaying, so that the horse and men could scarcely keep their balance." Entering Fredericksburg, the brigade moved to the west edge of the town. The day before, the frustrated, angry and to some extent malicious troops of Sumner's Corps had looted the town from the afternoon into the night. For hours, the Yankees had dragged the contents of Fredericksburg's homes into the streets and used it for their amusement. When the 83rd and the other regiments of Stockton's Brigade moved up, furniture, clothing, and all kinds of household goods was scattered all over the dark and deserted streets and Fredericksburg had an eerie look to it. As they reached Prince Edward Street, the last before the open slope began, Confederate artillery shells exploded in the air and in the fields just beyond the town, and the soldiers dropped their knapsacks and huddled against the houses for protection.[18]

The new surgeon of the 83rd, Dr.

IX. Mournful Cries in the Stillness of the Night

James P. Burchfield, observed the battle from a house commandeered for use as a hospital, and wrote; "While I was standing in the yard of a large house which had been taken for a hospital a shell came and struck near the root of a tree not more than 3 feet from me, I was a little frightened I tell you...." The bombardment went on for about an hour and as Burchfield continued, "The shells flew thick and fast ..." and exploded in the air, fell in the streets, or hit in the fields on the other side of the houses and threw great clouds of dirt on the soldiers. The men wore heavy wool overcoats but were wet with perspiration, and many shivered as they hugged the cold walls of Fredericksburg's homes during the shelling. Col. Vincent stood conspicuously in one of the streets with his sword in one hand, defying the enemy gunners with what Judson recalled was "a high and chivalrous sense of duty."[19]

As the day wore on, the divisions and brigades of the 5th Corps went into the battle in a series of piecemeal assaults or to relieve other units that were trapped on the hillside. Though his formations had consistently been shattered by concentrated Rebel fire, Burnside was sending in the 5th Corps based on the belief that a forceful assault could break the enemy line. This was similar to the mistake that Gen. John Pope had made at Manassas the previous August, when the latter general ordered attacks under the impression that the Confederates were about to retreat. Burnside had not been at Manassas to learn Pope's lesson. But at Antietam in September, less than a thousand fortified Georgians held up Burnside's Corps for hours and he should have known the difficulties of dislodging entrenched defenders by frontal assaults. Massed attacks over open ground were feasible in the era of inaccurate smoothbore muskets, but that day had passed. Infantry with rifles that fired the Minié bullet could destroy formations at ranges beyond 300 yards, and when entrenched and combined with artillery, such a force was nearly impossible to close with. By the late afternoon sixteen brigades had charged the stone wall and none had been able to break the Confederate line. Blue-coated dead and wounded blanketed the slope in front of Marye's Heights.

Col. Stockton reported that it was "just before sundown" when his brigade received orders to attack. An officer of the 44th later wrote, "It is doubtful if a single person in the Brigade indulged the hope that any real success could be obtained in making the movement." Whether the soldiers were reluctant or not, the bugle call for the advance cut through the sounds of exploding shells, and the regiments left the protection of the houses and fell into formation.[21]

Before the battle, the Rebel artillerymen had precisely measured the ranges to the streets where the Yankees were likely to emerge. As the 3rd Brigade came out from behind the buildings and into the open fields, the gunners zeroed in on the blue columns. Shells crashed into the ranks with increasing volume and accuracy. With his sword still in hand, Col. Vincent moved out in front of the regiment, commanded, "Forward 83rd!" and the troops pushed through the fire. Another officer of the brigade, Maj. Edward Hill, recalled their exit from Fredericksburg as "terror-inspiring." Soldiers in every regiment fell with each shell burst, but the brigade moved forward in column behind a skirmish line from Brady's Michigan Sharpshooters. The 17th New York took the lead, followed by the 12th New York, 20th Maine, 44th, 83rd, and the 16th Michigan last.[22]

Ahead of the soldiers, barely visible in the gray winter twilight and thick gunpowder smoke, was a field that rose to a low ridge, dipped, and then continued up to Marye's Heights. Orange flashes from the mouths of cannon and muskets formed a line in the distance that marked the stone

Above and on next page: Two photographs that show Mayre's Heights from Fredericksburg. The 83rd attacked up this slope on December 13th and moved up Hanover Street, on the right, on the night of the 15th. (National Archives)

wall. Except for the unfinished railway bed, the partially filled millrace, some rail fences and a few scattered houses, the ground was completely bereft of cover.[23]

Confederate field artillery from batteries on Marye's Heights, directly in front of Stockton's Brigade, and long-range guns on the hills southwest of Fredericksburg dropped shells on the Yankees from two directions as they started up the slope. The fences and houses broke up the advancing formation and the regiments lingered at the base of the hill as they adjusted their lines after each obstacle. The brigade's column formation subjected them to what Amos Judson remembered as "murderous artillery fire." When it reached open ground Stockton formed a line of battle with the 83rd in the center of the front rank, the 44th on their right and the 16th Michigan to the left. The 20th Maine and 12th and 17th New York made up the 2nd rank. Stockton indicated a small white house on the slope as the 83rd's objective to Col. Vincent, and the line went forward.

As the 83rd advanced it crossed the unfinished railroad bed, which was crowded with troops from the 10th New Hampshire taking shelter from the fire. Vincent's two companies on the far right of the line of battle were forced to walk through and over the men that were lying in the cut and the process caused them to slow and fall behind. The colonel halted the regiment on the far side of the railway bed as the companies caught up and advanced again, but the rest of the brigade had negotiated the flooded mill race and emerged soaked and out of alignment. Moving the regiment to the right, Vincent regained contact with the brigade and kept moving up the slope towards the first ridge. The remnants of earlier attacks littered the ground and the men of the 83rd grimly stepped over scattered equipment, severed limbs, the wounded and the dead.[24]

Ahead of the 83rd, three Confederate

brigades were in position and waiting behind the stone wall. The first ridge had shielded Stockton's Federals from some of the enemy guns, but as the troops came over the crest, the Rebels leveled their muskets and fired. The Confederates stood behind their wall in three ranks, and had enough men to continuously re-load muskets, pass them to the front, and fire much faster than the attacking Yankees. The 83rd immediately shot back, but the Rebel volleys were so effective that Col. Vincent reported: "The storm of shot and shell and musketry that now poured into us was exceedingly destructive. The enemy's guns completely commanded this ridge and its front slope. Officers and men fell rapidly, but there was not a waver of the line."[25]

With musket fire pelting the men from the front and artillery raining in from the left, Vincent wheeled the 83rd to the right towards the white house that Griffin had designated as their objective. The regiment halted at the base of the second ridge, the stone wall only a few dozen yards in front of them. The regiment's position below the hill provided some protection, and Amos Judson recalled, "For nearly an hour we laid close upon the ground and gazed upon the fiery messengers of death screaming over...."[26]

Lines of Union soldiers from the day's attacks lay all over the slope, intermixed and overlapping each other; some still fired at targets unseen in the night. Unidentified muzzle flashes flared all around the regiment. The situation would have been confusing for a veteran officer, and must have been even more difficult for Vincent, who was only in his second battle. Although the colonel took considerable steps to avoid mishaps, the regiment accidentally fired into the rear of the 9th New York, who were ahead of them on the slope and about ten yards short of the stone wall. Unable to see any targets, Vincent ordered the regiment to hold their fire to conserve ammunition.[27]

Full darkness fell and provided some concealment, but the Union troops were still within yards of the Confederates who fired at anything they perceived moving on the slope. Pinned down, retreat or relief was impossible. Whole divisions of men who had

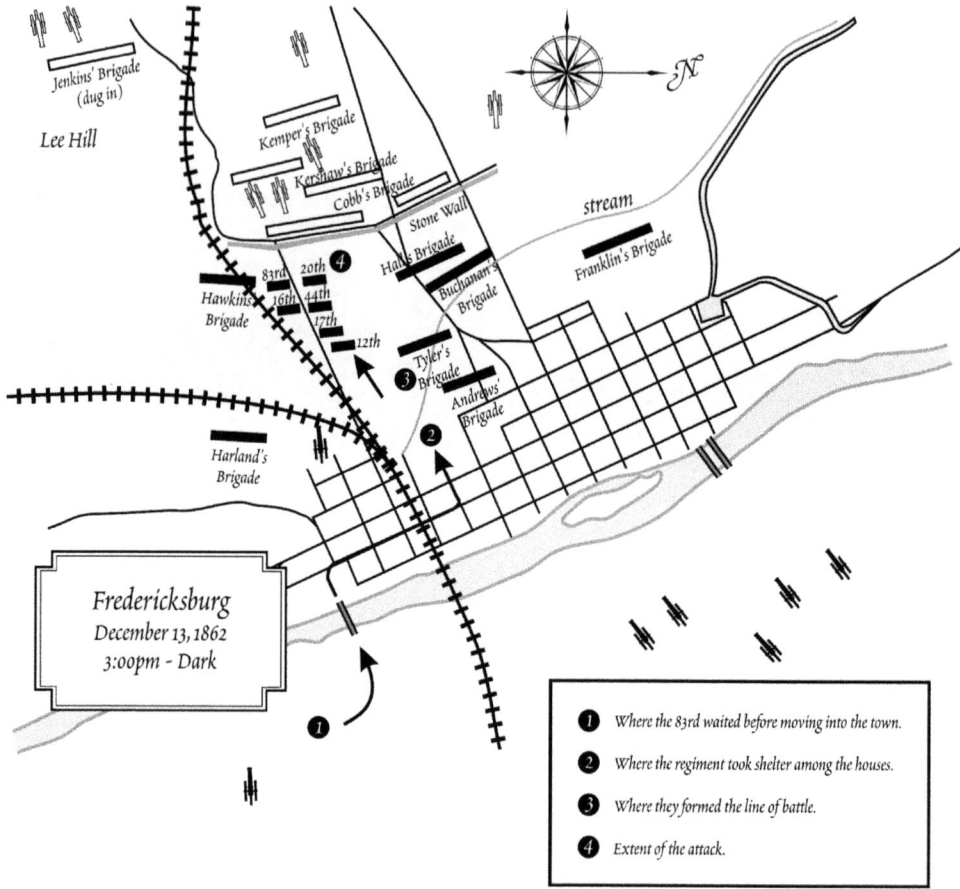

The late afternoon in front of Marye's Heights at Fredericksburg. (Adapted from a map by Frank O'Reilly and John Dove, 1997.)

attacked that day were trapped on the hill. Like them, the soldiers of the 3rd Brigade simply lay low on the slope. The Rebel fire ebbed away but temperatures had dropped after the sun went down and a bitter north wind blew along the slope. Wounded Northerners lay all over the hillside and as the anesthesia of shock wore off, the terrible pain, thirst, and cold set in. Amos Judson remembered, "Shortly after we had ceased firing, the cries of the wounded began to assail our ears. They had lain upon the field all day, and now their agonizing cries for help broke mournfully upon the stillness of the night." Probably because Vincent had called off their attack before a prolonged firefight with the Rebel infantry, only five of the 83rd had been killed. But there were thirty-two wounded, and their voices became part of the woeful chorus.[28]

All the Federal attacks of the day had been repulsed with heavy losses, but Gen. Burnside was determined to push the Rebels off Marye's Heights the next day. Gen. Griffin came to the line that night and told Col. Stockton that the 9th Corps was scheduled to continue the attack the next morning, and that the 1st Division was to hold their position on the slope until then. Wagons quietly delivered more ammunition, then just as quietly took away some of the 3rd Brigade's casualties.[29]

Those soldiers that stayed on the hillside had no choice but to remain lying in their ranks. Temperatures were near freezing. A cold wind and uniforms wet with perspiration made sleep difficult or impossible. Fires would have drawn enemy fire, and the soldiers' blankets had been left in their knapsacks in Fredericksburg. Each man made do as best they could, but it was a bitterly cold, miserable night for all on the slope on Marye's Heights.[30]

Thick fog in the early morning initially hid the men, but when it lifted the Confederate infantry resumed its fire and kept the soldiers pinned down. Any man that moved was a target, as Judson recalled: "The moment a head appeared above the brow of the hill, a dozen bullets came whizzing after it."[31]

Gen. Burnside also rose with the dawn and prepared to resume the attack, but senior generals convinced him of the futility of the effort. At first Burnside announced that he would lead his own 9th Corps in a charge on the enemy line, but the other generals convinced him that it would be a pointless gesture. He retired to his tent, despondent over the loss of life at his direction, and ordered the evacuation of Fredericksburg.[32]

The general's decision had little immediate effect on the men of the 83rd, who held their position while the appointed hour of the expected attack came and went with no action. As the Federal troops in Fredericksburg began pulling out in mid-morning, Vincent's men used the only tools they had—their tin plates and bayonets—to dig shallow breastworks. With some wood added from a nearby broken fence, the men were able to raise enough protection to move around at a crawl. Amos Judson recalled that the Confederates kept up a sporadic bombardment, but, "Their shots generally struck the brow of the hill and ricocheted off to the rear and exploded without effect." Although their second day on the slope was not as deadly as the first, Col. Stockton reported,

"The din of battle, the charge, and contest try most men's nerves, but that is nothing to what it is to be compelled to lie all day, scarcely sheltered at all, exposed to the shells and musketry of an ever-watchful enemy." Stockton also wrote that through all the trials of the day, he "saw no signs of fear in either officers or men. Each and all performed their duty well and promptly."[33]

A few troops volunteered to run back into Fredericksburg in pairs to fill canteens for the wounded, but Confederate sharpshooters in a small brick house on the slope tried to pick them off as they crossed the open field. Amos Judson recalled that the Yankees followed a shallow ditch back to town, which kept them nearly out of sight. "Our men, who were accustomed to be shot at and missed," wrote Judson, "dreaded running this gauntlet but little more than school boys dread to run the gauntlet of as many snowballs." The Pennsylvanians roared with laughter at each trip. Except for that, the only activity of the day was when a Confederate squad moved into some woods about 400 yards off the left flank of the regiment in an effort to fire lengthwise down the Yankee line. Vincent's men spotted them, fired, and the Rebels retreated to their own lines. The brigade still held its position when the sun went down. Col. Vincent took advantage of the darkness to bury the regiment's dead on the hillside.[34]*

At about 11:00 PM instructions to withdraw to Fredericksburg finally reached the 83rd, and the soldiers passed the orders along in whispers. The 3rd Brigade moved back down the slope the same way they had come up. The debris of the previous day's assaults covered the ground, and the men quietly picked their way among discarded equipment, destroyed gun carriages, and unburied dead. Reaching the town, the regiments bivouacked on the cold brick sidewalks of Caroline Street. Twice during the

---

*Vincent reported that the regiment lost 5 killed, 32 wounded at Fredericksburg.

night the troops were awakened to meet an expected attack and they had little sleep. When morning of December 15 came, the men rose cold, tired, and hungry, but marginally safer than they had been in the past two days. Breakfast that morning was cooked on the barren street.[35]

Federal soldiers had been plundering Fredericksburg since they entered it three days earlier. Even as the army withdrew, the town was still full of Union troops that waited for their orders. Hundreds continued looting the abandoned houses and shops and the activity infected soldiers all over the town. Amos Judson recalled, "Orders had been issued the day before to prevent all pillaging; but to strictly enforce such an order during the process of an engagement is impossible. Some of the 83rd went somewhere, got flour and commenced cooking pancakes in the streets.... Every body got something.... I saw several literary vandals pile up a large trunk full of books with which they intended to solace themselves during the leisure hours of winter quarters; but being in lack of transportation they were obliged to leave them. The day was spent in curiosity hunting by some, and in a sort of jollifiication by others till towards evening ...." Oliver Norton observed, "The streets were filled with a confusion of all things, splendid furniture and carpets, provisions, bottles, knapsacks, dead men and horses, blankets, muskets, the pomp of war and paraphernalia of peace mingled together. Men were ransacking every house." The reasons for the sacking of Fredericksburg have been the subject of much debate, but no single cause has been pinpointed. It is possible that the army's continuous losses and the pointless attacks on Marye's Heights brought morale to new lows and that the soldiers vented their frustrations on the defenseless town. No matter what their motivations, the looting of December 15 reached levels never before seen in the Army of the Potomac. It was a black mark on otherwise honorable soldiers. The men of the 83rd considered themselves a unit of high discipline, but if Judson's and Norton's accounts are true, the Pennsylvanians were as guilty as other soldiers were. And though the looting occurred in front of them, neither Oliver Norton nor Amos Judson showed any remorse for the soldiers' deprivations in their descriptions of it. The events do not even appear in Vincent's, Stockton's, Griffin's or Butterfield's reports, though their troops clearly took part in them.[36]

That night the 4th and 5th Corps were assigned as the rear guard to defend Fredericksburg while the rest of the army withdrew across the Rappahannock. Col. Vincent took command of the 3rd Brigade that night after Stockton, who had suffered severe exposure the previous day, was evacuated. Fredericksburg was still crowded with soldiers and equipment moving toward the river, and when Vincent's troops formed their ranks that evening, many thought their turn for evacuation had come. The evening was cold and windy, and freezing rain and sleet began as the 3rd Brigade marched against the tide of soldiers that headed to the bridges. They arrived at the northwest corner of the town at around midnight. Newspaperman Amos Judson noted that the 83rd occupied the former residence of a local newspaper editor while they waited for orders on their mission.[37]

Having now taken three positions in as many days, the men of the 83rd were even more confused than usual about their activity. Rumors spread that the army was pulling out, a concept supported by the troops they just passed moving towards the river. Some soldiers expected to leave Fredericksburg that night. Unfortunately, the 3rd Brigade's task to defend the town required them to move back up the slope of Marye's Heights in the darkness and hold their old position until the army was safely away. Judson recalled the soldiers' reaction: "What, then was our disappointment on finding that, instead of heading for the river, we were again heading for the front!"

Col. Vincent took his tired and dejected command out through the west side of town and back up to the slope where they had charged two days earlier. In some ways, their second trip up to the heights was as dispiriting and dangerous as the first. Confederate infantry still held the stone wall and would cut up any Federals on the hillside, so the column moved in silence to avoid detection. Moonlight illuminated the wreckage of battle that covered the ground. At one point, some men saw a line of blue-clad troops lying on their arms and asked them their unit in low whispers. No reply came, and the soldiers moved closer and realized that they had hailed lines of dead men, lying in neat rows and frozen stiff. They rolled them aside and continued on. When the brigade reached their position of the previous day they relieved a brigade of the 2nd Corps and sent out a picket line. The rest of the soldiers lay down on the ground and spoke in whispers if at all. Judson recalled, "Ugh! But wasn't it dismal out there this time? ... so gloomy were the associations connected with that slaughter-pen that I think I can safely say, that every soldier in the army was more anxious to get out of it as soon as he could."[38]

The 5th Corps finally received orders to withdraw across the river in the early morning. With more whispered commands, the soldiers rose and went into line to move back down the hill. With most of the army gone the brigade was especially vulnerable to attack or capture as it withdrew. Stealth was more important than ever. As the men got up to form ranks, clouds obscured the moon and provided a protective cover of darkness. Col. Vincent quickly ordered the brigade to move, and there was only the sound of rattling tin cups and equipment as they headed for Fredericksburg.[39]

The rest of the army had not completed pulling out, and Vincent formed the brigade in a line of battle on the west edge of the town to maintain their guard. A few stray shots from the Rebel lines cut the night air, probably fired by nervous sentries who detected some movement on the hillside. Judson recalled that the only other sound was that of a bloodhound baying, "as if he, too, had been set upon our tracks." A cold winter wind blew in more clouds and freezing rain, and for two more hours Vincent's men stood in their line as the army finished the withdrawal.[40]

The corps began pulling back to the river when there were no other troops left in the town except the provost guard patrolling for stragglers. At about daylight on Monday, December 16, Vincent's Brigade crossed back over the Rappahannock, one of the last units to leave Fredericksburg. Another cold rain fell as they reached the far side of the river, and Judson remembered; "The men were worn out from watching and fasting and were seemingly indifferent to the changes of fortune; yet it was easy to see that a gleam of satisfaction lighted up their weather-beaten countenances. And as for myself, I am free to confess that the moment I touched the earth I drew a long, strong and soul-reviving breath, and, from the bottom of my heart, thanked God that I had lived to get out of that infernal slaughter pen, and was once more safely landed on the other side of Jordan."[41]

The Confederates warily moved back into Fredericksburg when the fog lifted and they discovered that the Federals were gone. The Union army stayed in camps on Stafford Heights for the next three days. Over 12,600 soldiers had been killed, wounded, or were missing, sixty percent of them had fallen before the sunken road. Daniel Foote was still in a hospital in Virginia that filled up with the wounded in the days after the battle. He wrote to Julia; "Four men are just passing with a dead man for the dead house. He was able to walk around this morning. Disease Typhoid fever. Such is life."[42]

The Tempest and Whirlwind of Battle

As if paralyzed by defeat, the Army of the Potomac went back into the same camps it had occupied before the battle of Fredericksburg. The 83rd moved into the rough tents and huts that they had erected at Stoneman's Station, and with little indication of any action soon, prepared to stay the winter.

The battle of Fredericksburg was one of the most lopsided Southern victories of the war, and gloom permeated the Union. Burnside accepted full responsibility for the debacle and offered his resignation. The President sent a spiriting letter to the army with congratulations on what small gains that could be gleaned from the battle, but the message did little to console the veteran soldiers who knew that they had been beaten. The 83rd's casualties were not as severe as their previous battles, but the soldiers spent their 2nd Christmas of the war despondent over the defeats of the late summer and winter. Oliver Norton wrote to his sister soon after reaching his quarters; "We have had a terrible fight, but you have heard of that, and I need not give particulars. I don't feel like it, for it was nothing but humiliating defeat.... You may think I am talking bitterly. Well, I feel so. I'm sick of such useless slaughter."[1]

In addition to the soldiers, some of the army's generals complained openly about Burnside's incompetence. But Burnside's acceptance of responsibility was a far cry from the excuses offered by McClellan and Pope, and despite the objections of some senior officers and cabinet members, Lincoln left him in command.

Eager to vindicate himself and the army, Burnside developed another plan to take the army ten miles northwest, cross the Rappahannock at the United States Ford, and outflank the Confederates, who remained on the river's west bank. The offensive began on January 20, but as if ordered by the Rebels, a cold rain began just after dark and went on all night. The march and the downpour continued in the morning and the soldiers, horses, wagons, and cannon churned the roads into mud pits worse than any the soldiers had seen. Oliver Norton wrote home, "It beat all the Peninsula mud I ever saw ...." One officer of the 5th Corps wrote, "Indeed, a statement of the awful condition of the roads might exhaust all the adjectives in the English language and yet not exaggerate the actual condition of things."[2]

It was nearly impossible for infantrymen to march through the knee-deep muck in the freezing rain with soaked overcoats and equipment. The columns slowed, then stopped. Confederates on the opposite bank of the Rappahannock watched their coun-

150

terparts with great interest, and as the Union army ground to a halt, the Rebels yelled taunts at the Yankee pickets or put up signs that said "Stuck in the mud" or "This way to Richmond." Three days after setting out, Burnside realized that further movement was impossible and canceled the operation. The general's second attempt to defeat the Confederates would go down in history as "The Mud March" but Amos Judson termed it "The Great Katabasis," as he explained: "[The Greek word] Anabasis means an expedition into the up-country, or a *going up*; so, Katabasis means an expedition into the down-country, or a *going down*. And whether it is applied to an army going down to Richmond, or down into the bowels of the earth, the word is entirely appropriate in either case." The troops returned to their camps, and Gen. Burnside resigned.[3]

Back at Stoneman's Station, the men of the 83rd laid out their area with much of the same care that they had at Hall's Hill, but these winter quarters were considerably less comfortable than the camp of the previous year. The regiment officially owned roomy French tents, but no soldiers mentioned their presence on campaign. Instead, the Pennsylvanians built the more common winter quarters of huts made of log walls, four or five high, roofed with shelter tents or ponchos joined together, and a mud and stick fireplace at one end. Two or three soldiers stayed in each hut. Though the fireplaces often smoked and the roofs were not always completely weather proof, the huts were comfortable for men who had spent ten months on campaign.*

The winter of 1862-63 was cold and snow fell often. Except for some limited picket and guard duty, there was little activity through the snowy months. Living conditions worsened with the weather. Washing was irregular, and gray-back lice, a scourge of soldiers of both sides, bred in the soldiers' dirty clothes. Norton wrote of them that winter, "They grow to enormous size and are the most cunning and most impudent of all things that live.... I woke up the other night and found a regiment of them going through the manual of arms on my back. Just as I woke the colonel gave the command 'charge bayonets,' and the way they let drive at my sirloin was a proof of their capacity." Fresh rations were also scarce. Food was normally available from the sutlers, but Stockton's Brigade had not been paid for six months, and as Norton also noted, "The sutler won't come where there is no money, and of course we can't buy anything." At the end of December he had written home on some of his last few sheets of stationary, and lamented that pens, pencils, stamps, and ink—writing materials that are essential to the letters that can sustain a soldier's spirit—were in short supply.[4]

As it had at Hall's Hill, camp disease raged in the cramped and poorly ventilated quarters. The 83rd reported an aggregate strength of 715 soldiers in January 1863, but out of that number 256 were in the hospital with disease and another 40 sick men were still in the ranks. Thirty-five soldiers were discharged that month from wounds or sickness and four died from disease. The situation was much the same throughout the army, and the combination of the bitter weather and miserable conditions were so bad that the winter outside Fredericksburg would become known as "The Valley Forge of the Union Army."[5]

The soldiers' spirits plummeted. Desertion—always an indicator of low morale—was on the rise. The first desertions the 83rd ever suffered did not occur until November 1862, when two soldiers ran off.

---

*The 83rd's quarters are mentioned in Norton's letters of December 6, 1862, and Foote's letter to Julia Hill of February 23, 1863. The huts were a common type of winter quarters for the Army of the Potomac.

Union huts on the Rappahannock over the winter of 1862–63. The 83rd stayed in huts of similar construction. (LOC)

Perhaps spurred by the horrors of Fredericksburg, twenty-one men deserted in December, six left in January, and 23 bolted in February. January also saw one soldier in Capt. George Stowe's Company G charged with avoiding work details and acting "loud and boisterous" one evening, and another for striking Stowe when the captain attempted to enforce the soldier's attendance at duty. A court-martial found both men guilty of the charges and sentenced the requisite punishment.[6]*

Pvt. James Harris was in a hospital in Arlington, Virginia, known as "Camp Convalescent" and wrote home, "Under the treatment they receive here, soldiers have become mere brutes as it were. All the finer and nobler feelings of the man have lost sight of the brutal nature of a lower life; all, as if by some strange gravitating power are brought to one common level. Men who were the most honest and moral at home are brought down by the pressure of evil influence around them to the level of the beggar, the liar, and even thief." In contrast to the hero's welcome the soldiers received in Pennsylvania after the Peninsula Campaign, the men who returned in late 1862 or early 1863 may not have been welcomed as enthusiastically, as evidenced by the Erie *Weekly Gazette's* editorial on January 24: "The soldiers who return from the battlefield, crippled, diseased, and unfit for longer service, should be kindly dealt with by our people. Take them by the hand. Welcome them to their homes. Encourage them by cheerful words. Help them to good situations. Show by your acts that you truly appreciate their patriotism. We fear that there is too much neglect on this subject by

---

The regimental record of their courts-martial states that when Capt. Stowe ordered Pvt. Moses B. Hunter to keep the noise down, Hunter replied, "Commissioned officers can make as much noise as they choose when they get drunk, but privates are not allowed to fart." Hunter was also accused of dodging a work detail, was found guilty, and sentenced to police call for 12 consecutive days (Sundays excepted). Pvt. John Downing, who was found guilty of striking Stowe, was publicly reprimanded.

our citizens." Signs of demoralization were on the rise in the camps, hospitals, and at home.[7]

The task to build the army back into fighting shape was given to Maj. Gen. Joseph Hooker, whom President Lincoln appointed as Burnside's replacement at the end of January. Hooker was among the most popular generals of the Army of the Potomac. A West Point graduate, he fought the Seminoles and Cherokees, and was promoted for gallantry to lieutenant-colonel during the Mexican War. Hooker had resigned from the army, but garnered a brigadier's commission through political contacts and maneuvering soon after the war began. With blonde hair, clear blue eyes, a straightforward manner and a reputation for hard drinking, he became well known and had risen to command a division of the 3rd Corps in the Peninsula Campaign. He earned the nickname "Fighting Joe" at the Battle of Williamsburg in May 1862, and since then he had ably led his division on the Peninsula, commanded the 1st Corps in the worst of the fighting at Antietam, and the Right Grand Division at Fredericksburg. Hooker had been an outspoken critic of Burnside and the Lincoln administration, but he was a fighter, and the President put his trust in the profane, confident general for a badly needed Union victory.

An old soldier, Hooker took immediate steps to heal his army. The ration system was improved so the men received real bread (instead of old hardtack) four times a week and fresh vegetables twice a week. Aware of the army's living conditions, the general saw to it that camp sanitation was improved and the huts inspected to cut down on disease. Instead of allowing the men to sit idle, he ordered them out on en-

Maj. Gen. Joseph Hooker. (LOC)

gineering projects like road and bridge repair. To cut down on desertions, he established a liberal policy for furloughs (which Col. Vincent took full advantage of) and ensured the soldiers' back-pay was distributed.* Hooker also cleared away the remnants of Burnside when he scrapped the Grand Divisions and had corps commanders report to him through his new chief of staff, Gen. Butterfield. Maj. Gen. George Meade succeeded to command of the 5th Corps.

On the Peninsula, Hooker's fellow division commander in the 3rd Corps, Brig. Gen. Phil Kearney, had each of his men affix a square of red felt to the tops of their caps so they could be easily identified on the battlefield or on the march. Eventually known as the "Kearny Patch," the badges were hugely popular. Butterfield suggested expanding their use to improve unit esprit and aid identification of the wounded or stragglers. In mid–March each corps was assigned their own symbol to be cut from

---

*Since taking command of the 83rd, Col. Vincent had sent 28 men home on furlough in November, eight in December, and eight more in January. With Hooker's new policy, he sent ten men home in February, nine in March, and one in April. Amos Judson was one of the soldiers who took a medical furlough in January, when he was stricken with nephritis, an ailment of the kidneys.

cloth and stitched to the soldiers' caps. The 1st Division of each corps would be colored red, the 2nd Division white, and the 3rd Division blue. The 5th Corps' designation was the Maltese Cross, and as soldiers of the 3rd Brigade, 1st Division, the men of the 83rd fixed the red Maltese Cross symbols to their caps.[8]

By early spring the changes were taking effect. As Hooker ordered, the soldiers received their pay in February. In March the 83rd's sick list dropped to 150, none died from disease that month (although 48 men were discharged for disabilities), and desertions ceased. Col. Vincent made a concentrated effort to retrieve soldiers from unnecessary details or desertion. Even Lt. Israel Thickstun felt the heat of the colonel's efforts to rebuild the ranks. In March, Thickstun was up for promotion to captain, but the advancement required an endorsement from Vincent, his official regimental commander. After visiting the 83rd that month, Thickstun wrote home, "I was a little disappointed to find that the Col. had not sent for my commission. He is holding it from me until I shall be released from Signal duty.... I think I shall not make any further efforts to be returned to the regiment, and if I am not promoted I shall have him to thank." Col. Vincent may have discovered that there was a substantial difference between being a popular commander and a stern one. Thickstun stayed on Signal duty, but by the end of March there were 453 men in the ranks.[9]

Seth Waid was one of the men on authorized details who returned. Waid was passing a pleasant winter at his hospital in Philadelphia when in late January, an order came for all orderlies to return to their units. He wrote that when he departed the hospital that month, ladies and friends crowded the doors and windows to wave goodbye and it was "almost like leaving home." For a month Waid was kept at a replacement depot outside Washington called "Camp Distribution." He wrote of his delay, "It would suit me much better if I could be some where I could be more active Service for my country but I am on hand ready to go wherever and whenever sent, and if the US can afford to keep me here in idleness why I dont know as it is my fault." He did not reach the regiment until February 26, where he was happy to find two friends still in Company F. "I have been away from the company for one year," he wrote, "and ... what a change has been wrought in that time. I will not attempt to describe the difference in the company since a year ago but will leave that to be imagined and talked over by those who are lucky enough to go home."[10]

Another addition in the 83rd's camp was a beautiful new set of State Colors, the military version of the Stars and Stripes that every state issued to its regiments. The 83rd's first State Colors had been delivered at Hall's Hill and had flown in all of the regiment's campaigns. Worn by weather and rent by bullets and shell fragments, the flag was barely recognizable by the end of 1862. The previous November Col. Vincent wrote to the Pennsylvania Military Adjutant, "We have borne it through half a score of battles ... not without honor.... The remnant of which is left of its tattered silk and [shattered] lance proclaim the service it had seen." The request for a new flag was granted on the condition that the regiment return the old one, but Vincent wrote back, "You can easily understand how great a pride both the officers and men have grown to feel in the old color, which has so often victoriously waved over them in the fiercest of the fight—and believe they all love it the more because it is so sadly faded and riddled and torn.... Send us the new color, which we will carry side by side with the old." The new flag arrived sometime that spring.[11]

Morale throughout the army soared with Hooker's changes and the coming spring. Even with his continuing bouts of illness, Daniel Foote remained a resilient soldier. In December his family had apparently suggested he seek a medical discharge, but Foote could not (or would not) arrange the proper examination and wrote back to them, "You ask to much of me. Even if I could obtain a discharge it would not be my duty until I see whether I was ever going to be fit for duty again." In February he wrote again, "To receive a discharge by begging for it I would not do it. I am willing to use honorable means and none other." Though he had almost been killed at Gaines's Mill and spent months in the hospital with sickness, in late February he wrote Julia Hill, "My trust is in God. I think if there had not been more work for me to do there would of been a way for me to have got my discharge, therefore I am strong in the faith that I shall fully recover and do service for yet for a bleeding country who needs every man."[12]

Oliver Norton's family apparently also suggested that he seek a medical discharge. Though he fought in all the 83rd's battles and was wounded at Gaines's Mill, Norton still resisted the idea of a medical release. "I wouldn't take a discharge now if I could get it," he told them. "If I did want one, I fancy (pardon my vanity) I could play off on the doctors and get it, but I don't want it, and I would kick a man that would offer me one." In February, Norton was thrilled to be appointed color-bearer and bugler for Col. Vincent, who was the Brigade Commander while Col. Stockton recovered from the sickness he developed at Fredericksburg.[13]

In mid–March, Daniel Foote wrote, "All I know about Gen. Hooker is good.... He certainly has got the army under much better discipline than it was." Israel Thickstun echoed, "The army is getting stronger every day and is under stricter discipline than ever before and a feeling of confidence is growing rapidly." The army's celebration of St. Patrick's Day on March 17 seemed to confirm their new springtime vigor. In every

Top: Strong Vincent, photographed in Erie as Colonel of the 83rd in 1862. (Irwin Rider)
Bottom: Lt. John C. Vanetta of the 83rd, wearing a metal 5th Corps Badge. (USAMHI, Wendell Lang Collection)

camp there were sack races, pig chases, Irish music, all fueled by rations of whiskey and rum. A steeplechase where the soldier-riders wore full silk jockey dress and boots was the day's central event, and even Gen. Hooker served as one of the judges along with Gen. Meagher, commander of the 2nd Corps' famous "Irish Brigade." Foote wrote to Julia Hill the next day: "The Irish regiments had grand times yesterday around here, it being St. Patrick's day. In the morning they drank rum, [had] horse races and enjoyed themselves generally and in many cases laying dead drunk all night. The 9th R. Mass. Vol. had two men and two horses killed dead. The horses probably the greater loss."[14]

In the same letter, Foote optimistically related a camp rumor about an old farmer near Fredericksburg who owned a well that dried up three months before each of America's wars and ran again three months before they ended. As the story went, this fabled well had dried up three months before the firing on Ft. Sumter, and Foote wrote, "A short time ago it commenced to run. The old man they say is willing to bet his property that we will have peace in three months." In contrast, Col. Vincent wrote to his wife, "We must fight [the Confederates] more vindictively, or we shall be foiled at every step. We must desolate the country as we pass through it, and not leave the trace of doubtful friend or foe behind us; make them believe that we are in earnest; terribly in earnest; that to break this band in twain is monstrous and impossible; that the life of every man, yea, of every weak woman or helpless child in the entire South, is of no value whatever compared with the integrity of the Union." Having missed much of the horrors of the Peninsula and Bull Run campaigns, Vincent may not have dreaded more combat as much as his soldiers. Still, his assessment of the war's course was more realistic than Foote's, and his energy and devotion to the Union cause seem to justify Amos Judson's remembrance that the men of the 83rd emerged from their winter quarters, "robust, well-rested, and

Sketch by Edwin Forbes of St. Patrick's Day in the Army of the Potomac, 1863. (LOC)

X. The Tempest and Whirlwind of Battle 157

Top Left: The regimental colors of the 83rd. (Pennsylvania State Preservation Committee)

Top Right: The 83rd's State Colors. This was the third flag issued to the regiment. The 83rd received it in 1865 and it is unlikely that it ever saw combat. (Pennsylvania State Preservation Committee)

Bottom: The pennant of the 3rd Brigade, 1st Division, 5th Army Corps.

ready for any surprise that [Hooker] might ask of them." Company G's 1st Sergeant, Thomas Van Giesen, had been promoted to 2nd Lieutenant at the end of December and wrote his sister on April 10: "It is warm as summer & the mud is drying up very fast and I expect Gen. Hooker will soon give the word forward but still there isent no signs of moving yet."[15]

By the time Van Giesen wrote those lines, the Army of the Potomac had grown to over 130,000 soldiers, and President Lincoln was eager for a new offensive. Gen. Lee's 60,000-man army was stretched thinly from Fredericksburg to Port Royal, twenty-five miles southwest. Hooker planned to attack at Fredericksburg with the 1st and 6th Corps to pin the Confederates down while the 5th, 11th, and 12th Corps went twenty miles northwest, crossed Rappahannock at Kelly's Ford, then turned southeast to cross the Rapidan River and strike the Rebels' flank or force them to retreat. Lincoln promptly approved the plan.[16]

Early on the morning of April 27, the three infantry corps received their orders to march in what Judson called the "annual movement towards Richmond." By midmorning the 83rd was on the road and headed northwest. A dejected Oliver Norton, whose detail at Brigade Headquarters had ended earlier that month, marched with them. He had written his sister a week before the movement, "I am returned to the regiment. Colonel Vincent could not be satisfied to let me stay when I had a good berth, but insisted on my coming back. My

Color Sergeant Alexander Rogers holds the 83rd's first set of state colors in 1863. The tattered condition of the flag led Col. Vincent to request a new flag from Pennsylvania in the spring of 1863. Capt. Amos Judson presented this flag to the city of Erie after the battle of Gettysburg. Its remnants are now on display in the Erie County Historical Society. (Ronn Palm)

reward for strict attention to duty is this, retrograde promotion." Col. Vincent's term as Acting Brigade Commander had ended in March, and when he returned to the 83rd he had found the regimental bugler unsatisfactory. The colonel wrote to an officer on the Brigade Staff on March 24, "[The bugler] has grown authoritative ... and is no longer fit to do what he attempts. As there are a number of other buglers in the other regiments of the Brigade better than Norton.... I respectfully submit that ... the detail for that duty be taken from another regiment." Norton was soon packed off to re-join the 83rd, where he found parting with the comforts of the Brigade Headquarters a bitter pill to swallow. He went on, "Coming back to the regiment seems almost like leaving the comforts of a home and enlisting again. I did not realize half the privileges I did enjoy till I came to be deprived of them."[17]

Temperatures were mild when the army began its march on April 27 and humidity kept the dust down on the roads. A chilly rain began that evening but Gen. Meade's 5th Corps covered eight miles the first day and fifteen miles the next. On the morning of April 29 they crossed the Rappahannock without mishap and pressed on nine more miles to Ely's Ford on the Rapidan River. There the river was high and swift from spring rains, and the men waded across in water up to their arms. Keeping up their pace, they marched five miles on April 30. That afternoon Griffin's Division led the 5th Corps into the crossroads hamlet of Chancellorsville. The 11th and 12th Corps were not far behind Meade's column, and Gen. Couch's 2nd Corps was also crossing the river. Scattered Confederate brigades of Gen. A. P. Hill's Division skirmished with the Federals along the route, but fell back. Daniel Foote wrote home that the 83rd passed through a Rebel camp that had been so hastily evacuated that "their tents were left pitched and sick were in them." Over 50,000 Union soldiers covered nearly 40 miles in four days.[18]*

The rear of Lee's army at Fredericksburg was only eleven miles from the Federal formations at Chancellorsville, and Gen. Hooker had brilliantly led one of the most daring marches of the war.

Gen. Lee expected a Federal offensive. By the evening of April 30 he ascertained the direction of Hooker's attack. He ordered Gen. Jackson's four-division corps to move west against the Federals while a skeletal force held Fredericksburg. The Union advance to the east continued the next morning, but as the 12th Corps went forward it clashed with the Jackson's lead elements. Although the Yankees pushed the Confederates back, Hooker ordered his corps to pull back to Chancellorsville and prepare a defensive line.[19]

North of the 12th Corps' fight, the 5th Corps had also continued their advance northeast from Chancellorsville on the River Road. The 83rd had marched about eight miles by the time the orders to move back to the crossroads reached them in the late afternoon. At dusk, the 83rd followed the 17th New York along a winding path through the thick, second growth woods toward their assigned portion on the line. Visibility in some portions of this area, known to locals as "the Wilderness," was often limited to a few feet, and at some point of the march the New Yorkers took the wrong road. Confusion mounted as the regiments passed through a small forest fire and reached a climax when Rebel artillery shells unexpectedly exploded among the ranks. Seth Waid, who was seeing his first action, wrote in his diary, "We left double quick. For a few minutes the shell fell around us pretty fast." Col. Vincent eventually found Gen. Griffin, who sent a guide to lead the regiments back onto the right path. That night they bivouacked on the road with the intent of rejoining the 3rd Brigade the next morning.[20]

At about the same time that the 83rd groped its way through the woods, Generals Lee and Jackson finalized their plans to blunt Hooker's offensive. To overcome the Union strength in numbers, Lee decided to pin down Hooker's front with limited attacks while Jackson's Corps made a wide march around to the west to hit the Union line on its exposed flank. The attack was scheduled for the next afternoon.

Col. Vincent woke his men early on May 2 and moved the 83rd down the Mineral Spring Road until they found Griffin's Division. By the time the regiment arrived, all the Union corps had pulled back their troops and were set in the semi-circular defense around the crossroads. Meade's 5th Corps and the 2nd Corps faced east and Slocum's 12th Corps fronted toward the south. The 3rd Corps extended to the south and Maj. Gen. O.O. Howard's 11th Corps was about two miles west of Chancellorsville on the Orange Plank Road. Many of Howard's troops were German immigrants who had joined to serve with their countryman Maj. Gen. Franz Sigel, and their catch phrase was "I fights mit Sigel." Joining with the 2nd Corps, Griffin's Division formed the right of the 5th Corps and was busy preparing breastworks as the 83rd arrived that morning. As soon as the Pennsylvanians assumed their position with the 3rd Brigade, axes, picks, and shovels were issued and Vincent's men began digging their own works. Two artillery sections (usually two guns each) strengthened the regiment's line, and by the afternoon the soldiers had prepared what Vincent reported as "an impregnable position."[21]

---

*The incident gave more evidence that some of the 83rd had brought parts of their Zouave uniforms to the Peninsula. Foote stated that he came across "a good many old French knapsacks" in the camp, and Oliver Norton also wrote that a deserted Rebel camp (probably the same one) had "some of the French knapsacks and muskets we lost at Gaines' Mill."

Similar efforts had taken place all along the Union line and for most of the day the Confederates were barely seen or heard. That afternoon many Federal soldiers were preparing dinner and lounging behind their works when the relaxing air was split with the sounds of firing and the Rebel yell. Jackson's Corps had succeeded in making its wide flank march and had crashed into the open flank of the 11th Corps. Caught completely off guard, the Union troops recovered and fought back, but were overpowered by the Southerners' momentum. For five hours, Jackson's troops pressed their attack. Spoiling attacks on the Union line by Maj. Gen. Lafayette McLaws' Division held the 5th and 2nd Corps in place. The Federal 11th and 3rd Corps counterattacked against Jackson but took terrible casualties. By night the troops had given up two miles of ground and Hooker's line was bent back on itself like a hairpin.[22]

As the 11th Corps retreated, the battle lines closed to within a mile of the rear of Griffin's Division, close enough for Vincent's men to see and hear much of the action. Daniel Foote wrote, "For three hours there was as terrible a battle raged as ever a man heard…. At times there would be a lull in the storm, then you could hear the groans and shrieks of the wounded." Oliver Norton, who had ably described the worst battles before, wrote to his sister, "You must imagine the scene—I cannot describe it. The roar was unearthly; there is no better word for it. I shudder at the slaughter." Except for their skirmishers that sparred with McLaws' troops, the men of the 83rd had been relegated to the role of spectator.[23]

Darkness brought the battle to a close. By the end of May 2 Gen. Hooker had surrendered the initiative in his campaign, been surprised, and lost thousands of men, but fate delivered one gift to the Union cause that night. As Stonewall Jackson scouted ahead of his line for the next day's route of attack, nervous Confederate soldiers fired on his party thinking it was Federal cavalry and mortally wounded him. Had they been aware of it, the men of the 83rd would probably have taken some satisfaction in the knowledge that it had been Lane's North Carolina Brigade, their opponents at Hanover Court House, that had mistakenly killed one of the world's most gifted military commanders and committed a blunder from which they would never recover.[24]

The next morning Hooker adjusted his lines to front all the corps west towards the expected attack. The 5th Corps shifted their position to one that ran along the Little Hunting Run and joined with the 1st Corps to the north. The battered troops of the 11th Corps took over their trenches on the Mineral Spring Road as they moved out. Many soldiers derided the German regiments for their surprise and rout of the previous night, and Daniel Foote made fun of their previously popular phrase: "The Dutchmen in the 11th Corps said the morning they took our place that 'they fights mit Sigel and runs mit Howard.'"[25]

The 83rd built more breastworks on their new line, and the Confederates pressed their attack from the west. Gen. Meade requested permission to attack the Rebel flank, but Hooker, dazed from a wound suffered earlier in the day, denied permission. Later that day "Fighting Joe" called his generals together and announced that he was passing command to Gen. Couch and that the army would withdraw to a defensive line around the fords on the Rappahannock. Again Vincent's skirmishers traded shots with their Rebel counterparts throughout the day and the regiment took no greater part in the fighting.[26]

Monday, May 4, found six corps of the Army of the Potomac dug in to a "U" shaped perimeter with its open end toward the Rappahannock. The 5th Corps held the round end and faced southwest, with the 1st Corps on their right and the 3rd to the left.

North of the Rappahannock, thousands of wounded Union soldiers made their way toward hospitals in Falmouth and crowded the roads that led away from the battlefield. One soldier from the 83rd, who had been on detached service, was moving up from Stoneman's Station that day bound for the regiment and remembered, "The road was literally lined with wounded, returning from the battle-field of Chancellorsville; ambulances were loaded, baggage wagons were filled; some were on horses, many on foot, with faces black and daubed with blood just from the firey furnace of battle, some with broken legs had cut off the crotched branches of trees and using them for crutches were hobbling along, some had made up fires along the roads and were cooking a cup of coffee to revive their exhausted spirits." As in the days before, the 83rd's action that day was limited to some shelling and picket fire.[27]

The armies faced each other for two more days, but by May 5 Hooker admitted defeat and ordered the army back across the Rappahannock. Rain came that evening and covered the retreat. As the army's rearguard, the 5th Corps waited through the night and slowly pulled their lines in to cover the fords as the infantry corps crossed. Confederate skirmishers followed warily but Union pickets held them off. Many of Gen. Meade's troops knew that they had barely been engaged in the battle and wondered why the sudden retreat was ordered, as Oliver Norton wrote, "To say we were surprised would give but a feeble idea of our feelings." Confused or not, the 83rd headed for the river at about 2:00 the next morning. Foote recalled that he was forward of the regiment's line on picket duty while the withdrawal continued without them: "Just before day break an officer told us to leave our posts and go quickly and quietly to our lines. You may imagine my astonishment when there was not a man nor gun to be seen—only our squad of pickets." Foote and his group moved down the road toward the river and found the regiment about a mile further guarding the ford. Griffin's Division was the last across the pontoons that morning, and the army marched back to its camps in another soaking, mud-making rain.[28]

The 83rd reached its camp at near Stoneman's Switch that afternoon. Col. Stockton reported that the brigade was in "good spirits" as they moved into their old huts, but Daniel Foote wrote that the men were "as tired a set of boys as ever was seen." Most of the action at Chancellorsville had been in thick woods that limited the soldiers' view, and as the 5th Corps had been left out of most of it, the course of the fighting was a mystery to the men in the 83rd. The Union had lost over 17,000 men, the Confederates 13,000, and the battle of Chancellorsville was the bloodiest of the war up to that point, but Vincent's men knew none of these facts as they went back into their camp. The 83rd had suffered only one man wounded in the campaign, and the Pennsylvanians felt more confusion than anything else. Daniel Foote later wrote Julia Hill, "The object attained in this battle I cannot see. We took a good many prisoners and an immense amount of artillery. I suppose their loss must have been three to our one in killed and wounded. I suppose the object was to take the heights of Fredericksburg.... It is not a defeat nor is it really a victory.... I think Gen. Hooker has done well and is a good general, but I do not know a great deal about anything I did not see."[29]

If Foote had known the entire picture he would have thought differently. After his brilliant start, Gen. Hooker had allowed his army, nearly twice the size of Lee's, to be outmaneuvered and thrown back to its starting point. With the Army of the Potomac in its camps and the Confederates between them and Richmond, little had changed in the strategic situation since November. Senior generals and cabinet members called for Hooker's relief, but finding a new army commander was not so easy, and Lincoln decided to keep him.³⁰

In Virginia, the soldiers went back into a routine of drill and camp duties, and as an officer of the 44th New York wrote, "removing from the person and clothing a liberal accumulation of Virginia mud." Brig. Gen. James Barnes assumed command of the 1st Division of the 5th Corps. The 12th and 17th New York mustered out when their terms of enlistment expired. Col. Stockton resigned as commander of the 3rd Brigade. Col. Vincent succeeded him, and the Brigade was then composed of the 16th Michigan, 20th Maine, 44th, and the 83rd. Lt. Col. Hugh Campbell's leg had been amputated after his Bull Run wound, and he resigned from the army that month. Maj. Hugh Lamont was selected as an aide at the 1st Division headquarters, and command of the 83rd went to the senior captain, Orpheus Woodward.³¹

As was the custom, Vincent drew his brigade staff from his own regiment. He took Capt. Judson as an aide, Lt. John M. Clark as the Brigade Adjutant, Dr. Burchfield as the Brigade Surgeon, and Oliver Norton as his bugler and color-bearer. Norton was thrilled to be back at Brigade Headquarters, and especially pleased at the colonel's flag that it was his responsibility to carry. He wrote to his sister, "My horse is fat as a cub and sleek as mole and my flag—oh, I must tell you about the new flag; it is a quaint concern." He went on to describe it as a white triangle, six feet to each side, bordered by blue with a red Maltese Cross—the symbol of their division—in the center.³²

By the end of May, Gen. Hooker had positioned the army to watch the Confederates across the Rappahannock. The 5th Corps guarded several fords across the river. The regiments of Vincent's Brigade were split up into separate camps overlooking the river, and the 83rd was assigned the re-

Top: Amos Judson, pictured as a captain. (The Judson family)
Bottom: Orpheus Woodward of Company E, pictured as colonel of the 83rd (Irwin Rider)

sponsibility of watching Richard's Ford and Kemper's Ford. Simply watching for Rebel activity was light duty, and the soldiers enjoyed a leisurely early summer. Amos Judson wrote, "Nothing occurred, during our stay here, worthy of mention. The rebels were posted, likewise, at every ford along the river, and they and our men had nothing to do but to while away the time as easily as they could, smoke the pipe of peace and look lazily across the river at each other."[33]

While the Army of the Potomac whiled away the spring, Gen. Lee planned the next Confederate move. Despite the Army of Northern Virginia's successes, the South was still losing the war. On the Mississippi, U. S. Grant was closing in on Vicksburg. Another Union army pushed into eastern Tennessee, and still more Federals were steadily advancing from the coast in North Carolina and Virginia. Lee considered the best way to relieve the pressure from the South was to push into Pennsylvania to threaten Baltimore and Washington, and encourage foreign backing. Confederate President Davis and his cabinet immediately endorsed the plan and Lee made preparations for the campaign. One of Jackson's division commanders, Maj. Gen. Richard Ewell, succeeded to command the 2nd Corps. Gen. Longstreet retained the 1st Corps, and a third corps commanded by A.P. Hill was added. In early June, Lee launched his 75,000-man army on a march to the north behind the Blue Ridge mountains and around the right flank of the Federals.[34]

Intelligence of the Confederate movement reached the Union army, and rumors on the Rebels' destination and intent filled the camps. Hooker ordered the 1st Corps to be ready to move but it was not until early June, when Brig. Gen. Alfred Pleasonton's Cavalry Corps clashed with Confederates at the battle of Brandy Station, that he realized that Lee's troops had begun moving north. With orders to protect Washington, Hooker began to cautiously pull his corps out of the camps and head them north after the Rebels.[35]

Back on the Rappahannock, the 83rd broke camp on June 13 and picked up the march with rest of the 5th Corps the next day. In three days they reached Manassas Junction, thirty miles north. On the same day Ewell's Confederate corps crossed the Potomac River and moved into Maryland unopposed. Trying to head the Confederates off and guard Washington at the same time, all the Union commanders drove their troops at a tough pace. By June 17 the 83rd had covered almost twenty more miles and was at the town of Gum Spring, less than fifteen miles' march from the Potomac. Amos Judson remembered marching "through clouds of dust and beneath a scorching sun ... the men, sweating beneath the heat and burden of their knapsacks, fell out in crowds and could be seen lying along every little stream, where a drop of water could be found to quench their raging thirst, or a bush to shelter them from the rays...."[36]

Thirty miles to the west, Lee's troops moved into Maryland, guarded from Federal eyes by cavalry detachments that held the mountain passes in the Blue Ridge. On the evening of June 20 the 5th Corps arrived at the town of Aldie, Virginia, where Union horsemen recently fought with a division of Rebel troopers led by Gen. Jeb Stuart himself. The Yankee cavalry had pushed Stuart about five miles back towards Middleburg and Gen. Pleasonton, the Federal cavalry commander, planned to attack the Confederates in force the next day. Pleasonton asked the 5th Corps for infantry support. That night, Meade assigned the task to Barnes' Division, and Vincent's Brigade was attached to the cavalry while the other two brigades remained in reserve.[37]

The soldiers of the 83rd woke early in

the morning of Sunday, June 21, and marched to Middleburg. They met the troopers of Gen. Gregg's cavalry division at about 6:00 or 7:00 AM and moved into position on their left flank. Ahead of them, the turnpike led west to Ashby's Gap in the Blue Ridge, which dominated the horizon. Open fields extended on both sides of the road, broken by a small stream and some low stone walls that bounded the plots and met the road at right angles. Woods stood to the regiment's left. Dismounted Confederate cavalrymen of Brig. Gen. Fitzhugh Lee's Brigade with a battery of artillery crouched behind the stone walls on the south side of the road. As the Federal horsemen drew up alongside the 83rd, they also dismounted to make their attack on foot.[38]

When all the regiments were in place, Vincent sent the 16th Michigan forward. Lee's skirmishers put up stiff resistance, and Pleasonton called for more infantry. Vincent sent the 44th and the 20th Maine forward to clear the Rebels out. At the same time, Vincent sent the 83rd into the woods around to the left. Skirmishers' rifles cracked in the morning air as the Union line slowly moved forward. Concealed by the trees, Capt. Woodward moved the 83rd to a point just beyond the Rebel line and then turned right. The 44th and the 20th closed with the Confederates and opened fire, and the 83rd burst from the woods onto the enemy flank.

Overwhelmed, Lee's troopers quickly pulled out from their stone walls with the Union cavalry and infantry in pursuit. The Rebels made a stand on the banks of a small stream, but again Vincent flanked their position and drove them back. For four more miles, the Confederates retreated and the Union followed until Lee's horsemen reached Goose Creek and took position behind another stone wall on its far side.

Only one bridge led over the stream and a direct assault here would be difficult. Gen. Pleasonton ordered Vincent to take the position. With that, Vincent told the 83rd to "carry the bridge on the run" as he reported, while the rest of the brigade forded the stream to hit the Rebels' flank once more. Norton later wrote that Vincent yelled, "There they go boys; now give 'em hell!" Amos Judson recalled, "At a bound, the skirmishers of the 16th followed by those of the 83rd, dashed over the bridge with a general yell, and shouting 'Shoot them! Take them prisoners!'" Some of the Pennsylvanians splashed into the stream and scrambled up the banks. The Rebel cavalrymen fired back, but the wild Union men rushed the stone wall and drove them back again, capturing those that didn't get away.

Vincent's Brigade followed the Confederates for another ten miles to near the town of Upperville, but by that time they had covered nearly twenty miles since their early morning wake-up, and their attack lost momentum as the troops ran out of energy. At that point the Union cavalry continued the fight and pursued the Rebels back through Ashby's Gap, five more miles distant. The 1st Brigade relieved Vincent's that evening, and after a rest, the 3rd Brigade marched back to Middleburg. The 83rd had suffered only one man injured out of the brigade's twenty-one wounded, and the combined force took between fifty and sixty prisoners. Amos Judson later called the skirmish "one of the most exciting times we had ever yet experienced: when we were carried along, as it were, by the tempest, whirlwind and, I might say, joy of battle into the midst of the enemy's ranks."[39]

The battle at Aldie, though a significant event for Vincent's Brigade, was one of a series of clashes along the flanks of the Army of the Potomac as it shadowed the Confederate invasion of the North. The army was under orders to cover Washington and Baltimore and to strike the Rebels if they moved directly on either city, and the various corps took different routes north through Maryland. By the time the Federals gathered at Frederick in late June, the Confederates of Ewell's Corps were threatening Harrisburg, the other two corps of Lee's army were not far behind them, and the Northern states were in a panic. The government was gravely concerned that Lee would attain his objective of seizing Baltimore, Philadelphia, or even Washington. Militia units from all over New York and Pennsylvania were called out to contest the invasion (Erie County mustered one company).

Though Hooker remained popular with the soldiers, relations between the general and the War Department soured. Gen. Halleck closely controlled the army's movements, which Hooker perceived as undue interference. By the end of June, Hooker felt he could no longer freely command the army and asked to be relieved. Lincoln granted the request, and Hooker, the last of the Army of the Potomac's popular but inept leaders, was reassigned to the western theater. The President initially asked 1st Corps commander Maj. Gen. John Reynolds to command the army. Having seen Washington's overly tight control, Reynolds declined the offer. The 5th Corps' Gen. Meade had a solid battle record, but he was also known to have a short temper and he was not universally liked outside of his own corps. Still, Meade had the respect of his fellow officers and the government, and he was the next best candidate. On June 28 Lincoln named him as Hooker's successor. Maj. Gen. George Sykes, who had led the division of Regulars up to that point, took over the 5th Corps. For the first time, an unpopular, but competent, general commanded the Army of the Potomac. The men of the 83rd learned about the changes while camped at Frederick, and Amos Judson remembered, "As Gen. Meade was already regarded as one of the best general officers in the army, this change of commanders was

Maj. Gen. George G. Meade. Though he was unpopular with much of the Army of the Potomac, the men of the 83rd respected him as a dependable officer. (LOC)

received with quiet but apparent satisfaction."[40]

As Meade's army concentrated around Frederick, the cavalry and civilians reported that Ewell's Corps had been as far north as Carlisle and that Longstreet's and Hill's Corps were in southern Pennsylvania. In a circular to his new soldiers, Meade announced that a general engagement was imminent. Each corps was ordered to stay constantly ready to march. The soldiers received sixty rounds of ammunition and three days' rations.

The various corps continued north on their separate routes, keeping the inside track between the Confederates and Washington. The 5th Corps left Frederick on June 29 and by nightfall of the next day reached the town of Union Mills, five miles south of the Pennsylvania border. Although they had covered about thirty-five miles in two days, the weather was not overly warm and there was enough moisture to keep the dust on the roads down to an acceptable level for veteran soldiers. The men of the 83rd in particular found consolation in the fact that they were moving towards Pennsylvania, and this would be the first time many of the men would see their home state since leaving it nearly two years earlier. Amos Judson recalled, "During the whole march the spirits of the men of the 83rd had increased in confidence as they neared the boundaries of Pennsylvania, and when they found that they were about to enter the threshold of their native state and fight upon her soil, their enthusiasm knew no bounds." Corporal Henry Lytle, marching in the ranks with Judson's Company E, wrote home, "Let the invaders learn by experience that there is yet a sound core in the despised mudsills of the northern states ... let the defiant spirit of he old northlanders come forth.... I expect before the dawn to be on the way to meet the enemy, to help punish him for their audacity."[41]

July 1 dawned hot, but the 5th Corps' only task for the day was to march about ten miles to the town of Hanover, which would be half the distance they had walked in the last few days. The columns headed north early that morning and began crossing the border into Pennsylvania at around noon. The troops had been welcomed and hailed through Maryland, but the citizens of Pennsylvania lined the roads and gave out cool water or homemade delicacies to the men as they passed. When the 3rd Brigade crossed the state line, Col. Vincent sent back word to the 83rd, and Judson recalled: "In a moment Sergeant Rogers had unfurled the flag of the 83rd to the winds. The drum corps struck up our thrilling old national air of Yankee Doodle, and as the glorious old banner, shattered and rent by the shocks of a dozen battle fields, floated once more proudly upon the inspiring breezes of the old Keystone State, long and loud shouts of joy from ten thousand iron throats broke upon the morning air." Vincent pulled his staff off to the side of the road to watch the brigade pass, and when the colors of the 83rd came past, he doffed his hat and remarked to his adjutant, Lt. John Clark, "What death more glorious can any man desire than to die on the soil of Pennsylvania fighting for that flag!" The cheering and enthusiasm spread to other regiments all along the march, and soon regimental and brigade flags were flying and bands were playing all along the column as it continued on.[42]

It was late afternoon when the corps reached Hanover and the men pulled off the road to bivouac for the night. Soon after they settled in, a messenger on horseback from Gen. Meade's headquarters galloped into the camp and found Gen. Sykes. The officer told Sykes that two Union corps, the 1st and the 11th, were engaged with Confederates near the town of Gettysburg. Gen. Meade was concentrating the Federal army at Gettysburg as soon as possible, and sent orders for the 5th Corps to march for the town that night.

Gen. Sykes quickly briefed the division commanders on the situation and prepared the corps to continue their march. Within Barnes' Division, brigades actually raced to break camp and reach the road first in order to have the honor of leading the corps into battle. Within two hours the 5th Corps was on the road and headed toward Gettysburg, thirteen miles away to the west. The men could hear the artillery booming even then.[43]

The Rocky Hill

At about 3:30 AM on Thursday, July 2, Oliver Norton sounded the unwelcome notes of reveille for Vincent's Brigade.

After they left Hanover, the men of the 5th Corps had marched hard along the road that led west to Gettysburg. It was a cool evening and a bright moon shone on the troops as they tramped past the civilians that lined the roads well into the night. Confederate cavalry had been active in the area, and the citizens of Pennsylvania were grateful to see Union soldiers. Amos Judson rode along with Vincent and the 3rd Brigade headquarters, and recalled, "Passing through the villages on the way, the women came out and sang the Star Spangled Banner and other national airs, and were cheered in return by the soldiers." Pvt. Seth Waid walked in the ranks with Company F of the 83rd. Waid had been through the Chancellorsville campaign and in the past two weeks had walked from Falmouth, Virginia, to Pennsylvania with the regiment. Though he had only been in the field for a few months, he could at least call himself a veteran marcher. He recorded in his journal, "We have seen a verry different State of things than we find in Va or even Maryland, the people bringing water to us on the march and evry where showing signs of patriotism. we passed many towns last night and were evry where greeted with Cheers and demonstrations of joy. Women and children bringing us water and singing patriotic songs as we passed." Although the men were exceptionally tired from their long days on the road, it was an exhilarating night.[1]

Enthusiasm and good cheer can carry a soldier only so far and the troops were nearly exhausted. Gen. Sykes knew that his men could easily stumble upon Confederates as they came closer to the battlefield, and he halted the brigade sometime between 1 and 2 AM. With the weariness brought on by eighteen hours of marching, the soldiers dropped their knapsacks, threw blankets over themselves, and slept at the side of the road. They were about five miles from Gettysburg.[2]

The men rose to the sounds of the bugle tired, sore, and hungry. There was a quick breakfast of hardtack and coffee and then they pulled their aching bodies up from the roadside, fell back into formation and continued the march. A red sun rose into an overcast sky, and although a slight breeze helped blow the dust off the road, it was already 74 degrees an hour into the march, and it looked like July 2 would be hot day. The column followed the Hanover Road for a while, turned south on the Low Dutch Road, and then northeast on the Baltimore Pike, and about an hour into the march the 1st Division's lead troops came within sight of the crossroads town of Gettysburg. The soldiers swung off the road at the farm owned by the Deardorff family, stacked arms, and sat down for a rest while the officers went to seek instructions. The men were no doubt relieved to know that they would not have a long march in the heat of the day, but the occasional artillery shots, picket firing, troops moving into position, and galloping messengers were signs that the previous day's battle was likely to continue. Soon, word of the situation arrived.[3]

Two days earlier, while the 83rd was still in Maryland, Confederates had penetrated into Pennsylvania as far north as the town of Carlisle. Though the three corps of the Army of Northern Virginia were scattered from the Pennsylvania border to the area just south of Harrisburg, Lee's army was in position to turn southeast toward Philadelphia, Baltimore, or Washington. The Confederate cavalry, under Gen. Stuart's command, was supposed to watch the Union army and keep Lee informed about their movements, but Stuart had taken his men on a wide-ranging ride around the Federals and had not reported for days. Lee's troops moved into Pennsylvania unopposed, but also unaware that the 95,000-man Army of the Potomac was closely following them. Federal cavalry shadowed the Rebel movements, for although Gen. Meade had kept his formations between the Confederates and the major cities, he could not consolidate them to strike until the Rebels turned and disclosed their intended target. The day the battle of Gettysburg started, the seven corps of the Army of the Potomac were steadily moving north but were widely separated on different routes.

Thirty-five miles southeast of Harrisburg and between the two armies was the town of Gettysburg. It was a quiet town, typical of the hamlets that dotted southeastern Pennsylvania. About 2,000 citizens called it home and worked the farms that followed the rolling ridges and hills of the surrounding area. A few hundred yards south of the town rose the flat-topped Cemetery Hill. Cemetery Ridge extended south from the hilltop for about two miles, gradually decreasing in height until it blended into the farmland. A mile to the west and somewhat lower in elevation was a similar feature named Seminary Ridge for the Lutheran school located at its northern end. Just east of Cemetery Hill was the somewhat smaller and wooded Culp's Hill. South of where Cemetery Ridge ended, an oval-shaped hill known as Little Round Top rose 150 feet above the countryside. Big Round Top, which was about fifty feet higher, was just to its south.

As long as the opposing armies moved north and east, Gettysburg lay out of their direct path and was unimportant to either side. But on June 29, Lee learned that the Army of the Potomac was in Pennsylvania and that his dispersed columns were vulnerable to being cut up piecemeal by the more numerous Federals. He quickly canceled the advance on Harrisburg and ordered his three corps to converge at Gettysburg or six miles west at Cashtown.

But the Federal cavalry covered the eastern flank of the Army of the Potomac. By June 30th they had identified that the Rebels were concentrating near Gettysburg and reported the information to Meade's headquarters. On the afternoon of June 30, Meade sent orders to the Union corps to march towards Gettysburg.

These orders put the 5th Corps and the 83rd on the road to Hanover on the morning of July 1, and in the day that it took the Pennsylvanians to reach their objective much had happened. The Confederates had clashed with the Union cavalrymen near Gettysburg on the morning of July 1st. More units from both armies arrived throughout the day, and although Gen. Lee did not intend it, a battle developed. The Union troops held off their attackers for much of the day. But in the late afternoon, Gen. Ewell's Confederate Corps arrived and pushed the Yankees back through Gettysburg. By the end of the day the battered remnants of the Union 1st and 11th Corps had withdrawn to Cemetery

Hill, where the Federal artillery held off further Confederate attacks.

Gen. Meade ordered all seven corps of his army to march to the town with haste and other troops rushed to Gettysburg as the 5th Corps had. The 2nd, 12th, and 3rd Corps arrived through the night. Meade also rode in and positioned the units along the area's high ground. By the time the 5th Corps arrived the morning of July 2, the Federal line was shaped like a fish hook, the shank running down Cemetery Ridge and the hook curving around Cemetery and Culp's Hills. Firmly based on the high hills and ridges and also with the interior lines that would allow reinforcements to rapidly shift from one place to another, the Union army was in a secure defensive position. Meade could afford to wait for the Confederates to attack.

As the Federal corps arrived at Gettysburg, so did the rest of the Confederates of Gen. Hill's and Ewell's Corps. Lee believed that an aggressive attack by the bulk of his army could push the Union off the ridgeline and force them into retreat. Longstreet's corps was moving up that morning, and most of the 75,000 man Army of Northern Virginia took positions that mirrored Meade's.

To dislodge the Federals from their high ground, Gen. Lee planned to launch two of Longstreet's divisions against the weakest part of the Union line on the southern end of Cemetery Ridge. Simultaneously, Gen. Ewell's Corps was to launch a diversionary attack at Culp's Hill on the northern end of the Union position. Once Longstreet's men seized the commanding heights of the Round Top hills, they could smash the Union flank and buckle the line. Longstreet's Corps was the farthest away from Gettysburg when the Confederates were ordered to concentrate and his units were the last to arrive at the battlefield. Gen. Hood's and McLaws' Divisions, Longstreet's units that were slated to make the attack, were making a forced march to reach the battle on the morning of July 2. Lee's assault would begin when they arrived.[4]

On the Union side, Gen. Meade had designated the 5th Corps as the army's reserve that morning. Waiting to be called upon, the 5th Corps troops relaxed east of Cemetery Ridge near the Deardorff farm. Units moved all over the battlefield, but the men of Vincent's Brigade had marched over sixty miles in the last three days with little sleep and they were probably too tired to notice the activity. One officer of Vincent's Brigade remembered that many of the soldiers were so exhausted that few even knew the time of day or where they were. Since an attack was expected, the brigade formed a line of battle. Nothing developed that morning, and the men stacked arms and fell asleep in their ranks. Most of the Union army had taken position and a 3rd Brigade officer recalled that the battlefield "was still as death.... The whole army seemed to be sleeping in the hot July sun while they waited the attack of the enemy."[5]

In mid-morning the Union 6th Corps arrived and took the place of the 5th. Barnes's Division moved to a position behind the 2nd Corps in the center of the Union line, then to another north of Little Round Top near the George Weikert farm. The soldiers of the 83rd probably found the morning's shifting of position an annoyance that deprived them of precious sleep, and there was most likely some grumbling and cursing as the division reached its third destination of the day. The men went back to sleep in the sunshine. Seth Waid's anxious entry in his diary hints at the tension that was in the air: "In line of battle near Gettysburg Pa. [We] have been marching and manovering about all the forenoon. there was fighting here yesterday and we are expecting to have fighting to do soon." Late morning passed into the early afternoon and the heat rose into the low-nineties. As Vincent's men lounged, the Confederates of

Longstreet's Corps moved into position about a mile to the southwest and prepared for their attack.[6]

About 3:30 or 4:00 PM, Confederate artillery opened fire and signaled the advance of McLaws' and Hood's Divisions. As Lee planned it, both divisions would cross the fields west of Cemetery Ridge in a roughly northeast direction and hit the southern end of the Union line *en echelon*, like a 1-2-combination punch. But unknown to Lee, the Federal 3rd Corps had moved off the ridge and occupied the ground that Longstreet's men were to advance across. Within minutes of beginning their attack, the Confederate troops hit unexpected and stiff resistance. The sounds of the fight reached the 83rd, less than a mile behind the Union line, and the men lifted their heads to see what the commotion was about.

The noise also surprised Gen. Meade, who at that time was riding along Cemetery Ridge with his staff. He turned to the army's Chief Engineer Officer, Maj. Gen. Gouverner Warren, and told him to investigate the cause of the firing. Little Round Top loomed ahead of the party, and it was the best vantage point to observe the battlefield. Warren spurred his horse toward the hill.

As Warren reached the summit of Little Round Top, Longstreet's attack was unfolding below him. Directly west, among the wheat fields and farm roads, Confederate skirmishers pushed into the Federal 3rd Corps. Behind the gray skirmish line, the four brigades of McLaws' Division advanced in line of battle. The firing increased as the main Rebel force collided with the Union brigades, and Warren's view became quickly obscured by thick clouds of gunpowder smoke and bursting shells.

Earlier in the day, Gen. Meade had instructed Maj. Gen. Dan Sickles to place his 3rd Corps along Cemetery Ridge, which would have included Little Round Top. Through some confusion, Sickles had moved his troops west of the ridge into the lower farmland, which actually positioned it well to block Longstreet's attack but left Little Round Top uncovered. As Warren viewed the spectacle below him, the hill was only occupied by a small semaphore team who was signaling reports of the Confederate movements to Meade's headquarters. Worse, an officer with the team told Warren that there were more Rebel troops forming in the woods to the west.

As a professional army engineer and former regimental commander with a good combat record, Gen. Warren was a well-qualified judge of militarily significant terrain. He recognized that artillery placed on Little Round Top would be in a position to fire down the length of the Union line and if infantry seized the height, they would have a clear avenue into the rear of Meade's position or could roll up its flank. Warren later wrote that he considered the hill "the key of the whole position."

A Federal artillery battery was set up near the base of Little Round Top, positioned to fire into a field strewn with boulders known as the Devil's Den. Warren quickly rode down to the battery and asked the commander to fire a shot into the woods on Seminary Ridge to see if it brought a response from the Confederates and disclosed the positions that the signal officer suspected. The cannon sent out a single shot that landed in the tree line, and Warren noticed the distinct glint from rifle barrels and bayonets as Rebel troops took shelter from the round. His suspicions confirmed, he rode back up to the hill and sent an aide to report to Gen. Meade that Little Round Top was in immediate danger and to rush a division to hold the hill. At around the same time, Gen. Hood walked out in front of his ranks as they formed on Seminary Ridge and made a short speech to the troops that ended with, "Fix bayonets, my brave Texans; forward and take those heights!" One of Hood's staff officers gestured toward

Left: Maj. Gen. Gouverner K. Warren, who discovered that Little Round Top was undefended and sent the messages that brought Vincent's Brigade to the hill. (LOC)
Right: Maj. Gen. George Sykes, commander of the 5th Corps at Gettysburg. There is controversy over his role in how Vincent's Brigade arrived on Little Round Top. (LOC)

Little Round Top, and as some of the men shouted, "We'll do it!" the line stepped out of the trees and went forward.

Another of Warren's aides, Lt. Ranald Mackenzie, galloped to Gen. Sickles and asked for a unit to hold Little Round Top, but the general refused, probably stating that his corps was too hard pressed to spare a brigade. Mackenzie then rode to find Gen. Sykes of the 5th Corps and repeated Warren's plea for troops. Not long before, Meade had ordered Sykes to send his corps in to shore up the 3rd Corps line, and as this request seemed to fit in with Meade's intent, Sykes quickly consented. He sent one of his aides to instruct Gen. Barnes, the commander of the 1st Division, to occupy Little Round Top.[7]

By then Sickles' and Longstreet's Corps were fully engaged less than half a mile from where Barnes's Division rested. Columns of Union troops rushed toward the line and went into the fight, and the thundering artillery, crash of musketry, shouted orders and screams of the wounded clearly carried to the soldiers in Vincent's brigade while the men waited in their ranks, expecting action at any minute. Vincent and Norton were on their horses at the head of the brigade when, as Norton later remembered it, they saw a rider coming their way from the direction of the firing. Vincent recognized the man as one of Sykes's aides, and the colonel spurred his horse toward the officer with Norton close behind.

When the two intercepted the courier, they reined up and Vincent asked, "Captain, what are your orders?" The question would have elicited an immediate response from anyone in his brigade, but staff officers sometimes do not recognize any authority except their own general, regardless of their rank, and the captain only answered, "Where is General Barnes?" Col. Vincent, the disciplinarian who grew up working in a foundry, had survived the Chickahominy Fever and the frozen heights of Fredericksburg, knew his own authority as a brigade commander, a full third of the strength of the division, and retorted, "What are your orders? Give me your orders." Overpowered, the messenger answered, "General

Sykes directs General Barnes to send one of his brigades to occupy that hill yonder." The captain gestured toward the hulking rock of Little Round Top, which dominated the sky from less than a mile away to the south. Vincent glanced at the hill for a moment and told him, "I will take the responsibility myself of taking my brigade there," and with that he and Norton turned and sped back to their waiting soldiers.[8]*

Vincent's assertiveness is commendable in hindsight, and even more amazing since it was completely unauthorized and potentially dangerous. Gen. Barnes had been away from the division for some time, and Vincent had no knowledge of his commander's intent or intentions. Vincent's troops might have been needed elsewhere and the move to Little Round Top could easily have put them in the wrong place at the wrong time. If the 3rd Brigade had gone to the hill and seen no action, he would have been guilty of a court-martial offense. Other officers had committed lesser violations and been cashiered.

Whether Vincent thought about any of this is unknown, but as soon as they reached the brigade he found Col. Rice of the 44th New York and told him, "Colonel, bring the brigade as quickly as possible on to that hill. Double quick where the ground will permit." Vincent sent his staff down the line to repeat the orders to the other regiments, and he and Norton galloped off towards Little Round Top with the brigade pennant flapping in the breeze. Around the same time, the men of Hood's Division were moving through the fields and headed for the same hill. It was about 4:30 PM.

Vincent and Norton came upon Little Round Top from the northwest and tried to ride up the slope, but the ground was too broken and rocky for the horses to negotiate. They swung around to the east side of the hill to a point near the Bricker farmhouse where the ground was less rocky, and rode over the spine of the height and broke out of the trees onto the cleared western slope. Norton and his commander were alone on Little Round Top as they halted and first saw the ground the 3rd Brigade was coming to hold.[9]

Little Round Top juts violently out of the low farms that surround it. To the west, a brook known as Plum Run runs through the boulder field called the Devil's Den. The hill rises out of the Devil's Den, continues at a shallow ascent for about fifty yards or so to a rock shelf, and then up at a steeper angle to a collection of boulders that form the summit. Warren and the signal crew were at the north end of this highest elevation, and the boulders blocked their view of the southern end, where Norton and Vincent sat on their horses. Big Round Top is about 100 yards to the south, and the bases of the two hills meet to form a small valley. The west slope of Little Round Top was barren and

---

*The story related here is how Oliver Norton remembered the events, but is not reflected in any other documents, including the official reports of the battle. That Warren identified that the hill was unoccupied and sent his aides to find troops to hold it is not disputed, but accounts of what happened after that conflict. Gen. Barnes reported that he was with Sykes when "General Warren, of the staff of General Meade, came up, riding rapidly from the left, and pointed out the position of the elevation known as the Round Top, not far off an toward the left, urged the importance of assistance in that direction. General Sykes yielded to his urgent request, and I immediately directed Colonel Vincent, commanding the 3rd Brigade, to proceed to that point with his brigade." Gen. Sykes also stated Barnes directed Vincent to the hill, although he was not present at the scene and may have based that on Barnes' report. Vincent's aide, Capt. Judson, skips over the event in his memoir. None of the regimental commanders of the 3rd Brigade mention how Vincent received his orders. Only Vincent, Norton, and the unknown aide could have overheard the conversation. After the war, Norton tried to identify which aide he and Vincent spoke with and by a process of elimination, concluded that it was Lt. Ranald Mackenzie of Warren's staff. His conclusion was never confirmed. Norton was a devout champion of Col. Vincent until the end of his days, but in light of the colonel's many qualities, it seems unlikely that Norton would have had to concoct this story to bring praise to his commander. The actions seem consistent with Vincent's strong character and tactical abilities.

Top: A sketch of Little Round Top, left, and Big Round Top, right, as seen from the Confederate lines at Gettysburg. (LOC)
Bottom: Little Round Top from the west. Vincent's line cut across the slope in the left center of the photograph. (LOC)

the east half was completely wooded, as was Big Round Top. Although cleared of trees, the rock shelf and hundreds of other boulders made the ground exceptionally rugged. Judson remembered that the hill "consisted of a huge, solid rock covered over with a thousand other loose boulders of every size and shape...." It was probably the best defensive site on the entire battlefield.[10]

Vincent and Norton had barely enough time to take a look around before a shell exploded near them, followed by two or three more in quick succession. With the large 3rd Brigade banner flying in the breeze, the two figures in blue made a conspicuous target for Confederate artillery, and Vincent barked, "Down with that flag, Norton! Damn it, go behind the rocks with it!" The private obligingly trotted his horse into the trees, dismounted, and tucked the colors against a boulder. In another minute the colonel followed, handed Norton the reins of his horse, and went back out to analyze the ground.[11]

Although Little Round Top was an excellent defensive position, Vincent still faced the problem of where to position his brigade. The 3rd Corps line was 200 yards away to the west. To the east, the Taneytown Road ran north and straight into the Union rear. There was probably a thousand yards of open ground, but stretched to their thinnest line, Vincent's 1,336 soldiers in four regiments would only cover about 400 yards. Unless he positioned his brigade to block the Confederates effectively, the Rebels could easily outflank his brigade, seize the height and be in a perfect position to crush the flank of the Union line. Vincent probably examined Little Round Top from the viewpoint of his enemy, and thought of where he would maneuver if the 3rd Brigade were attacking the hill instead of defending it. From the attacker's perspective, the west slope offered a difficult route since it gave defenders clear fields of fire, and the rocky ledges would break up the lines of battle. Big Round Top was steep, heavily wooded, and also made a poor platform for an advance into the Union rear. But the valley between the two hills had a gradual slope with plenty of cover and formed a natural course for an infantry attack. The valley was the most likely avenue for a Confederate advance, and Vincent decided to place his brigade at the base of Little Round Top to cover the vale.[12]

Within minutes, Norton heard the 3rd Brigade coming over the top of the hill from the north. The 44th was in the lead, followed by the 16th Michigan, then the 83rd, and the 20th Maine brought up the rear. Col. Rice of the 44th rode forward to meet Vincent and along with Norton, they went out into the cleared area. Vincent intended to form a line of battle which faced south and west by the standard method where each regiment swings out of the column and into line in the order it arrived. Indicating the area for the 44th, Vincent told Rice, "Form your regiment here, Colonel, with the right against the rock" (which must have been a significant slab among the field of boulders). Vincent's positioning would have placed the New Yorkers on the right of the line, with the 16th in between them and the 83rd. Rice answered him, "In every battle in which we have been engaged, the 83rd and the 44th have fought side by side. I wish it might be so today."

It had been almost two years since the night the Pennsylvanians had welcomed the 44th to Hall's Hill. Since then they had suffered together in the trenches at Yorktown, faced merciless combat, marched hundreds of miles, and endured endless camp miseries together. Rice and Vincent had begun the war as second in command to their respective regiments and now Vincent, the younger of the two, was Rice's commander. The bond between the two units, "Butterfield's Twins," was strong by this time of the war, and something of these images must have been in the two officers' minds as they formed to fight on northern territory. Vincent answered Rice, "All right, let the 16th pass you," and the Michigan troops moved around the 44th and took the right flank of the brigade while the other regiments filed onto the line.[13]

With all four regiments now in position, the 3rd Brigade's line of battle curved around the southern face of Little Round Top in a semi-circle. On the right, the 16th Michigan and the 44th faced roughly west and were in open ground that was relatively level. To the New Yorkers' left, the 83rd's line bulged out a few paces in a quarter-circle and straddled the tree line. The brigade's junior regiment, the 386-man 20th Maine, was on the far left where they faced directly into the valley between the two hills. Col.

The area where Little Round Top, left, meets Big Round Top, right, which would become known as "the Valley of Death." This is the view that the Confederate regiments of Law's Brigade had as they rushed into the alley on July 2 and into the waiting guns of the 83rd. (National Archives)

Chamberlain later reported, "Colonel Vincent indicated to me the ground my regiment was to occupy, informing me that this was the extreme left of our general line, and that a desperate attack was expected in order to turn that position, concluding by telling me I was to 'hold that ground at all hazards.'"[14]

Each regiment sent skirmishers out for warning of the expected attack. Capt. D. P. Jones led the 83rd's D Company forward into the valley. There was significant ground to cover between Little Round Top and the 3rd Corps line, and the 16th Michigan sent two companies to fan out over the base of the hill. Capt. Charles Hazlett's battery of 5th Corps artillery, which had fired in support of the 3rd Brigade at Hanover Court House, Gaines's Mill, Malvern Hill, and Bull Run, had also been rushed to Little Round Top and arrived not long after the infantry. The rough ground made it nearly impossible for the horse teams to pull the guns up the hill, and Capt. Woodward let a few men loose to help. Pvt. J. B. Potter was one of them, and he remembered that the soldiers hauled the guns up "using ropes and muscle only...." which was exceptionally difficult work in the hot, humid afternoon. Within minutes Hazlett's guns opened fire on the Confederate formations that were coming towards Little Round Top. It was now nearing 5:00 PM.[15]

After leaving Seminary Ridge, Hood's Division had headed across the fields and towards the Devil's Den. A brigade of Alabama infantry commanded by Brig. Gen. Evander Law and another brigade of Texans led by Brig. Gen. Robertson were tasked to pass in front of Big Round Top and swing north onto what they thought was the Federal flank. Both units began their advance in good order, but the ground over which they passed was scattered with fences, streams, rocks, and other obstacles which broke Law's formation as the men maneuvered around them and periodically adjusted their lines. Robertson's Brigade fell behind Law's, and to make matters worse, Union artillery and sharpshooters fired on the Southerners as they struggled across the fields. Gen. Hood was wounded by an exploding shell and was taken to the rear. The advancing brigades took casualties before they even saw the Federal troops on Little Round Top.[16]

With Hood wounded, command of his division fell to Law, who moved to the rear to assume control. Before leaving, he left instructions for Col. William Oates, commander of the 15th Alabama, to control the movements of his own regiment and the 47th Alabama, but no officer was left in command of the rest of the brigade. Law's four regiments continued the advance but with no one to direct their movements, they drifted right and up the slope of Big Round Top. Instead of skirting the hill as was intended, the 15th and 47th Alabama headed for the crest while the other two regiments of the brigade, the 4th and 48th Alabama, went up the western slope. With Robertson's Brigade already behind, the slip of the Alabama regiments to the right increased the gap between the units, and Robertson also shifted his troops to the right to close the distance. The combination of the rough terrain, Union artillery, sharpshooter fire, and the lack of command in Law's Brigade caused the Alabama and Texas regiments to cross over each other's paths. By the time the line headed up Big Round Top, two of Robertson's regiments, the 4th and 5th Texas, advanced alongside three of Law's, the 4th, 15th and 47th Alabama. One of the troops in Robertson's Brigade, twenty-one year old Valerius C. Giles of the 4th Texas, recalled, "The fire from the enemy, both artillery and musketry, was fearful. In making that long charge, our brigade got jammed. Regiments lapped over each other, and when we reached the woods and climbed the mountains as far as we could go, we were a badly mixed crowd." Like Little Round Top, the slope of Big Round Top was covered with rocks and underbrush and was a difficult ascent for the Rebels. As the line came to the crest of the hill, men fainted from the heat, exertion, and lack of water. Though over 2,000 Confederates in five regiments headed for Little Round Top, they were disorganized, had little direction and were nearly exhausted.[17]

Col. Oates halted to wait for a detail of men to bring up canteens of water. From the crest of Big Round Top, he had a clear view of Little Round Top and the rear of the Union army. A lightly guarded Federal wagon park (possibly the train for Hazlett's battery) was below him to the right near the Taneytown Road. Although he couldn't see Vincent's Brigade, the idea of attacking such a strong position as Little Round Top daunted the veteran colonel. "Within half an hour I could convert it into a Gibraltar that I could hold against ten times the number of men that I had," he later wrote. An aide from Gen. Law arrived at the top of the hill and asked why the line was halted. Oates explained the difficulty of taking Little Round Top but the aide repeated Law's instructions for the attack to go forward. With no choice but to attack, Oates dressed the lines of the two regiments before they continued their advance down the north slope of the hill. To their left, the Texas regiments had already passed over the base of Big Round Top and were rushing up the valley towards Little Round Top and Vincent's thin line of Union skirmishers. Rifle shots echoed up the vale as the two lines met and exchanged fire.[18]

Strong Vincent's brigade had barely finished taking its position when scattered shots from the skirmish line alerted the troops to action. From the 83rd's position, the men stared down the rock-strewn slope of the hill towards the valley and looked for the waves of infantry in tattered gray or butternut uniforms. The late-afternoon sun burned over their right shoulders and the men had a clear view through the sparse woods all the way to the base of Big Round Top. The skirmishers came through the trees, calmly retreating and firing as they went, and the men on the main line saw three columns of Rebels with fixed bayonets charging towards them at a run. Shells from Hazlett's battery burst in the Confederate formations and men fell with every explosion, but the others closed their ranks and still headed for Little Round Top.

Col. Vincent turned to the Brigade Adjutant, Lt. John Clark, and told him, "Go and tell Gen. Barnes to send me reinforcements at once; the enemy are coming against us with an overwhelming force." He also sent aide Amos Judson off to find additional troops, and then Vincent climbed to a rock behind the line from where he could oversee the brigade. The men finished loading their muskets, and Capt. Woodward probably prepared the 83rd to "fire by rank," where the front line would discharge a volley to be closely followed by the soldiers in the rear line. With Woodward's command, there was the sound of 274 hammers being cocked and the soldiers brought their weapons to chest-height at the "ready" position. The company officers stood next to their ranks making last-minute directions, and the soldiers stared through the trees at the Rebels that came up the valley toward their line.[19]

Amos Judson recalled that the when the Rebels reached the base of Little Round Top, they charged with "a loud, fierce, distant yell ... as if all pandemonium had broken loose and joined in the chorus of one grand universal war-whoop." The 4th Alabama had outpaced the other regiments and rushed up the base of the hill towards the 83rd and 44th. Woodward's men waited anxiously as the Rebel line came closer. The rocks proved to be a real asset, and the Southerners had to work their way around boulders or into narrow defiles that allowed only four or five men to pass at a time. They dressed their lines and came on a few paces more and Woodward ordered "Aim!" The soldiers' muskets were shouldered and pointed into the mass of gray and butternut that came steadily on. The Pennsylvanians peered over their sights down the slope at the Confederates that came ever closer, sweating, gasping for air, tripping over and around rocks. It must have seemed like an eternity before Woodward shouted "Fire!" and the rifles of the front rank exploded in a volley with an ear-splitting crash. The Rebel line disappeared in a cloud of smoke. The rifles of the 44th ripped into the Confederates at almost the same time, and as the smoke slowly drifted off the Pennsylvanians and New Yorkers saw the dead and wounded enemies littering the ground.[20]*

The 4th Alabama pulled back a few yards and dressed their lines. The 5th and 4th Texas arrived and joined the attack on their left. The line came forward again, this time walking over the bodies of their comrades who fell in the previous rush. The sound of the Rebel yell and the sight of the charging Confederates may have shaken less seasoned regiments, but the veterans of the 83rd and 44th knew how to put up a tough defense. Pvt. Philander Platt of the 83rd's Company G remembered that fighting on Pennsylvania soil moved him to vow "never [to leave] this position alive while there is an enemy in front." One soldier of the regiment, described as "overgrown and uncouth," overexposed himself to Rebel fire. An officer told the fellow to get down, and the man answered, "I am on the soil of Pennsylvania now, and if they get me down they'll have to shoot me down." Woodward's men had no intention of giving up ground in their home state, and they fired as fast as they could into their attackers. Pvt. Seth Waid of the 83rd's Company F later

---

*There is no record of the firing method that Woodward chose, but this is a tactically accurate method of firing for a regiment in the defensive. The commands for "Fire by Rank" have also been simplified for clarity, but the positions the men took and their actions on the commands are correct.

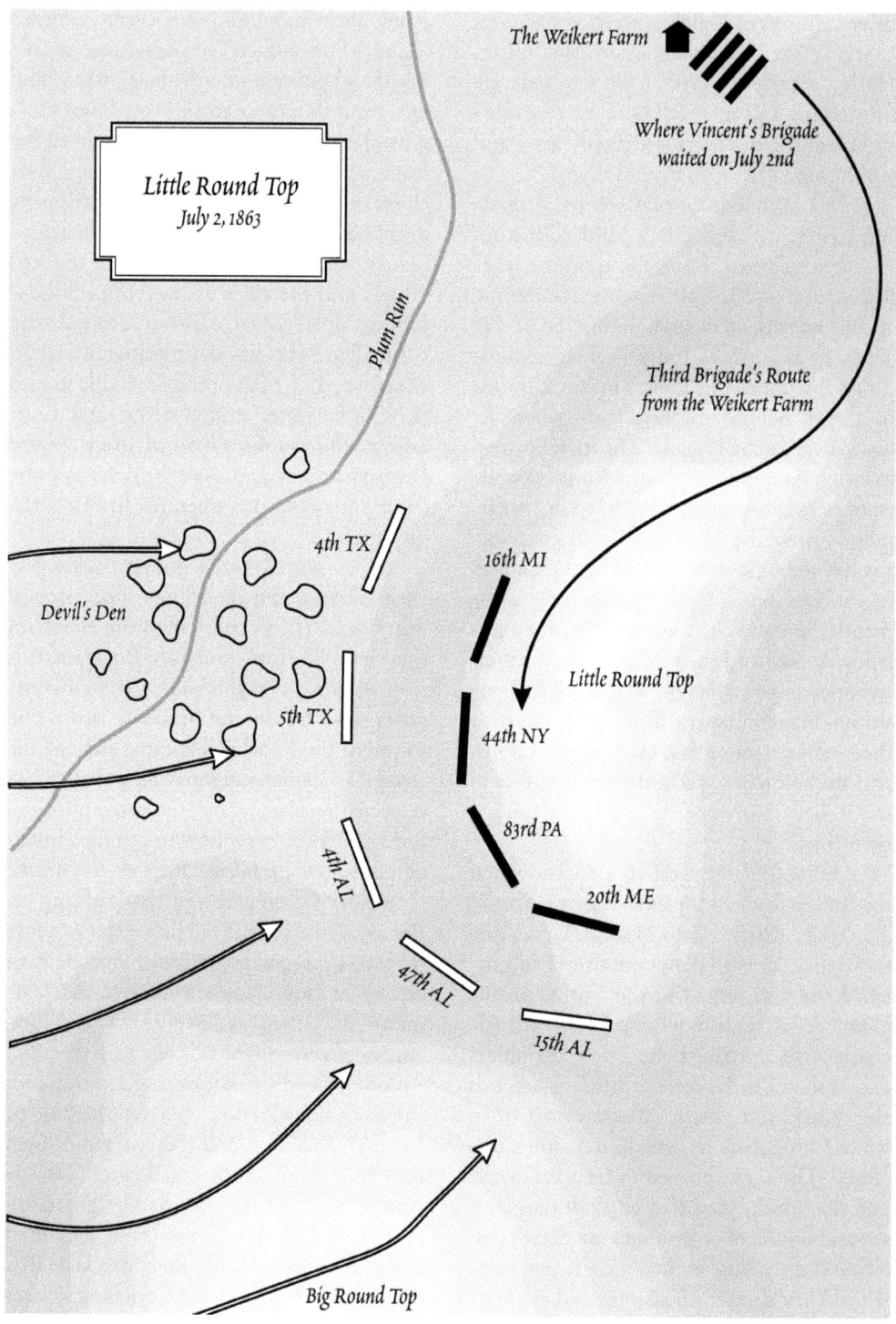

The fight for Little Round Top on July 2, 1863, where Vincent's Brigade arrived just in time to block the Confederate attack.

wrote, "The Rebs came on in great numbers but were hansomely met by our Boys. We poured the minnie into them with terrible effect killing and wounding verry many...." Alabama captain W. C. Ward remembered that as his regiment advanced toward the line of Pennsylvanians and New Yorkers, one Southern soldier called, "Come on boys; come on! The Fifth Texas will get there before the Fourth! Come on boys; come on!" When they reached Little Round Top and went into the charge, Ward recalled, "[We] received the first fire from the hidden Federals. A long line of us went down, three of us close together." Ward was one of the wounded. He recalled that when he regained consciousness a few minutes later, "Minie balls were falling through the leaves like hail in a thunderstorm." John Stevens of the 5th Texas wrote that the men of his regiment reached the hill "almost out of breath and the weather hot as a furnace ... we got a plunging volley from the enemy, who [were] posted behind the rocks on the crest. They [were] not more than 25 or 30 steps away and well protected behind the rocks, while we are exposed to their fire." "Oh, what firing and yelling!" later wrote a member of Hazlett's Battery, who observed Vincent's line as the Confederates charged again.[21]

The first attack of the 4th Alabama, 4th Texas, and 5th Texas had hit the Union line with energy but not much coordination. When the line moved forward a second time, the three regiments were cooler and more concentrated. This time the assault spread and engaged the 16th Michigan. But the Yankees fought hard and despite the efforts of the Confederate officers to hold their men in place, the attackers fell back again. By this time the Rebels were running out of steam and instead of going immediately forward again, the regiments dressed their formation lines at the base of the hill. Both lines traded volleys at close range. Casualties in Vincent's Brigade were light up to this point, but the men were fatigued by their long night's march and the rush to Little Round Top. They were running low on ammunition. Although the Union held the upper hand, the battle was taking a toll on both sides.[22]

As the other three regiments traded volleys with the Yankees, the 15th and 47th Alabama came down into the valley after their run down the north slope of Big Round Top. One of the regiments of Law's Brigade that had been detoured in the advance, the 48th Alabama, came out of Devil's Den and joined the fight on the left of the 4th Texas. Now with six regiments, the entire Confederate line went forward at once.

The 48th Alabama and 4th Texas concentrated their attack on Vincent's right, where the 16th Michigan held, and the 5th Texas, 4th Alabama and 47th Alabama pushed against the center, the position of the 83rd and 44th. The 15th Alabama went forward against the Union left. Vincent needed every man to repel this attack. The 83rd's color guard and musicians threw their flags and instruments aside and grabbed muskets from the wounded. Oliver Norton left his flag perched on a rock and joined the 44th's line. All four of Vincent's regiments fired into the Confederates at point-blank range.[23]

The 4th Alabama could get no farther than the base of the hill and halted a few yards away from the 83rd and 44th. With the pressure in front of them momentarily relieved, both Yankee regiments directed their fire to the left into the seven companies of the 47th Alabama as it rushed the line. The 47th was also probably raked by fire from the 20th Maine, and was forced back. Seeing the regiment retire, Col. Oates steered his 15th Alabama to the left and took up the attack from the stricken 47th. The Pennsylvanians and Maine men kept up their volleys and shredded the advancing gray ranks. Col. Oates later wrote that the

An Alfred Waud sketch with the notations, "The Devil's Den, Gettysburg. Vincent's brigade driven in." This may show the brigade's picket line retreating from the advancing Confederates, or the withdrawal of the 16th Michigan, which Vincent stemmed, on July 2. (LOC)

fire was so fierce that his line of troops "wavered like a man trying to walk against a strong wind, and then slowly, doggedly, gave back a little...."[24]

The 4th Alabama held its position in the rocks but still returned the fire of the 83rd. The two Texas units and the 48th Alabama surged up the hill towards the right of Vincent's line while Oates' two Alabama regiments continued pressure on the left. Despite the volleys from the 20th Maine, the 15th Alabama slipped around the 20th's left flank and pressed their attack. Chamberlain's men held their line, but the Alabama troops had faced the rear of Vincent's Brigade and their fire went beyond the 20th and into the ranks of the 83rd. As the 4th Alabama was still in front of Capt. Woodward's position and still returning fire (probably along with portions of the 5th Texas and 47th Alabama), the men of the 83rd had the terrifying experience of bullets zipping into their line from the front and behind. On Vincent's right, the 16th Michigan had barely 150 men and was forced back by the weight of the Confederate attack. The 3rd Brigade line was in danger of collapse on both ends.[25]

Sergeant Charles Sprague of the 44th was wounded and on his way to a hospital when he was suddenly surrounded by retreating soldiers of the 16th Michigan. Although bleeding, Sprague yelled at the men to stay. As he later wrote, "The men of the 16th stared at me curiously, but I think they saw someone behind me, Vincent, coming up on foot with his wife's little riding whip in his hand. He touched me lightly with his left hand, saying, 'That will do, Sergeant Sprague; I'll take hold of this.'" With that, Vincent waded into the rush of men and implored them to hold their line. The tide of retreating men slowed as the 16th turned to face their attackers.[26]

Sharpshooters of both armies made officers their primary targets, and that day Devil's Den swarmed with Confederate marksmen. Vincent, standing on the rocks and yelling at the retreating troops, was an obvious and easy mark for one of them. As the 16th went back into line, a bullet smashed into his left hip and stopped in his right thigh. Bones broke all along its path, and Vincent collapsed. "This is the fourth or fifth time they have shot at me," he told the troops who reached to pick him up, "and they have hit me at last." As the soldiers carried their colonel to the rear on a stretcher, the 140th New York regiment came over the top of the hill in the lead of Brig. Gen. Weed's Brigade of the 5th Corps' 2nd Division. The force of the counterattack, coupled with Vincent's timely halting of the 16th's retreat, was enough resistance to blunt the Confederate attack, and the three Rebel regiments slowly gave ground and went back down the slope of Little Round Top.[27]

Unaware of his colonel's wounding, Capt. Woodward of the 83rd saw that if the Rebels pressed the 20th Maine any farther the left half of the brigade would collapse and cut off the 83rd's only avenue of retreat. He dispatched the Adjutant, Lt. Gifford, to find Col. Chamberlain and see if the 20th could hold. Gifford found the colonel and learned that the Confederates were indeed close to breaking the line. The men of the 20th were fighting hand to hand in some places, and squads of Southerners were forcing their way through the line. Nearly overwhelmed, Chamberlain asked the 83rd to detach a company to come to his aid. With at least two Rebel regiments still to his front, Woodward could not let a company loose. Instead, the captain offered to elongate his line to the left to allow the 20th to do the same. Chamberlain concurred, and Woodward ordered the bulging line of the 83rd back a few paces and then the men shifted left. Corporal J. B. Potter of Company H recalled that the regiment executed the movement "still facing the enemy not 20 feet from us and firing as we went."[28]

In front of the 83rd, the 4th Alabama was tired and low on ammunition. Its commander, Lt. Col. Scruggs, later wrote that the Federal position was "impossible to carry." An officer of the 47th Alabama on their right recalled that he saw a wounded soldier walking to the rear who pleaded, "Adjutant, a handful of men can't drive those Yankees from that place. Can't you get Major Coleman to call the boys off before all are killed?" On the 4th Alabama's left, Maj. Bryan of the 5th Texas saw his commander, Col. James Powell, fall wounded. Bryan rushed to his aid and he too was hit in the arm, and command fell to another major. All over the Confederate line, fire slackened as the exhausted Rebels ran out of energy, officers, and ammunition.[29]

Col. Oates's Alabama troops were also tired, burning with thirst, and nearly out of cartridges, but the colonel formed his two regiments for another charge in the valley and started them back up the slope. At the same time, the 20th Maine had also expended its ammunition, and as Oates's men came back, Col. Chamberlain ordered his regiment to fix bayonets. With a tremendous shout, the Yankees charged down the slope and into the Confederate line. The force of the counterattack drove the Rebels back and Chamberlain's men followed, taking prisoners along the way. As the 20th came past the 83rd's line, the Pennsylvanians cheered and also charged after the retreating Confederates. In front of the 83rd, the 4th Alabama had run out of ammunition and "retired in good order," as its commander reported, but suffered eighty-seven men killed, wounded, or captured. Maj. Bryan of the 5th Texas wrote, "The command to fall back came from some unknown source, and, finding that the regiments on our right and left had retired, it became necessary to follow." Bryan ordered his men to turn about, and they moved off Little Round Top with 211 casualties. Capt. Nash of Vincent's staff later wrote that the enemy regiments "disappeared behind the banks of smoke and the lowering dusk of evening." The 83rd eventually captured nearly sixty Rebels, part of the 3rd Brigade's total of over 500 prisoners.[30]

The Rebel units withdrew towards Big Round Top. Troops from all the regiments of Vincent's Brigade pursued them, firing as they went. At the base of the hill, the Confederates stopped and set up a hasty defense among the rocks. Pvt. Giles of the 4th Texas recalled, "Every tree, rock and stump that afforded any protection from the rain of Minie balls that were poured down upon us from the crest above us, was soon appropriated.... By this time order and discipline were gone. Every fellow was his own general. Private soldiers gave commands as loud as the officers. Nobody paid attention to either."[31]

Nearly overextended, the Union troops broke off their pursuit and returned to Little Round Top. Col. Rice of the 44th had taken command of the brigade on Vincent's wounding, and one of his first acts had been to send "every officer and man in the rear not engaged, whether known or unknown," out with requests for ammunition and reinforcements. The results of Vincent's and Rice's pleas for troops was realized when five regiments of the Pennsylvania Reserves from the 3rd Division arrived just as the 3rd Brigade pushed their attackers back to Big Round Top. The rest of Weed's Brigade had also reinforced the northern half of the hill. The Confederates were exhausted, out of ammunition, and now on the defensive. By 7:00 PM, Little Round Top was firmly in the hands of the Union.[32]

As evening fell, Col. Rice ordered details out to bury the dead and bring in the wounded that still lay between the lines. Sgt. Sturdevant of the 44th recalled that "the scene where our first volley struck the enemy's line was one of sickening horror. Their dead and wounded were tumbled together, so that it was difficult to cross the

In the Valley of Death, photographed just after the battle. (LOC)

line where they fell without stepping on them." Capt. Amos Judson had returned from his hunt for ammunition and found the wounded Col. Bulger of the 47th Alabama. Judson recalled that the colonel "spoke and acted as if he was evidently tired of the war." Lt. David Rodgers of Company A captured Col. Powell of the 5th Texas and took the colonel's sword and revolver. Rodgers wrote that the colonel protested that the items cost over $75 and that Powell "did not like to give it up." Judson came across Powell later and recalled that the Rebel officer was "a man of quite a different stamp. He was one of your morose, sullen men, who imagine that to be insolent in the hour of defeat and humiliation is to be brave and resolute. 'You have peppered us pretty badly,' he observed with an air of self-satisfaction to Captain Woodward, 'but you'll get the worst of it before it's over!'"

Fire from Rebel sharpshooters made caring for the wounded dangerous work. Even as the attack ended, Pvt. Philip Grine of Company H left the 83rd's line and carried in a wounded Confederate. Before going out again he asked others for help. A few men followed Grine but lost heart when they came within sight of the enemy on Big Round Top. Grine told them that there was no danger from the Rebels and to follow on, but as he raised another injured man, a shot came from somewhere, and both fell to the ground dead. Acts like his generated Seth Waid's remembrance, "It was *affecting* to see our men when the firing partially seaced go out and bring in the wounded Rebs, Carrying the badly wounded on their backs and supporting others as they limped along."[33]

Judson remembered hearing groans come from a Rebel sergeant and private that were brought in. Going to help, he wrote, "I ... found them lying upon their blankets in a pool of blood, their limbs shivering with the cool night air, and the young sergeant incapable of moving without wrenching his broken bone, so as to send a thrill of agony through his whole body.... 'Oh, sir,' he exclaimed brokenly, 'I am glad you have come to my assistance; will you please give me a drink of water and help me to turn over; I am lying on my broken limb, and cannot help myself.'" Judson let the man drink from his canteen and with another soldier, made the pair a bed of leaves, bound their wounds with handkerchiefs and covered them with a blanket. Any movement made one man yell in agony, "Oh men, for God's sake, do be careful. Oh my mother!" Both thanked the Northerners, but Judson protested, "We told them that they need not feel themselves under any obligations for anything we had done, for though we might be foes on the field of battle, yet it was no more than the duty of every soldier to give assistance to a fallen foe in the hour of his misfortune." Before the night was over both were carried to the hospital, but Judson also hoped that "they lived to repent and abandon the errors of their ways." The Federal soldiers would pass an uneasy night surrounded by hundreds of wounded from both sides that had not been brought in. A sergeant of the 44th wrote of his time on the picket line: "The ground was literally covered with dead and wounded. It was the worst picket duty I ever performed. Will never forget it.... It was terrible, some crying, some praying, some swearing and all wanting help."[34]

Ten soldiers of the 83rd had been killed on Little Round Top, and most were buried on the hill that night. Another forty-five men had been wounded and taken to the farmhouses that the 5th Corps surgeons had commandeered as hospitals. Many from Vincent's Brigade went to the Leonard Bricker farm, which was half a mile east of Little Round Top. The Bricker farm probably filled up rapidly during the fighting, and other soldiers went to Jacob Weikert's farm, the Fiscel house or over a mile east to the home of Lewis Bushman, where Strong Vincent was carried.[35]

After the battle, Col. Rice sent Oliver Norton to look for ambulances and stretcher-bearers at the hospitals, but the private found no help. At last he noticed Lt. Col. Welch of the 16th Michigan outside the Bushman house, and Welch told him that Col. Vincent was inside. Norton went in and saw his colonel lying among the casualties in extreme pain from his hip wound. Norton wrote home, "He was very weak, but he held out his cold hand to me and asked 'if I had just come from the front.' When I told him yes, and how well the boys had fought, his eye brightened, but he was too weak to talk much." Norton later wrote that words failed him at that point. Stunned with emotion for the twenty-six year old lawyer who was in agony with a crippling, if not mortal wound, Norton hurried from the house to gather the stretchers he had been sent to find. Aside from Vincent, the 83rd's only loss among officers was Company I's commander, Capt. John M. Sell. Sell had been the acting Provost Marshal of the Division and was away from the regiment with his small guard force when the 3rd Brigade went to Little Round Top. When the 1st and 2nd Brigades were thrown into the fight to reinforce the 3rd Corps, Sell took his guards forward and was hit in the leg by a solid cannon shot. He died from the effects of amputation the next day.[36]

The Confederate attempts to take Cemetery Ridge had failed. Longstreet's assaults had initially broken the 3rd Corps, but Meade quickly reinforced the line with brigades from the 5th and 6th Corps and checked the advance. Limited Rebel attacks by Gen. Ewell's Corps on the northern end of the line at Culp's Hill were also repulsed. Little Round Top, what Gen. Warren had called "the key to whole position," firmly anchored the southern flank of the Union line, and the other high ground that dominated the battlefield—Culp's Hill, Cemetery Hill, and Cemetery Ridge—were also in Federal hands. Although the Army of the Potomac had lost some insignificant ground and taken thousands of casualties, it ended July 2 in a much stronger defensive position than it had in the morning. But Gen. Lee, despite the fact that his divisions had lost over 7,000 men, still believed that with the proper coordination, another series of attacks would break the Union line. As his hospitals filled with wounded, Lee planned to launch both wings of his army against the Federals the next day. Ewell's Corps would attack Culp's Hill while three divisions of Longstreet's and Hill's Corps made a direct assault on the center of the Union line on Cemetery Ridge. Maj. Gen. George Pickett's Division of Longstreet's Corps had recently arrived on the field and was still fresh. His troops would spearhead the attack the next day.[37]

Later that evening, Col. Rice felt that the enemy might use Big Round Top as an advanced stronghold the next day. With Little Round Top sufficiently held by three brigades, he sent the 20th Maine up to the top of the wooded hill to keep it out of enemy hands. Some of the Pennsylvania Reserves that had arrived were supposed to reinforce the 20th, but through some confusion, the order was not carried out. The Rebel regiments that had attacked that afternoon were still in position at the base of Big Round Top, and Chamberlain felt his regiment was too exposed to hold the hill alone. He asked Rice for reinforcements, and Rice sent the 83rd and the 44th up sometime around midnight. The Reserves eventually made their way to the hill and joined with the 20th, and by morning a solid line of Union troops extended across both hills.[38]

Firing from the area of Culp's Hill, the beginning of Lee's attacks, woke the men of the 83rd early on July 3. As it became clear that the action would be elsewhere that day, Col. Rice had the brigade's prisoners bury the dead that still lay on the field. One of the details found the 83rd's Pvt. Grine lying where he was killed the day before while helping to bring in the wounded, the Rebel he had tried to pick up was beside him. Sometime before noon, the 1st Brigade relieved Rice's troops, and the brigade moved about a half mile north to the end of Cemetery Ridge, in reserve again. Pvt. Seth Waid noted: "We were relieved before the middle of the forenoon and came to the rear to rest, and *oh* how we needed it."[39]

The men had an easy few hours while they were off the main line, but in the early afternoon, Confederate artillery opened fire on Cemetery Ridge in preparation for the grand assault. The 3rd Brigade's position was almost a mile from the intended point of the attack, but unfortunately for Rice's men, many of the Rebel gunners fired too high and their shells arched over their targets into the Union rear, where the men of the 83rd now hugged the ground. Amos Judson recalled: "The earth shook like an earthquake, and the air was filled with missiles of death, screaming, hissing and whiling in every direction over the field.... Hundreds burst over and around us, hurling their fragments in every direction." Despite the fury of the two-hour bombardment, the 83rd took no serious casualties.[40]

When the barrage ended, three Confederate divisions came out of the trees on Seminary Ridge and advanced toward the Union line in what is now known as Pickett's Charge. The 3rd Brigade was not called forward, but Amos Judson used his freedom as a mounted aide to go back to Little Round top to observe the battle. Two batteries of rifled Parrot guns lobbed explosive shells at Rebel artillery and infantry from the crest of the hill, and the ground that the men had fought so hard for was being put to good use. "Mount Sinai in all its glory, never thundered, nor belched forth such volumes of smoke and lightning, as did the grand little citadel upon this memorable day," Judson remembered. The Rebel assault reached its unsuccessful climax in the late afternoon and the Confederates retreated to Seminary Ridge under fire from the batteries on Little Round Top. Col. Vincent's soldiers had made their contribution to stopping Pickett's Charge a day before it occurred.[41]

Earlier that day, Gen. Meade telegraphed Washington and recommended Vincent for promotion to brigadier-general for "gallant conduct on the field." Meade stated, "[Vincent] is mortally wounded, and it would gratify his friends, as well as myself. It was my intention to have recommended him with others, should he live." Behind the lines at the Bushman House, Strong Vincent was in great pain. Gen. Butterfield, who had been slightly wounded in the battle, visited Vincent and told him of Meade's recommendation. Vincent told his old commander that he wished to leave for home at once, and Butterfield authorized Lt. Clark to take him by ambulance to the hospital at Westminster and then by train to Baltimore. When the 3rd Brigade surgeon informed the colonel that his wound made movement impossible, Vincent asked for someone to send for his wife. Clark fulfilled his request (though the telegraphs did not reach Erie for three days) but Vincent's injuries were beyond the capabilities of the field surgeons to repair and the new general was not recovering. Any movement that jarred his broken leg must have been excruciating, but the new general stoically concealed his pain and told one visitor, "I presume I have done my last fighting."[42]

The next day, Gen. Lee expected the Federals to counterattack immediately, but Meade's army held their ground. They had repulsed the Confederate attacks and inflicted nearly 25,000 casualties, but the Army of the Potomac had also lost 23,000 men and was badly disorganized. The remaining troops were low on ammunition and exhausted. The army was in no shape to immediately counterattack the Rebels, and Meade was content to let his men recover. Rain came in the middle of the day. The 3rd Brigade relieved some 2nd Corps troops and picketed, but there was no fighting—the men of both sides were too tired to shoot at each other.[43]

With his fighting strength left on the fields of Gettysburg, Gen. Lee began pulling his army off Seminary Ridge and back into Virginia. The downpour covered the retreat, and it was not until the next morning, Sunday, July 5, that the Federals discovered that the Rebels had slipped away. After a year of being beaten and retreating from the Confederates, Oliver Norton was at last able to write home, "We had one of the greatest battles of the war, and a great victory too"— words that he had never used before to describe his own army's actions. Lt. Israel Thickstun of the 83rd, still on detached duty with the Signal Corps, wrote home: "Our army never was [better] handled before on a battlefield.... The Rebel army [was] thoroughly whipped...."[44]

The Army of the Potomac marched south in pursuit of the Lee's army two days later. Their victory gave some men hope that they had broken the Confederates, and Seth Waid wrote before the 83rd left, "How earnestly I hope that this is the last of the Rebellion."[45]

On July 7, the day the Union army left Gettysburg, Strong Vincent died at the Bushman House as he whispered the Lord's Prayer.[46]

There were two more years of war.

For None Others Can Know

Adjutant Clark's telegrams to Elizabeth Vincent, sent from Hanover and Westminster on July 2, finally reached the Vincent home on July 5 or 6. It is unknown how much Clark explained in the messages, but the fact that Strong had called for his wife could only mean that the colonel was gravely wounded and possibly dying. Bethel Boyd Vincent immediately left Erie for the battlefield to care for his son. Lizzie Vincent could not travel. She was seven months pregnant.

B. B. Vincent reached Gettysburg on July 8 and began searching for his son among the twenty thousand wounded. Working his way to the 5th Corps hospitals, he found a soldier who informed him that Strong was dead. Lt. Clark had left Gettysburg that morning with the general's remains.

It was on the evening of July 10 that the train carrying Clark and Vincent arrived in Erie. The funeral, which began at the Vincent home, included former members of the Three Months Regiment, officers of the 83rd home on leave, a detachment of Regulars, Mehl's Band, and members of the Erie Bar and Furnace Molders.

On July 13, the same day as Vincent's funeral in Erie, the Army of Northern Virginia crossed the Potomac River into Virginia. Gen. Meade's army continued their pursuit two days later. By the end of the month both armies had moved to the banks of the Rappahannock River. Lee's army, though it had suffered greatly at Gettysburg, was intact and still blocked a Federal advance to Richmond. Another campaign, this one would become known as the "Mine Run" campaign, began, and Seth Waid's wish for the end of the war did not come true.

In pursuit of the Rebels, Norton wrote that the army was "barefooted, hungry, lousy, and faint.... The horse are worn out, every day's march killing from five to twenty in each battery," and there was not much difference in the men of the 83rd from their state of a year before when they were on the Peninsula. But the nature of the war was changing.[1]

Lee's second invasion of the North had been broken at Gettysburg. Though Gen. Meade came under some criticism for not completely destroying the Rebels after Gettysburg, he had proven himself a competent commander. He led the army without the timidity of McClellan, the ineptitude of Burnside, or the political overconfidence of Hooker. Cautious as well as tough and tenacious, Meade would stay in command of the Army of the Potomac until the end of the war. In the west, Gen. Grant's army had taken the city of Vicksburg on July 4, giving the Union uncontested control of the Mississippi River and splitting the Confederacy. A Federal army under Maj. Gen. William Rosecrans secured Tennessee. These

Union successes and the Emancipation Proclamation (officially announced in January 1863) eliminated the possibility that foreign powers would intervene on the behalf of the Confederacy. Spirits in the South sank as those in the North rose. Though the war was far from over and some of the hardest fighting was still ahead, victory for the Union was inevitable after the summer of 1863, as long as the North maintained the will to fight.

But the losses of the first three years of the war were more than the Union could expect to replace through voluntary enlistment and lenient conscription. Through disease and battle, regiments fielded, on average, 643 men in the summer of 1863. Officer vacancies were particularly high. To keep the armies manned, Congress passed a new conscription law that applied to all males aged twenty to forty-five and allowed for enforcement through local Provost Marshal Offices. Such an extensive draft was met with much opposition in the North. Riots erupted in New York City. Despite the opposition, the drafts continued.[2]

Previous draft laws had issued quotas to congressional districts, and the districts could meet their requirements by volunteer enlistment or with men who joined for a bounty. Under that system, Erie County had always met its quotas for volunteers in the first two years of the war. But by 1863, the same counties that had spawned the 83rd had sent soldiers into the 39th, 42nd, 58th, 111th, 113th, 145th, 151st, 159th, 182nd, 193rd and 211th Pennsylvania Infantry Regiments, as well as the 14th and 21st Cavalry. Most of the men who would join the army out of patriotism or solely for cash were already gone, and northwestern Pennsylvania would not be able to escape the draft of 1863.

As Provost Marshal of the northwestern congressional district, Col. Hugh Campbell, the former commander of the 83rd who had lost a leg at the Second Battle of Bull Run, presided over the area's first draft, held in Erie on August 24. A crowd watched as Campbell and the draft board drew lottery numbers. Aware of the discord the draft had caused in other cities, especially New York, Campbell took the precaution to post a company of Regular Army troops for security at the site. The Erie *Observer* reported that the crowd cheered with each name announced, and "all of them appeared to take it in the best humor possible." But the Democratic-leaning paper also opined that the crowd "consisted mostly of Republicans."[3]

With such a large number of men being raised by the draft, single towns or counties would no longer bear responsibility for entire regiments, and the men conscripted in the northwestern portion of the state were not necessarily destined for the 83rd or one of the other regiments from that area. The first allotment of conscripts that reached the 83rd in mid–August was raised from the southeastern corner of Pennsylvania. The soldiers who had joined the army out of patriotism had always disdained those who were compelled into service, but the conscripts of 1863 were worse than any the army had yet received. Amos Judson, who was posted to recruitment duty in Philadelphia that summer and commanded the first lot of draftees, said that those sent to the 83rd were "mostly procured in the market at Philadelphia. There were men among them from almost every nation of Europe." The commander of Company G, Capt. George Stowe, accepted about 150 new soldiers in Philadelphia and took them to join the regiment at its camp on the Rappahannock, but several deserted along the way and Stowe arrived at the regiment's camp on the Rappahannock River with only 127 men. When the 83rd's adjutant turned in a list of the deserters to the Provost Marshal, he wrote in bold and underlined, "Drafted men and substitutes," lest they become confused with the veteran members of the regiment.[4]

The new soldiers raised the 83rd's strength to 404 men, and 146 more arrived in September. October saw 131 more. But their value as fighting men was doubtful. Judson noted that many would fight bravely in the coming battles, "but the majority of them were the grandest scoundrels that ever went unhung." It was rumored that many had joined to escape punishment for arson, robbery, and murder. Daniel Foote wrote, "They are from every nation under the sun. English, Irish, French, Germans, Russians, Danes and Swedes. One is a murderer, others rebel deserters." Short on patriotism, the new men brawled often and skulked away when battle was imminent. The law allowed drafted men to buy substitutes to take their place for the price of $300, and "Bounty jumpers"—men who made a business out of continually deserting their regiments and then offering themselves as paid substitutes in other states—were common. In addition to the men that never made it to the regiment, the 83rd saw five desertions in September, seventy-three in October, and twenty-four in December. Such troublesome men were not missed, and when they deserted, Judson called it "thanks to a kind Providence, or some other invisible power of redemption."[5]

Desertions were so rampant that five men of the 1st Division received a sentence of death, the maximum punishment allowed under the Articles of War, in late August. To leave the soldiers with a vivid impression of what awaited deserters, the entire 5th Corps was formed to observe the execution by firing squad. The men stood in silence as the prisoners, with their arms pinioned behind their backs, were marched to the foot of five open graves. A bugle sounded, and the commands of ready, aim, fire rang clear over the field. The five men fell back on their coffins. Witness Daniel Foote wrote, "That is a good beginning. I hope they will catch the 30 that has deserted and shoot them all at once." Seth Waid wrote that some of the substitutes talked of how the penalty was too harsh, but the veterans told them that it was a just penalty, one that "*we hoped* every deserter might receive for his folly and crime."[6]

The draftees swelled the ranks of the 83rd to over 560 in the fall of 1863, but though the regiment was larger than it had been in over a year, there was little test of its new strength. The Army of Northern Virginia had retreated all the way to the Rapidan River, north of Richmond, and Gen. Meade kept the Federal formations north of the Rappahannock. Spurred by the President, Meade maneuvered his corps in a series of moves designed to get around the Rebel flanks. As they had in previous campaigns, the men of the 83rd took part in a series of marches, the object of which they were never informed. The weather was wet and the roads were muddy. Only enemy pickets were seen, and by December, the 83rd had declared an unofficial truce with their opposite numbers and the men traded coffee and tobacco over the lines. Gen. Lee parried each of the Union attempts to turn his flank, and in early December Meade gave up the campaign and sent the army into winter quarters on the Rappahannock River.

The winter on the Rappahannock was uneventful. Elections were held in the 83rd in January 1864; Capt. Woodward was officially installed as the colonel, and Capt. DeWitt McCoy was made the lieutenant colonel. But the majority of the army consisted of men who had enlisted for three-year terms in 1861. Their service would expire just as the new campaigns began in the spring of 1864. As most of the men had seen more war than they had ever imagined, they were not likely to voluntarily re-enlist without significant incentive. To avoid a mass exodus of the ranks, in the fall of 1863 the War Department offered each veteran who re-enlisted a bounty of $400, a 30-day furlough, a promotion and the right to call

Three veterans of the 83rd, John Shields, George Mallory, and Brownlee Zuver (L-R), pose with the shredded remnants of the regiment's state colors sometime after the war. In 1884, Zuver returned to Gettysburg to mark the 83rd's position there and promised to return with a doll for his daughter. Zuver was killed in a train accident during the trip, and afterward, his daughter sent his story to a Washington newspaper. When the paper printed the tale, veterans' groups from all over the United States, north and south, mailed the girl dolls of every type. (The Zuver family)

themselves "Veteran Volunteers." These bonuses were presented to the soldiers in the most patriotic manner with speeches, songs, and often in rallies with alcoholic beverages. Nearly 27,000 men, enough to hold the army together, took the government's offer.[7]

The terms for the 83rd's soldiers would expire within a year. Out of about 360 of the original members left in the regiment that fall, 169 re-enlisted and became Veteran Volunteers over the winter of 1863-64. Daniel Foote also elected to stay on, though he had tired so much of infantry service that he had applied for a transfer to the Signal Corps. The transfer was disapproved, and Foote accepted a promotion to corporal in Company K instead. Israel Thickstun continued his service in the Signal Corps. David Rodgers also re-enlisted. George Bedient, the private in Company I who helped Capt. Hiram Brown at Gaines's Mill, re-enlisted as a corporal. Amos Judson and Seth Waid were two of the men who had joined with John McLane that did not elect to stay on.[8]

The formation of regiments of free blacks was another of the North's efforts to man their armies in the field and had been announced in the Emancipation Proclamation. White officers led the regiments. In May 1863, Oliver Norton had responded to the government's request for officer volunteers in the United States Colored Troops. It was October when he received word to go to Washington for examinations on his fitness for a commission.[9]

Norton was sure of his qualifications, but as far as the War Department was concerned, a successful officer applicant had to pass a physical examination and oral tests on Casey's tactics manual, geography, history, arithmetic, algebra, geometry, Army Regulations and forms, and the Articles of War. Apprehensive, he spent two weeks in Washington studying. Norton's turn for the orals came in late October. He wrote without shame that he cheated slightly on the eye examination, and the veteran probably suppressed a laugh when the doctor asked him if he could march twenty-five miles without becoming sick. "I told [the surgeon] I could and had," he wrote his father, "and he seemed satisfied." Norton also went sightseeing at the Patent Office and the Smithsonian Institution. He told his mother, "I won't try to tell you what I saw there. It set my brain a whirl...." Though he was confident that he had passed, Norton was still assigned to the Third Brigade headquarters and he rejoined the brigade on the Rappahannock. It was not until November that he finally received his commission as a first lieutenant in the 8th United States Colored Troops, then quartered in Philadelphia. Within a day, Norton packed his baggage, said goodbye to the soldiers he had served with for two years, and left to join his new regiment.[10]

In March, President Lincoln appointed Gen. Grant as the commander of all the Union armies. Planning to lead from the field, he joined the Army of the Potomac in its camp that spring.

For three years, the operations of the Army of the Potomac had focused on capturing Richmond or stopping Confederate invasions of the North. But by 1864 Lincoln realized that victory could only come through killing or capturing the Rebel armies themselves. Instead of taking Richmond, Grant's objective was the destruction of the Army of Northern Virginia.

In May, Grant took his army across the Rapidan River and attempted to move around the Confederates' flank. In the series of actions that became known as the Wilderness Campaign, both sides suffered huge numbers of casualties. But instead of returning to his camps as previous Union generals had, Grant kept his army on the offensive. Battles followed at Spotsylvania, North Anna and Cold Harbor. Though the casualties were high, Grant's relentless attacks had pushed the Rebels south. Cold Harbor—where Grant attacked and was repulsed in June—was the same village where the 83rd had camped in the summer of 1862, and Federal forces were once again less than ten miles from Richmond. When the Confederates entrenched around the critical railroad junction-city of Petersburg, south of Richmond, the Union army dug mirroring siege lines. By the fall both armies were locked in a stalemated siege of the city. They remained there for the rest of 1864.

The 83rd, under the command of Lt. Col. DeWitt McCoy, was outside Petersburg in early September when the three-year enlistments of its original members expired. Excluding the men who had re-enlisted with the Veteran Volunteers, about 170 of the men who joined Col. McLane in 1861 were still in the regiment and subject to discharge. Capt. Amos Judson, who had returned to the 83rd in June after his service on the Third Brigade staff, was one of them. On September 7, Lt. Col. McCoy loaded them on a steamer on the James bound for Washington. A few days later they arrived in Harrisburg. There they remained for a few more weeks while the paperwork mustering them out was completed, and the men made their ways back

Lt. Oliver Norton, 8th U.S. Colored Troops.

home. Reporting that the soldiers' tours were ending, the editor of the *Erie Weekly Gazette* told readers, "Let a cordial reception be extended to the brave men of it *who are left* on their arrival at this place. They really deserve honor and gratitude at our hands." If the city officially honored the men when they reached home, there was no mention of it in the paper.[11]

Like Judson, Seth Waid also went home that fall. In October 1863 he had gone back into the division hospital from a sickness he contracted on the march into Virginia, possibly jaundice. He spent a month in another hospital in Washington and returned to the regiment in December. With his usual reflection, he mused that month, "So we pass through the journey of life youth and its freshness and beauty is soon gone then comes middle life, then old age, and death. Then a new race fills the place of that which has passed and gone, and we are forgotten."

In the spring of 1864 Waid was diagnosed as having a "cistic tumor" and declared unfit for duty in the field. That May he went to another hospital in Philadelphia and was assigned nurse's duties again while he waited for a surgeon to operate on his tumor. For some reason the doctors were reluctant to operate, and it was eventually lanced and that relieved Waid's discomfort. Waid stayed at the hospital over the summer. On September 3 the doctor told Waid he was relieved from all duties and to be mustered out. He received his papers that night and began his journey home. Within days he arrived back at his farm in Crawford County, where he wrote, "*I am at home. Who can describe the deeply interesting emotions of the Soul, as it passes over the road described in the forgoing? I cannot. My pen is too feeble, my lips to dumb for the task, and I leave it to be imagined, aye, to be experienced by those who are of like Sencibilitys for none others can know.*" It was the last entry in his war diary.[12]

With the departure of the old-timers, there were less than 300 soldiers—the Veteran Volunteers (like Daniel Foote), the few volunteers who had joined in 1862, and the conscripts—assigned to the 83rd. Army Regulations dictated that such a small number of men did not justify the title of "regiment." Those remaining were re-organized into six companies and re-named the 83rd "Battalion." Chauncey P. Rogers, who had formerly commanded Company D and had been wounded at Malvern Hill, was appointed a lieutenant colonel and commanded the unit. After that, the men settled into their winter quarters outside Petersburg. Skirmishing continued despite the poor weather, and thirteen men were lost in a small battle at Hatcher's Run in February 1865. In March, four new companies of conscripts, raised near Harrisburg, were added. With a full complement of men, the battalion was re-designated as the 83rd Pennsylvania Regiment again.[13]

Though the 83rd was back up to fighting strength, the end of the Army of Northern Virginia was near. In March, Union troops moved around the Confederate works at Petersburg and the Rebels pulled out of their trenches in an attempt to escape to the west. The Federals pursued, and by the end of the month Lee's army was reduced to 28,000 men and had been cornered. When the 5th Corps marched thirteen miles and cut off the retreating Rebels at Five Forks, Virginia, on March 31, Pvt. Alva Higley, who had joined Company H the previous March, was the regiment's sole casualty and last death in battle.

By early April the Confederates were cut off, greatly outnumbered, and worn out. Daniel Foote excitedly wrote home that the Fifth Corps had taken 20,000 prisoners. The men of the 83rd, he said, were "in fine spirits and dreaming of home every night. We shall soon be through this war, God continuing to grant mercies to our victorious army." The regiment passed thousands of prisoners on the roads and rumors of surrender flew through the camps.[14]

The rumors came true on April 11, when Gen. Lee met Grant at a farmhouse near Appomattox Court House and surrendered the Army of Northern Virginia. The ceremony was scheduled to take place on April 12, and the 1st Division, 5th Corps, was awarded the honor of forming the Union honor guard. Joshua Chamberlain, former commander of the 20th Maine who had held Little Round Top with the 3rd Brigade, by then commanded the Division's 1st Brigade. Twice wounded and promoted for bravery, it was he who was appointed to accept the surrender of the Confederate regiments. With a special sentimentality for his old unit, Chamberlain asked that the 3rd Brigade compose the honor guard at the surrender site. When the Army of Northern Virginia passed through the lines of Yankee soldiers and laid down their arms, the 83rd stood in salute with Chamberlain.[15]

Three days later, the 5th Corps began its return march to Washington. The same day rumors ran through the ranks that the President had been assassinated. The rumors were confirmed on April 19. The Army suspended all operations in mourning, and the bands played funeral dirges all day. Daniel Foote called it "the nation's saddest day for years.... It is a sad, sad thing for that noble man to die after years of hard labor just completed, but undoubtedly it is for the best for the nation or it would not have been permitted by our Wise Ruler."[16]

The corps continued its march to Washington the next day. As it had been all throughout the war, the men moved with little information. There were rumors that they were going to join the western armies who were still fighting with Gen. Joe Johnston's Confederates in southern Virginia. On May 6 they passed through Richmond, the target of their earliest campaign, and saw Libby Prison, already famous as a jail for captured Union officers. Amos Judson had been held there during his captivity. Lt. Plympton White, who had demanded the enemy surrender at Gaines's Mill, had been captured in June 1863 and also imprisoned there. White had escaped in February 1864, been re-captured, and confined in a dark basement cell at Libby. Transferred to Macon, Georgia, and then to a hospital in Charleston, South Carolina, White had died of disease in September 1864.

The same day, they followed the road out of Richmond to Mechanicsville and on to Hanover Court House. That night, they camped on the field of their first battle. It was a reverse-march of the Peninsula Campaign and it would have been an eerie event if there were enough of the men who had lived through the events present to appreciate it. If Daniel Foote felt any queer feelings as they returned to the fields where he first saw men killed, he did not write about it. Col. Rodgers was one who definitely remembered the area, and as the column passed Gaines's Mill he took a detachment and disinterred Col. McLane's remains from the hasty battlefield grave where they had lain for three years. Rodgers had the body transported to Washington and then on to Erie, where it arrived on May 13. On May 19, Col. John McLane was laid to rest at the Erie Cemetery, not far from his young friend, supporter, and successor, Strong Vincent.[17]

Even in victory, the men kept a grueling pace. They covered seventeen miles on May 3; nineteen on the eighth; twenty-four on the ninth; seventeen on the tenth; and thirty-two miles on May 11, when they arrived at Fairfax Station on a rainy afternoon. Daniel Foote, who had been in all the Army of the Potomac's campaigns for the last four years, was now returning to the city for the third time of the war. A long march was by then a routine task for him, and he said the journey was "a distance of 120 miles carrying bed and board with us as usual."[18]

On May 12 the regiment reached the outskirts of Alexandria and camped near the Fairfax Seminary (near Alexandria and Leesburg Pike), on land that was rumored to belong to Gen. Lee himself. By then Jefferson Davis had been captured, and Daniel Foote hoped they would hang Davis, and wrote: "I have thought that Mr. Lincoln was to easy with the traitors of our country who have in a measure brought on this war, when he has had them in his power." Even though Foote wished for stern treatment of the Southerners, he noted that he was in favor of pardoning all rebels except the "leaders." "There has been bloodshed enough already," he wrote home.[19]

With significant Confederate resistance in all the theaters of war ended, the Union armies' sole task was to parade before their grateful public and government in front of the White House. On May 23, the 83rd woke early and marched into Washington. Along with the rest of the 5th Corps, the men marched down Pennsylvania Avenue surrounded by cheering crowds. As soon as they returned to their camp in Alexandria, rumors about when the troops would be released ran through the camps.[20]

The 5th Corps began mustering troops out the next day and would be finished within two days, but the process of mustering out was not just a matter of giving men their papers and sending them home. All the regiment's equipment and supplies were Government property and required proper accounting. The mass of finance books, roll books, equipment and payroll receipts and other military paperwork also needed proper care. The 83rd began releasing soldiers in small groups as early as May 29, but much of the regiment was still in uniform in mid–June, probably because of the bureaucratic burden of leaving Federal service. It was not until June 27 that all of the men were officially mustered out, but even then they had to go to Harrisburg to receive their discharge papers and final pay. Daniel Foote had been promoted to the second lieutenant's position in Company K, and when the final orders for discharge came his commander was absent. In command of the company, it fell to Foote to stay on after all the men left and settle the accounts of government property. His own pay in arrears, Foote had to ask his father to send $20 so he could buy his new officer's uniform and sword. Foote cleared up the company books quickly, and his military record shows that he was also released on June 28. By July, the entire regiment was mustered out and had returned to their homes.[21]

※ ※ ※

There had been over 3,000,000 men listed in militia organizations before the Civil War. In 1893, there were 112,000. Perhaps deterred by the stories of combat from old soldiers, the military spirit that supported the volunteer armies waned in the latter nineteenth century.

Though the volunteers of 1861 hated the concept, conscription had enabled the Union to man its huge armies and defeat the Confederacy. The close-knit, community-based volunteer regiments like the 83rd had fought bravely, but as the Government's mid-war recruitment efforts had shown, the cities, towns and counties that had supplied the early units were incapable of supporting them through a long war.

Though these lessons were clear, the United States retained the volunteer concept and used it again in the Spanish-American War in 1898 with limited success. Post-war reviews revealed that the Army had repeated many of the mobilization mistakes of the Civil War. Even after that, the Army's mobilization concept still relied on the Regulars, the National Guard (the successor to the militia) and volunteers. The War Department tested the concept during a series of crises with Mexico from 1911 to 1917 and found that the system was incapable of manning a modern army. When the United States entered the First World War in 1917, the War Department quickly opted to raise a "National Army" composed of a mix of Regulars, National Guardsmen and conscripts. The drafts had supplied six percent of the total Union Army in the Civil War; but by 1918, 67 percent of the troops were conscripts. The Civil War was the last to be fought by huge volunteer armies.[22]

By the time the old Army died, most of the men of the 83rd had gone with it.

Amos Judson, who had left the regiment when his term of enlistment expired in September 1864, accepted an appointment in the War Department in January 1865 and moved to Washington. Although he was not on active service with the regiment, Gov. Curtain appointed him a major in the 83rd and he received a brevet commission as lieutenant colonel from President Andrew Johnson. Judson's position at the War Department gave him easy access to the records of the war. Within weeks of the regiment's disbanding, he gathered the 83rd's official reports and muster rolls and began writing his history of the unit. It was one of the first Civil War unit histories published and remains renowned for its candor, humor and sound literary style. In 1866, Judson transferred to the Treasury Department and in 1870, married the former Clementine Crouchet. The couple settled in Washington and had five children. Judson died in 1913 and was buried in the District of Columbia. His eulogizer remembered, "Of such stuff are heroes made." His descendants still live in the Washington area.[23]

Seth Waid returned to farming and spent the rest of his days in Randolph Township. He died in 1905, three years after his wife passed away.[24]

David Rodgers married Julia Porter in December 1863. Wounded in the Spotsylvania Campaign, he had been discharged for disabilities in the fall of 1864. After the war he farmed in Chautauqua, New York, and Ashtabula, Ohio. When Julia's father died in 1867, he returned to their home in Pleasantville, Pennsylvania, and managed the Porter farms. He later drilled for oil, and rose to become a respected operator in the petroleum business. He and Julia had four children. He died in 1917.[25]

George Bedient, who had been wounded in the throat at Gaines's Mill and helped Capt. Hiram Brown across the Chickahominy, served with the regiment until it disbanded. He married in 1866 and fathered a son. Bedient lived in Erie until 1879, moved to Pittsburgh, then Baltimore in 1893. His injury caused what doctors termed "partial paralysis of the throat" and it troubled him constantly. Bedient's first wife died in 1889, and he re-married in 1900. A daughter was born the same year, but Bedient died in 1910 at the age of 62. His second wife raised the child.[26]

Orpheus Woodward, who had risen from command of Company E to colonel of the regiment, had his right leg amputated above the knee after his wounding in the Wilderness in May 1864. He returned to Erie, and after the war served two terms in the Pennsylvania House of Representatives. Woodward had married in September 1861, and in 1868 he and his wife moved to Woodson County in southeastern Kansas. There he entered the hardware business, farmed, and served four years in the Kansas Senate. Later biographies called him "one of the most prominent men of Woodson County." He had three children, suffered several light strokes in later life, and died in Neosho Falls, Kansas, in June 1919.[27]

Hugh Campbell, also former commander of the 83rd, completed his service as Erie County's Provost Marshal when the war ended. Along with his wife and three children, he moved to Paola, Kansas, in 1867 and engaged in real estate. By 1883 he owned extensive property in Miami County but his wounds caused chronic rheumatism that confined him to his home. Campbell's condition worsened and he eventually contracted blood poisoning. He died from the condition in August 1890 at the age of 61.[28]

Daniel Foote returned to Wattsburg after mustering out in June 1865. That October, he married Julia Hill, his faithful correspondent of the war. He operated his own dry goods company in Wattsburg until 1872, and then sold his interests and entered the meat and grocery business. Foote's business expanded into a two-building concern with a full line of dry goods, groceries and school supplies, and an 1884 synopsis of their township said he and Julia "by their courtesy and strict business habits ... have built up a first-class trade." The Footes had three children, and an 1884 the family moved to Harrisburg. The effects of his leg wound and the rheumatism he contracted during the campaigns bothered him for the rest of his life, and after examining him in 1903, a surgeon stated, "There is marked debility ... he is older than a man of 64." Foote died in Harrisburg at the age of 70 in November 1911.[29]

Oliver Norton served the rest of the war with the 8th U.S. Colored Troops and saw more action at the battle of Olustee in Florida in February 1864. He spoke highly of the bravery of the soldiers in his company, but Norton was unimpressed by the regiment's inept officers. They spent the spring and summer of that year garrisoning the city of Jacksonville, and in August the 8th U.S.C.T. went back to Virginia to join Maj. Gen. Butler's Army of the James as part of the campaign around Petersburg. By the end of the month Norton succumbed to the effects of sunstroke that he had suffered in Florida, and for the first time of the war he was sent to the hospital. "I am weak and enervated," he wrote his sister from Ft. Monroe, "unable to endure fatigue as I used to in the old campaigns." He returned to the regiment in October and was assigned as the Acting Regimental Quartermaster. He wrote home, "I have had a good share of duty in the line and can afford to let some one else win the glory now while I take it easy."[30]

Norton was in Baltimore when Lee's Army surrendered. Days later he went into Richmond, and wrote his father, "To-day completes the fourth year of my efforts to reach Richmond, and I am here." His regiment crossed paths with the 5th Corps as the Army of the Potomac returned to Washington in May. When the 83rd passed, Norton wrote, "I should never have known it for the same regiment. Not a dozen of the old men who were in the ranks when I left remained, but there were a few that greeted me joyfully." He called the day "one of the happiest" he had ever experienced in the Army.[31]

Though the 83rd went home, the 8th U.S.C.T. went to Texas to garrison forts along the Rio Grande. There he was fascinated by Mexican culture, especially the ladies, and delighted that he was known as "Don Olivero el Quartelmaestro." In November his regiment also mustered out, and Norton returned to his home in Springfield.[32]

Norton went to work at the Fourth National Bank of New York City after the war. In 1869, he and his brother Edwin moved to Toledo, Ohio, and opened a can and sheet metal manufacturing company. They moved the business to Chicago in 1870 and there they pioneered automatic machinery for can making. Oliver married Lucy Fanning of Brooklyn, New York, the same year and the couple eventually had five children. One boy was named Strong Vincent Norton. The company expanded to other cities and eventually merged with the American Can Company in 1901.

By then Norton was 62 years old and his eyesight was failing. He retired soon after the company's merger. In 1903 he published a collection of his wartime correspondence as *Army Letters, 1861-1865*. Though almost totally blind, he dictated his next book, *The Attack and Defense of Little Round Top*, which came out in 1912. The book was an earnest analysis of the events of July 2, 1863, and relied on the official reports of the units involved on both sides and post-war histories of the battle. It was also an unabashed attempt to bring honor to Strong Vincent for his quick seizure of Little Round Top. Norton's last book, *Strong Vincent and His Brigade at Little Round Top*, repeated some of the same arguments. Norton remained an advocate of Vincent's until his death in Chicago in 1920, at the age of 80.[33]

Norton kept in close contact with Vincent's widow, Lizzie Vincent. Distraught after her husband's death, Lizzie had remained with the Vincent family in Erie. Often dreaming of Strong's death, she dreaded sleep. On September 29, 1863, she gave birth to a daughter, Blanche Strong Vincent. The child enlivened Lizzie's spirits, but Blanche died the next September nine days before her first birthday. Lizzie stayed with the Vincents for the rest of her life. The family moved to Pittsburgh, then Cincinnati, where she was active in the church and young women's charities. She died in 1914 and was buried alongside Strong and their daughter in the Erie Cemetery. In her will, she left Oliver Norton $250, which was to be spent on "the best cigars he can buy."[34]

Though military ardor ebbed in the latter half of the nineteenth century, the soldiers of the Civil War cherished their memories of the conflict. Veteran's organizations like the Grand Army of the Republic, the Military Order of the Loyal Legion, and local regimental associations thrived. For years after the war the various groups gave veterans opportunities to meet and relive their experiences that had been terrible, but faded with time. Daniel Foote, Oliver Norton, Orpheus Woodward and Amos Judson all regularly attended the annual meetings of the 83rd Regimental Association. In 1889, Pennsylvania commissioned a monument to the 83rd on the slope of Little Round Top. The monument was placed a few yards behind the regiment's line of July 2, and topped by a likeness of Vincent. Oliver Norton read the dedication for the monument. In 1911, at the 83rd's fiftieth anniversary, 273 men attended. Sixty-six members attended the encampment of the Grand

Army of the Republic and the Confederate Veterans at Gettysburg for the fiftieth anniversary of the battle in 1913, and the veterans of the 3rd Brigade met on Little Round Top. Oliver Norton took his bugle to the summit and blew the 3rd Brigade call, "Dan, Dan, Dan, Butterfield," and the veterans gathered from all around with tears in their eyes.[35]

For years afterward, Erie newspapers reported the annual meetings of the 83rd Regimental Association. The group met in ever-decreasing numbers, and at their meeting in 1930, only six members attended out of thirty-nine living veterans of the regiment throughout the United States.[36]

There were no more reports about the meetings after that.

NOTES

Chapter I: Here Am I, Let Me Go

1. William F. Fox, *Regimental Losses in the American Civil War* (Albany, New York: Albany Publishing Company, 1889), 282; Monthly Returns of the 83rd Pennsylvania for August, 1862 and June 1863, Records of the Adjutant General's Office, Record Group 94, National Archives; Oliver Norton to Father, July 9, 1862, Oliver W. Norton, *Army Letters, 1861–1865* (1903; reprint, Dayton, Ohio: Morningside House, 1990), 97; John W. Busey and David G. Martin, *Regimental Strengths and Losses at Gettysburg* (Hightstown, New Jersey: Longstreet House, 1994), 248.

2. Fox, *Regimental Losses*, 282.

3. Allan Nevins, *The War for The Union, Volume I, "The Improvised War, 1861–1862"* (New York: Charles Scribner's Sons, 1959), 94.

4. Lt. Col. Marvin A. Kriedberg and Lt. Merton G. Henry, *History of Military Mobilization in the United States Army 1775–1945* (Department of the Army: Washington, 1955), 92; Nevins, *War for the Union*, 77–78.

5. Helene Smith and George Swetnam, *A Guidebook to Historic Western Pennsylvania* (Pittsburgh: University of Pittsburgh Press, 1991), 102–103, 149, 165, 256, 283, 293; Mary M. Muller, *A Town at Presque Isle: A Short History of Erie, Pennsylvania to 1980* (Erie, Pennsylvania: Erie County Historical Society, 1991), 7–12.

6. Samuel P. Bates, *History of Mercer County, Pennsylvania* (Chicago: Warner and Beers Company, 1888), 147, 191; Smith and Swetnam, *Historic Western Pennsylvania*, 149–150, 256–257, 283–284, 293–294; Jonathan E. Helmreich, *The First 100 Years: Settlement and Growth in Crawford County, Pennsylvania* (Meadville, Pennsylvania: Crawford County Historical Society, 1987), 1–18; John L. Androit, *Population Abstract of the United States* (McLean, Virginia: Androit Association, 1980), 692–694; *Population of the United States, 1860* (Washington, 1861), 406–408. The number does not include Forest County, which would also contribute some soldiers to the 83rd Regiment. Forest County had 274 men of military age.

7. Muller, *Town at Presque Isle*, 11–13, 17–19, 26–32; H.W. Hulbert, *Erie City Directory for the City of Erie and the Vicinity Adjacent* (Erie, Pennsylvania, n.p., 1861), 4; Samuel P. Bates, *History of Erie County, Pennsylvania* (Chicago: Warner and Beers Company, 1884), 381, 433, 499; Douglas V. Shaw, "Erie's Population in 1850: A Demographic Analysis," *The Journal of Erie Studies*, Spring 1984, 24–26; *Population of the United States*, 408–411.

8. Bates, *History of Erie County*, 491; Hulbert, *Erie City Directory*, 7; "The Military Bill," and "Sheriff's Sales," *Erie Weekly Gazette*, April 18, 1861, and "Local Paragraphs," *EWG*, April 4, 18, and 25, 1861.

9. "Local Paragraphs," *EWG*, April 18 and 25, 1861.

10. Dan Maille, *A Popular History of Harborcreek, A Vignette: Colonel John W. McLane* (Harborcreek, Pennsylvania: Harborcreek Historical Society, 1994), 1–3; "The Time has Come!" *Crawford Journal*, April 19, 1861; "Local Paragraphs," *EWG*, April 25, 1861.

11. "The Time has Come!" *CJ*, April 19, 1861; "Local News," *CJ*, April 30, 1861; "Local Paragraphs," *EWG*, April 18, 25, 1861; Amos Judson, *History of the 83rd Regiment Pennsylvania Volunteers* (1865; reprint, Dayton: Ohio, Morningside House, 1986), 10. "To Our Soldiers," *Warren Ledger*, May 1, 1861; "A Soldier's Kit," *CJ*, April 30, 1861.

12. S. B. Nelson, *Nelson's Biographical Dictionary and Historical Reference Book, Volume I, Erie County* (Erie: S. B. Nelson, 1896), 201; Judson, *History of the 83rd*, 10.

13. "The Time has Come!" *CJ*, April 19, 1861; "Local Paragraphs," *EWG*, April 18 and April 25, 1861; "Local News," *CJ*, April 30, 1861; Judson, *History of the 83rd*, 8–9.

14. Nelson, *Bio Dictionary*, 202; Judson, *His-*

tory of the 83rd, 10; "Arrival of the Erie Regiment," *EWG*, May 2, 1861.

15. "Letter from Camp Wilkins," *EWG*, May 16, 1861; "A Visit to Camp Wilkins," *EWG*, May 23, 1861.

16. "Letter from Camp Wilkins," *EWG*, June 6, 1861; "The Erie Regiment," *EWG*, June 20, 1861; Judson, *History of the 83rd*, 11–12; "Local Paragraphs," *EWG*, June 27, 1861.

17. "The Erie Regiment," *EWG*, June 20, 1861; Kriedberg, *Military Mobilization*, 93; "Letter from Camp Wright," *EWG*, June 30, 1861; Plympton A. White to J. L. Beers, May 10, 1861, "A Union Rookie at Camp Wilkins, 1861," *Western Pennsylvania Historical Magazine* Vol. 37 (March 1954), 60.

18. "Our Regiment Coming Home!" *EWG*, July 4, 1861; "Letter from Camp Wright," *EWG*, June 30, 1861; "Speech of Col. McLane at Camp Wright," *EWG*, July 18, 1861; Judson, *History of the 83rd*, 13–14.

19. Nevins, *The War for the Union*, 232; Judson, *History of the 83rd*, 15–16; "Return of the Erie Regiment," *EWG*, July 25, 1861.

20. "Recruits Wanted!" *CJ*, July 30, 1861.

21. War Department, *Revised Regulations for the Army of the United States, 1861* (1861; reprint, Harrisburg, Pennsylvania: National Historical Society, 1980), 519.

22. Bruce Catton, *Reflections on the Civil War*, ed. John Leekley (New York: Berkley Books, 1981), 49–50.

23. Muster Roll of Company G, RG 94; Judson, *History of the 83rd*, 17–20; Linda Susko, "Tionesta Ranger's Reunion," *JES*, Spring 1993, Volume 22, No. 1, 94–96.

24. Keidberg and Henry, *Military Mobilization*, 94; Judson, *History of the 83rd*, 17–20; "Local Paragraphs," *EWG*, August 9, 1861.

25. The following sources provided information on the officers' occupations and lives: Capt. Knox, Lt. Stowe, Lt. Clark, Lt. Jones and Lt. Saeger are found in the company Descriptive Books, RG 94. Capt. Austin: *Erie City Directory*, 1861, 18; Capt. Campbell: A.T. Andrea, *History of the State of Kansas* (1883; reprint, Acheson County Historical Society, 1976), 882; Lt. Judson: autobiography provided by the Judson family, n. d., and *Memorial of Amos M. Judson of Burnside Post, No. 8, Department of the Potomac, G.A.R., Address of Comrade F.J. Young at the Memorial Service of the Post, April 23, 1913* (the Judson family, Washington D.C.); Lt. White: Judson, *History of the 83rd*, 71: Capt. Woodward; L. Wallace Duncan and Charles F. Scott: *History of Allen and Woodson Counties, Kansas* (Iola, Kansas: Iola Register, 1901), 882; Capt. Brown: "Brevet General Hiram L. Brown," *Journal of Erie Studies*, Vol. 4, No. 1, 73–75; Lt. Clark: *Erie City Directory*, 37.

26. James H. Nevins and William B. Styple, *What Death More Glorious: A Biography of General Strong Vincent* (Kearny, New Jersey: Belle Grove Books, 1997), 11–27.

27. Company descriptive books of the 83rd Pennsylvania, RG 94, National Archives. The averages and percentages of occupations are based on a compilation of soldiers that mustered-in between July and September 1861. Since soldiers indicated their occupations in a variety of terms, I have generalized them for clarity; Benjamin A. Gould, *Military and Anthropological Statistics of American Soldiers* (New York: Hurd and Houghton, 1869), 210.

28. Company descriptive books of the 83rd Pennsylvania, RG 94.

29. War Department, *Revised Regulations*, 130–131. Soldiers' ages are taken from their ages at enlistment as indicated in Company Descriptive Books, RG 94.

30. *The War of the Rebellion: A Compilation of the Official Records of the Union and Confederate Armies* (Washington: Government Printing Office, 1880–1901) (hereafter cited as *OR*, Series I unless otherwise noted), Series III, Vol. 1, 68. The average age for the officers was computed using twenty-one known samples (excluding McLane and Faulkner), as indicated in the following sources: McLane; Maille, *Col. John W. McLane*, 1. Vincent; J. Nevins and W. Styple, *What Death More Glorious*, 11. C.P. Rogers, Israel Thickstun, O. Woodward; Officers Commissions, Regimental Orderly Book, RG 94. The ages of D. P. Jones, Knox, Stowe, Clark, McCoy, Smith, Stebbins, Austin, Bates, Reed, Carpenter, Wilson, Thickstun and Sigler are found in the Company Descriptive Books, 83rd Regiment, RG 94. Amos Judson's age was provided by the Judson family. Hiram Brown is found in "Brevet General Brown," 73.

31. The Van Giesen relation information is provided by their ancestor, Ms. Cynthia Freedman; the Wittich family story is found in Nelson, Biographical Dictionary, 632; nationalities are found in the Company Descriptive Books, RG 94.

32. Nelson, *Bio Dictionary*, 201; Nevins, *War for the Union*, 232; Judson, *History of the 83rd*, 17–18.

33. Robert Ilisevich and Jonathan Helmreich, ed., *The Civil War Diaries of Seth Waid III* (Meadville, Pennsylvania: Crawford County Historical Society, 1993), vi, 12.

34. "Local Paragraphs," *EWG*, August 19, 1861.

35. Bates, *History of Erie County*, 189; Daniel Foote to Julia Hill, September 27, 1861, Foote Papers, U.S. Army Military History Institute, Carlisle, PA; Seth Waid, Entry for September 13, 1861, *Civil War Diaries of Seth Waid*, 11.

Chapter II: It Seemed a Little Like War

1. Nevins, *The War for the Union, Vol. I*, 223–224; James M. McPherson, *Battle Cry of Freedom* (New York: Ballantine, 1988), 348–349.

2. Nevins, *The War for the Union, Vol. I*, 266–267.

3. J. Montre, "Letter from Washington—Arrival of the Erie Regiment." *EWG*, September 26 1861.

4. Foote to Julia Hill, September 27 1861; Judson, *History of the 83rd*, 18; J. Montre, "Letter from Washington—Arrival of the Erie Regiment," *EWG*, September 26, 1861.

5. Seth Waid, Entry for September 20, 1861, *Civil War Diaries of Seth Waid*, 20; Judson, *History of the 83rd*, 18; "Extract of a Letter from a Member of McLane's Regiment," *EWG*, October 17, 1861.

6. Judson, *History of the 83rd*, 18.

7. *Ibid*; Israel Thickstun to Mother, October 4, 1861, Thickstun Papers, U.S. Army Military History Institute, Carlisle, PA.

8. Letter from Brig. Gen. G. W. McCall, Commanding Pennsylvania Reserves, September 16, 1861, Regimental Letters Book, RG 94; Judson, *History of the 83rd*, 18.

9. William H. Powell, *The Fifth Army Corps (Army of the Potomac), A Record of Operations During the Civil War in America, 1861–1865* (1896; reprint, Dayton, Ohio: Morningside House, 1984), 2–9.

10. *Ibid.*, 11–12.

11. Donald A. Wise, "Bazil Hall of Hall's Hill," *The Arlington Historical Magazine* (Arlington, Virginia, 1982), 20–23; Norton to Sister L, September 30, 1861, *Army Letters*, 24

12. Brig. Gen. Silas Casey, *Infantry Tactics for the Instruction, Exercise, and Maneuvers of The Soldier, A Company, Line of Skirmishers, Battalion, Brigade or Corps D'Armee* (1862; reprint, Dayton: Morningside House, 1985), Plate 1, Plate 4.

13. The War Department published Casey's Manual with the intention of ensuring standard training practices, but other manuals, especially Hardee's "Rifle and Light Infantry Tactics," were also commonly used in 1861. It is unknown which manual McLane's regiment used, but the movements and tactics called for in the manuals were basically the same, and Casey's is used here to illustrate the War Department's official standards and the difficulty the men would have in reaching them. Casey's manual officially replaced Hardee's in 1862 and remained the training standard for the remainder of the war.

14. *Ibid.*, 9–64, 42–48, 63–64.

15. Bates, *History of Erie County*, 1,000; Seth Waid, Entries for September 10 and September 13, 1861, *Civil War Diaries of Seth Waid*, 8, 10.

16. Casey, *Infantry Tactics*, 90–103; William P. Craighill, *The Army Officer's Pocket Companion, Principally Designed for Staff Officers in the Field* (New York: D. Van Nostrand, 1863), 88–97; Judson, *History of the 83rd*, 21.

17. Casey, *Infantry Tactics*, 105–128.

18. Eugene A. Nash, *History of the Forty-fourth Regiment New York Volunteer Infantry in the Civil War, 1861–1865* (1910; reprint, Dayton, Ohio: Morningside House, 1988), 49–50; Judson, *History of the 83rd*, 21; Casey, *Infantry Tactics*, 227–230; May to Cousin Grace, October 24, 1861.

19. Waid, Entry for September 23, 1861, *Civil War Diaries of Seth Waid*, 23; Norton to Sister L., September 30, 1861, *Army Letters*, 23, and to Friend P., October 8, 1861, *Army Letters*, 28.

20. Judson, *History of the 83rd*, 21, 240–241; Nash, *History of the Forty-Fourth*, 49–50; Casey, *Infantry Tactics*, 227–230; 83rd PVI Descriptive Books, RG 94.

21. Fred A. Shannon, *The Organization and Administration of the Union Army, 1861–1865, Vol. I*, (Cleveland, Ohio: Arthur H. Clark Co., 1928), 199; Norton to Friend P, October 8, 1862, *Army Letters*, 28; *Revised Regulations*, 76–77.

22. Judson, *History of the 83rd*, 21; Brigade Circular dated October 10, 1861, Third Brigade Orders Book, RG 393, National Archives; Alexander May to Mr. Seneca Chambers, October 4, 1861, private collection, the estate of Irwin Rider, Erie, Pennsylvania.

23. Norton to Friend P., October 26, 1861, *Army Letters*, 29; Waid, Entry for October 14, 1861, *Civil War Diaries of Seth Waid*, 34.

24. Foote to Julia Hill, October 31, 1861; Norton to Friend P., October 26, 1861, *Army Letters*, 29.

25. Norton to Sister L., September 30, 1861, *Army Letters*, 23; "Extract of a Letter from a Member of McLane's Regiment," *EWG*, October 17, 1861; Waid, Entry for October 9, 1861, *Civil War Diaries of Seth Waid*, 32.

26. Gregory A. Coco, *The Civil War Infantryman: In Camp, On the March, and in Battle* (Gettysburg: Thomas Publications, 1996), 24–27.

27. Waid, Entries for October 3, 13, 22, 27, November 16, 28, 1861, *Civil War Diaries of Seth Waid*, 29–43.

28. Norton to Friends, October 4, 1861, *Army Letters* 26; and to Sister L., December 19, 1861, *Army Letters*, 38; Norton to Cousin L., February 11, 1862, *Army Letters*, 50; Van Giesen to Brother James and Sister Jane, October 15, 1861.

29. Foote to Julia Hill, November 17, 1861.

30. Norton to Friends, October 4, 1861, *Army Letters*, 26.

31. Norton to Friends, October 4, 1861, 26; "Extract of a Letter from a Member of McLane's Regiment," *EWG*, October 17, 1861.

32. Nash, *History of the Forty-Fourth*, 7–45.

33. Nash, *History of the Forty-Fourth*, 46; Foote to Julia Hill, October 31, 1861; May to Cousin Tip, November 14, 1861.

34. *OR*, Series I, Vol. 5, 650; Bates, *History of Pennsylvania Volunteers*, 1249; Judson, *History of the 83rd*, 22; Nash, *History of the Forty-Fourth*, 55.

35. "Correspondence," *Crawford Journal*, November 26, 1861.

36. Theodore J. Karle, "The Erie Regiment's Fancy French Uniform," *Journal of Erie Studies*, Fall 1990, Vol. 19, No. 2, 70.

37. Norton to Friend P., November 15, 1861, *Army Letters*, 33; Foote to Julia Hill, November 17, 1861.

38. Judson, *History of the 83rd*, 23–24; Norton to Sister L., December 8, 1861, *Army Letters*, 36.

39. Norton to Sister L., December 19, 1861, *Army Letters*, 37; May to Cousin Grace, December 6, 1861.

40. McLane to Butterfield, undated, and Special Orders, Regimental Orders Book, RG 94.

41. Masiker to Eliza, November 22, 1861; Cleeland to Sister, November 30, 1861; Van Giesen to Brothers and Sisters, November 28, 1861.

42. Judson, *History of the 83rd*, 26; Foote to Julia Hill, November 28, 1861; Norton to Sister L., January 17, 1862, *Army Letters*, 40.

43. Masiker to Eliza, November 22, 1861; Cleeland to Sister, November 30, 1861.

44. Rodgers to Julia Porter, October 28, 1861; Bates, *History of Pennsylvania Volunteers*, 1287; May to Cousin Grace, October 24, 1861; Joseph J. Woodward, M.D., *Outlines of the Chief Camp Diseases of the United States Armies, As Observed During the Present War* (1863, reprint, San Francisco: Norman Publishing, 45; George W. Adams, *Doctors in Blue: The Medical History of the Union Army in the Civil War* (New York: Henry Schuman, 1952), 196; May to Cousin Grace, October 24, 1861.

45. Waid, Entries for November 27–29, December 25–26, 1861, *Civil War Diaries of Seth Waid*, 43–44; Norton to Sister L., December 19, 1861, *Army Letters*, 38; Regimental Return for November 1861, RG 94.

46. Regimental Orders Book, RG 94; Foote to Julia Hill, November 28, 1861; Report of 1st Lt. John Wilson, December 1, 1861, RG 94.

47. Norton to Sister L., December 19, 1861, *Army Letters*, 38; Judson, *History of the 83rd*, 25; Richard A. Sauers, *Advance the Colors! Pennsylvania Civil War Battleflags* (Harrisburg, Pennsylvania: Capitol Preservation Committee, 1987), 202; Thickstun to Gilbert, December 25, 1861; Cleeland to John and Elisibeth Cleeland, December 27, 1861.

48. Cleeland to John and Elisibeth Cleeland, December 27, 1861.

Chapter III: Hard Marches to Yorktown

1. Foote to Julia Hill, January 19, 1862; Norton to Friend P., February 3, 1862, to Sister L., February 8, 1862, and to Cousin L., February 27, 1862, *Army Letters*, 45–53.

2. May to Cousin Grace, February 14, 1862; "Army Correspondence," *CJ*, February 11, 1862; Third Brigade Circular, January 21, 1862, Fifth Army Corps Letters, RG 393, National Archives; G.A. Goodell to Francis Waid, February 13, 1862; Rice to Hiram, January 21, 1862. Lt. Hanrahan's story is found in Col. McLane's endorsement of his resignation in the regimental orders book, January 25, 1862.

3. *OR*, Series 1, vol. 5, 76; Regimental Return for February 1862, RG 94; Waid, entries for February 9–10, 1862, *Civil War Diaries of Seth Waid*, 45–46.

4. Regimental return for February 1862, RG 94; *Crawford Journal*, February 4, 11, 1862; Lt. Yale's recruitment results are in a February 25 letter in the regimental orders book at the National Archives.

5. Stephen W. Sears, *To the Gates of Richmond: The Peninsula Campaign* (New York, Ticknor & Fields, 1992), 3–12.

6. Norton to Friend P., March 5, 1862, *Army Letters*, 56; Foote to Julia Hill, March 8, 1862; David Rodgers to Friends, January 21, 1862, private collection of Jean Rodgers Hall, Camp Hill, Pennsylvania.

7. Norton to Cousin L., February 11, 1862, *Army Letters*, 49.

8. Sears, *Gates of Richmond*, 6–10.

9. Sears, *Gates of Richmond*, 5–10; Powell, *Fifth Army Corps*, 9–11, 25–26.

10. Judson, *History of the 83rd*, 27.

11. Sears, *Gates of Richmond*, 12–17; Norton to Cousin L., March 17, 1862, *Army Letters*, 59.

12. John Rice to Parents, March 11, 1862, private collection of Charles Alcorn, Chapel Hill, North Carolina.

13. Foote to Julia Hill, March 19, 1862; Norton to Cousin L., March 17, 1862, *Army Letters*, 59.

14. Sears, *Gates of Richmond*, 16–17, Judson, *History of the 83rd*, 27–28; Norton to Cousin L., March 17 1862, *Army Letters*, 59.

15. Sears, *Gates of Richmond*, 18–20.

16. Judson, *History of the 83rd*, 29; Norton to Cousin L., March 17, 1862, *Army Letters*, 59.

17. Judson, *History of the 83rd*, 30; Foote to Julia Hill, March 19, 1862.
18. William J. Miller, "Scarcely any Parallel in History: Logistics, Friction, and McClellan's Strategy for the Peninsula Campaign," *The Peninsula Campaign of 1862, Yorktown to the Seven Days,* Volume 2 (Campbell, California: Savas Woodbury, 1997), 134; Sears, *Gates of Richmond*, 23; Foote to Julia Hill, March 19, 1862.
19. Sears, *Gates of Richmond*, 24; Judson, *History of the 83rd*, 30; Norton to Sister L., March 26, 1862, *Army Letters*, 61; Foote to Julia Hill, April 12, 1862, Rodgers to Julia Hill, April 11, 1862; Cleeland to Parents, April 21, 1862.
20. Sears, *Gates of Richmond*, 28; Norton to Sister L., March 26, 1862, *Army Letters*, 62; Foote to Julia Hill, April 12, 1862.
21. Sears, *Gates of Richmond*, 30–31.
22. Judson, *History of the 83rd*, 31–33; Norton to Sister L., March 29, 1862, *Army Letters*, 63–64; *OR*, Series 1, vol. 14, 47.
23. Sears, *Gates of Richmond*, 35–36; Judson, *History of the 83rd*, 34; *OR*, Series 1, vol. 11, 287.
24. Sears, *Gates of Richmond*, 25–38.
25. Sears, *Gates of Richmond*, 58.
26. *OR*, Series 1, vol. 11, part 1, 384.
27. Judson, *History of the 83rd*, 36; Norton to Sister L., April 27, 1862, *Army Letters*, 73.
28. Judson, *History of the 83rd*, 36; Snyder to Friend C. Brown, May 30, 1862; Foote to Parents, April 21, 1862; Norton to Sister L., April 21, 1862, *Army Letters*, 72.
29. Norton to Sister L., April 21, 1862, *Army Letters*, 72–73.
30. Sears, *Gates of Richmond*, 48; Norton to Cousin L., April 14, 1862, *Army Letters*, 66.
31. Judson, *History of the 83rd*, 37–38; Foote to Julia Hill, April 12, 1862; Rice to Sarah, April 22, 1862.
32. Norton to Sister L., April 21, 1862, *Army Letters*, 72; Foote to Julia Hill, April 12, 1862.
33. William J. Miller, "Weather Still Execrable: Climatological Notes on the Peninsula Campaign, March through August 1862," *The Peninsula Campaign of 1862, Yorktown to the Seven Days, Volume 3* (Campbell, California, Savas Woodbury, 1997), 180–182, 191; Judson, *History of the 83rd*, 37; Snyder to Friend C. Brown, May 30, 1862; Regimental Return for April 1862, RG 94.
34. Coco, *The Civil War Infantryman*, 25; William J. Miller, "Scarcely any Parallel in History," 137–143.
35. Brigade Circular of March 25, 1862, Third Brigade Orders Book, RG 393; Norton to Cousin L., April 14, 1862, *Army Letters*, 66–67.
36. Rice to Sarah, April 22, 1862; Cleeland to Father, undated; Foote to Julia Hill, April 12, 1862; Norton to Sister L., April 21, 1862, *Army Letters*, 69.

37. Sears, *Gates of Richmond*, 60–61.
38. *OR*, Series 1, vol. 11, part 1, 311; Foote to Julia Hill, May 3, 1862; Judson, *History of the 83rd*, 38.
39. *OR*, Series 1, vol. 11, part 1, 311; May to Father and Mother, May 12, 1862; Rice to Folks, May 18, 1862.

Chapter IV: A Promise of Perfect Success

1. Sears, *Gates of Richmond*, 65–86.
2. Sears, *Gates of Richmond*, 86; Rodgers to Julia Porter, May 12, 1862; Norton to Friends, May 26, 1862, *Army Letters*, 81; Foote to Julia Hill, May 20, 1862.
3. Rodgers to Julia Porter, May 12, 1862; Judson, *History of the 83rd*, 39–48.
4. Judson, *History of the 83rd*, 48; Foote to Julia Hill, May 20, 1862.
5. Sears, *Gates of Richmond*, 89–95.
6. *Ibid.*, 98–107.
7. Sears, *Gates of Richmond*, 109–110; Judson, *History of the 83rd*, 48; Norton to Sister L., May 23, 1862, *Army Letters*, 78.
8. Coco, *The Civil War Infantryman*, 82–86; Craighill, *Army Officer's Pocket Companion*, 95.
9. Miller, "Weather Still Execrable," 183–184; Rice to Folks, May 18, 1862.
10. Foote to Julia Hill, March 19, 1862; Miller, "Weather Still Execrable," 183–184; May to Father, May 30, 1862.
11. John J. Pullen, *The Twentieth Maine, A Volunteer Regiment in the Civil War* (Dayton, Ohio: Morningside House, 1991), 90.
12. Norton to Father, May 20, 1862, *Army Letters*, 78.
13. Sears, *Gates of Richmond*, 95–96, 112–113.
14. Judson, *History of the 83rd*, 48; Norton to Sister L., May 23, 1862, *Army Letters*, 78; Norton to Friends, May 26, 1862, *Army Letters*, 81.
15. Sears, *Gates of Richmond*, 96-97; Robert E. L. Krick, "Prelude to the Seven Days; The Battle of Slash Church (Hanover Court House) May 27, 1862, *The Peninsula Campaign of 1862, Yorktown to the Seven Days, Essays on the American Civil War, Volume 2* (Campbell, California, Savas Publishing, 1997), ed. William J. Miller, 2–4.
16. Sears, *Gates of Richmond*, 113–114; Krick, "Slash Church," 4; Judson, *History of the 83rd*, 48.
17. Judson, *History of the 83rd*, 48–49; Norton to Friends, May 30, 1862; *Army Letters*, 82; Nash, *History of the Forty-fourth*, 73.
18. *OR*, vol. 11, pt. 1, 698; Norton to Friends, May 30, 1862, *Army Letters*, 82; *OR*, vol. 11, pt. 1, 722.
19. *OR*, vol. 11, pt. 1, 740; *OR*, vol. 11, pt. 1, 743; Krick, "Slash Church," 9–13.

20. Krick, "Slash Church," 11; "Letter from Capt. Austin of the 83d Regiment," *EWG*, June 12, 1862.
21. Krick, "Slash Church," 13–14.
22. *OR*, vol. 11, pt. 1, 723; *OR*, vol. 11, pt. 1, 733.
23. *OR*, vol. 11, pt. 1, 733; Judson, *History of the 83rd*, 49; *OR*, vol. 11, pt. 1, 743; Krick, "Slash Church," 14.
24. Norton to Friends, May 30, 1862, *Army Letters*, 83; *OR*, vol. 11, pt. 1, 699.
25. *OR*, vol. 11, pt. 1, 733–734; *OR*, vol. 11, pt. 1, 744; Norton to Friends, May 30, 1862, *Army Letters*, 83; Judson, *History of the 83rd*, 49.
26. *OR*, vol. 11, pt. 1, 744; Rodgers to Julia Porter, May 31, 1862; Judson, *History of the 83rd*, 49.
27. *OR*, vol. 11, pt. 1, 734; *OR*, vol. 11, pt. 1, 723; Judson, *History of the 83rd*, 49.
28. Krick, "Slash Church," 17–19.
29. Judson, *History of the 83rd*, 50; *OR*, vol. 11, pt. 1, 723.
30. Foote to Parents, May 30, 1862; Norton to Brother and Sister, June 2, 1862, *Army Letters*, 85.
31. *OR*, vol. 11, pt. 1, 724; Judson, *History of the 83rd*, 50; Foote to Parents, May 30, 1862.
32. Judson, *History of the 83rd*, 50.
33. Judson, *History of the 83rd*, 50; Krick, "Slash Church," 26–27; *OR*, vol. 11, pt. 1, 734.
34. *OR*, vol. 11, pt. 1, 734.
35. Krick, "Slash Church," 27–29; *OR*, vol. 11, pt. 1, 734.
36. Judson, *History of the 83rd*, 50; Foote to Parents, May 30, 1862; *OR*, vol. 11, pt. 1, 735; May to Parents, May 30, 1862.
37. *OR*, vol. 11, pt. 1, 735; Judson, *History of the 83rd*, 51; May to Parents, May 30, 1862; Foote to Parents, May 30, 1862.
38. *OR*, vol. 11, pt. 1, 735; *OR*, vol. 11, pt. 1, 724; May to Parents, May 30, 1862; Norton to Brother and Sister, June 2, 1862, *Army Letters*, 85.
39. *OR*, vol. 11, pt. 1, 735; Judson, *History of the 83rd*, 51; Norton to Brother and Sister, June 2, 1862, *Army Letters*, 85.
40. Powell, *Fifth Army Corps*, 68.
41. Adams, *Doctors in Blue*, 66–68, 114–118; Coco, *The Civil War Infantryman*, 103.
42. Krick, "Slash Church," 32; Coco, *The Civil War Infantryman*, 141; *EWG*, Letter from Capt. Austin, June 12, 1862.
43. Foote to Parents, May 30, 1862; Bates, *History of Pennsylvania Volunteers*, 1285; *EWG*, Letter from Capt. Austin, June 12, 1862.
44. Powell, *Fifth Army Corps*, 68; *OR*, vol. 11, pt. 1, 742; *OR*, vol. 11, pt. 1, 724; *OR*, vol. 11, pt. 1, 679; *OR*, vol. 11, pt. 1, 680; *Crawford Journal*, June 24, 1862.
45. *OR*, vol. 11, pt. 1, 735.
46. Norton to Brother, May 30, 1862, *Army Letters*, 85.
47. Judson, *History of the 83rd*, 52; Norton to Brother and Sister, May 30, 1862, *Army Letters*, 85; May to Miss Grace, June 21, 1862; *EWG*, Letter from Capt. Austin, June 12, 1862.
48. Foote to Julia Hill, June 4, 1862.
49. *OR*, vol. 11, pt. 1, p. 700; Judson, *History of the 83rd*, 52–53.
50. Cleeland to Parents, May 30, 1862; May to Miss Grace, June 21, 1862; Foote to Julia Hill, June 4, 1862. Norton to Sister L., June 10, 1862, *Army Letters*, 88.

Chapter V: You Will See Enough of Them Before Night

1. Sears, *Gates of Richmond*, 117–133.
2. Judson, *History of the 83rd*, 54.
3. Sears, *Gates of Richmond*, 145, 149.
4. *Ibid.*, 156–158.
5. Foote to Parents, June 8, 1862, and to Julia Hill, June 24, 1862; May to Miss Grace, June 21, 1862. Rice to Friends, June 23, 1862.
6. Sears, *Gates of Richmond*, 160; Norton to Sister L., June 10, 1862, *Army Letters*, 87.
7. May to Miss Grace, June 21, 1862; Norton to Sister L., June 10, 1862, *Army Letters*, 87.
8. Norton to Mother, June 16, 1862, *Army Letters*, 89.
9. Sears, *Gates of Richmond*, 163–64; Thickstun to Brother Comp, July 6, 1863.
10. RG 94, Monthly returns of the 83rd Pennsylvania from March to June 1862. As the returns were normally filled out at the end of each month, the figures for June include those men who incurred illness during the Seven Days battles, June 25–July 1. Though probably skewed somewhat by the battle, they are still indicative of the Army of the Potomac's sickness rate in mid–June; *EWG*, "Local Paragraphs," May 22, 1862; Nevins and Styple, *What Death More Glorious*, 35; Foote to Parents, June 8, 1862.
11. Sears, *Gates of Richmond*, 153–156, 174, 181–183, 196; Judson, *History of the 83rd*, 54.
12. Sears, *Gates of Richmond*, 183–204.
13. *OR*, vol. 11, pt. 2, p. 272; *OR*, vol. 11, pt. 2, p. 315; Judson, *History of the 83rd*, 55–56; Thickstun to Brother Comp, July 2, 1862; *OR*, vol. 11, pt. 2, p. 344.
14. Sears, *Gates of Richmond*, 207–208; *OR*, vol. 11, pt. 2, p. 316.
15. Sears, *Gates of Richmond*, 210–211; Powell, *Fifth Army Corps*, 82–83.
16. Sears, *Gates of Richmond*, 213; *OR*, vol. 11, pt. 2, p. 344.
17. Judson, *History of the 83rd*, 57.

18. *OR*, vol. 11, pt. 2, p. 272; *OR*, vol. 11, pt. 2, p. 224; *OR*, vol. 11, pt. 2, p. 316; Judson, *History of the 83rd*, 58.
19. *OR*, vol. 11, pt. 2, p. 316; *OR*, vol. 11, pt. 2, p. 326; Judson, *History of the 83rd*, 58; Sears, *Gates of Richmond*, 214–215.
20. *OR*, vol. 11, pt. 2, p. 344; Judson, *History of the 83rd*, 59; Powell, *Fifth Army Corps*, 90; Sears, *Gates of Richmond*, 215.
21. *OR*, vol. 11, pt. 2, p. 316; *OR*, vol. 11, pt. 2, p. 344; Judson, *History of the 83rd*, 59; Norton, *Army Letters*, 339.
22. Sears, *Gates of Richmond*, 212, 218–219.
23. Sears, *Gates of Richmond*, 219–221; *OR*, vol. 11, pt. 2, p. 757; *OR*, vol. 11, pt. 2, p. 780; *OR*, vol. 11, pt. 2., p. 324; Judson, *History of the 83rd*, 60.
24. Sears, *Gates of Richmond*, 222–224; Judson, *History of the 83rd*, 60.
25. Judson, *History of the 83rd*, 60.
26. *OR*, vol. 11, pt. 2, p. 344; Judson, *History of the 83rd*, 61.
27. *OR*, vol. 11, pt. 2, p. 780; Judson, *History of the 83rd*, 61.
28. Judson, *History of the 83rd*, 61; George Bedient, "The 83d PA. at Gaines's Mill," *The National Tribune*, June 22, 1905.
29. Sears, *Gates of Richmond*, 228–233.
30. *OR*, vol. 11, pt. 2, p. 767; Judson, *History of the 83rd*, 61; Bedient, "83d at Gaines's Mill;" Issac Moorehead, *A Brief History of Monroeville* (n.p.), 149–150. Moorehead was an Erie journalist who met McGehee while touring the 83rd's battlefields after the war.
31. Bedient, "83d at Gaines's Mill;" *OR*, vol. 11, pt. 2, 224; Sears, *Gates of Richmond*, 223–226; *OR*, vol. 11, pt. 2, 492–493.
32. Sears, *Gates of Richmond*, 236–241.
33. *OR*, vol. 11, pt. 2, 344; The size and position of Longstreet's attack is taken from a series of unpublished maps by Edward S. Bearss, in the holdings of the Richmond National Battlefield Park.
34. *OR*, vol. 11, pt. 2, 291; *OR*, vol. 11, pt. 2, 317; *OR*, vol. 11, pt. 2, 291.
35. Judson, *History of the 83rd*, 63; Bedient, "83d at Gaines's Mill."
36. Bedient, "83d at Gaines's Mill;" Judson, *History of the 83rd*, 64.
37. Judson, *History of the 83rd*, 64; Foote to Julia Hill, July 18, 1862.
38. Norton to Friends, July 4, 1862, *Army Letters*, 91; Bedient, "83d at Gaines's Mill."
39. Judson, *History of the 83rd*, 64.
40. Judson, *History of the 83rd*, 65; *EWG*, "Letter from the Potomac Army," July 11, 1862.
41. *OR*, vol. 11, pt. 2, 323; *OR*, vol. 11, pt. 2, 339.
42. *OR*, vol. 11, pt. 2, 317; Judson, *History of the 83rd*, 65.
43. *OR*, vol. 11, pt. 2, 345; Judson, *History of the 83rd*, 65; Foote to Julia Hill, July 18, 1862.
44. Judson, *History of the 83rd*, 66; *OR*, vol. 11, pt. 2, 345; James J. Baldwin III, *The Struck Eagle: A Biography of Brigadier General Micah Jenkins, and a History of the Fifth South Carolina Sharpshooters and the Palmetto Sharpshooters* (Burd Street Press, 1996), 123–124.
45. *OR*, vol. 11, pt. 2, 345; Baldwin, *Struck Eagle*, 124; Bedient, "83d at Gaines's Mill."
46. Norton to Friends, July 4, 1862, *Army Letters*, 91.
47. Judson, *History of the 83rd*, 66–67; *OR*, vol. 11, pt. 2, 345.
48. Judson, *History of the 83rd*, 67; Bedient, "83d at Gaines's Mill."
49. Judson, *History of the 83rd*, 68.
50. Judson, *History of the 83rd*, 68; *OR*, vol. 11, pt. 2, 340.
51. Norton to Friends, July 4, 1862, *Army Letters*, 91.
52. Foote to Julia Hill, July 18, 1862; "Interesting from the Ellsworth Regiment—Events and Experiments of the Battlefield," *Buffalo Morning Express*, July 16, 1862; *Memorial of Amos M. Judson*, 2; Judson, *History of the 83rd*, 68–69.
53. Bedient, "83d at Gaines's Mill."
54. Sears, *Gates of Richmond*, 244–248.
55. Judson, *History of the 83rd*, 69.

Chapter VI: Revenge for McLane

1. "Concerning Col. McLane and Maj. Nahgel," *EWG*, September 4, 1862.
2. Sears, *Gates of Richmond*, 249–252.
3. Bedient, "83d at Gaines's Mill."
4. "Concerning Col. McLane," *EWG*, Sep. 4, 1862.
5. Judson, *History of the 83rd*, 72–73; Foote to Julia, July 18, 1862.
6. Sears, *Gates of Richmond*, 256–257, 274–275.
7. Sears, *Gates of Richmond*, 275; Judson, *History of the 83rd*, 74–75; *OR*, Series 1, Vol. 11, Report No. 128, 319; *OR*, Series 1, Vol. 11, Report No. 93, 227–228.
8. Sears, *Gates of Richmond*, 310–311; *OR*, Series 1, Vol. 11, Report No. 93, 229.
9. Sears, *Gates of Richmond*, 311–312.
10. Sears, *Gates of Richmond*, 310; Foote to Julia Hill, July 18, 1862.
11. Foote to Julia Hill, July 18, 1862; Sears, *Gates of Richmond*, 291–292; *OR*, Series 1, Vol. 11, Report No. 128, 319.
12. Sears, *Gates of Richmond*, 314–317.
13. *OR*, Series 1, Vol. 11, Report No. 112, 275; *OR*, Series 1, Vol. 11, Report No. 128, 319.

14. *OR*, Series 1, Vol. 11, Report No. 128, 320; *OR*, Series 1, Vol. 11, Report No. 119, 293; *OR*, Series 1, Vol. 11, Report No. 136, 346.

15. Sears, *Gates of Richmond*, 321–324. The direction of the Confederate assault is also taken from a series of unpublished maps of the battle by Edwin C. Bearss, held at the Richmond National Battlefield Park.

16. *OR*, Series 1, Vol. 11, Report No. 128, 319; *OR*, Series 1, Vol. 11, Report No. 136, 346; Bearss, map showing activity of 4:00–6:00 PM, July 1 1862.

17. *OR*, Series 1, Vol. 11, Report No. 128, 320; *OR*, Series 1, Vol. 11, Report No. 136, 346; Norton to Brother, July 26, 1862, *Army Letters*, 107.

18. *OR*, Series 1, Vol. 11, Report No. 136, 346; Judson, *History of the 83rd*, 77; Norton to Brother, July 26, 1862, *Army Letters*, 107; *OR*, Series 1, Vol. 11, Report No. 313, 814.

19. *OR*, Series 1, Vol. 11, Report No. 136, 347; Norton to Brother, July 26, 1862, *Army Letters*, 108; *OR*, Series 1, Vol. 11, Report No. 128, 320.

20. Bearss, map of 6:00–7:30 PM; Sears, *Gates of Richmond*, 334; Norton to Brother, July 26, 1862, *Army Letters*, 108; Norton to Friends, July 4, 1862, *Army Letters*, 92; Foote to Julia Hill, July 18, 1862; Judson, *History of the 83rd*, 77–78.

21. *OR*, Series 1, Vol. 11, Report No. 136, 347; Memoirs of Pvt. E. Franklin Faison, North Carolina Department of Archives and History, Georgia Faison Collection.

22. *OR*, Series 1, Vol. 11, Report No. 128, 320; *OR*, Series 1, Vol. 11, Report No. 136, 347; Col. Strong Vincent to Mr. Frank Moon, April 22, 1863, Regimental Orders Book, RG 94, National Archives; "Interesting from the Ellsworth Regiment—Events and Experiments of the Battlefield," *Buffalo Morning Express*, July 16, 1862.

23. Bearss, map of 6:00–7:30; *OR*, Series 1, Vol. 11, Report No. 128, 320; *OR*, Series 1, Vol. 11, Report No. 136, 347; Norton to Brother, July 26, 1862, *Army Letters*, 108, Norton to Cousin L., July 5, 1862, *Army Letters*, 94.

24. Sears, *Gates of Richmond*, 334.

25. *OR*, Series 1, Vol. 11, Report No. 136, 347; Judson, *History of the 83rd*, 78–79; Foote to Julia, July 18, 1862.

26. Sears, *Gates of Richmond*, 335–336.

27. Judson, *History of the 83rd*, 79–80.

28. Sears, *Gates of Richmond*, 344–345.

29. Sears, *Gates of Richmond*, 345; *OR*, "Organization of Troops and Return of Casualties in the Army of the Potomac during Operations before Richmond, Virginia, June 26–July 2, 1862"; *OR*, Series 1, Vol. 11, Report No. 128, 322.

30. Sears, *Gates of Richmond*, 339–341.

31. Judson, *History of the 83rd*, 81; Bates, *History of Pennsylvania Volunteers*, 1276, 1295.

32. Sears, *Gates of Richmond*, 346.

33. Sears, *Gates of Richmond*, 347–348.

34. 83rd Pennsylvania monthly return for July 1862, RG 94; Thickstun to Comp, July 22, 1862, and to Sister, July 29, 1862; Foote to Julia Hill, July 18, 1862; Norton to Father, July 9, 1862, *Army Letters*, 97.

35. Norton to Cousin L., July 5, 1862, *Army Letters*, 92–94; Foote to Julia Hill, July 18, 1862; Norton to Father, July 9, 1862, *Army Letters*, 99; Cleeland to Parents, July 14, 1862.

36. Foote to Julia Hill, August 24, 1862; "Local Paragraphs," *EWG*, July 24, 1862; Norton to Brother, July 13, 1862, *Army Letters*, 100–103.

37. Norton, "Two Bugle Calls," *Army Letters*, 323–329.

38. Sears, *Gates of Richmond*, 350–353.

39. Powell, *Fifth Army Corps*, 193; Norton to Father, August 14, 1862, *Army Letters*, 116; Judson, *History of the 83rd*, 83–84.

40. 83rd Pennsylvania monthly returns for March and July, 1862, RG 94; Judson, *History of the 83rd*, 84; Norton to Father, August 14, 1862, *Army Letters*, 117.

Chapter VII: An Unlucky Field

1. "Letter from Washington," *EWG*, July 17, 1862; "The 83d Regiment—List of the Sick, Wounded and Prisoners," *EWG*, August 24, 1862.

2. Foote to Julia Hill, August 24, 1862.

3. *Crawford Journal*, July 22 and August 5, 1862; "Local Paragraphs," *EWG*, August 7, 1862.

4. Waid, entries for February 10 to May 2, 1862, *Civil War Diaries of Seth Waid*, 45–47.

5. Catton, *Reflections on The Civil War*, 64–66.

6. Waid, entries for May 12 to August 16, 1862, *Civil War Diaries of Seth Waid*, 48–57.

7. *Revised Army Regulations*, 141; Foote to Parents, August 17, 1862; G. J. Foote to Parents, August 19, 1862; Bates, *History of Pennsylvania Volunteers*, 1260, 1302; *EWG*, August 24, 1862; Judson, *History of the 83rd*, 84; "Letter from the Army," *EWG*, August 28, 1862; Regimental Return for July and August 1862, National Archives, RG 94.

8. David G. Martin, *The Second Bull Run Campaign, July–August 1862* (Conshohocken, PA, 1997), 17–44, 85–94.

9. Martin, *Second Bull Run*, 85; *OR*, Series 1, Vol. 16, No. 86, 465.

10. Martin, *Second Bull Run*, 85–106.

11. Wilson A. Greene, *The Second Battle of Manassas* (Eastern National, 1995), 9–15.

12. Judson, *History of the 83rd*, 85; *EWG*, "From the 83d Regiment," September 18, 1862.

13. Greene, *Second Battle of Manassas*, 13–23; Martin, *Second Bull Run*, 159.
14. Martin, *Second Bull Run*, 176–178.
15. Greene, *Second Battle of Manassas*, 26–27.
16. Judson, *History of the 83rd*, 85; Martin, *Second Bull Run*, 179.
17. Martin, *Second Bull Run*, 181–207.
18. *OR*, Series 1, Vol. 16, No. 9, 474; Judson, *History of the 83rd*, 86.
19. Martin, *Second Bull Run*, 207; *OR*, Series 1, Vol. 16, No. 9, 474; *OR*, Series 1, Vol. 16, No. 94, 476.
20. Powell, *Fifth Army Corps*, 225. The 83rd's casualties are a compilation of the official returns and a report of the regiment's killed, wounded, and missing in the *Erie Weekly Gazette*, July 17, 1862.
21. Judson, *History of the 83rd*, 86; "From the 83d Regiment," *EWG*; Nash, *History of the Forty-Fourth New York*, 99.
22. Martin, *Second Bull Run*, 209–210.
23. *OR*, Series 1, Vol. 16, No. 97, 480; *OR*, Series 1, Vol. 16, No. 95, 478.
24. Judson, *History of the 83rd*, 86–87; Greene, *Second Battle of Manassas*, 39.
25. "From the 83d Regiment," *EWG*; John J. Hennessy, *Return to Bull Run: The Campaign and Battle of Second Manassas* (Dayton, 1993), 339–340.
26. Hennessy, *Return to Bull Run*, 340.
27. Hennessy, *Return to Bull Run*, 345–347; *OR*, Series 1, Vol. 16, No. 94, 476; "From the 83d Regiment," *EWG*.
28. Judson, *History of the 83rd*, 87; "From the 83d Regiment," *EWG*.
29. John J. Hennessy, *Historical Report on the Troop Movements for the Second Battle of Manassas, August 28 through August 30, 1862* (Dept. of the Interior, 1985), 532–533; *OR*, Series 1, Vol. 16, No. 174, 666; *OR*, Series 1, Vol. 16, No. 97, 480; *OR*, Series 1, Vol. 16, No. 94, 477.
30. Hennessy, *Return to Bull Run*, 347–348; "From the 83d Regiment," *EWG*; *OR*, Series 1, Vol. 16, No. 97, 480.
31. Hennessy, *Return to Bull Run*, 348–349.
32. "From the 83d Regiment," *EWG*; Judson, *History of the 83rd*, 87.
33. Hennessy, 356–357; "From the 83d Regiment," *EWG*.
34. Martin, *Second Bull Run*, 218–222.
35. *OR*, Series 1, Vol. 16, Report No. 97, 481; Judson, *History of the 83rd*, 87–88; "From the Erie Regiment," *EWG*.
36. Judson, *History of the 83rd*, 88; "From the 83d Regiment," *EWG*; Hennessy, *Return to Bull Run*, 358–359.
37. Hennessy, *Return to Bull Run*, 358–360; Judson, *History of the 83rd*, 88.
38. Hennessy, *Return to Bull Run*, 358; Judson, *History of the 83rd*, 89; "From the 83d Regiment," *EWG*.
39. *OR*, Series 1, Vol. 16, No. 97, 481; Nelson, *Biographical History of Erie County*, Volume II, 585, 632; Judson, *History of the 83rd*, 89; John D. Chapla, *48th Virginia Infantry* (Lynchburg, 1989), Letter of Pvt. Andrew Johnson, 36–37.
40. Greene, *Second Battle of Manassas*, 51.
41. Judson, *History of the 83rd*, 89; "From the 83d Regiment," *EWG*.
42. Greene, *Second Battle of Manassas*, 52; Judson, *History of the 83rd*, 90; "From the 83d Regiment," *EWG*.

Chapter VIII: Armies Broken and Divided

1. Norton to Sister L., September 8, 1862, *Army Letters*, 118; Foote to Julia Hill, September 6, 1862.
2. *OR*, Series 1, vol. 16, No. 94, 477, No. 95, 479, No. 96, 479; Nash, *History of the Forty-Fourth*, 101. Foote to Julia Hill, September 6, 1862.
3. Powell, *Fifth Army Corps*, 251.
4. Norton to Sister L., September 8, 1862, *Army Letters*, 118.
5. Shelby Foote, *The Civil War: A Narrative, Volume I: Fort Sumter to Perryville* (New York, 1986), 662–663; Nevins, *The War for the Union*, Volume II; *War Becomes Revolution*, 217.
6. Powell, *Fifth Army Corps*, 259.
7. Powell, *Fifth Army Corps*, 259–262, 303–304; Pullen, *The Twentieth Maine*, 20.
8. S. Foote, *The Civil War, Vol. I*, 672; Judson, *History of the 83rd*, 91; War Record of Amos Judson, Memorandum from Prisoner of War Records No. 356, National Archives; Nash, *History of the Forty-Fourth*, 104; Norton to Sister L., September 23, 1862, *Army Letters*, 119.
9. S. Foote, *The Civil War, Vol. I*, 667–676.
10. S. Foote, *The Civil War, Vol. I*, 683. *OR*, Series 1, vol. 19, 338.
11. Norton to Sister L., September 23, 1862, *Army Letters*, 120.
12. S. Foote, *The Civil War, Vol. I*, 700.
13. S. Foote, *The Civil War, Vol. I*, 701–703; Powell, *Fifth Army Corps*, 506; 83rd Pennsylvania Infantry Field and Staff Muster Roll for September 1862, RG 94.
14. Judson, *History of the 83rd*, 94–95; Powell, *Fifth Army Corps*, 295.
15. S. Foote, *The Civil War, Vol. I*, 704.
16. Judson, *History of the 83rd*, 96; Norton to Brother, September 26, 1862, *Army Letters*, 121; Co. G. Orderly Book, RG 94; Van Giesen to brother James and sister Jane, October 10, 1862.
17. Regimental return for September and October 1862, RG 94; Nevins, *What Death More*

Glorious, 36–41; "Local Paragraphs," *EWG*, October 9 1862.

18. Judson, *History of the 83rd*, 96; Norton to Brother, September 26, 1862, *Army Letters*, 124; Van Giesen to James and Jane, October 10, 1862.

19. Foote to Julia Hill, September 29 1862; Regimental Orderly Book, RG 94.

20. Powell, *Fifth Army Corps*, 309; S. Foote, *The Civil War, Vol. I*, 751–752.

21. Norton to Brother, September 26, 1862, *Army Letters*, 123. Judson, *History of the 83rd*, 93.

22. Judson, *History of the 83rd*, 97; Powell, *Fifth Army Corps*, 311–316; Foote to Julia Hill, November 10, 1862.

23. S. Foote, *The Civil War, Vol. I*, 752–754.

24. Judson, *History of the 83rd*, 98.

25. Judson, *History of the 83rd*, 98–99; S. Foote, *The Civil War, Vol. I*, 757; Norton to Sister L., December 6, 1862, *Army Letters*, 128.

26. Powell, *Fifth Army Corps*, 322–323.

Chapter IX: Mournful Cries in the Stillness of the Night

1. Norton to Sister L., December 6, 1862, *Army Letters*, 128.
2. *Historical Times Illustrated Encyclopedia of the Civil War*, ed. by Patricia L. Faust (New York, 1986), 96–97.
3. Nevins, *The War for the Union*, 343–344; William Marvel, *The Battle of Fredericksburg* (Eastern National Park and Monumental Association, 1993), 3–4.
4. Powell, *Fifth Army Corps*, 355–359.
5. Powell, *Fifth Army Corps*, 359–361; Marvel, *Battle of Fredericksburg*, 4.
6. Nevins, *The War for the Union*, 345.
7. Nevins, *The War for the Union*, 344–346; Marvel, *Battle of Fredericksburg*, 7–10.
8. Powell, *Fifth Army Corps*, 363; Judson, *History of the 83rd*, 99; Norton to Sister L., December 6, 1862, *Army Letters*, 129; Pullen, *Twentieth Maine*, 43.
9. Nash, *History of the Forty-Fourth*, 112.
10. Powell, *Fifth Army Corps*, 370–374; Marvel, *Battle of Fredericksburg*, 11–15.
11. Nash, *History of the Forty-Fourth*, 114; Judson, *History of the 83rd*, 101.
12. Nevins, *The War for the Union*, 347–348; Marvel, *Battle of Fredericksburg*, 17; Judson, *History of the 83rd*, 101.
13. Judson, *History of the 83rd*, 101.
14. William Marvel, "The Making of a Myth: Ambrose E. Burnside and the Union High Command at Fredericksburg," in *The Fredericksburg Campaign: Decision on the Rappahannock*, ed. by Gary W. Gallagher (Chapel Hill, 1995), 18.
15. Nevins, *The War for the Union*, 348–349.
16. Judson, *History of the 83rd*, 101–102; Nash, *History of the Forty-Fourth*, 115; Thickstun to Brother Leonard, December 18, 1862; Hooker is quoted from Nevins, *The War for the Union*, 350.
17. Marvel, "Burnside," 19; "Battle of Fredericksburg," 44. *OR*, Series 1, vol. 21, No. 170, 399.
18. Pullen, *Twentieth Maine*, 52; Edward Hill, "The Last Charge at Fredericksburg," Proceedings of the Third Brigade, First Division, Fifth Corps, Army of the Potomac Association, held at the National Encampment of the Grand Army of the Republic, Washington, D.C., September 21, 1892 (New York, 1892), 34; Judson, *History of the 83rd*, 102.
19. James P. Burchfield, Letter of December 15, 1862; Judson, *History of the 83rd*, 102.
20. Marvel, *Battle of Fredericksburg*, 46–47.
21. *OR*, Series 1, vol. 21, No. 178, 411; Nash, *History of the Forty-Fourth*, 115; Judson, *History of the 83rd*, 103.
22. *OR*, Series 1, vol. 21, No. 178, 411; Judson, *History of the 83rd*, 103; Hill, *Last Charge at Fredericksburg*, 35.
23. Hill, *Last Charge at Fredericksburg*, 34–35.
24. *OR*, Series 1, vol. 21, No. 179, 413; Judson, *History of the 83rd*, 103; Pullen, *Twentieth Maine*, 53.
25. *OR*, Series 1, vol. 21, No. 179, 413.
26. Judson, *History of the 83rd*, 103.
27. *OR* Series 1, vol. 21, No. 179, 413; *OR*, Series 1, vol. 21, No. 130, 336. Judson, *History of the 83rd*, 103.
28. Judson, *History of the 83rd*, 103.
29. *OR*, Series 1, vol. 21, No. 178, 411; Hill, *Last Charge at Fredericksburg*, 37.
30. Hill, *Last Charge at Fredericksburg*, 37.
31. Judson, *History of the 83rd*, 105.
32. Nevins, *The War for the Union*, 350.
33. Judson, *History of the 83rd*, 105; *OR*, Series 1, vol. 21, No. 178, 412.
34. Judson, *History of the 83rd*, 105–106; *OR*, Series 1, vol. 21, No. 179, 413.
35. Pullen, *Twentieth Maine*, 56; Hill, *Last Charge at Fredericksburg*, 39.
36. Judson, *History of the 83rd*, 106–107; Norton to Sister L., December 30, 1862, *Army Letters*, 130.
37. Powell, *Fifth Army Corps*, 393–394; *OR*, Series 1, vol. 21, No. 179, 412; Hill, *Last Charge at Fredericksburg*, 40; Judson, *History of the 83rd*, 107.
38. Hill, *Last Charge at Fredericksburg*, 41; Judson, *History of the 83rd*, 107.
39. Judson, *History of the 83rd*, 108; Hill, *Last Charge at Fredericksburg*, 42.
40. Judson, *History of the 83rd*, 109.
41. Judson, *History of the 83rd*, 109; Pullen, *Twentieth Maine*, 59.

42. Marvel, "Fredericksburg," 52; Foote to Julia Hill, December 18, 1862.

Chapter X: The Tempest and Whirlwind of Battle

1. Powell, *Fifth Army Corps*, 404; Ernest B. Ferguson, *Chancellorsville 1863: The Souls of the Brave* (New York, 1993), 12–13; Norton to Sister L., Dec. 20, 1862, *Army Letters*, 129.
2. Ferguson, *Chancellorsville*, 12–13; Powell, *Fifth Army Corps*, 406–408; Norton to Sister L., January 25, 1862, *Army Letters*, 133.
3. Powell, *Fifth Army Corps*, 409; Judson, *History of the 83rd*, 111.
4. Norton to E., February 6, 1863, *Army Letters*, 136.
5. 83rd Pennsylvania regimental return for January 1863, RG 94; Ferguson, *Chancellorsville*, 11.
6. 83rd Pennsylvania regimental returns for November 1862 to January 1863; Records of Courts-Martial are in the Regimental Orderly Book, RG 94.
7. "Convalescent Camp Life," *EWG*, January 1, 1863; "Local Paragraphs," *EWG*, January 24, 1863.
8. Ferguson, *Chancellorsville*, 20–35.
9. 83rd Pennsylvania monthly returns for February and March 1863, RG 94; Thickstun to Brother Leonard, March 11, 1863.
10. Waid, entries for January 22, to February 27 1863, *Civil War Diaries of Seth Waid*, 75–83.
11. Vincent to Military Adjutant of Pennsylvania, Nov. 21, 1862, RG 94; Sauers, *Advance the Colors!*, 226–227.
12. Foote to Parents, December 19, 1862; to Parents, February 15, 1862; to Julia Hill, February 23, 1863.
13. Norton to E., February 6, 1863, *Army Letters*, 135; to Sister L., January 25, 1863, *Army Letters*, 133.
14. Ferguson, *Chancellorsville*, 55; Foote to Julia Hill, March 18, 1863; Thickstun to Brother Leonard, March 11, 1863.
15. Foote to Julia Hill, March 18, 1863; J. Nevins, *What Death More Glorious*, 57; Judson, *History of the 83rd*, 111; Van Giesen to Sister, April 10, 1863.
16. Ferguson, *Chancellorsville*, 63–67, 88.
17. Judson, *History of the 83rd*, 112; Norton to Sister L., April 8, 1863, *Army Letters*, 147–148; Vincent to Capt. Estes, March 24, 1863, Regimental Orderly Book, RG 94.
18. Ferguson, *Chancellorsville*, 91–96, 107; Foote to Dear Friends, May 8, 1863.
19. Ferguson, *Chancellorsville*, 110–111, 123–130.
20. *OR*, Series 1, Vol. 25, No. 175, 521–522; Waid, entry for May 2, 1863, *Civil War Diaries of Seth Waid*, 92; Judson, *History of the 83rd*, 112–113.
21. Ferguson, *Chancellorsville*, 138–143, 152; *OR*, Series 1, Vol. 25, No. 175, 522; Judson, *History of the 83rd*, 113.
22. Ferguson, *Chancellorsville*, 152, 172–195.
23. Norton to Sister L., May 8, 1863, *Army Letters*, 150; Foote to Julia Hill, May 8, 1863.
24. Ferguson, *Chancellorsville*, 202.
25. Ferguson, *Chancellorsville*, 218; Foote to Julia Hill, May 25, 1862.
26. Ferguson, *Chancellorsville*, 242, 304; *OR*, Series 1, Vol. 25, No. 175, 522.
27. Ferguson, *Chancellorsville*, 270; "Letter from the 83d Regiment," *EWG*, May 21, 1862. The writer identified himself only by the name "SUM."
28. Ferguson, *Chancellorsville*, 313; Judson, *History of the 83rd*, 115; Norton to Mother, May 10, 1863, *Army Letters*, 151; Foote to Dear Friends, May 8, 1863.
29. Judson, *History of the 83rd*, 115; Foote to Julia Hill, May 8, 1863.
30. Ferguson, *Chancellorsville*, 330–332.
31. Nash, *History of the Forty-Fourth*, 135; Judson, *History of the 83rd*, 115–116.
32. 83rd Pennsylvania regimental return for May 1863, RG 94; *OR*, Series 1, Vol. 27, Part 1, No. 194, 615; Norton to Sister L., May 27, 1863, *Army Letters*, 155.
33. Powell, *Fifth Army Corps*, 496; Judson, *History of the 83rd*, 116.
34. Powell, *Fifth Army Corps*, 490; S. Foote, *The Civil War, Vol. II*, 431–441.
35. S. Foote, *The Civil War, Vol. II*, 448.
36. Judson, *History of the 83rd*, 117.
37. *OR*, Series 1, Vol. 27, Part 1, No. 336, 911; Series 1, Vol. 27, Part 1, No. 189, 598; Judson, *History of the 83rd*, 117–118.
38. Judson, *History of the 83rd*, 118–119; *OR*, Series 1, Vol. 27, Part 2, No. 565, 688.
39. *OR*, Series 1, Vol. 27, Part 1, No. 194, 614–615; Norton, "Our Fallen Comrades, *Army Letters*, 341; *OR*, Series 1, Vol. 27, Part 1, No. 344, 954; Judson, *History of the 83rd*, 119–120.
40. Harry W. Pfanz, *Gettysburg, the Second Day* (Chapel Hill, 1987), 12; Ferguson, *Chancellorsville*, 347; Judson, *History of the 83rd*, 122.
41. Pfanz, *Gettysburg*, 12–13; Judson, *History of the 83rd*, 123; Henry Lytle to Dear Brother, June 28, 1863, Lewis Lehigh Collection, Book 42, U.S. Army Military History Institute.
42. *OR*, Series 1, Vol. 27, Part 1, No. 189, 600–601; Judson, *History of the 83rd*, 123; Oliver Norton, *The Attack and Defense of Little Round Top, Gettysburg, July 2, 1863* (reprint, Gettysburg, 1992), 285.
43. Pfanz, *Gettysburg*, 40–51.

Chapter XI: The Rocky Hill

1. Nash, *History of the Forty-Fourth*, 141; Judson, *History of the 83rd*, 124; Waid, entry for July 2 1863, *Civil War Diaries of Seth Waid*, 103; Pfanz, *The Second Day*, 51.

2. Pfanz, *The Second Day*, 52; Judson, *History of the 83rd*, 124; Nash, *History of the Forty-Fourth*, 141.

3. Pfanz, *The Second Day*, 61–62; Nash, *History of the Forty-Fourth*, 141.

4. S. Foote, *The Civil War, Vol. II*, 489–492.

5. Pfanz, *The Second Day*, 63–64; 1st Lt. Edward Bennett, Co. A, 44th New York, "Fighting Them Over" *National Tribune*, May 6, 1886.

6. Pfanz, *The Second Day*, 63; Judson, *History of the 83rd*, 124; Waid, entry for July 2, 1863, *Civil War Diaries of Seth Waid*, 102–103.

7. Pfanz, *The Second Day*, 150–208.

8. Norton to Frank Huntington, September 28, 1888, *Army Letters*, 359.

9. Norton to Huntington, *Army Letters*, 360; James R. Wright, "Time on Little Round Top," Gettysburg Magazine, January 1, 1990, 53.

10. Judson, *History of the 83rd*, 125.

11. Norton to Sister L., July 21, 1863, *Army Letters*, 167; Oliver Norton, *The Attack and Defense of Little Round Top* (1913; Dayton, Ohio: reprint, Morningside House, 1992), 265.

12. The analysis of the ground is my own. The strength of Vincent's Brigade comes from John W. Busey and David G. Martin, *Regimental Strengths and Losses at Gettysburg* (Hightstown, New Jersey, 1994), 248.

13. Norton, *ADLRT*, 265.

14. *OR*, vol. 27, pt. 1, 623. The strength of the Twentieth Maine comes from Busey, *Strengths and Losses at Gettysburg*, 248.

15. Judson, *History of the 83rd*, 126; Pfanz, *The Second Day*, 214; Thos. Scott, Battery D, Fifth U. S. Artillery, "On Little Round Top; A Batteryman's Reminiscences of Gettysburg," *The National Tribune*, August 2, 1894; J. B. Potter, Sergeant, 83d Pennsylvania, "Gettysburg; A Comrade Who Helped Drag Artillery up Round Top," *National Tribune*, October 29, 1891; Wright, "Time of Little Round Top," 53.

16. Pfanz, *The Second Day*, 168–173.

17. Pfanz, *The Second Day*, 173, 217; *Rags and Hope, The Recollections of Val C. Giles, Four Years With Hood's Brigade, Fourth Texas Infantry, 1861–1865*, compiled by Mary Laswell (New York: Coward-McCann, Inc., 1961), 179; Busey, *Regimental Strengths and Losses*, 280.

18. Pfanz, *The Second Day*, 217–219.

19. Judson, *History of the 83rd*, 126; Norton, *ADLRT*, 269; Pfanz, *The Second Day*, 222.

20. Pfanz, *The Second Day*, 219–222; Judson, *History of the 83rd*, 26–127.

21. Pfanz, *The Second Day*, 219–222 (the "uncouth soldier" is also quoted from Pfanz); Philander Platt, Cos. D and F, 83d Pennsylvania, "On Little Round Top," *National Tribune*, April 11, 1907; Waid, entry for July 3, 1863, *Civil War Diaries of Seth Waid*, 103–104; Capt. W. C. Ward, Company G, Fourth Alabama, "Incidents and Personal Experiences on the Battlefield at Gettysburg," *Confederate Veteran*, August, 1900, 347–348; Jno Stevens, *Reminiscences of the Civil War* (Hillsboro, Texas: Hillsboro Mirror Print, 1902), 114; Scott, "On Little Round Top," *National Tribune*.

22. Pfanz, *The Second Day*, 221–227.

23. Pfanz, *The Second Day*, 229–231; Judson, *History of the 83rd*, 127; Norton to Sister L., July 21, 1863, *Army Letters*, 167.

24. Pfanz, *The Second Day*, 230–231; William C. Oates, *The War Between the Union and the Confederacy and Its Lost Opportunities, with a History of the Fifteenth Alabama Regiment and the Forty-eight Battles in Which it Was Engaged* (New York: Neale Publishing Company, 1905), 218.

25. Pfanz, *The Second Day*, 227–231; Judson, *History of the 83rd*, 128–129.

26. Sprague to Norton, January 16, 1910, *Army Letters*, 363; Judson, *History of the 83rd*, 127–128.

27. Judson, *History of the 83rd*, 128; Nevins, *What Death More Glorious*, 77; Pfanz, *The Second Day*, 228–230.

28. Judson, *History of the 83rd*, 129; Pfanz, *The Second Day*, 232–233; J.B. Potter, "Fighting Them Over; Another Story as to the Defense of Round Top," *National Tribune*, February 15, 1892.

29. *OR*, Vol. 27, pt. 2, 391; R. T. Coles, *From Huntsville to Appomattox, R. T. Cole's History of the 47th Regiment Alabama Volunteer Infantry, C. S. A., Army of Northern Virginia*, Jeffery Stocker, ed. (Knoxville, University of Tennessee Press, 1996), 109; *OR*, vol. 27, pt. 2, 412; Pfanz, *The Second Day*, 230.

30. Pfanz, *The Second Day*, 231–235; Judson, *History of the 83rd*, 130; *OR*, vol. 27, pt. 2, 391; *OR*, vol. 27, pt. 2, 412; Busey, *Regimental Strengths and Losses*, 280; Nash, *History of the Forty-Fourth*, 147; *OR*, vol. 27, pt. 1, 632; *OR*, vol. 27, pt. 1, 618.

31. Pfanz, *The Second Day*, 235–238; Giles, *Rags and Hope*, 180.

32. *OR*, vol. 27, pt. 1, 618; Wright, "Time on Little Round Top," 53–54.

33. Judson, *History of the 83rd*, 130–133; Nash, *History of the Forty-Fourth*, 153; Rodgers to Julia, July 6, 1863; Waid, entry for July 3, 1863, *Civil War Diaries of Seth Waid*, 104.

34. Judson, *History of the 83rd*, 134–136; Nash, *History of the Forty-Fourth*, 151.

35. *OR*, Vol. 27, pt. 1, 632; Judson, *History of the 83rd*, 134; Gregory A. Coco, *A Vast Sea of Misery: A History and Guide to the Union and Confederate Field Hospitals at Gettysburg, July 1–November 20, 1863* (Gettysburg: Thomas Publications, 1988), 68, 70–72, 98–99; John W. Busey, *These Honored Dead: The Union Casualties at Gettysburg* (Hightown, New Jersey: Longstreet House, 1988), 212.

36. Norton, *ADLRT*, 244; Norton to Sister L., July 12, 1863, *Army Letters*, 162; Judson, *History of the 83rd*, 133.

37. S. Foote, *The Civil War, Vol. II*, 513, 529–531.

38. *OR,* vol. 27, pt. 1, 625.

39. Nash, *History of the Forty-Fourth*, 148; *OR*, vol. 27, pt. 1, 618; Judson, *History of the 83rd*, 131; Waid, entry for July 4, 1863, *Civil War Diaries of Seth Waid*, 104.

40. Judson, *History of the 83rd*, 136–137; *OR*, vol. 27, pt. 1, 618.

41. Judson, *History of the 83rd*, 137.

42. *OR*, vol. 27, pt. 1, 1041; Judson, *History of the 83rd*, 139; Manuscript order from Butterfield, July 3, 1863, Regimental Letters Book, RG 94.

43. S. Foote, *The Civil War, Vol. II*, 576–578, 582–587.

44. S. Foote, *The Civil War, Vol. II*, 587; Norton to Sister L., July 12, 1863, *Army Letters*, 161; Thickstun to Brother, July 6, 1863.

45. Waid, entry for July 4, 1863, *Civil War Diaries of Seth Waid*, 104.

46. Judson, *History of the 83rd*, 140.

Epilogue: For None Others Can Know

1. Norton to Friends, July 17, 1863, *Army Letters*, 165; Judson, *History of the 83rd*, 151–155.

2. Gould, *Anthropological Statistics*, 594; Lt. Col. Marvin Kreidberg and Lt. Merton Henry, *History of Military Mobilization in the United States Army, 1775–1945* (Department of the Army, 1955), 104; Russell F. Weigley, *History of the United States Army* (Indiana University Press, 1984), 207–209.

3. "The Draft," *Erie Observer*, August 29, 1863.

4. Judson, unpublished autobiography, and *History of the 83rd*, 148–151; 83rd Pennsylvania descriptive list of deserters, RG 94, National Archives; Foote to Dear Friend, August 24, 1863.

5. Judson, *History of the 83rd*, 152.

6. Foote to Parents, August 30, 1863; Waid, entry for August 29, 1863, *Civil War Diaries of Seth Waid*, 118.

7. Weigley, *History of the U.S. Army*, 210.

8. Judson, *History of the 83rd*, 190, 243, 285, 301; George Bedient Pension File, National Archives; Foote to Parents, September 30, 1863;

9. Weigley, *History of the U.S. Army*, 211; Norton to Sister L., October 15, 1863, *Army Letters*, 183.

10. Norton to Mother, October 15, 1863, *Army Letters*, 185–86; and to Father, October 28, 1863, *Army Letters*, 186–87.

11. Judson, *History of the 83rd*, 229–231; "Local Paragraphs," *EWG*, September 15, 1864.

12. Waid, entries for 1864, *Civil War Diaries of Seth Waid*, 133–141.

13. Judson, *History of the 83rd*, 238–231.

14. Foote to Parents, April 8, 1865; Diary of Chaplain O. B. Clarke, entries for April 6–8, 1865.

15. Powell, *Fifth Army Corps*, 863.

16. Clarke, April 15; Foote to Parents, April 19, 1865.

17. Clarke Diary, April 20–May 13 1865; Judson, *History of the 83rd*, 70; *Erie Weekly Gazette*, May 16, 1865.

18. Clarke War Diary, May 3–11, 1865; Foote to Parents, May 15, 1865.

19. Clarke War Diary, May 12, 1865, Foote to Parents, April 19, 1865.

20. Clarke War Diary, May 23, 1865; Powell, *Fifth Army Corps*, 871; Foote to Parents, June 16, 1865.

21. Powell, *Fifth Army Corps*, 872; Clarke War Diary, May 29–31, 1865; Judson, History of the 83rd, 239; Foote to Father, June 18, 1865; Daniel Foote Pension File, National Archives.

22. Weigley, *History of the United States Army*, 216, 282, 356–357, 365; Kreidberg, *History of Mobilization*, 90–91, 172–173, 201.

23. Judson, autobiography; *Memorial of Amos M. Judson*, 6.

24. Robert Ilisevich and Jonathan Helmreich, Preface to *Civil War Diaries of Seth Waid*, viii.

25. Courtesy the Rodgers family.

26. George Bedient Pension File, National Archives.

27. Orpheus Woodward Pension Files, National Archives; *History of Allen and Woodson Counties*, 882–884.

28. Andrea, *History of Kansas*, 882.

29. *History of Erie County*, 189; Daniel Foote Pension File, National Archives.

30. Norton to Sister L, August 22, 1864, *Army Letters*, 226, and October 9, 1864, *Army Letters*, 237.

31. Norton to Brother and Sister, April 15, 1865, *Army Letters*, 256; to Father, April 19, 1865, *Army Letters,* 257; to Sister L., May 7, 1865, *Army Letters*, 258.

32. Norton to Sister L., August 27, 1865, *Army Letters*, 277.

33. *Memorials of Deceased Companions of the Commandery of the State of Illinois*, Illinois Commandery of the Loyal Legion, Military Order of

the Loyal Legion of the United States, Vol. 13D (Chicago, 1923), 606–610.

34. Nevins, *What Death More Glorious*, 86–88; Will of Elizabeth C. Vincent, *Army Letters*, 363.

35. Records of the 83rd Regimental Association and Fiftieth Anniversary, September 15, 1911, Erie County Historical Society; Norton, "Our Fallen Comrades," *Army Letters*, 337–334.

36. "Reunion of the 83rd Regiment," *Erie Observer*, July 14, 1913, and "83rd Infantry Met in Erie for Reunion," *Erie Observer*, September 22, 1930.

BIBLIOGRAPHY

Adams, George Worthington. *Doctors in Blue: The Medical History of the Union Army in the Civil War*. New York: Henry Schuman, 1952.

Anderson, Frank S. "Brevet General Hiram L. Brown," in the *Journal of Erie Studies*, Volume 4, No. 1, Spring 1975.

Andreas, A.T. *History of the State of Kansas*. 1883; reprint, Acheson County Historical Society, 1976.

Androit, John L. *Population Abstract of the United States*. McLean, Virginia: Androit Association, 1980.

Baldwin, James J. III. *The Struck Eagle: A Biography of Brigadier General Micah Jenkins and a History of the Fifth South Carolina Volunteers and the Palmetto Sharpshooters*. Burd Street Press, 1996.

Bates, Samuel P. *History of Erie County, Pennsylvania*. Chicago: Warner and Beers Company, 1884.

_____. *History of Mercer County, Pennsylvania*. Chicago: Warner and Beers Company, 1888.

_____. *History of the Pennsylvania Volunteers, 1861-1865*. Five volumes. Harrisburg: D. Singerly, Harrisburg: State Printer, 1869.

Bearss, Edwin C. Unpublished maps of the Peninsula Campaign. Richmond National Battlefield Park, Richmond, Virginia.

Burchfield, James P. Letters. Gettysburg National Military Park, Gettysburg, Pennsylvania.

Busey, John W. *These Honored Dead: The Union Casualties at Gettysburg*. Hightstown, New Jersey: Longstreet House, 1988.

Busey, John W., and Martin, David G. *Regimental Strengths and Losses at Gettysburg*. Hightstown, New Jersey: Longstreet House, 1994.

Casey, Silas. *Infantry Tactics for the Instruction, Exercise, and Maneuvers of the Soldier, A Company, Line of Skirmishers, Battalion, Brigade, or Corps D'Armee*. 1862; reprint, Dayton, Ohio: Morningside House, 1985.

Catton, Bruce. *The Civil War*. Boston: Houghton Mifflin, 1960.

_____. *Reflections on the Civil War*. Edited by John Leekley. New York: Berkley Books, 1981.

Chapla, John D. *48th Virginia Infantry*. Lynchburg, Virginia: H. E. Howard, Inc., 1989.

Cleeland, Arthur K. Letters. Private collection, Karen Steinlight, Sandlewood, Georgia.

Coco, Gregory A. *The Civil War Infantryman: In Camp, On the March, and in Battle*. Gettysburg, Pennsylvania: Thomas Publications, 1996.

_____. *A Vast Sea of Misery: A History and Guide to the Union and Confederate Field Hospitals at Gettysburg, July 1–November 20, 1863*. Gettysburg: Thomas Publications, 1988.

Coles, R. T. *From Huntsville to Appomattox: R. T. Coles' History of the 47th Regiment Alabama Volunteer Infantry, C. S. A., Army of Northern Virginia*. Edited by Jeffery Stocker. Knoxville: University of Tennessee Press, 1996.

Craighill, William P. *The Army Officer's Pocket Companion, Principally Designed for Staff Officers in the Field*. New York: D. Van Nostrand Co., 1863.

Crawford County Herald. Issue of June 18, 1862.

Crawford Journal. Issues of April 19, April 30, July 30, November 26, 1861; February 11, 1862.

Erie City Directory, 1861-62. Erie, Pennsylvania: H. W. Hulbert, 1861.

Erie Weekly Gazette. Issues of April 4, 18, 25; May 2, 23; June 6, 20, 27, 30; July 4, 18, 25; August 9, 19; October 17, 1861.

Foote, Daniel B. Letters. Foote Papers, U.S. Army Military History Institute, Carlisle, Pennsylvania.

_____. Letters. Foote Collection, Erie County Historical Society & Museum.

Foote, Shelby. *The Civil War: A Narrative*. Three volumes. New York: Vintage Books, 1963.

Fox, William F. *Regimental Losses in the American Civil War*. Albany: Albany Publishing Company, 1889.

Furgurson, Ernest B. *Chancellorsville 1863: The Souls of the Brave*. New York: Vintage Books, 1993.

Gerrish, Rev. Theodore. *Army Life, A Private's*

Reminiscences of the Civil War. Reprint, Baltimore: Butternut and Blue, and Gettysburg: Stan Clark Military Books, 1995.

Giles, Valerius. *Rags and Hope: The Recollections of Val C. Giles, Four Years with Hood's Brigade, Fourth Texas Infantry, 1861-1865.* Edited and compiled by Mary Lasswell. New York: Coward-McCann, 1961.

Goodell, G. A. Letters. Crawford County Historical Society, Meadeville, Pennsylvania.

Gould, Benjamin Apthorp. *Investigations into the Military and Anthropological Statistics of American Soldiers.* New York and Cambridge: Riverside Press, 1869.

Greene, A. Wilson. *The Second Battle of Manassas.* Eastern National, 1995.

Helmreich, Jonathan E. *The First 100 Years: Settlement and Growth in Crawford County, Pennsylvania.* Meadeville, Pennsylvania: Crawford County Historical Society, 1987.

Hennessy, John J. *Historical Report on the Troop Movements for the Second Battle at Manassas, August 28 through August 30, 1862.* Washington: Department of the Interior, 1985.

_____. *Return to Bull Run: The Campaign and Battle of Second Manassas.* Dayton, Ohio: Morningside House, 1993.

Hill, Edward. *The Last Charge at Fredericksburg. Proceedings of the Third Brigade, First Division, Fifth Corps, Army of the Potomac Association, Held at the National Encampment of the Grand Army of the Republic, Washington, D.C., September 21 1892.* New York: 1892.

Historical Times Illustrated Encyclopedia of the Civil War. Edited by Patricia L. Faust. New York: Harper & Row, 1986.

History of Allen and Woodson Counties, Kansas. Edited by L. Wallace Duncan and Chas. F. Scott. Iola, KS: 1901.

Judson, Amos E. *History of the 83rd Regiment Pennsylvania Volunteers.* 1865; reprint, Dayton, Ohio: Morningside House, 1986.

Karle, Theodore J. "The Erie Regiment's Fancy French Uniform," in *The Journal of Erie Studies*, Volume 19, No. 2, Fall 1990.

Katcher, Philip. *Civil War Uniforms: A Photo Guide.* London: Arms and Armour Press, 1990.

Krick, Robert E. L. "Prelude to the Seven Days: The Battle of Slash Church (Hanover Court House), May 27, 1862," in *The Peninsula Campaign of 1862, Yorktown to the Seven Days,* Volume Two, edited by William J. Miller. Campbell, California: Savas Woodbury, 1997.

Kreidberg, Lt. Col. Marvin A., and Henry, 1st Lt. Merton G., *History of Military Mobilization in the United States Army, 1775-1945.* Department of the Army Pamphlet 20-212. Washington: 1955.

Lytle, Henry. Letter. Lewis Leigh Collection, Book 42, U.S. Army Military History Institute, Carlisle Barracks, Pennsylvania.

McPherson, James M. *Battle Cry of Freedom.* New York: Ballantine, 1988.

Maille, Dan. *A Popular History of Harborcreek, A Vignette: Colonel John W. McLane.* Harborcreek, Pennsylvania: Harborcreek Historical Society, 1994.

Martin, David G. *The Second Bull Run Campaign, July–August 1862.* Conshohocken, Pennsylvania: Combined Books, 1997.

Marvel, William T. *The Battle of Fredericksburg.* Eastern National Park and Monument Association, 1993.

_____. "The Making of a Myth: Ambrose E. Burnside and the Union High Command at Fredericksburg," in *The Fredericksburg Campaign: Decision on the Rappahannock.* Edited by Gary W. Gallagher. Chapel Hill: University of North Carolina Press, 1995.

Masiker, James H. Letters. Crawford County Historical Society, Meadeville, Pennsylvania.

May, Alexander. Letters. Private collection. Irwin Rider, Erie, Pennsylvania.

Miller, William J. "Scarcely Any Parallel in History: Logistics, Friction, and McClellan's Strategy for the Peninsula Campaign," in *The Peninsula Campaign of 1862, Yorktown to the Seven Days,* Volume 2. Campbell, California: Savas Woodburg, 1997.

_____. "'Weather Still Execrable': Climatological Notes on the Peninsula Campaign, March through August, 1862," in *The Peninsula Campaign of 1862, Yorktown to the Seven Days,* Volume Three, edited by William J. Miller. Campbell, California: Savas, 1997.

Moore, James A. Letter. Civil War Miscellaneous Collection. U.S. Army Military History Institute, Carlisle, Pennsylvania.

Muller, Mary M. *A Town at Presque Isle: A Short History of Erie, Pennsylvania to 1980.* Erie, Pennsylvania: Erie County Historical Society, 1991.

Nash, Eugene A. *A History of the Forty-fourth Regiment New York Volunteer Infantry in the Civil War, 1861-1865.* 1910; reprint, Dayton, Ohio: Morningside House, 1988.

National Tribune. Issues of November 23, 1882; May 6, 1886; August 4, 1887; October 29, 1891; February 25, 1892; August 2, 1894; December 19, 1895; June 22, 1905; April 11, 1907.

Nelson, S. B. *Nelson's Biographical Dictionary and Historical Reference Book of Erie County.* Two volumes. Erie, Pennsylvania: S. B. Nelson, 1896.

Nevins, Allan. *The War for the Union.* Three volumes. New York: Charles Scribner's Sons, 1959.

Nevins, James H., and Styple, William B. *What Death More Glorious: A Biography of General Strong Vincent.* Kearny, New Jersey: Belle Grove, 1997.

Norton, Oliver W. *Army Letters 1861-1865*. 1903; reprint, Dayton, Ohio: Morningside House, 1990.

_____. *The Attack and Defense of Little Round Top, Gettysburg, July 2, 1863*. 1913; reprint, Dayton, Ohio: Morningside House, 1992.

Oates, William C. *The War Between the Union and the Confederacy and Its Lost Opportunities, with a History of the 15th Alabama Regiment and the Forty-eight Battles in Which it Was Engaged*. New York and Washington: Neale Publishing Company, 1905.

Pfanz, Harry W. *Gettysburg, the Second Day*. Chapel Hill, North Carolina: University of North Carolina Press, 1987.

Powell, William H. *The Fifth Army Corps (Army of the Potomac), A Record of Operations During the Civil War in the United States of America, 1861-1865*. 1896; reprint, Dayton, Ohio: Morningside House, 1984.

Pullen, John J. *The Twentieth Maine, A Volunteer Regiment in the Civil War*. Dayton, Ohio: Morningside House, 1991.

Records of the Third Brigade, First Division, Fifth Army Corps, including letters, orders, and notes. Record Group 393, National Archives, Washington.

Regimental Records of the 83rd Pennsylvania, including muster rolls, descriptive books, letters, orders, reports, and returns. From records of the War Department, Office of the Adjutant General, in the National Archives, Record Group 94, Washington.

Rice, John. Letters. Private collection. The Alcorn family, Chapel Hill, North Carolina.

Rodgers, David R. Letters. Private collection. Mrs. Jean R. Hall, Camp Hill, Pennsylvania.

Sauers, Richard A. *Advance the Colors! Pennsylvania Civil War Battleflags*. Harrisburg, Pennsylvania: Capitol Preservation Committee, 1987.

Sears, Stephen W. *To the Gates of Richmond: The Peninsula Campaign*. New York: Ticknor & Fields, 1992.

Shannon, Fred Albert. *The Organization and Administration of the Union Army 1861-1865*, Vol. I. Cleveland, Ohio: Arthur H. Clark Co., 1928.

Shaw, Douglas V. "Erie's Population in 1850: A Demographic Analysis," in *The Journal of Erie Studies*, Spring 1984.

Smith, Helene, and Swetnam, George. *A Guidebook to Historic Western Pennsylvania*. Pittsburgh, Pennsylvania: University of Pittsburgh Press, 1991.

Snyder, Jacob. Letters. Private Collection. Gerald English, Erie, Pennsylvania.

Stevens, Jno. *Reminiscences of the Civil War; A Soldier in Hood's Texas Brigade, Army of Northern Virginia*. Hillsboro, Texas: Hillsboro Mirror Print, 1902.

Susko, Linda. "Tionesta Rangers' Reunion," in *The Journal of Erie Studies*, Volume 22, No. 1, Spring 1993.

Thickstun, Israel H. Letters. Thickstun Family Papers. U.S. Army Military History Institute, Carlisle, Pennsylvania.

Van Giesen, Thomas J. Letters. Private Collection. Cynthia Freedmann, Boston, Massachusetts.

Waid, Seth. *The Civil War Diaries of Seth Waid III*. Edited by Robert Ilisevic and Jonathan Helmreich. Meadville, Pennsylvania: Crawford County Historical Society, 1993.

War Department. *Atlas to Accompany the Official Records of the Union and Confederate Armies*. Washington: War Department, 1891-1895.

_____. *Revised Regulations for the Army of the United States, 1861*. 1861; reprint, Harrisburg, Pennsylvania: National Historical Society, 1980.

_____. *War of the Rebellion: A Compilation of the Official Records of the Union and Confederate Armies*. 70 Volumes in 28 Parts. Washington: War Department, 1880-1891.

Ward, W. C. "Incidents and Personal Experiences on the Battlefield at Gettysburg," in *Confederate Veteran*, August 1900.

Warren Ledger. Issue of May 1, 1861.

Weigley, Russell F. *History of the United States Army*. Bloomington: Indiana University Press, 1984.

White, Plympton A. Letter as it appears in "A Union 'Rookie' at Camp Wilkins," in *Western Pennsylvania Magazine of History and Biography*, March 1954, edited by Robert Rutland.

Wise, Donald A. "Bazil Hall of Hall's Hill" in *The Arlington Historical Magazine*. Arlington, Virginia: Arlington Historical Society, 1982.

Woodward, Joseph Janvier, M.D. *Outlines of Chief Camp Diseases of the United States Armies, As Observed During the Present War*. 1863; reprint, San Francisco: Norman Publishing, 1992.

Wright, James R. "Time on Little Round Top," in *Gettysburg Magazine*, January 1, 1990, Issue No. Two.

Young, F.J. "Memorial of Amos M. Judson of Burnside Post, No. 8, Department of the Potomac, G.A.R., Address of Comrade F.J. Young at the Memorial Service of the Post, April 23, 1913." Washington, D.C.

INDEX

Italic numbers indicate pages with photographs, drawings, charts, diagrams, or maps. Names of commanders may include troops serving under them.

Accidents among soldiers 35
Adjutant's role 34
Akerly, Nicholas 135
Alcohol 44, 46, 135
Aldie, Virginia 163–164
Alexandria, Virginia: camp at Shuter's Hill 52; camp on return to Washington at end of war 194; Union march to 51–52
Allabach, Col. *131*
Ambulances 76, 77
Ames, Adelbert 131
Ammunitions *see* Firearms
Anderson, G.B. 110
Anderson, Joseph 67
Anesthetics 77
Antietam, battle of 133–134
Appomattox surrender 193
Armistead, Lewis, Brigade of Virginia under, at Malvern Hill 106, 107
Army Medical Department's powers 117
Army of Northern Virginia *see* Lee, Robert E.
Army of the Potomac: Burnside made commander of 136; call for more troops 81; campaigns 3–4; casualties and wounded 111; formation of 28; Hooker made commander of 153; McClellan as commander of 51; McLane's troops joining 29; move from peninsula 118–119; reorganization by McClellan 64; reorganization into Grand Divisions 138; St. Patrick's Day celebration (1863) 155–156, *156;* as of September 1862 129; size of 52, 132, 157; Yorktown siege *see* Yorktown, Virginia; *see also*

specific battles, corps, brigades, and regiments
Army of Virginia 114, 118; transferred to Army of the Potomac 130; *see also* Pope, John
Austin, Henry 68, 77, 78, 79
Austin, James 44
Austin, Thomas 20

Badges 153–154, *155*
Balloons, hot-air, used to observe enemy movements 82
Baltimore, protection of 164
Banks, Nathaniel 118, 134
Barnard, Brig. Gen. (McClellan's chief engineer officer) 85
Barnes, James: commander of 1st Brigade of 1st Division, 5th Corps *131;* commander of 1st Division of 5th Corps 162; at Gettysburg, *172; see also* Barnes' Division
Barnes' Division: at Aldie 163; at Gettysburg 169; march to Gettysburg 166
Battle tactics, 30–32; lying still while under artillery fire 105; officers' knowledge of 33; regiment in column of companies *31;* regiment in line of battle *31*
Battles *see* names and locations of specific battles
Baylor, Will 126
Beauregard, P.G.T. 18, 26
Bedient, George: death of 196; on Gaines's Mill battle 90, 91, 92, 93–94, 96, 100–101; life after Civil War 195–196; on McLane's death at Gaines's Mill 94; re-enlistment of 190; wounded at Gaines's Mill battle 97, 99, 100
Benson, Henry 68, 69

Berdan, Hiram 105, 123
Big Bethel, Virginia reconnaissance 53–54
Big Round Top (Gettysburg): Confederate ascent 176; Confederate retreat from Little Round Top to 182; description of 7, 9–10, 174, 176; sketch of, as seen from Confederate lines *173*
Black regiments 190–191, 196–197
"Bounty jumpers" 189
Bowen, exchange re stolen pig 60
Brady's Michigan Sharpshooters 143
Branch, Lawrence 67, 68, 73, 74, 76, 77
Brandy Station, battle of 163
Brawls among troops in camp 46
Bricker, Leonard 183
"Brogans" 37
Brown, Hiram: background of 20; at Hanover Court House battle 74; life after Civil War 196; wounded at Gaines's Mill battle 94, 100–101
Bryan, King 181–182
Buchanan, Lt. Col. *131*
Buchanan as commander of 2nd Brigade in 5th Army Corps, 2nd Division 65
Bugler playing "Taps" 114
Bulger, Col. of 47th Alabama 183
Bull Run, First Battle of 18–19, 26
Bull Run, Second Battle of 11, 119–128, 129; casualties and wounded 4, 11, 128; retreat of Union soldiers 127–128
Burchfield, James P. 143, 162
"Burgettstown Blues" 14
Burnside, Ambrose E.: Army of the Potomac command given to 136; background of 137–138;

217

complaints about 150; Fredericksburg strategy 138, 139, 140, 141, 142, 143, 146, 147, 150; photo of *138;* resignation of 150, 151; successful battles in early 1862 47; *see also* 9th Corps
Bushmen, Lewis 184
Bushnell, Henry 37, 44
Butler 196
Butterfield, Daniel: appointment to 5th Corps staff 131; background of 30; on casualties and wounded in the Seven Days 112; chief of staff under Hooker 153; commander of brigade 30; commander of 3rd Brigade in 5th Army Corps, 1st Division 65; commander of 5th Corps 138; complimenting 83rd Pennsylvania 38, 78; on discipline and drill needed while in camp 46; at Fredericksburg 148; at Gaines's Mill 87, 90, 94; guard post orders from 35; Hanover Court House battle and strategy 68, 69, 73, 74; at headquarters near Gaines's Mill 101; at Malvern Hill battle 105, 107, 108, 109; at Mechanicsville battle 85; orders at end of Hanover Court House 76; photo of *30;* on pillaging 60; at Second Bull Run 121, 123, 127; "Taps" for lights out devised by 114; training of officers by 33; uniforms demanded by 37; visit to dying Vincent 185; wounded at Gettysburg 185
Butterfield's Brigade: at Big Bethel action 54; at Gaines's Mill 86, *88,* 88–99, 91; at Hall's Hill camp 30; at Hanover Court House 69, 72; prisoners taken by at Hanover Court House 77; sickness and disease 47; as 3rd Brigade of 1st Division 50
"Butterfield's Thieves" 131
"Butterfield's Twins" 38, 101, 174

Calvin, Samuel 23
Camp arrangements and conditions: Camp Leslie near Washington 34–35; Hooker's improvements 153; Shuter's Hill camp in Alexandria, Virginia 52; Stoneman's Station winter quarters 151; Thanksgiving scene in a Union camp near Washington *40;* Union soldiers crowding a sutler's wagon *41;* Union soldiers stealing fence rails *40*
Camp Leslie 30–35, 38; hygiene at 43–44; night at 43; return to, from Second Bull Run retreat 128; winter at 42, 44–45, 46

Camp Winfield Scott (Yorktown) 56; Union soldiers leaving *57*
Campbell, Hugh: apportioning new recruits among companies 118; background of 20; commander of 83rd Pennsylvania at Malvern Hill 107, 108; conducting draft in Erie 188; death of 196; on death of McLane at Gaines's Mill battle 94; election to lieutenant-colonel 112; on Gaines's Mill 85, 87, 90, 92; life after Civil War 196; on Malvern Hill 105, 107, 108, 109, 110, 111; recruiting drive in Erie by 113, 117; resignation following amputation of leg 162; retreat from Gaines's Mill 97, 99, 101; at Second Bull Run 122, 124; taking command at Gaines's Mill battle 94, 95, 96, 99; wounded at Malvern Hill 108; wounded at Second Bull Run 124
Canister shot 124
Caps, symbols on to identify corps and division 153–154
Carter, Elizabeth 21, 22; *see also* Vincent, Elizabeth
Casey, Silas 32, 33
Catholics 52
Cavalry's scouting missions 132
Centreville, Virginia: Confederate troops positioned at (1861) 47, 48, 50, 51; Union soldiers' march to pre-Peninsula campaign 50–51; Union soldiers' retreat to after Second Bull Run 128
Chamberlain, Joshua 142, 175, 180, 181, 184, 193
Chambers, Ezekial 23
Chancellorsville, battle of 157–161; casualties 161; march to 157–158; Union retreat ordered 161
Chapman as commander of 2nd Brigade in 5th Army Corps, 2nd Division 65
"Chickahominy Fever" 82
Chickahominy River (Virginia): Army Engineers' bridge over *83;* bridges over 80; camping at, after Hanover Court House 80; description of 67; disease-carrying insects along 82; Gaines's farm as camp of 83rd Pennsylvania near 82, 85, 86; march from Yorktown to 64–65; retreat to, after Union loss at Gaines's Mill 98–99, 101
Christmas celebration at Camp Leslie 45
Civil War, purpose of 2, 8
Clark, Daniel 20, 59, 60
Clark, John M.: adjutant job of 34; background of 20; as

Brigade Adjutant for Vincent 162; at Gettysburg 177; summoning Vincent family to Strong Vincent's deathbed 185, 187; traveling to Erie with Strong Vincent's remains 187
Cleeland, Arthur: death of, due to disease 113; on desire for no further battles 113; on drilling 42; on Hanover Court House battle 79; on letter-writing 43; on possible future battle 45; on river trip to Chesapeake Bay 52; on Springfield muskets 45; on visions of return home 60; on Yorktown siege 60
Cobb's Brigade 141
"Coffee grinder" (forerunner of machine gun) 82
Cold Harbor: battle of (under Grant) 191; camp (near Chickahominy River, Virginia) 65, 67, 79; 3rd Brigade advance to 84–85
Coleman, Major 181
Colored troops *see* Black regiments
Colors as battle trophy 110
Colors of the 83rd 154, *157, 158,* 162, 166, *190; see also* Flags and pennants
Commissary Sergeant's role 34
Compromise of 1850 2
Confederates: First Bull Run victory of 18; illness among troops 83; Johnston's troops in Virginia 48; losing war, strategy to turn tide (1863) 163; Pennsylvania strategy 168; positioning at Little Round Top and Big Round Top 10–11; prisoners of *see* Prisoners taken by Confederates; reorganization of troops 138; veterans 198; *see also specific battles, commanders, and regiments*
Conscription of troops 117, 188, 195; hiring substitutes 189; immigrants 188–189
Cooking 36
"Corduroy Roads" 57–58
Couch, Darius 104, 107
Couch's 2nd Corps 158, 160; *see also* 2nd Corps
Court(s) martial: of men in Stowe's company 152; of Porter 136
Cowan, Edward 45
Crouchet, Clementine 195
"Crowd poisoning" 43
Culpeper, Virginia 138
Curtain, Andrew 15, 16, 18, 82, 195
Cutler, Charles 24

Davis, Jefferson 163, 194
Death sentence for deserters 189

Deaths: disease as cause of 47, 129; *see also specific battles for casualties*
Deschrya, Francis 23
Desertions 151–152, 154, 188, 189
Devil's Den, Gettysburg *180*
Discharge: disease as cause of 47; end of three-year term 191–192
Disease *see* Sickness and disease
Downing, John 152
Draft *see* Conscription of troops
Drake, Edwin 13
Drinking 44, 46, 135

Eastern Theatre of Operations (1861–1865) *49*
Edison, Abner 23
18th North Carolina 73
83rd Pennsylvania Infantry Regiment: after first year in War 129; at Appomattox surrender 193; backgrounds of enlistees 22–24; casualties and wounded 4, 11–12, 77, 99, 111, 112, 129, 133, 146, 147, 151, 161, 164, 183, 193; colors of 45, 154, *157, 158*; desertions 151–152, 154, 188, 189; discharge of men at end of three-year term 191–192; draftees joining after Antietam 134; draftees joining after Gettysburg 188; elections of officers after Gettysburg 189; elections of officers after the Seven Days campaign 112; first battle of *see* Hanover Court House, battle of; formation of 3; monument to, on Little Round Top 197; mustering out 194; name change from Battalion back to Regiment 193; name change from Regiment to Battalion 192; name given to 38; number in October 1862 134; number in January 1863 151; number in fall 1863 189, 192; as part of Butterfield's Brigade 50; as part of 5th Corps, 1st Division 64, *65*; as part of Vincent's 3rd Brigade 162; prisoners of Confederates 129; re-enlisting upon end of three-year term 190; sickness and disease suffered by 11, 82, 112–113, 129, 151, 154; survivors of Peninsula Campaign 115, 117; veterans of 197–198; *see also specific battles, commanders,* 3rd Brigade, and 5th Corps
11th Corps: at Chancellorsville 158, 159, 160; at Gettysburg 168
Elliot, Robert 122
Ellsworth, Elmer 37
"Ellsworth Avengers" 37, 122; *see also* 44th New York

Emancipation Proclamation 188, 190
Equipment and kits 41; lack of writing utensils 151; orderly books showing re-equipping after Antietam 134; storage of excess 50; at Yorktown siege 60
Erie, Pennsylvania: draft 188; history of 12–14; hometown of 83rd Pennsylvania 3; militia 14–16; population of 14; quota of volunteers from 117, 188; recruiting in 47; welcome of returning soldiers 152, 192
Erie Regiment of Colonel McLane, failure to be called to action 16–18
Eriez (Eries) tribe 12–13
European military observers 82
Ewell, Richard: at Gaines's Mill battle 90; at Gettysburg 168, 169, 184; at Harrisburg 165; monitoring Union retreat from Gaines's Mill 102; successor to Stonewall Jackson 163

Fairfax, Virginia 51
Faison, E. Franklin 109
Fales, George 135
Fanning, Lucy 197
Faulkner, William 23, 44
Fear 2, 72, 108
Featherston, Winfield 87
Field, Charles 126
Field hospitals 76–77, 100; at Gettysburg 183; at Savage's Station after battle of Gaines's Mill *103*
15th Alabama 176, 179, 180
5th Corps: at Antietam 133, 135; cap symbol to identify 154; casualties and wounded in the Seven Days 112; at Chancellorsville campaign 158, 159, 160; at Chickahominy River and Mechanicsville 80, 83–84; end of war march to Washington 193–194; at Fredericksburg 143, 148, 149; at Gaines's Mill 100; *see also* Gaines's Mill, battle of; at Gettysburg 167, 169, 184; Hooker taking command of 136; at Malvern Hill 104, 107 *see also* Malvern Hill, battle of; Meade as commander of 153; organization (May 18, 1862) 64, *65*; organization (September 16, 1862) *131*; part of Center Grand Division 138; Peninsula Campaign return 119; Porter relieved of his command of 136; prisoners taken in spring 1865 193; in pursuit of Lee in Virginia (October/November 1862) 135; as reserve for Maryland battles 131; retreat after Gaines's Mill 102; at

Second Bull Run 120, 122, 123, 128; at Sharpsburg 132; size of 81; Sykes as commander of 165; *see also specific brigades and regiments constituting*
5th South Carolina 95
5th Texas 176, 177, 179, 180
5th Vermont 101
Fighting among soldiers in camp 46
"Finney Guards" 19
Firearms: ammunition for Hanover Court House battle 67, 68; "coffee grinder" (forerunner of machine gun) 82; Minié bullets 75, 143; muskets 31, 33, 45
1st Brigade *see* Martindale's 1st Brigade
1st Corps: at Antietam 133; at Chancellorsville 160; at Gettysburg 168; located near Fredericksburg 118; ordered into Maryland 131; ordered to remain in Washington 56; part of Left Grand Division 138; at Second Bull Run 120; at Sharpsburg 132
1st Division: desertions 189; at Fredericksburg 146; *see also* Morell's Division
1st U.S. Sharpshooters *65,* 123
1st Virginia 125
Fisher 94
Flags and pennants: as battle trophy 110; color bearer killed at Malvern Hill 108; later presentations to 83rd 154, *157, 158*; Norton's description of 162; original presented to 83rd at Hall's Hill 45, 154; placed at Big Bethel 54; veterans of 83rd with *190*; Vincent having unfurled on march into Pennsylvania 166
Fleming, Capt. 20, 28
Flower, Josiah 63, 113–114
Food and rations 36–37; for Hanover Court House battle 67, 78; Hooker's improvements 153; for march 50; at Stoneman's Station winter camp 151; Union soldiers crowding a Sutler's wagon *41*; at Yorktown siege 59–60
Foote, Daniel: on accidental shooting of soldier 35; on alcohol excess of soldiers 135; background of 24–25; on Chancellorsville 158, 160, 161; on Chaplain Flower 113; on Confederate dead 63; on conscription and his brother, George 117; correspondence with family and Hill 43 *see also* Hill, Julia; on Davis' capture and pardon of rank-and-file Confederates 194; death of 197; on deserters 189;

on desire to do battle 48; on diminished ranks of Company K 83, 113; on discharge from service, refusal to seek 155; on drinking by the troops 44; on escaped slave 79; on foraging 37; on 44th New York Regiment 38; on Gaines's Mill battle 90, 93, 94, 95, 98; on Hampton, Virginia 52; on Hanover Court House battle 73, 74, 75, 77; on Hooker 155; illness and hospital confinement 116, 149, 155; on immigrant conscripts 189; life after Civil War 197; on Lincoln's assassination 193; on loads carried by marching soldiers 66; on Malvern Hill battle 104, 109, 111; marriage to Julia Hill 196; on McLane's death at Gaines's Mill 94; mustering out 194; nearly killed at Gaines's Mill 93; on packs 51; photo of 25; on picket duty 81; on predictions of end of War 156; promotion to corporal 190; on pursuit of Lee from Maryland to Virginia (October/November 1862) 136; re-enlistment of 190; on retreat from Gaines's Mill 102; return to 83rd after release from hospital 129–130; on Richmond approach 63, 65, 78; on Richmond area camp 81; on Shuter's Hill camp 52; on Stoneman's Station camp 151; on survivors of 1862 summer campaigns 130; on survivors of Gaines's Mill 102; on survivors of the Seven Days 112–113; on Washington, D.C. 28; on Washington march at end of war 194; on winning zouave uniform in drill competition 41; on winter weather 46; on Yorktown siege 57, 59, 60, 61
Foote, George (brother of Daniel) 117
Foraging, 37, 44; at Fredericksburg 142, 148; at Hanover Court House 78; 3rd Brigade's habitual stealing of Rebel property 131; at Yorktown siege 60
Ft. Monroe: strategy of McClellan 51; troops moved to after Peninsula Campaign 115
4th Alabama 176, 177, 179, 180, 181
4th Corps: at Chickahominy River 80; at Fredericksburg 148; at Malvern Hill 104
4th Michigan: at Malvern Hill 104; part of 5th Corps, 1st Division 65
4th Texas 176, 177, 179, 180

42nd Virginia 125
44th New York Regiment 37–38; at Aldie 164; dispute with 83rd over flag captured at Malvern Hill 110; at Fredericksburg 143, 144; at Gaines's Mill 86, 87, 90, 94, 97, 98, 99; at Gettysburg 174, 177, 184; losses of 1862 summer campaigns 130; at Malvern Hill 108, 110; part of 5th Corps, 1st Division 65; part of Porter's Division 50; part of Vincent's 3rd Brigade 162; retreat from Gaines's Mill 101; at Second Bull Run 123, 124, 127; *see also* "Ellsworth Avengers"
47th Alabama 176, 179, 180
48th Alabama 176, 179, 180
48th Virginia 125, 126, 128
Franklin, William: as commander of Left Grand Division (1st & 6th Corps) 138; as commander of 6th Corps 64; *see also* Franklin's Grand Division
"Franklin Pierce Rifle Guards" 14
Franklin's Division 62
Franklin's Grand Division: at Fredericksburg 139, 140, 141, 142
Fredericksburg, battle of 11, 138–149; burying dead at 147; casualties and wounded 147, 149; description of locale 138, 140; evacuation ordered 147, 149; fog at 141, 147; looting of town 142, 148; Marye's Heights *144, 145*; river crossing 140, 142
Fremont, John C. 118
Furloughs 116, 153

Gaines, William 86
Gaines's farm as camp of 83rd Pennsylvania 82, 85, 86
Gaines's Mill: battle of 2, 11, 86–99, 100; Boatswain's Swamp *88;* breakthrough and retreat *93;* Butterfield's Brigade position *88;* casualties and wounded 4, 94, 97, 99, 100; Confederates sweeping field at dusk *98;* death of McLane at 94, 100; first attacks by the 83rd *89;* plateau of *95;* 6th Corps relieving 83rd and 44th after battle 101; smoke and noise problems 95; Union retreat 94–95, 97–99, 100; Watt House as Porter's headquarters 91, *98*
Garland, Samuel 109, 110
General Orders accompanying Military Act 23
German enlistees 43, 159, 160
Gettysburg, battle of 166–186; casualties 184, 185 *see also* Little Round Top (Gettysburg); Cemetery Ridge 7, 8, 170, 185;

Confederate retreat 185, 186; Culp's Hill 184–185; description of locale 168; Devil's Den, 170, *180;* importance of 11; maneuvering during 7–11; march to 166–167; Pickett's Charge 185; Union victory 184; Valley of Death, just after the battle *182; see also* Big Round Top; Little Round Top
Gifford, Lt. 181
Giles, Valerius C. 176, 182
Goodell, G.A. 46
Graham, Captain 68, 126, 127
Grand Army of the Republic 197, 198
Grant, Benjamin 16
Grant, Ulysses S.: appointment as General-in-Chief 191; Appomattox surrender of Lee to 193; Shiloh victory 60; strategy of 191; at Vicksburg 163, 187; victories in early 1862 47
Gregg 164
Griffin, Charles: at Chancellorsville 158, 159, 160, 161; at Chickahominy River battle 84; as commander of 2nd Brigade in 5th Army Corps, 1st Division 65, *131;* as commander succeeding Morrel 138; at Fredericksburg 145, 146, 148; *see also* Griffin's 2nd Brigade
Griffin's 2nd Brigade: at Hanover Court House 74–75; at Malvern Hill 107, 108; part of 5th Army Corps, 1st Division 65; at Second Bull Run 120, 121
Grine, Philip 183, 185
Groveton, Battle of 120
Grower, William 122
Guard posts 35, 44
Guides 65

Hall, Bazil 30
Halleck, Henry 118, 128, 130, 138, 165
Hall's Hill, camp at *see* Camp Leslie
Hampton, Virginia 52; 83rd Pennsylvania march to Big Bethel from 53; Union troops landing at the beginning of Peninsula Campaign (drawing) *53*
Hanover Court House, battle of 11, 67–79; burying of Confederate dead 78; casualties and wounded 76, 77; map *70;* prisoners taken 77; Rebel cannon abandoned at *71,* 72; retreat of Rebel troops 72–73, 74; sketch by eyewitness *71;* Union march to 67–68
Hanrahan, Pierce 46

Index

Harris, James: on first meeting 83rd Pennsylvania upon enlisting 118; on hospital treatment 152; on march to Bull Run 119; on Second Bull Run 122, 123, 124, 125, 126, 127; on Second Bull Run retreat 128

Harrison's Landing: Lincoln's visit to McClellan and troops at 114; Union burial at *113*; Union move to after Malvern Hill battle 111–112

Hatch, Daniel 94, 123, 124, 126

Hatcher's Run 193

Hays, Chauncy 117

Hays, Jairus 117

Hazlett, Charles 76, 175, 176, 177

Heavy artillery: canister shot 124; at Gaines's Mill 86; at Gettysburg 175; soldiers lying still while under artillery fire 105; at Yorktown 57, *58*

Heintzelman, Samuel P. 48, *50*, 53, 54, 121

Higley, Alva 193

Hill, A.P. 84, 87, 88, 158, 163, 165, 169

Hill, D.H. 84, 87, 107

Hill, Edward 143

Hill, Julia: correspondence from Foote to 25, 38, 41, 43, 63, 81, 113, 116, 130, 149, 151, 155, 156, 161; friend of Foote 24; marriage to Foote 196

Holmes, Theophilus 104

Hood, John B.: Brigade of Texas under, stopping Union troops in Virginia 62; division at Gettysburg 11; at Gaines's Mill 92; at Gettysburg 169, 170, 172, 175; wounded at Gettysburg 175–176

Hooker, Joseph "Fighting Joe": background of 153; Chancellorsville strategy of 157, 159, 160, 161; commander of Army of the Potomac 153; commander of Center Grand Division (3rd & 5th Corps) 138; criticism of 161–162, 165; on Fredericksburg 142; Lincoln retaining after Chancellorsville 162; morale, improvements aimed at 153–154; photo of *153*; post–Chancellorsville strategy 162, 163; request to be reassigned from Army of the Potomac 165; retreat ordered at Chancellorsville 161; at St. Patrick's Day festivities 156; taking command of 5th Corps 136; wounded at Chancellorsville 160; *see also* Hooker's Grand Division

Hooker's Grand Division 139

Hospitals 116–117; *see also* Field hospitals

Hot-air balloons, used to observe enemy movements 82

Howard, O.O. 159; *see also* 11th Corps

Humphreys, Andrew A. 131, *131*

Hunter, Moses B. 152

Hurlbert, Egbert 77

Huson, William 122

Hygiene 43

Immigrants among troops 24, 188–189; Germans, help in letter-writing 43; Germans fighting at Chancellorsville 159, 160

"Infantry Tactics" (Casey) 32, 33

"Invincibles" 14

"Irish Brigade" 110, 111

Islett, Samuel *39*

Jackson, Thomas J. "Stonewall": at Cedar Mountain battle 118; at Chancellorsville 159; at Fredericksburg 139, 140, 141, 160; at Gaines's Mill battle 95; promotion to Lt. General 138; at Second Bull Run 119–128; Shenandoah Valley location of troops in Virginia 138; strategy coordinated with Lee 83–84, 87; Washington approach by 55; wounded by Confederate men at Fredericksburg 160

Johnson, Andrew 195

Johnson, Bradley T. 125, 126, 128

Johnston, Albert Sidney 60

Johnston, Allen 23

Johnston, Joe: concern over Union troops nearing Richmond 67; Confederate commander of forces in Virginia 47; at end of war 193; strategy for attack on Union troops on Chickahominy 80; wounded in battle 81

Johnston's troops: at Centreville, Virginia 47, 48, 50; retreat to Richmond 62, 64; size of 52, 64, 81; withdrawal to line behind Rappahannock 51, 52; at Yorktown, Virginia 55, 61

Jones, David P. 20, *72*, 135, 175

Judson, Amos: as aide to Vincent 162; on Aldie 164; on "annual movement towards Richmond" 157; background of 20; on Big Bethel action 53, 54; on Camp Leslie winter 42, 44; captured by Confederates 102, 103; on Chickahominy River 80; on Chickahominy River battle 85; on Cold Harbor camp 67; as Confederate prisoner 102, 103, 132, 193; on conscripts after Gettysburg 188; death of 195; discharge chosen over re-enlistment 190, 191; election to captain of Company E 112; flag of 83rd donated to Erie by 158; on following Pope in northern Virginia 119; on foraging 78; on Fredericksburg 141–142, 143, 144, 145, 146, 147, 148–149; furlough taken by 153; on Gaines's Mill battle 87, 89, 90, 92, 94, 95–96; on Gettysburg 167, 172, 173, 177, 183, 185; on guard posts 35; on Hanover Court House battle 67, 73, 74; history of 83rd Pennsylvania by 4, 195; on immigrant conscripts 189; life after Civil War 195, 197; on marching in Virginia 51, 54, 163; on McClellan's competence 135; on Meade as commander of Army of the Potomac 165; on Mechanicsville battle 86; on mud 151; on Pennsylvania march 166; photo of *21, 162*; on pursuit of Lee from Maryland to Virginia (October/November 1862) 135–136; on readiness to fight 156; on receiving marching orders 50; release from Confederate prison 132; on retreat at Gaines's Mill 97; on Second Bull Run retreat 127; on Second Bull Run strategy 120–121, 122; on Seven Pines battle 84; on Shepardstown Ford battle 134; on Stoneman's Station camp 163; War Department position (1865) 195; on Washington, D.C. 28; wounded at Gaines's Mill battle 99; on Yorktown siege 58–59, 61

Judson, George 128

Kearney, Phil 153

"Kearney Patch" 153

Kerr, John 43

Kershaw's Brigade 110, 141

Keyes, Gen. 54

Knox, David S. 20

Lamont, Hugh 125, 126, 162

Lamont, William 112

Lane, James 68, 69, 72–73

Lane, William S. (law partner of Strong Vincent) 22

Lane's North Carolina Brigade 160

Lansing, Hugh 50, 121, 122, 127

Law, Evander 175, 176, 179

Lee, Fitzhugh 164

Lee, Robert E.: Antietam strategy and retreat 133–134; Appomattox surrender by 193; Chancellorsville strategy 159; commander of Army of Northern Virginia 81; concern over Union troops nearing Richmond 67; on duty 2; Fredericksburg strategy

139, 157; Gaines's Mill strategy 87, 90, 91; Gettysburg retreat 186; Gettysburg strategy 169, 170, 184, 185; Malvern Hill strategy 104, 105, 106, 107, 111, 112; Pennsylvania strategy 168; Rappahannock (August 1862) strategy 119; Richmond protection strategy 83–84, 85, 118, 136; Second Bull Run strategy 121, 123; strategy after Chancellorsville 163; strategy after Gaines's Mill battle 102; strategy after Gettysburg 187; strategy after Second Bull Run 130, 132; Washington or Baltimore as possible objective of 165; Yorktown strategy 55
"Lee's Lost Order" 132
Letter-writing 43; lack of utensils for 151
Lewis, Charles 23
Libby Prison (Richmond) 132, 193
Lice 151
Lieutenants' role 33; *see also* Officers
Life of soldiers: at camp *see* Camp arrangements and conditions; during training 33–34; *see also specific camps*
"Lights Out in Camp" tune 114
Lincoln, Abraham: appointment of Burnside to command Army of the Potomac 137–138; appointment of Grant as General-in-Chief 191; appointment of Halleck as General-in-Chief 118; appointment of Hooker to command Army of the Potomac 153; appointment of McClellan as General-in-Chief 26, 27, 47; appointment of Meade as commander of Army of the Republic 165; approval of Burnside's Fredericksburg strategy 138, 139; approval of McClellan's plan against Johnston's troops 47, 48, 50, 51; approval of offensive under Hooker 157; asking Reynolds to head Army of the Potomac 165; assassination of 193; concern over Union losses in summer of 1862 130; considering withdrawing Union troops from Peninsula Campaign 114; creation of Army of Virginia with Pope as commander 118; disillusionment with, leading to removal of, McClellan 51, 114–115, 136; Hooker relieved from Army of the Potomac command 165; Hooker retained by 162; letter to troops after Fredericksburg 150; ordering McClellan to pursue Lee in Virginia 135; protection of Washington as concern of 48, 55–56; raising troops 19 *see also* Military Act of 1861; visit to McClellan and troops at Harrison's Landing 114
Line of battle 31
Little Round Top (Gettysburg) 2, 4, 170–183; burying dead at 182–183, 185; casualties and wounded of 83rd 183; Confederate advance toward 175–181; Confederate casualties, wounded and captured 181, 182; description of 7, 9–10, 172–173; diagram of battle on July 2, 1863 *178*; importance of position 9, 170, 172, 184; monument to 83rd Pennsylvania on 197; Norton with Vincent 8, 9, 171–174, 179; photo, from the west *173*; reinforcements' arrival 182; seeking troops to hold 170–171, 172; sketch of, as seen from Confederate lines *173*; Valley of Death, where Little Round Top meets Big Round Top *175*; veterans meeting on 198; Vincent wounded at 181; Vincent's actions 8–11, 172–181; Warren on summit of 170, 172
Loads carried by marching soldiers 66
Longstreet, James: commander of Confederate 1st Corps 163; at Fredericksburg 139, 140; at Gaines's Mill 88, 90, 91, 92, 95, 97; at Gettysburg 169, 170, 171, 184; at Hagerstown, Maryland 132; promotion to Lt. General 138; at Rappahannock 118, 119; at Second Bull Run 120, 121; in southern Pennsylvania 165; strategy to counter Union troops near Richmond 84, 87
Lovell, Maj. *131*
Lowe, Thaddeus 82
Lying still while under artillery fire 105
Lytle, Henry 166

Mackenzie, Ranald 171, 172*n*
Magruder, John B. 52, 54, 107
Mahone, William 107, 108, 109, 110
Mail 43
Mallory, George *190*
Malvern Hill, battle of 11, 103–111; artillery fire 105, 111; battlefield 103–104, *106, 107;* casualties and wounded 4, 11; Confederate colors captured 110; men lying still under artillery fire 105; mistakes by Lee at 107; Morell's Division's position at 11 a.m. *106;* movements during *109*

Manassas *see* Bull Run
Maps and diagrams: Eastern Theatre of Operations (1861–1865) *49;* Fredericksburg, battle of *146;* Gaines's Mill, battle of *89, 93;* Hampton and Yorktown area *55;* Hanover Court House, battle of *70;* Little Round Top (Gettysburg) *178;* Porter's attack on the railroad cut (Bull Run) *125;* Washington, D.C., and northern Virginia (1861) *27*
Marches 2, 65–66
Martindale, James: commander of 1st Brigade in 5th Army Corps, 1st Division *65;* at Gaines's Mill battle 92; at Hanover Court House 73; on Malvern Hill 105; *see also* Martindale's 1st Brigade
Martindale's 1st Brigade: at Gaines's Mill 99; at Hanover Court House 78; at Malvern Hill 105, 106, 107; at Mechanicsville 84
Masiker, James 42, 43
Mason and Slidell affair 42
May, Alexander: death at Gaines's Mill 99; on equipment 41; on 44th New York Regiment 38; on guard posts 35; at Hanover Court House 76; at Hanover Court House battle 75, 79; on hot-air balloons 82; on inaction during winter 46, 47; on letters taken from Rebel dead 78; on marching 66; on Richmond area camp 81; on sickness among troops 44; on training maneuvers 33; on uniforms 42; on visions of return home 81; on Yorktown siege 61
McBride, Frank 77
McCall, George W. 29, 81, 84, 86, 117
McClellan, George B.: animosity toward Pope 118; Antietam strategy 133; appointment as army commander 26, 27, 47; arrival at Ft. Monroe 54; background of 26; blame for Second Bull Run placed on 130; complimenting 83rd Pennsylvania 38; decline in popularity of 47; discipline and training 28; failure to pursue Confederates after Malvern Hill 111, 112; failure to pursue Lee into Virginia after Antietam 134; on Hanover Court House victory 77, 80; at headquarters near Gaines's Mill 101; likeness on stationery 43; at Malvern Hill 104; Maryland strategy 131–132; Mechanicsville strategy 84; nickname of "Little Mac" 27; order to occupy Hall's

Hill from 30; ordered to remove troops to Ft. Monroe 115; photo of *39*; proclaiming Mechanicsville victory 85; public scorn for 135; rallying troops 27, 51; on readiness to fight 47; relieved by Lincoln on November 5, 1862 136; removal from post as General-in-Chief 51; retreat after Mechanicsville 85; retreat from Gaines's Mill 102, 103; retreat from Malvern Hill 111, 112; review of troops by 38; review of troops to present Wittich with captured flag 112; Richmond strategy 48, 50, 51, 64, 67, 81, 84, 85, 114; on Seven Pines battle 81; at Sharpsburg 132–133; on uniforms 37; Yorktown strategy 56, 57, 60–61, 62; *see also* Army of the Potomac

McCoy, DeWitt: election of lieutenant colonel 189; Finney Guards under 19; at Petersburg, Virginia 191; photo of *126*; recruiting drive led by 47; on Second Bull Run 125–126; wounded at Gaines's Mill battle 94

McDowell, Irvin.: commander of Union troops in Washington 18, 26, 56; demotion of 26; failure to attack Confederates near Gainesville 120; Fredericksburg soldiers under 67; *see also* McDowell's 1st Corps

McDowell's 1st Corps: placed under Pope's Army of Virginia 118; at Second Bull Run 121

McGehee, son of Wilmer (Pvt. in Pickett's Brigade) 91

McKinley, Color-Sergeant 54

McLane, John W.: background of 15, 23; at Big Bethel action 53, 54; body recovered from battlefield 101; commander of 83rd Pennsylvania 3; commander of Erie Regiment 15–18; death at Gaines's Mill battle 94, 99, 100; disinterment of remains and return to Erie 194; on failure of troops to be Federalized 18; at Gaines's Mill battle 89, 92, 94; at Hanover Court House 76; at Hanover Court House battle 67, 69, 74, 75, 78, 96; illness of 82; leadership positions under 20; photo of *15*; on pillaging 60; praised by Butterfield 78; recruiting of troops by 19, 47; revenge for death of 100–115; Richmond approach of 65; training of officers by 33; on uniforms 42

McLane's Regiment: arrival in Washington, D.C. (1861) 28; assignment to Porter's Division 29; at Gaines's Mill 90, 92; at Hanover Court House 72, 73; renamed 83rd Pennsylvania 38; welcoming 44th New York Regiment 38

McLaws, Lafayette 160, 169, 170

McPherson, James 4

Meade, George G.: at Chancellorsville, 160, 161; commander of Army of the Potomac 165, 187; commander of 5th Corps 153; commending Vincent for bravery at Gettysburg 185; Gettysburg strategy 163, 166, 168, 169, 170, 171, 172, 184, 185, 186; Mine Run campaign 189; photo of *165*; pursuit of Lee after Gettysburg 186, 187; *see also* 5th Corps

Meagher, Thomas 110, 156

Mechanicsville, battle of 84–85, 86

Mehl, Michael 34, 187

"Mephitic effluvia" 43

Merrimac 55

"Mess" 36

Mexican War 1, 12, 15

"Michigan Independents" *see* 16th Michigan

Military Act of 1792 12

Military Act of 1861 19, 23

Military Order of the Loyal Legion 197

Militia, pre- and post–Civil War 195

Miller, James 23

Minié bullets 75, 143

Minors as enlistees 23, 47

Moorehead, Isaac 100*n*

Morale: after Fredericksburg 150, 151, 153; after Gettysburg 188; after Hanover Court House victory 79; after losses of 1862 summer campaigns 130; battle expectations 53; eagerness to fight 47–48; Fredericksburg campaign 148, 149; Hooker's efforts to improve 153–154; mail and 43; on march to Frederick 132; Shiloh victory, upon news of 60

Morell, George W.: as commander of 1st Division of 5th Corps *131*; division commander of 5th Army Corps 64, *65*; on Hanover Court House battle 69; on losses at Malvern Hill 112; at Malvern Hill 105; at Mechanicsville 84; photo of *72*; at Second Bull Run 121, 127; transfer to forces on upper Potomac 138; withdrawal orders from Malvern Hill 111

Morell's Division: at Antietam 133; at Gaines's Mill 86, 92, 100; at Hanover Court House 67–69, 77; at Malvern Hill 104, 108, 110; at Mechanicsville 84; retreat from Gaines's Mill 100, 102; at Seven Pines 80; at Second Bull Run 120, 136; at Sharpsburg 132; at Shepardstown Ford 133; *see also* 5th Corps

Morris, John F. 88, 94, 116

"The Mud March" 151

Muskets *see* Firearms

Nahgel, Louis: death at Gaines's Mill battle 94, 98, 99, 100; election to major 28; at Hanover Court House battle 73

Nash, Eugene 38, 182

Navy 55, 56, 62

New York City riots against draft 188

9th Corps: at Antietam 133; at Fredericksburg 146, 147; ordered into Maryland 131; part of Right Grand Division 138; at Sharpsburg 132

9th Massachusetts 74, 75; part of 5th Corps, 1st Division 65

9th New York 145

Norton, Edwin 197

Norton, Oliver: on Aldie 163; on Antietam 133; on approaching battle 35, 79, 135; *Army Letters, 1861-1865* by 4; background of 8, 22; on Big Bethel action 53, 54; books on Civil War by 197; as bugler and color-bearer 8–9, 155, 158, 162, 198; on Camp Leslie beautification 44; on Chancellorsville 160, 161; on Chaplain Flower 114; on Cold Harbor camp 67; Colored Troops, officer position with 191, 196–197; on colors of 83rd 162; on Confederate camp, recovering Union equipment and uniforms at 159; on Confederate dead 63, 78; correspondence with family 43; departure from 3rd Brigade 191; on desire to do battle 48, 67; on discharge from service, refusal to seek 155; on 83rd marching to Washington at end of war 197; on equipment and outfitting 41, 42; on European military observers 82; on food 36, 151; on foraging 37, 60; on Fredericksburg strategy 137, 150; on Gaines's Mill battle 93, 94, 96, 97; at Gettysburg *see* Little Round Top (Gettysburg); on Gettysburg victory 186; on guard posts 35; on Hampton, Virginia 52; on Hanover Court

House battle 68, 69, 72, 73, 76, 78; on hospitalization with sunstroke 196; on inaction at Camp Leslie 47–48; on lice 151; life after leaving 83rd and after Civil War 196–197; on looting at Fredericksburg 148; on losing position as bugler 157–158; on losses of summer of 1862 130; on Malvern Hill battle 108–109, 110; on Maryland march 132; on McClellan's competence 135, 136; on McLane's death at Gaines's Mill battle 94; on Mine Run campaign 187; on move to Ft. Monroe after Peninsula Campaign 115; photo of *23, 192*; on possible Richmond attack 65, 79; on preventing his brother from joining up 113; on purpose of Civil War 8; retreat at Gaines's Mill 97–98; on return to 83rd from Brigade Headquarters 158; on Second Bull Run defeat 129; on seeing rebel camps in Virginia 30; on severe conditions faced by soldiers 11, 33; on Sharpsburg camp after Antietam 134; on Stoneman's Station camp 140, 151; on survivors after the Seven Day campaign 113; "Taps" played by 114; on uniforms 66; on Vincent's deathbed conversation 184; on Virginia march 50, 51, 52; on visions of return home 60; waking troops for march to Gettysburg 167; on winning Zouave uniform in drill competition 41; on winter at Camp Leslie 42, 46; on Yorktown siege 56, 57, 58, 59

Norton, Strong Vincent (son of Oliver Norton) 197

Oates, William 176, 179–180, 181
Occupations of enlistees 22–23
Officers: age of 23; election of *see* 83rd Pennsylvania Infantry Regiment; experience and training of 32–33; preferential treatment at field hospital 100; as target of marksmen at Gettysburg 181; uniforms of 37, 41–42; vacancies 188
Older men as enlistees 23
"Onadaga Regiment" 50
140th New York 181

Palmetto Sharpshooters 95, 96
"Parallels" 56
Pay: Hooker's distribution of back-pay 153, 154; re-enlistment incentives 189; Stockton's Brigade not paid for 6 months 151

Peninsula Campaign 46–61; Confederate withdrawal to line behind Rappahannock 51, 52; map of area *49, 55; see also specific locations* (e.g., Hampton, Virginia)
Peninsula formed by the York and James rivers 63
Pennants *see* Flags and pennants
Pennsylvania, history of northwest area 12–13
Perry, Oliver Hazard 14
"Perry Artillery Company" 14
Petersburg, Virginia 191; Confederate retreat from 193; 83rd at 193
Physicians 76–77; *see also* Field hospitals
Picket duty: at Camp Leslie 35, 44; at Camp Winfield Scott 57; at Malvern Hill 104; at Richmond area camp 81
Pickett, George 90, 91, 184, 185
Pickett's Charge 185
Piepenbrink, Pvt., of 44th New York 110
Pierce, Franklin 14
Pillaging *see* Foraging
Platt, Philander 177
Pleasonton, Alfred 163, 164
Pope, John: Army of Virginia under 114, 115, 118; background of 118; charges against Porter for disobeying orders at Bull Run 130, 136; fighting Stonewall Jackson's troops 118–120, 121; relieved of duty and sent to Minnesota 130; Second Bull Run strategy 121, 123, 128, 143
Porter, Fitz-John: advice to McClellan on taking Richmond 41; Antietam strategy 133; background of 29; closing Sutler and banning sales of alcohol 44; commander of division 29; as commander of 5th Corps *131*; court martial for Bull Run actions 136; criticism of, by Pope 130, 136; drill competition held by 41; 5th Corps under, 64, *65 see also* 5th Corps; at Gaines's Mill battle 86, 87, 89, 90, 91, 99; at Hanover Court House battle 67, 68, 74, 77, 79; at Malvern Hill battle 104, 110, 111; at Mechanicsville battle 85, 86; photo of *30*; relieved from command of 5th Corps 136; Second Bull Run strategy 120–121, *125*, 126–127, 136; Shepardstown Ford strategy 133–134; at siege of Yorktown 56, 61; *see also* 5th Corps; Porter's Division
Porter, Julia *29*; Rodgers' correspondence with 62; wife of Rodgers 195

Porter's Division: Big Bethel reconnaissance 53–54; chasing Confederates to Richmond 62; as 1st Division of 3rd Corps for battle in Virginia 48; organization of 50; at Rappahannock (August 1862) 119; reorganization into 5th Corps 64 *see also* 5th Corps; trip to Hampton, Virginia 51–52; at Yorktown siege 56
Potter, J.B. 175, 181
Powell, James 181
Prim y Prats (Spanish Army General) 82
Prisoners taken by Confederates: 83rd Pennsylvania 129, 134; Judson as 102, 103, 132; Libby Prison (Richmond) 132, 193; White as 193
Prisoners taken by Union: taken at Gettysburg 181–182; taken at Hanover Court House 77; taken in spring 1865 193
Pryor, Roger 87, 88, 90, 91

Quartermaster's role 34, 36

Railroads, destruction of 78
Rapidan River 158
Rappahannock: battle (August 1862) 119; Confederate withdrawal to line behind in 1861 51, 52; winter quarters (December 1863 & January 1864) 189; *see also* Chancellorsville, battle of; Fredericksburg, battle of
Rations *see* Food and rations
Recruiting of troops: by Campbell in Erie 113, 117; by McLane 19, 47; regimental commanders to find recruits 117
Re-enlistment incentives 189–190
Reynolds, John 165
Rice, James (of 44th New York Regiment): at Gettysburg (Little Round Top) 10, 172, 174, 184, 185; moving 83rd Pennsylvania away from Gaines's Mill 99; opinion on continuing to fight at Gaines's Mill 97; after retreat from Gaines's Mill 101; taking command at Second Bull Run 127; taking command at Gettysburg 182
Rice, John (Pvt.): on drunk soldier 46; killed at Gaines's Mill 111; on marching 50–51, 66; on picket duty 81; on Yorktown siege 59, 60, 61
Richmond, Virginia: Confederate protection of *see* Lee, Robert E.; Confederate retreat to 62, 64; Johnston's strategy regarding 64; McClellan's strategy regarding

Index

48, 50, 51, 64, 67, 81; siege of 81, 84
Roberts, Charles 123
Roberts' 1st Brigade at Second Bull Run 123
Robertson, Jerome B. 175, 176
Robinson, Stephen 23
Robinson, William 23
Rockwell, John C. 34
Rodgers, David: on Confederate dead 62; death of 195; disinterment of McLane by 194; at Gettysburg 183; on Hanover Court House battle 73; on inaction at Camp Leslie 48; life after Civil War 195; photo of *29*; re-enlistment of 190; on Richmond march 63; on seasick soldiers 52
Rogers, Alexander 108, *158*, 166
Rogers, Chauncey P. 32, 192
Rosecrans, William 187
Ruehle, Lt. Col. of 16th Michigan 88

Saeger, Daniel 20, 116
Saeger, James 34
Savage's Station: Confederates overtaking 102; field hospital at *103*
Schlachback, William 24
Schlaudecker, Matthias 16
Scholl, Joseph 22
Scruggs, L.H. 181
Second Bull Run *see* Bull Run, Second Battle of
2nd Corps: at Chancellorsville 158, 159, 160; at Chickahominy River 80; at Fredericksburg 149; at Gaines's Mill 99; at Gettysburg 169, 186; at Malvern Hill 104, 110; at Mechanicsville 84; ordered into Maryland 131; part of Right Grand Division 138; retreat after Gaines's Mill 102; at Sharpsburg 132; at Yorktown, Virginia 54, 56
2nd Division of 5th Corps *see* Sykes' Division
2nd Maine Infantry 47; part of 5th Corps, 1st Division 65
Sell, John M. 110, 184
Seneca tribe 12–13
"The Seven Days" 111
Seven Pines, battle of 80, 82
17th New York: 72, 78, 86; at Chancellorsville 159; expiration of term 162; at Fredericksburg 143, 144; part of 5th Corps, 1st Division *65;* at Second Bull Run 122, 124, 125
Seward, William 63
Sharpsburg, Maryland: fighting at 132; Union camp at after Antietam 134
Shaw, Capt. 19

Shepardstown Ford 133–134
Sherman, William Tecumseh 1
Shields, John *190*
Shiloh victory of Union forces 60, 64
Ships and water transport for Army of the Potomac 52
Shriver, Jacob 77
"Sick Call" 44
Sickles, Dan 170, 171
Sickness and disease 11, 43–44, 46–47, 188; at Harrison's Landing 112; at Richmond siege 82; at Stoneman's Station winter camp 151; at Yorktown siege 59
Siege of Yorktown 56–61
Sigel, Franz 120, 134, 159
16th Michigan ("Michigan Independents"): at Aldie 164; at Fredericksburg 143, 144; at Gaines's Mill 86, 87, 94, 96, 97; at Gettysburg 174, 175, 179, 180; at Hanover Court House 69; at Malvern Hill 107; part of Porter's Division 50; part of Vincent's 3rd Brigade 162; at Second Bull Run 122, 124
6th Corps: at Chickahominy River 80; creation of, under Franklin 64; at Gaines's Mill 86, 101; at Gettysburg 169; at Malvern Hill 104; ordered into Maryland 131; part of Left Grand Division 138; return from Peninsula Campaign 119
62nd Pennsylvania: at Hanover Court House 74; part of 5th Corps, 1st Division 65
69th New York Infantry 52
Skirmish line 31
Slaves, escaped, working as servants for Union soldiers 79
Smith, Bryon 22
Smith, Joel 23
Smith's Division of 6th Corps 101
Snow 42, 46
Snyder, Jacob 57, 59
Solid shot 124
Spanish-American War 195
Sprague, Charles 180
Springfield muskets 45
Starke, W.E. 124
State colors of the 83rd *see* Colors of the 83rd; Flags and pennants
Stealing *see* Foraging
Stebbins, Thomas 33
Stevens, John 179
Stewart, James 117
Stockton, T.B.W.: commander of 3rd Brigade 131, *131,* 138; commander of 16th Michigan 50; at Fredericksburg 143, 146, 147, 148; resignation of 162; retreat from Gaines's Mill 94; sickness

of 155; on troops after Chancellorsville 161
Stockton's Brigade at Fredericksburg 140, 142, 144, 145
Stoneman's Station camp (Fredericksburg) 139, 150, 151; Union huts on the Rappahannock, winter of 1862-63 *152*
Stowe, George 20, 68, 152, 188
Stretcher bearers 76
Strong, Sarah 20
Stryker, S.W. 50
Stuart, J.E.B. 83, 102, 120, 138, 163, 168
Sturtevant, Seth 94, 101
Sumner, Edwin 138
Sumner's Grand Division at Fredericksburg 139, 140, 141, 142
Supplies: burning of supplies at Gaines's Mill 87; training on system 34; Washington, D.C. area (1861) 27, 28; *see also* Food and rations
Surgeons 76–77; *see also* Field hospitals
Sykes, George 172; at Antietam 133; commander of 5th Corps 165; consenting to hold Little Round Top at Gettysburg 171; at Gettysburg 9; march to Gettysburg 166, 167; photo of *171*; regiments under command of 64, *65, 131; see also* Sykes' Division
Sykes' Division: at Chickahominy River 84; at Gaines's Mill 86, 87, 91; at Malvern Hill 104; retreat from Gaines's Mill 100; at Second Bull Run 123, 127; at Shepardstown Ford 133

Taliaferro, Alexander 126
"Taps" for lights out 114
Tents 34, 42
Thanksgiving scene in a Union camp near Washington *40*
Thickstun, Israel: on Chickahominy River battle 84; on Christmas celebration 45; combat injury of 59; on Fredericksburg 142; on Gettysburg victory 186; on illness 82, 112; on morale under Hooker 155–156; re-enlistment of 190; on seeing secessionist territory 29; on Vincent's treatment 154
3rd Brigade, 1st Division, of Union Army: at Appomattox surrender 193; casualties and wounded in the Seven Days 112; at Fredericksburg 146, 147; at Gaines's Mill 86; at Gettysburg 8, 182, 185, 186; infantrymen of 9; losses of 1862 summer campaigns 130; at Malvern Hill battle 110; at Mechanicsville battle

84, 85; organization under Vincent 162; at Second Bull Run 122, 123, 127; *see also specific regiments*
3rd Corps: at Chancellorsville 159, 160; at Chickahominy River 80; at Gettysburg 170, 171, 174, 175, 184; at Hampton, Virginia 53; at Malvern Hill 104; at Mechanicsville battle 84; part of Center Grand Division 138; return from Peninsula Campaign 119; at Second Bull Run 123; at Yorktown, Virginia 54
37th North Carolina 73
"Tionesta Rangers" 20
Training of troops 24, 28; drilling maneuvers 32, 33; manual for 32, 33; need for 30; winning drill competition 41
Tripler, Charles 46–47
Truce: 83rd and Confederates engaging in unofficial truce 189
12th Corps: at Antietam 133; at Chancellorsville 158; expiration of term 162; ordered into Maryland 131; at Sharpsburg 132
12th New York Infantry 69; at Fredericksburg 143, 144; at Gaines's Mill 86, 88, 92; losses of 1862 summer campaigns 130; at Malvern Hill 108, 110; part of 5th Corps, 1st Division 65; part of Porter's Division 50; at Second Bull Run 122, 124, 125
20th Maine Volunteer Infantry Regiment 131; at Aldie 164; at Fredericksburg 143, 144; at Gettysburg 174, 179, 181, 184; part of Vincent's 3rd Brigade 162
21st Virginia 125
25th New York Regiment 68; part of 5th Corps, 1st Division 65; at Second Bull Run 123
28th North Carolina Regiment 68, 69, 78
Tyler, Brig. Gen. *131*

Uniforms 37, 38–39, *39*, 41–42; recovering from Confederates 159; storage of excess 50; at time of march to Richmond (May 1862) 66
Union army: Lincoln's proclamation calling on militias to serve 12, 15; volunteers *see* Volunteer soldiers; *see also specific armies by name, corps, brigades, regiments, etc.*

Vader, Frank, 23
"The Valley Forge of the Union Army" 151
Van Giesen, Charles, 23
Van Giesen, John, 23

Van Giesen, Thomas: on food 36; promotion of 157; on readiness for battle 42, 157; on regiment's dead 135; on Sharpsburg camp after Antietam 134; siblings serving with 23
Vanetta, John C. *155*
Veterans' organizations 197–198
Victory parade in Washington 194
Vincent, Bethuel Boyd (father of Strong Vincent) 20, 21, 187
Vincent, Blanche Strong (daughter of Strong Vincent) 197
Vincent, Boyd (brother of Strong Vincent) 21
Vincent, Elizabeth (wife of Strong Vincent) 187, 197; *see also* Carter, Elizabeth
Vincent, John (grandfather of Strong Vincent) 20
Vincent, Strong: at Aldie 164; background 8, 20–22, 23; biography of 5; on Chancellorsville 159; command of 3rd Brigade taken at Fredericksburg 148; commander of 3rd Brigade (promotion) 162; commendation for bravery at Gettysburg 185; death and funeral of 186, 187; election to colonel 112; election to lieutenant-colonel 28; election to major 20; at Fredericksburg 143, 144, 145, 146, 147, 148, 149; furlough of soldiers allowed by 153; at Gettysburg, 8, 171 *see also* Little Round Top; at Gettysburg field hospital 184, 185; at Hanover Court House 69, 73, 78; illness of 82, 94, 116, 134; on march into Pennsylvania 166; meeting troops arriving in Washington, D.C. 28; monument to, on Little Round Top 197; on need to win 156; Norton's books about 197; order to close Sutler in afternoon 44; photo of *21, 155*; praised by Butterfield 78; promotion to general while on deathbed 185; on purpose of Civil War 2, 8, 22; rebuilding ranks by 154; removing Norton as bugler 158; return to action after illness 134; Richmond march 63, 65; second-in-command of 83rd Pennsylvania 3; wounded at Gettysburg 181; at Yorktown siege 56; *see also* Little Round Top (Gettysburg); Vincent's 3rd Brigade
Vincent's 3rd Brigade 148, 162; at Aldie 163, 164; at Gettysburg *see* Little Round Top (Gettysburg); march to Gettysburg 169
Volunteer soldiers 8, 12, 117, 188, 195

Von Vegesack, Major 79, 95, 96, 97

Waid, Seth: background of 24; on Chancellorsville 159; death of 195; on death sentence for deserters 189; discharge chosen over re-enlistment 190, 192; on food 36; on Gettysburg 167, 169, 177–178, 183, 185; on guard posts 35; on hard life of the soldier 2, 33; illness of 44, 47, 192; life after Civil War 195; on officers 33; on patients in military medical hospital 117; Philadelphia military hospital job of 116–117; on preparation for battle 36; on return home 192; return to 83rd Pennsylvania 154; on supplies 28; on vision of life after war 25; wish for end of war 186, 187
Ward, W.C. 179
Warren, Gouverner: as commander of 3rd Brigade in 5th Army Corps, 2nd Division 65, *131;* at Gettysburg 170; on Little Round Top at Gettysburg 170, 172, 184; photo of *171*
Warrenton, Virginia 135, 136, 139
Washington: victory parade 194
Washington area: map of (1861) *27;* march of 5th Corps to at end of war 193–194; protection of 26–27, 48, 51, 55–56, 163, 164; retreat from Second Bull Run to 128
Watt House: field hospital at Gaines's Mill 100; photo today *98;* Porter's headquarters for battle at Gaines's Mill 91
Waud, Alfred: Devil's Den, Gettysburg *180;* Hanover Court House battle *71;* Union soldiers stealing fence rails *40*
"Wayne Grays" 15
"Wayne Guards" 14, 15
Weapons *see* Firearms
Weather: Camp Leslie winter 42, 45, 46; during Fredericksburg campaign 139, 140, 147; during Gettysburg retreat of Lee 186; during Hanover Court House battle 67, 68; during march in Virginia (Peninsula Campaign) 51–52, 54, 66; during Richmond siege 82; at Stoneman's Station winter quarters 151; during Yorktown siege 59
Webber, J.B. 110
Webster, Daniel 2
Weed's Brigade of 5th Corps, 2nd Division 181, 182

Weeks, H.A. 50, 125, 127n; background of 122; at Second Bull Run 122, 124; wounded at Bull Run 127
Weikert, George 169
Weikert, Jacob 183
Welch 184
Wells, John 23
"Westchester Chasseurs" 50
White, Plympton: background of 20; as Confederate prisoner 193; death of 193; at Gaines's Mill battle 92; surrender incident at Gaines's Mill 95–96; on three-year enlistment 17
White, William 100, 101
Whiting, W.H.C.: at Gaines's Mill 92; at Malvern Hill 107
Wilcox, Cadmus 87
Wilderness Campaign 191
Wilson, John 44, 74
Winchester, Virginia 134, 135
Wittich, Frederick 24, 128
Wittich, William 24, 110, 112, 128
Woodward, Orpheus: at Aldie 164; background of 20; commander of 83rd 10, 162; death of 196; election of colonel 189; firing line at Gettysburg 177; at Gettysburg 175, 177, 180, 181; life after Civil War *162*, 196, 197
World War I 195
Wright, Ambrose 107, 108, 109, 110

Yale, Lt. of Company C 47
Yorktown, Virginia: heavy siege mortar in position near *58;* map of Union positions *55;* marches to 46–61; siege of 56–61; Union strategy at 54, 56

Zouave style uniforms 38, *39,* 41, 66; recovering from Confederates 159
Zuver, Brownlee *190*

www.ingramcontent.com/pod-product-compliance
Ingram Content Group UK Ltd.
Pitfield, Milton Keynes, MK11 3LW, UK
UKHW050531150426
5217IPUK00026B/1885